# Kovels'

## AMERICAN ART POTTERY

# Kovels'

## AMERICAN ART POTTERY

### The Collector's Guide to Makers, Marks, and Factory Histories

Ralph and Terry Kovel

CROWN PUBLISHERS, INC.

NEW YORK

Published by Crown Publishers, Inc.,
201 East 50th Street,
New York, New York 10022.
Member of the
Crown Publishing Group.

Random House Inc.
New York, Toronto, London,
Sydney, Auckland

CROWN is a trademark of
Crown Publishers, Inc.

Manufactured in
Japan

Library of Congress
Cataloging-in-Publication Data

Kovel, Ralph M.
Kovels' American art pottery /
Ralph & Terry Kovel.
p.    cm.
Includes bibliographical references
and index.
1. Art pottery, American.  2. Art
pottery—Collectors and collecting.
3. Pottery—Marks.  I. Kovel, Terry.
II. Title.
NK4005.K68  1993
738.3'0973—dc20        92-20638
CIP

ISBN 0-517-58012-8

10 9 8 7 6 5 4 3 2 1

First Edition

*(Title page) A LeCamark vase,
"Tiffany/Roman Gold," similar to the
J. B. Owens Company's Soudanese
line. It was made in 1927 and stands 8
inches high. (Collection of David Edwin Gifford; photograph by Gene Taylor, courtesy of the Old State House
Museum, Little Rock, Arkansas)*

The potters in this book are remembered for their artistry but
also as special people with special drives and talents. We dedicate
this, our sixty-fifth book, to our children, Lee, Kim, and Al and
our granddaughters, Zoe and Cloe, who have some of the creativity of George Ohr, the business sense of Sam Weller, the
independence of Maria Longworth Nichols, and the perseverance
of Frederick Rhead.

LESSEll

DEC 1993

# Contents
~

# Acknowledgments

~

Many people helped us with the research for this book, spent time and effort answering questions, gave us suggestions, and helped us choose photographs. Thank you to the Art Institute of Chicago (Lieschen Potuznik); Brooklyn Museum (Barry Harwood and Karen Tates); Bryce Bannatyne Gallery, Santa Monica, California (Bryce Bannatyne, Jr.); Cincinnati Art Galleries (Michelle and Randy Sandler); Cincinnati Art Museum (Joy Payton); Collector's Sales & Services, Middletown, Rhode Island (Linda and David Arman); David Rago Arts & Crafts Gallery, Lambertville, New Jersey (David Rago and Grace Van Dyke); Dedham Historical Society (Robert Hanson); Detroit Institute of Art (Marianne Letasi); Early Auction Co., Milford, Ohio (Roger R. Early); Erie Art Museum (John L. Vanco); Everson Museum of Art (John E. Rexine, Jr.); David Edwin Gifford; Frank L. Hahn; Henry Ford Museum and Greenfield Village (Fran Carroll); High Museum of Art (Jessica Laughlin); Jane Addams' Hull House at the University of Illinois at Chicago Circle (Mary Ann Johnson); June Greenwald Antiques, Cleveland Heights, Ohio; Moravian Pottery and Tile Works, Mercer, Pennsylvania (Vance A. Koehler); Museum of Modern Art (Gina C. Guy); Neal Auction Company, New Orleans, Louisiana (Gary L. Hume); Newark Museum (Margaret C. DiSalvi); Newcomb College at Tulane University (Sally Main); Robert Wyman Newton; William D. Noonan; North Carolina Museum of Art (Carrie Hastings Hedrick); Pisgah Forest Pottery (J. Thomas Case); Skinner, Inc., Bolton, Massachusetts (Sarah M. Hamill); Smithsonian Institution, National Museum of American History, Division of Ceramics and Glass (Bonnie Lilienfeld); Stan Hywet Hall and Gardens (Margaret A. Tramontine); Strong Museum (Carolyn T. Block); Barbara Wamelink; Western Reserve Historical Society (Dean M. Zimmerman); and Wolf's, Cleveland, Ohio (Kathryn Isenhart).

We thank again all those who helped with the research for our first book about art pottery in 1974. Their help led to the newer research and information.

Our gratitude also to Benjamin Margalit, who took the cover photograph and most of the color photographs in the book. To Marcia Goldberg, who closed all the last minute special research details for us. An extra thanks to Sharon Squibb, our editor, Ken Sansone, creative director, and Kim Hertlein, senior production editor, Bill Peabody, production manager, and Peggy Goddard and Nancy Kenmore, designers, who worked so hard to make the finished book our best ever.

And to Michelle Sidrane, publisher of the Crown group, and Betty Prashker, editor-in-chief, who have always encouraged our book-writing efforts, we once again express our appreciation.

We give special tribute to the authors of the 1900–1950 studies of American pottery, Edwin Atlee Barber, Evan Purviance, and E. Stanley Wires. These men collected pottery and wrote about the potters of their day, and their writing became the basis for all later studies. Their work has lived after them.

*(Opposite page) A 7-inch vase with raised flowers and leaves made by Faience Manufacturing Company. (Private collection)*

# Introduction

Though there may be more than one definition for the term *art pottery*, everyone agrees American art pottery was first made in Cincinnati, Ohio, during the 1870s. Art pottery pieces were hand-thrown, hand-decorated artistic products. Later products, also considered part of the art pottery movement, were made with underglaze slip decoration, matte glaze, high-gloss glaze, carved, molded, or applied decoration, and with a variety of other techniques. Many of the art potteries started as one-man or one-woman operations and then grew to become large successful financial ventures with hundreds of employees, until the art pottery movement in America ended in the 1930s. Overlapping with the art pottery movement were the studio potters of the 1920s and after. A studio potter usually had a small pottery with one or two potters.

We have emphasized those aspects of each pottery manufacturer that would be of interest to collectors. Makers, artists, dates, marks, and lines of pottery are described in detail. There is a general history of each pottery. For further information, a bibliography has been included at the back of the book. Many potters, chemists, designers, and plant managers moved from England to New England to the Midwest and to the West Coast in search of a job. We have tried tracing their travels, because the men and women who worked in a pottery often took their ideas to other factories. The similarity of two different wares can often be attributed to those travelers.

This book has been written for collectors. Pictures include both the best and the average wares of the art potters. Artist marks and factory marks have been dated as accurately as possible, but, unfortunately, some history has been lost. If an exact year could not be used, the date is just a time range. We also included many mysterious marks of artists. Some artists who used marks that were unknown in our first art pottery book are now identified. New research, rediscovered catalogs and records, archaeological digs, and family histories have yielded new information. If two reliable sources had conflicting information, we included both in the text with our opinion about the accuracy of each. All facts have been checked and rechecked from many sources, including magazines and newspapers of the period, factory records, interviews with employees and relatives, study collections at museums, experts who have studied individual potteries, and other possible sources.

Many of the chapters have been read by experts who specialized in research in one factory; their corrections or comments on accuracy were most appreciated. All of these experts are referred to in our comments or included in the bibliography. Some information has come from readers of our newsletter *Kovels on Antiques and Collectibles* or our nationally syndicated newspaper column. Some readers wrote to us that a family member was a workman or artist at the factory, and we were able to see catalogs, pictures, and even family treasures. Sometimes luck was a factor. We went to dinner at a collector's home and noticed some North Dakota pottery vases on the mantel. The collector's aunt was an artist at the pottery and she had family pictures and records that added to our research.

The book is in alphabetical order by factory. Tile factories are listed in the second section of the book. The pottery is described, but we do not attempt to evaluate artistic worth. That is a job for each collector or for a trained artist or museum historian. We began collecting art pottery in the 1960s while working on our first art pottery book, published in 1974. At that time, Ohr was unknown, Fulper and Roseville were ignored, and only Rookwood and Grueby were recognized for artistic worth by the major art museums. Today, many potteries are represented in museum collections and pieces sell for thousands of dollars. We, like all collectors, still search in out-of-the-way places for an art pottery treasure. After all, the Rookwood pottery sold many pieces from its museum collection in the 1940s and the flower arrangers of Ohio and neighboring states bought examples to use as vases. We own several pieces that we purchased with the chicken-wire flower holders still inside. The Dedham pottery sale at Gimbels in New York in 1943 scattered some of the factory's finest pieces to all parts of the country. And in 1972, when a dealer found thousands of pieces of pottery by George Ohr, a collector willing to buy the then-unknown works could find good pieces from $10 to $50.

We welcome any comments or additional facts about art pottery. Our research is never completed.

Ralph and Terry Kovel

Art Potteries

The art pottery movement in America started in the 1870s. Though there were a few earlier attempts to make artistic pottery, experts say the birth of the movement was at the 1876 Centennial Exhibition in Philadelphia. Many artists who eventually worked for art potteries were inspired by the exhibition. Mary Louise McLaughlin, an amateur potter from Cincinnati, Ohio, saw the French Haviland pottery. Hugh Robertson, later with Chelsea Pottery in Massachusetts, was inspired by sang de boeuf-glazed (red) pieces in the Chinese exhibit. Susan Frackelton of Wisconsin won a medal for a piece at the Centennial. William Long, a druggist from Steubenville, Ohio, who started the Lonhuda Pottery in 1892, became interested in making pottery because of displays in Philadelphia. Ideas that inspired art potters were found not only in ceramic displays but also in designs used in other countries. The philosophy of William Morris and John Ruskin of England suggested the advantages of making objects by hand. The unfamiliar designs of China and Japan led to the creation of exotic decorations by American potters.

Scholars define American art pottery as a type of ware made from about 1870 to 1920. English art pottery, Haviland pottery, and some other examples from Europe were all made with the same arts and crafts movement design inspiration. The pottery was handmade or primarily handmade. It was produced to be a thing of beauty and not just as a commercial vessel. In those early days, some companies made both art pottery and commercial florist wares. Pieces were designed and decorated by artists, but often the pottery vase was actually thrown on the wheel by a workman who specialized in that art. Women, sanitarium patients, and young girls were often trained as artists. Nineteenth-century women were considered frail and artistic. The heavy, dirty work was usually the man's job. Decorating pottery was one of the few means of employment that were socially acceptable for women who had to or wanted to work outside the home. Many different factors led to the development of the art pottery movement as a whole. The inspiration of the Centennial, the need for jobs for artistic women, the interest in home decorating and amateur china painting, the displays in newly founded art museums in major cities, and the establishment of several new art schools were all elements that came together in the 1870s.

Collectors have a slightly different definition of the words *art pottery*. The term refers mostly to the works of the many companies that made some pieces of art pottery during the 1870–1930 era. Sometimes it includes the studio potters' work from the 1920s through the 1940s. California potteries started much later than those on the East Coast, so collectors often include in the definition of art pottery works made in the West as late as the 1940s.

Included in this listing are the potteries that made what most collectors call "art pottery." The history of a firm is traced from its beginning to its end even if its production changed from art pottery to commercial or florist pottery in later years.

*This Arc-en-Ciel urn is glazed with the popular iridescent copper-colored glaze. The vase is 10¾ inches tall and 5⁵/₁₆ inches in diameter at its widest point. It is marked with the incised name of the pottery. (Smithsonian Institution)*

# Alberhill Pottery
### *Alberhill, California*

Because clays of good quality were available in the Alberhill region of California, the Alberhill Coal and Clay Company hired Alexander W. Robertson in 1912 to make art pottery. Although Robertson left the company in 1914, some of the art pottery received a gold medal at the 1915 Panama-California Exposition. The company soon abandoned the production of art pottery, and the only pieces that remained were the small group of experimental designs by Robertson.

Early pieces were marked "A.C.C.CO.Cal." Later pieces were marked "Alberhill" or with Robertson's initials.

# Albery Novelty Pottery
### *Evanston, Illinois*

Duane F. Albery and his wife, Frances Huxtable Albery, built a pottery in their backyard in Evanston, Illinois, in 1913. Duane graduated from Ohio State University with a ceramic engineering degree and worked at the Gates laboratory (see Teco Gates).

The Alberys made vases, wall vases, and novelties. The popular handmade Chicago silver of the day featured special-order monograms, and the couple adapted the idea, using monograms as part of their designs. Pieces were glazed with black or colored matte or with glossy glazes. One color was similar to the Teco matte green.

The pottery closed in 1915. Albery moved to a terra-cotta company in New Jersey, then in 1922 returned to work at the Northwestern Terra-Cotta Company.

# American Art Clay Works
### *See Pauline Pottery*

# Arc-en-Ciel
### *Zanesville, Ohio*

*Arc-en-Ciel* is the French word for rainbow. The finest products of the firm were the iridescent gold luster vases made only until 1905. The art pottery was not a success, so the firm began making cooking ware in stippled blue, brown, green, or mottled brown and yellow glaze. The cooking ware was known as the Brighton line.

The Arc-en-Ciel Pottery Company was founded in Zanesville, Ohio, in 1903. The factory had originally been built by Albert Radford, who made pottery there for about six months before Arc-en-Ciel purchased the facility. Some sources contend Radford built the pottery for Arc-en-Ciel, and because of a delay, Radford operated the pottery before the final sale. But the records show a trustee for the A. Radford Company, so perhaps the plant had some money difficulties and Radford was forced to sell.

*Impressed in mold.*
*Initials of A. W. Robertson.*

**ALBERHILL**

*Impressed in mold.*

ALBERY

*Mark in the mold.*

**ALBERY**

*Impressed in mold.*

*Ink-stamped mark.*

J. C. Gerwick was president of Arc-en-Ciel and C. G. Dillon was secretary. John Lessell (see Weller), another of the incorporators, managed the plant. Arc-en-Ciel changed its name to The Brighton Pottery Company in 1905 and made cooking ware and other dishes until the plant closed in 1907.

## Arequipa
### *Fairfax, California*

~

In 1911 some twenty-five patients at Arequipa, a tuberculosis sanatorium near San Francisco, California, began making pottery with encouragement from the director of the sanatorium, Dr. Philip King Brown. Sales from their finished work furnished some extra money for the patients. The patients were trained by Frederick Hürten Rhead, who had worked at the Roseville Pottery from 1904 to 1908, and his wife, Agnes. Since Arequipa was the name of the sanatorium, it was decided that the pottery should be marked with the same name.

A workman was hired to throw the clay and do the jobs that required strength or exposure to clay dust, while the patients, tubercular young women, were able to decorate the pottery sitting in a well-ventilated, sunny room. The decorator-patients were paid for their work.

Frederick Rhead continued supervising the technical aspects of the pottery work until 1913. From 1908 until 1911 (between Roseville and Arequipa), Rhead was employed at University City in St. Louis, Missouri, where he worked on porcelains with other well-known potters, including Adelaide Alsop Robineau, editor of *Keramic Studio* magazine. After Arequipa, Rhead founded Rhead Pottery in Santa Barbara, California (1914–1917).

Arequipa Potteries was incorporated as a separate commercial establishment in 1913. (The corporation was dissolved in 1915, but

AREQUIPA
☷☷☷
CALIFORNIA

*Impressed or incised or painted under glaze.*

*An Arequipa paper label.*

*Grayish plum glaze covers this 8-inch vase. (Smithsonian Institution)*

*A "Persian blue" glaze covers this vase, which is 2½ inches high and is marked "AP." The tree and jug symbol and a paper label are on the bottom of the piece. (Smithsonian Institution)*

the pottery continued working.) Albert L. Solon, a ceramic engineer and the son of Louis Marc Solon, an English ceramist and the author of books about English pottery, replaced Rhead at Arequipa in 1913. Under Solon, the pottery produced new shapes, clay bodies, and glazes such as Persian faience. They also began making tiles. Pieces were sold in department stores in Chicago, Boston, and New York.

The pottery had just begun to make money when Solon left in 1916 to take a teaching job at San Jose State College. Frederick H. Wilde, a successful English potter with experience making tiles in California, took over Arequipa. Wilde introduced a line of hand-made, Spanish-inspired tiles.

America's entry into World War I in 1917 led to the closing of the company the following year. The sanatorium, however, remained open until 1957.

Most Arequipa pottery was made from local clays in kilns using fuel. Pieces were thrown, pressed, or cast. Some were glazed and some had incised or raised designs. Pieces had a thick, sturdy look.

*An iridescent orange and gray matte glaze highlights this vase. It is 6 inches in diameter and 8 inches high. (Smithsonian Institution)*

*This Arequipa vase was purchased by the Smithsonian in 1916. It has a bright yellow iridescent glaze over a modeled, then cased, form. It is 4³⁄₈ inches high. (Smithsonian Institution)*

*This 10¹⁄₂-inch vase decorated by Frederick H. Rhead is marked with the incised jug under a tree and "1912 Arequipa California." (Collection of William Noonan; photograph by Robert Lowry from the Erie Art Museum, Erie, Pennsylvania)*

*This covered jar, 16¹⁄₄ inches high and 11¹³⁄₁₆ inches in diameter at its widest point, is incised "Arequipa California J.J.X.X." (Smithsonian Institution)*

# Avon

*Incised mark.*

*This rose-colored Avon Pottery mug is 4¼ inches high by 3⅛ inches in diameter. (Smithsonian Institution)*

*"Avon, 1902" is the mark on this vase. The vase, 5 inches tall and 6 inches wide, is glazed in shades of green and blue with a raised white decoration. (Private collection)*

*Mermaids are modeled on this 12½-inch-high vase with yellow to brown glaze. It dates from about 1905. The bottom is marked "Vance F. Co." (Harriet and Alan Goldner)*

## Avon Pottery
### Cincinnati, Ohio

The Avon Pottery was founded in Cincinnati, Ohio, in January 1886 by Karl Langenbeck, who had worked at the Rookwood Pottery. Artus Van Briggle, who later worked at Rookwood and at his own Colorado pottery, was one of Avon's artists.

The firm made a ware from yellow Ohio clay using modeled and incised decorations, colored slip, and a dull finish. Another type of ware was made from white clay featuring painted designs on the biscuit and a transparent glaze. Gradual shadings of pink, olive, violet, blue, and brown were blended on the white body. Some of these pieces were made with modeled handles, such as the ram's horn and elephant's head found on a few pieces. One line of pottery resembled the Rookwood standard glaze line. The pottery closed in 1888. The glazed pieces were marked "Avon."

Langenbeck continued in the pottery field, working for American Encaustic Tiling Company, Mosaic Tile Company, and the Grueby pottery. See also Avon Works.

## Avon Works (Vance/Avon)
### Wheeling, West Virginia

Although Edwin Barber in his 1904 book *Marks of American Potters* is very clear about the difference between the Avon Pottery of Cincinnati and the Avon Works of Wheeling, West Virginia, later writers have confused the records.

A cooperative pottery that made yellowware and Rockingham ware was founded in Tiltonsville, Ohio, in about 1880. From 1882 to 1884 the firm was known as the Tiltonsville Pottery Company. Soon the product line was expanded with the addition of novelties. There

*Incised.*

*Incised.*

*Printed.*

*Incised.*

*Incised.*

were about six more changes in ownership before November 1900, when a new company was organized as the Faience Pottery Company, owned by J. N. Vance and Sons of Wheeling, West Virginia. This company planned to make faience, jardinieres, pedestals, and umbrella stands. Several other types of wares were made and sold as well.

In 1902, the name of the pottery was changed to the Avon Faience Company and William P. Jervis of England became manager (see Craven Art Pottery). Frederick Hürten Rhead also worked at the company (see Arequipa). According to Barber, in January 1903 the Wheeling Potteries Company was organized by combining the Wheeling, La Belle, Riverside, and Avon potteries. Each of these four potteries became a department of the Wheeling Potteries Company. Artware was made at the Avon department. The artware was discontinued by 1905, and the firm went into receivership in 1908.

One of the lines made by Avon was a glazed ware decorated with white slip. It is thought to be the forerunner of the Weller Jap Birdimal line that was later introduced by Rhead. He made a similar ware at Roseville.

Several marks were used by the Vance and Avon potteries. Early pieces were marked "Vance" (1900–1902); later the firm used at least three marks with the word "Avon" (1902–1905).

*A Vance/Avon vase 6 inches high by 4 inches in diameter is inscribed "The Sweet Forget-me-nots That Grow for Happy Lovers." Frederick Rhead signed the body of the vessel with his last name. The piece is also incised "Avon WPTr(?) Co. 190." (Photograph by Mark Fainstein, Erie Art Museum, Erie, Pennsylvania)*

*This Jardiniere is marked "Avon B 1902." (Western Reserve Historical Society)*

# Edwin Bennett
## *Baltimore, Maryland*

~

*Painted under glaze.*

*This 13-inch-high two-handled green-glazed vase was made by the Edwin Bennett Pottery Company, Inc., of Baltimore, Maryland. It is marked "E. Bennett, 1896, KB, Albion." (Smithsonian Institution)*

The early history of the potteries founded by Edwin Bennett forms a backdrop to the history of American art pottery. James Bennett, Edwin's brother, lived in Derbyshire, England, and worked in many potteries there before coming to the United States. In 1834 he obtained a job at the Jersey City Pottery.

He later went to Troy, Indiana, where he worked at the Indiana Pottery Company. He left because he had malaria and hoped that an East Liverpool, Ohio, location would be healthier. With some money advanced from Anthony Kearns and Benjamin Harker, property owners in the area, James built a pottery in 1839. His pottery company made yellowware pieces, including mugs, pans, and other kitchen wares. The work was financially successful from the beginning, and James Bennett sent for his three brothers, Daniel, Edwin, and William, who arrived in 1841. As Bennett and Brothers, they produced yellowware and Rockingham ware. The success of this firm led to the founding of many other firms in the East Liverpool area, such as the Harker Pottery founded in 1840 by Benjamin Harker; Salt and Mears; Knowles, Taylor and Knowles; John Goodwin's pottery; Woodward, Blakely & Co.; and Vodrey.

In 1844, Edwin left the firm and moved to Pittsburgh, Pennsylvania. In 1845, he started his own pottery, the E. Bennett Chinaware Factory, in Baltimore, Maryland. His brother William joined him two years later, and the firm became E. & W. Bennett until 1856, when William left. Edwin continued to make pottery under the name Edwin Bennett Pottery from 1856 to 1890. From 1887 to 1890, he also owned the Chesapeake Pottery in Baltimore (see Chesapeake Pottery). Bennett's company was incorporated in 1890 and continued to do business as the Edwin Bennett Pottery Company Inc. until 1936. Edwin died in 1908.

The firm, which continued operating through changes in name and personnel, made all types of pottery, including the famous "Rebekah at the Well" teapot, Parian ware, Rockingham ware, porcelain, art pottery, majolica, a type of Belleek, and others.

The art pottery made at the factory was produced for only a short time—from 1895 to 1897. It was discontinued because of its poor sales. The line, called "Albion," was a slipware decorated with colored liquid clay. The body of each piece was green clay. After the design was built up from the colored glazes, the entire piece was covered with a clear glaze. Kate DeWitt Berg was the chief decorator for the art pottery line. Her wares featured figures of hunting scenes in the desert and in the jungle, and often pictured horses, camels, elephants, oriental figures, and related subjects. Another decorator of Albion ware was Annie Haslam Brinton. All pieces were marked "E. Bennett," and included the date, the word "Albion," and often the initials of the artist.

## John Bennett
*New York, New York*

~

John Bennett, born in England in 1840, trained there as a china painter in the Staffordshire potteries before 1873. Then he moved to London. Henry Doulton of the Doulton pottery hired Bennett in 1873 to establish a painted faience department. The design was painted in colored slip, then a clear shiny glaze was added over the slip decoration. Some of this pottery was displayed at the Philadelphia Centennial Exhibition in 1876, and was so popular that Bennett moved to New York City in 1877 to make his own pottery. At first he imported English pieces that he decorated at his studio, then soon built his own kilns and hired potters to make a cream-colored ware from native clays. He decorated this cream ware and also worked with a white ware made in Trenton, New Jersey.

Bennett's work was soon in great demand and brought high prices. It was exhibited and sold in many cities, including Boston, New York, Cincinnati, and San Francisco. Edwin Barber wrote in *The Pottery and Porcelain of the United States* (pp. 305–8):

> The shapes were simple and generally devoid of handles or moulded ornaments. The decorations consisted chiefly of flowers and foliage, drawn from nature in a vigorous and ornate style and painted with very few touches. A background was worked in after the painting, in loose touches and delicate tints, and finally the whole design was boldly outlined in black or very dark color. The glaze was brilliant, even, and firm, and the coloring exceedingly rich, the mustard yellows, deep blues, and browns tinged with red giving the ware a bright and attractive appearance. He also produced some pieces in the style of the so-called Limoges faience by applying colored slips to the unfired clay.

Bennett taught classes in pottery decoration in 1878, and moved to West Orange, New Jersey, in 1883. He died in 1907.

The mark used on his earlier pieces (1877–1883) was "J. Bennett, N.Y.," and usually included the date and street address.

## Biloxi Art Pottery
*See George E. Ohr*

~

## Charles Fergus Binns
*Alfred, New York*

~

Professor Charles F. Binns (1857–1934) ran the first ceramic school in the United States. He was the first director of the New York State School of Clay-working and Ceramics in Alfred, New York, from 1900 to 1931. Binns, who was born in Worcester, England, was the son of the director of the Royal Worcester Porcelain works. By the age of fourteen he was an apprentice at the works.

*Painted under glaze.*

*This drawing of a Bennett faience piece was pictured in Edwin Barber's 1893 book* The Pottery and Porcelain of the United States.

*Incised mark.*

In 1897 he moved to the United States to head a school in New Jersey and three years later became the director of the New York State School in Alfred. Binns, who was a potter as well as a teacher, made glazed stoneware. Examples of his work can be found at the New York State College of Ceramics at Alfred University, the Smithsonian Institution, and other museums. Binns usually signed his pieces with his initials and the date. Many important American potters trained under Binns, including Arthur Baggs, Paul Cox, Elizabeth Overbeck, R. Guy Cowan, and Frederick Walrath.

## Brouwer and Middle Lane
### Long Island, New York

The Middle Lane Pottery began operating on Middle Lane in East Hampton, Long Island, New York, in 1894. Its founder, Theophilus A. Brouwer, Jr., experimented with luster glaze and made pottery with unusual colors and metallic effects. He did all of the work at the pottery, from making molds and turning wares to casting and decorating. He made five types of wares. One type, made with a glaze over gold leaf, was appropriately named "Gold Leaf Underglaze." Another type, called "Fire Painting," was a biscuit pottery covered with a glaze that appeared to be a solid color until it was fired in the kiln. When a hot piece was removed and put on a heated iron plate, an iridescence with a variety of colors appeared. Mottled pieces with a high-gloss surface of red and yellow, pale green and gold, or cream with mother-of-pearl were just a few of the possible color effects created by Fire Painting. No decoration was needed beyond the natural variation in glaze colors.

A third type of pottery Brouwer made was called "Iridescent Fire Work." The pieces were glazed with a heavy coating, and the glaze and the metallic iridescence were the same color. Extreme

*Impressed or incised.*

*Used after 1903, incised.*

*Incised.*

*A black and purple iridescent glaze is used over a lighter green glaze on this 7¼-inch vase. It is marked with the M under a whalebone arch. (Smithsonian Institution)*

*A snake decorates this 5-inch-diameter iridescent vase. The piece was made by the Middle Lane Pottery, East Hampton, Long Island. (Smithsonian Institution)*

*Three Brouwer-Middle Lane pieces. At left is a 3½-inch-high vase with mouse in cheese; center, a vase 8½ inches high; and right, a pink vase 7½ inches high. (Smithsonian Institution)*

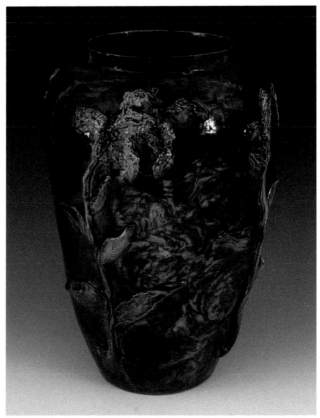

*This 12½-inch-high Brouwer vase is decorated with four applied goldenrod on a brown and gold iridescent flame-painted background. (David Rago Arts & Crafts Gallery)*

*A fiery orange, yellow, and brown glaze with iridescent effects covers this 7¼-inch vase. It is marked with the incised M under a whalebone arch, and the name Brouwer. The vase was made about 1903–1910. (Private collection; photograph from The Art Museum, Princeton University, Princeton, New Jersey)*

heat created a finished piece that resembled ancient rough glass. Pieces were made in various colors. "Sea-Grass Fire Work" was another glazed ware that was decorated through the action of the heat of the kiln. Lines that look like sea grass appear in green, brown, or gray on the plain glaze. "Kid Surface" ware was a pottery made with a solid-colored glaze. Blue, white, brown, green, and gray were used. "Flame" was a special type of pottery made by combining several techniques. Each piece has a unique design and the mold was destroyed after a fine piece was made. Brouwer considered Kid Surface ware his best product.

The factory moved to a new plant in Westhampton, Long Island, around 1903. It was usually referred to as The Brouwer Pottery. There was a gate to the grounds made of a jawbone of a whale caught near Long Island. The company used a symbol of this bone plus the letter *M* as a trademark that was impressed on each piece. The name Brouwer was incised on the pieces that were made at Westhampton. Some pieces were also marked with the word "Flame" or a picture of a flame.

Although Brouwer continued to make pottery, he had other business interests. He made a special type of "stone" figure from concrete, and in 1918 he made concrete boats. In 1925, he incorporated The Ceramic Flame Company to make and sell pottery and tiles. Brouwer died in 1932. The corporation was dissolved in 1946.

## Brush Guild
### New York, New York

The Brush Guild was organized in New York City around 1897 by the students of George de Forest Brush. The artists modeled the art pottery pieces after prehistoric patterns and used a black or blackish brown finish. Some pieces were even made with a black clay similar to black basalt.

Decorations were inspired by ancient Etruscan pottery. Annie F. Perkins and her daughter Lucy F. Perkins were part of the group and continued making the ware in Bridgeport, Connecticut, after 1908.

## Brush Pottery
### Roseville and Zanesville, Ohio

In 1901, George S. Brush went to work as editor of the *Owens Monthly*, a publication of the J. B. Owens Pottery of Zanesville, Ohio. After a short time he became the sales manager of the pottery, and in 1906 he left the company to found his own firm, the Brush Pottery Company.

Brush started his firm in a plant that had been used by the Union Pottery Company. He used Union's molds to make bowls and kitchen wares. His firm continued in business until 1908, when it

*1915–1925, found on papers, but many never have been used on pottery.*

*Revised 1927,*
*used 1958–1968,*
*paper label.*

*1965–1972,*
*paper label.*

*1930–1933,*
*paper label.*

*Used 1927–1929;*
*revised, used*
*1958–1968;*
*ink stamp.*

*After 1938,*
*mark in mold*
*or incised.*

was destroyed by fire. In 1909, Brush became manager of the J. W. McCoy Pottery of Roseville, Ohio. In 1911, the firm became the Brush-McCoy Pottery (see J. W. McCoy Pottery Co. for a listing of Brush-McCoy and Brush pottery lines).

The Brush-McCoy Pottery was later reorganized, and in December 1925 changed its name to Brush Pottery. The company's offices were moved from Roseville to Zanesville, and George Brush was its president from 1931 until his death in 1934. The plant closed in 1982.

Just as there were two separate companies named Brush Pottery Company (one from 1907 to 1908, the other from 1925 to 1982), there were two McCoy potteries: one, the J. W. McCoy Pottery, operating from 1899 to 1911 (when it changed its name to Brush-McCoy); the other, the Nelson McCoy Pottery, which was founded in 1910 by J. W. McCoy and his son Nelson as the Nelson McCoy Sanitary & Stoneware Company. This firm changed its name to the Nelson McCoy Pottery around 1933, and became part of the Mount Clemens Pottery in 1967.

*c. 1940,*
*in mold.*

*c. 1948,*
*impressed.*

*c. 1952,*
*in mold.*

*Two similar 4½-inch majolica-glazed vases with molded amaryllis decorations. (Private collection)*

# Buffalo Pottery/Deldare
*Buffalo, New York*

~

*Emerald Deldare stamped mark; year varied.*

*Stamped mark used on pitchers; year varied.*

*Stamped mark used on many pieces, including pitchers; year varied.*

*Stamped Deldare mark; year varied.*

The Buffalo Pottery Company made many types of pottery. Its famous Deldare pottery is now being classified with many of the art potteries, although it was not hand-potted or a uniquely decorated product, but rather a limited production line from a firm that made many types of chinaware. Deldare and another line called "Abino" were hand-decorated. Most of the other wares by Buffalo Pottery were decorated with decalcomanias, designs transferred from specially treated paper.

The Buffalo Pottery was founded by the Larkin Soap Company and built in Buffalo, New York, in 1901. John Larkin and his brother-in-law Elbert Hubbard manufactured soap and sold it through a premium-purchase plan. Their main purpose for establishing the pottery was to make dishes that could be given in exchange for certificates from Larkin soap. The Buffalo Pottery company, now Buffalo China, Inc., is still in business.

The art pottery of most interest to today's collector is Deldare ware. The manager of the pottery was Louis Brown; the superintendent, George H. Wood. William Rea, a ceramic engineer, perfected the body. Rea developed an olive green base clay by adding oxide of chrome to body clay made of English and Tennessee ball clay. The name Deldare refers to the clay color and not to the decoration. The first pieces were made in 1908 or 1909, although pitchers with the Deldare-colored body and black outline decorations are known dated 1906 and 1907. A later series is dated 1923, 1924, and 1925.

Pieces were decorated with English scenes from two old books, *The Vicar of Wakefield* and *Cranford*. The etchings were copied and hand-painted on the artware in mineral colors. A second series with

*This sample plate was used to advertise Buffalo Pottery Deldare ware.*

(Left to right) *Deldare ware: bowl, "Ye Village Tavern," 9½ inch diameter; chop plate, "An Evening at Ye Lion Inn," 14 inch diameter; mug, "Ye Lion Inn," 4½ inches tall; and candlesticks, 9 inches tall. (Wolf's)*

The Dutch jug (left) was made in 1906 and 1907. It measures 6¹/₈ inches and is marked "1906." The Gaudy Willow pitcher (right) is not one of the special pitchers, but belongs to the Gaudy Willow dinnerware sets. This 6⁵/₈-inch-high pitcher has an indistinct date mark. The fence on the front of the picture is dark blue, although the similar Blue Willow piece has a lattice fence. It was made about 1907. (Private collection)

The Buffalo Pottery made full sets of dishes in the Willow pattern. The sugar is 5¹/₂ inches tall; the creamer, 3¹/₂ inches. (Private collection)

The Fox Hunt (left) is a 7-inch-high pitcher marked "1907." It was offered for sale in the 1905 catalog but was also available in later years. The Roosevelt Bears Pitcher (right) was made in 1906, 1907, and 1908. This piece is marked "1907." The pitcher has pictures of the bears made popular through children's books illustrated by Floyd Campbell. (Private collection)

*The Emerald Deldare candleholder with a shield back is marked "1911." It is 6¾ inches high.*

*This Deldare humidor was made in 1909. On one side it says, "There was an old sailor and he had a wooden leg/He had no tobacco, nor tobacco could he beg." The other side says, "So save up your money and save up your rocks/And you'll always have tobacco in your own tobacco box." The humidor is 7½ inches high. (Private collection)*

its own backstamp was made in 1909 with the "Fallowfield Hunt" scenes. The only known piece of Deldare made in 1910 was a calendar plate. A third series was made in 1911 with copies of etchings from *Tours of Dr. Syntax*. This series featured a different Deldare ware called "Emerald Deldare." Some Deldare, as noted above, was made in 1923, 1924, and 1925, but the cost of manufacturing made it unprofitable and the line was discontinued. The later Deldare was made in the same manner and often by the same artists; the only difference is the date on the bottom.

Deldare ware was made in complete dinner sets, dresser sets, vases, pitchers, candleholders, punch bowls and mugs, and other shapes.

## LIST OF KNOWN DESIGN TITLES

*Ye Olden Days, 1908, 1909, 1923, 1924, 1925:* "All You Have to Do to Teach the Dutch English," "An Evening at ye Lion Inn," "At ye Lion Inn," "Breaking Cover," "Dancing ye Minuet," "The Great Controversy," "Heirlooms," "His Manner of Telling Stories," "Scenes of Life in Olden Days," "Scenes of Village Life in ye Olden Days," "Street Scenes," "Their Manner of Telling Stories," "This Amazed Me," "To Advise Me in a Whisper," "To Demand My Annual Rent," "To Spare an Old Broken Soldier," "Travelling in ye Olden Days," "Village Life in ye Olden Days," "Welcome Me with Most Cordial Hospitality," "Which He Returned with a Courtesy," "With a Cane Superior Air," "Ye English Village," "Ye Lion Inn," "Ye Village Gossips," "Ye Village Parson," "Ye Village Schoolmaster," "Ye Village Street," "Ye Village Tavern."

*Fallowfield Hunt, 1908, 1909:* "At the Three Pigeons," "Breakfast at the Three Pigeons," "Breaking Cover," "The Dash," "The Death," "The Hunt Supper," "The Return," "The Start." Other pictures in this series are just entitled "The Fallowfield Hunt" or are uncaptioned. All of these pictures were done originally as prints by Cecil Aldin about 1900.

## DESIGNS

Emerald Deldare was made in 1910 and 1911. The *Dr. Syntax* scenes by the English caricaturist Thomas Rowlandson were copied on the Emerald Deldare with minor alterations. The borders of the ware are Art Nouveau style or geometric. Some pieces have an Art Nouveau central design instead of the Dr. Syntax picture.

## ABINO WARE

Abino ware was made in 1911, 1912, and 1913, after Deldare. The shapes were the same as Deldare, but it had a transfer-printed, hand-decorated design showing boats, sea scenes, and windmills. The scenes picture Point Abino, a Canadian beach near Buffalo. The designs are misty and soft, with pale green and rust the main colors. Abino was marked with hand-printed black letters plus the date and a series number.

## PITCHERS

It seems necessary to include the pitchers made by Buffalo Pottery from 1905 to 1909, although these were not art pottery. These pitchers were made of semivitreous china. Twenty-nine patterns are known today. The decorations are transfer-printed and often hand-decorated. Many pieces had gold at the top edge and on the handles. The twenty-nine patterns include:

*The blue and white sailor pitcher is dated 1906. It is 9¼ inches high.*

Art Nouveau . . . . . . . . . . 1908.

Blue Geranium . . . . . . . . 1905.

The Buffalo Hunt . . . . .undated.

Canton Blue Flowers . . . . 1905.

Chrysanthemum. . . . . .undated.

Cinderella . . . . . . . . . . . .1907 (offered for sale 1905–1909 in Larkin catalogs).

Dutch Jug . . . . . . . . 1906–1907.

The Fox Hunt and the Whirl of the Town . . . . . . . 1908.

George Washington . . . . . . 1907.

Gloriana . . . . . . . . . 1907–1908.

The Gunner . . . . . . . .undated.

Holland . . . . . . . . . . . . . . 1908.

Hounds and Stag . . . . . . . 1906.

John Paul Jones . . . . . . . . 1907.

The Landing of Roger Williams . . . . . . . . 1907.

Mason Jug . . . . . . . . . . . . 1907.

Melon-shaped China Pitcher . . . . . . . . . . . . . . 1909.

The Old Mill . . . . . . . . . . 1907.

Orchids . . . . . . . . . . . .undated.

Pilgrim . . . . . . . . . . . . . . 1908.

Rip Van Winkle . . . . . . . . 1907.

Robin Hood . . . . . . . . . . . 1906.

Roosevelt Bears . . . . . . . . 1907.

Sailing Ships and Lightship. . . . . . . . . . . . 1906.

Sailors and Lighthouse . . . . . . . . . . . 1906.

Triumph (annual poppy) . . . . . . . . . . . .undated.

Vertical Stripe . . . . . . . . . 1906.

The Whaling City— New Bedford Massachusetts . . . . . . . . . 1907.

Wild Ducks . . . . . . . . . . . 1907.

*The Deldare designs were used in later years on a pink background pottery called Rouge Ware. This 11-inch plate is decorated with the scene "Morgan's Red Coach Tavern." The ware was made after 1928. (Private collection)*

# Byrdcliffe
## *Woodstock, New York*

*Impressed mark.*

An art colony was founded in Woodstock, New York, in 1902 by Ralph Radcliffe Whitehead, a student of the English art critic John Ruskin and his philosophy. The colony members endeavored to replace the factory system with the craft system. Their art and designs reflected nature. They made furniture, metalwork, textiles, read poetry, and painted. Whitehead supported the colony, which never became financially self-sustaining.

The colony began to make pottery in the summer of 1903. The Byrdcliffe Pottery was founded soon after by Edith Penman and Elizabeth R. Hardenbergh. Others working there were Charles Volkmar and Mabel Davidson. The pottery was made by hand without a wheel, and work was fired in an open-air kiln. The pieces usually had dull glazes of blue, green, or rose.

Zulma Steele, who had come to the colony about 1904 to work on furniture, ran the pottery after 1923. It continued until at least 1928. Another pottery, White Pines, was established about 1915 near the Byrdcliffe colony by Jane Byrd Whitehead and her husband, Ralph. Ralph was responsible for the mold making and production. Jane had studied with Frederick Hürten Rhead in 1913, and some White Pines pieces may have been decorated on Rhead blanks. Most pieces were inspired by oriental shapes. Light sea-green matte glaze and red, orange, rose, black, and turquoise glazes were used. Vases were marked "White Pines" or "RRW," or with a paper label featuring a stylized pine tree. The White Pines pottery operated until at least 1926.

# California Faience
## *Berkeley, California*

*Impressed.*

California Porcelain

*Impressed.*

Potteries often remained in the same building but kept changing owners or names. One example was Thomas & Bragdon, a pottery and shop started in about 1916 in Berkeley, California, by William V. Bragdon and Chauncey R. Thomas. The partners were trained in the ceramic and metal industries.

Bragdon, born in Pittsburgh, Pennsylvania, in 1884, had graduated from the New York State School of Clay-working and Ceramics in Alfred, New York, and worked at the University City Porcelain Works in St. Louis. Thomas (1877–1950) was a metalworker and teacher. The shop moved to a new location in Berkeley by 1922 and was renamed The Tile Shop, although tile and art pottery were both made. In 1924, the business formally became California Faience.

The pottery was cast and generally covered with monochrome matte glaze. Tiles were hand-pressed in molds and embellished with polychrome decorations. Red clay was often used for tiles. A local designer, Stella Loveland Towne, helped with the tiles.

The company, in association with the West Coast Porcelain Manufacturers of Millbrae, California, made a special line marked "California Porcelain" for the giftware trade in 1925, and also made some of the tiles for William Randolph Hearst's castle at San Simeon, California, in 1927. Production of the artwares stopped around 1930, during the Depression, although some tiles were made in 1932. Bragdon bought out Thomas in the late 1930s and continued to operate the pottery as a studio for local artists and decorators. Bragdon sold the business about 1955. He died in 1959.

The impressed mark "California Faience" was used even before the shop adopted the name.

## Camark Pottery
### Camden, Arkansas

Camden Art Tile and Pottery Company, known by its trademark Camark Pottery ("Cam" for Camden and "Ark" for Arkansas), was founded by Samuel J. (Jack) Carnes in Camden, Arkansas, in 1926. The pottery needed an experienced art director, and Carnes hired John Lessell to head the art department. Lessell had worked at Owen China Co., J. B. Owens Pottery Company, and Weller Pottery in Zanesville, Ohio. He established the Art China Company of Zanesville in 1924 and moved the company to Newark, Ohio, the following year.

Carnes shipped some Arkansas clay to Ohio for testing by Lessell before the Camden pottery started operating. The first Ohio-made pieces, signed "Lessell," were sent to Camark in 1926. There is some evidence that Lessell and his wife, Jenny, visited Camden early in 1926.

Lessell used the Arkansas clay to produce several lines of art pottery for Camark. He probably worked with another prospective Camark employee, Alfred P. Tetzschner, who had previously been with the Fraunfelter China Company of Zanesville, Ohio. The pottery pieces were made as duplicates of lines Lessell had designed for Owens and Weller. Another line was similar to a type of pottery made by Owen China Company, where Lessell may have worked about 1905. Camark's goal was apparently to use Arkansas clay and labor to produce unique "reproductions" of popular wares made in Ohio. The designs already had customer approval and were known to sell well.

Camark's best-known lines are those Lessell produced based on his Weller Marengo and LaSa lines. The Camark Old English Rose pieces, often signed "Lessell" or "LeCamark" on the decorated surface, are nearly identical to the Marengo line, while Camark's Bronze looks like LaSa and also like Owen China Company's Swastika Keramos. Camark also reproduced the black and gold Sudanese and Opalesce lines Lessell made for J. B. Owens, as well as other versions of Swastika Keramos.

*LeCamark, signed, 1927; pieces are also signed Camark.*

### CAMARK

*Impressed die stamp, 1927–mid-1930s.*

*English script, Arkansas outline, red-and-white paper label, mid-1930s–1960s. Similar mark impressed, 1928–1929.*

*Gold ink stamp, 1927–1928; black ink stamp, early 1930s; impressed die stamp, 1928–1929; similar paper label, solid gold, 1927; brown and gold, 1930s; blue and gold, 1940s–1960s.*

*Mold mark, mid-1930s–1960s.*

## CAMARK

*This Old English Rose lamp base was made by Lessell about 1926. The pattern is almost identical to the Marengo pattern Lessell designed for Weller. (June Greenwald Antiques)*

*A Camark 16-inch "Blue and Gold" matte vase, hand-thrown in 1928. (Collection of David Edwin Gifford; photograph by Gene Taylor, courtesy of the Old State House Museum, Little Rock, Arkansas)*

Lessell died in Ohio in December 1926, but when the plant in Camden was completed in 1927, Carnes hired John's wife and daughter Billie to head Camark's art department. The Lessells continued for a short time to decorate the lines John Lessell had developed for Camark. These were often signed "LeCamark."

The Lessells left Camark in December 1927 and the pottery produced less lusterware. A modernistic line was introduced and more reproduction lines were added. Pieces resembling Weller's Frosted Matte, Cloudburst, and Barcelona were copied. Camark hired Boris Trifinoff, a Muncie Pottery employee, to mix glazes; some Muncie lines were copied. (Muncie Pottery, founded by Charles Benham, operated in Muncie, Indiana, from about 1922 to 1951.)

Camark's production of art pottery stopped by the late 1920s. Instead, the firm manufactured pastel cast and molded florist ware and novelty pieces until it closed in the 1960s.

Most Camark art pottery items are marked with paper labels. "Genuine Camark" in an Arkansas state outline label, red on white, was used in 1927. An oval gold and blue metallic label was used during the 1950s and 1960s. Some pieces have the word "Camark" incised on the bottom. John Lessell signed many of the pieces he designed for Camark.

# Cambridge Art Pottery
### Cambridge, Ohio

A small art pottery in the southern Ohio area was the Cambridge Art Pottery of Cambridge, Ohio. The firm was started in 1900 and worked until 1908. Pieces made were similar to the other brown-glazed decorated wares of the area, such as Weller Louwelsa, Owens Utopian, or Rookwood. Floral decorations and some portraits were used to decorate the pieces, which were made from local clays. Artists who worked at this factory seemed to have been well traveled and many of them also decorated at other Ohio factories. Charles B. Upjohn of the Weller Pottery was hired as a designer and modeler.

The pottery also made slip-decorated wares called "Terrhea," and a brown-glazed line called "Oakwood." Beginning in 1902, Cambridge Art Pottery made various cooking wares, including a brown ware with white lining, until 1907–8, when the firm again returned to art pottery. That year the pottery made a matte green glazed ware called "Otoe." The company changed its name to Guernsey Earthenware Company in 1909.

The word "Oakwood" was used as a mark by several companies: Cambridge Art Pottery used the incised word "Oakwood." "Oakwood Pottery, Dayton, Ohio" was used by another pottery working about 1877. Advertisements from 1900 for the Oakwood Art Pottery of Wellesville, Ohio, show artwares, but no marked pieces are known. There was also an Oakwood Pottery in East Liverpool, Ohio, about 1902, but again no marked pieces are known.

TERRHEA

OAKWOOD

CAMBRIDGE  Guernsey

Acorn  OAKWOOD

*Cambridge marks can appear either by themselves or with the acorn and/or cipher. When the name appears alone, it is impressed. When the acorn and/or cipher appears with the name, the mark is printed.*

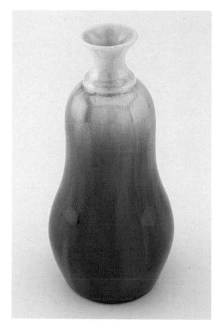

*"Oakwood" is impressed on the bottom of this Cambridge Art Pottery vase. The vase is 6¾ inches high and glazed in mottled yellow to green to brown shades. (Private collection)*

*A 7½-inch-high Cambridge vase glazed in shades of dark brown to tan. It is also marked "Oakwood." (Private collection)*

*This Cambridge Art Pottery vase, mottled brown, green, and yellow, stands 10 inches high. (Private collection)*

## Chesapeake Pottery
### *Baltimore, Maryland*
❧

Henry and Isaac Brougham started the Chesapeake Pottery in Baltimore, Maryland, in 1880. They sold the company in 1882 to David Francis Haynes, a salesman of many types of pottery and porcelain. He hired two Englishmen, Frederick Hackney, who had worked with Josiah Wedgwood and Sons, Limited, of Stoke-on-Trent, and Lewis Taft, who had worked at the Brownfield factory of Staffordshire. They developed the majolica look-alike Clifton ware and the ivory-colored Avalon ware. Other Chesapeake lines were Calvert ware, a blue or green-glazed ware with horizontal bands of decoration, calvertine, a gray, pink, or olive ware, and Severn ware, a gray-brown earthenware decorated with raised metallic bands.

Though the company grew, by 1887 money troubles led to a sale to Edwin Bennett of Baltimore. In 1890 Haynes became a partner of Bennett's son, and the firm was named Haynes, Bennett and Company until 1895, when Bennett retired. Frank R. Haynes, David's son, then became a partner, and in 1896 the name became D. F. Haynes and Son. In 1924 the company was closed.

*This Pilgrim vase with transfer-printed floral design is of semiporcelain with an acid-etched vellum finish. It measures 18½ inches high by 12¼ inches wide by 5½ inches long. (High Museum of Art, Atlanta, Georgia; Virginia Carroll Crawford Collection)*

*Ink-stamped.*     *Ink-stamped.*     *In mold or ink-stamped.*

# Cincinnati Art Pottery Co.

### Cincinnati, Ohio

*1890–1891, impressed.*

*1879–1886, printed in red or impressed.*

## KEZONTA

*1886–1891, printed in red or impressed.*

The Cincinnati Art Pottery Company was founded in Cincinnati, Ohio, in 1879 as a joint-stock company with Frank Huntington as president. Thomas J. Wheatley of T. J. Wheatley & Co. worked for the firm until 1882. At first the company made underglaze-decorated ware and Barbotine ware. Barbotine was discontinued and replaced by a ware called "Hungarian Faience," which had an overglaze decoration on white clay. Portland Blue Faience was a dark blue glazed ware with gold decorations. The most important product of the company was Kezonta ware, an ivory-colored faience with natural floral colors and gold scrollwork decorations.

The name Cincinnati Art Pottery was not used often after 1882, when T. J. Wheatley left. The factory closed in 1891. The manager of the company at that time, William Dell, obtained the molds and glazes and continued to make Hungarian Faience at William Dell Pottery. These pieces are signed with his name. Several marks were used by the firm, including "Kezonta" and "CAP Co." This pottery should not be confused with the Pottery Club of Cincinnati.

*The Cincinnati Art Pottery's "Hungarian Faience" as pictured in* Popular Science Monthly, *January 1892.*

White crackle glaze with cloisonné decorations of natural-colored flowers on a sky-blue background decorate this gold-trimmed Kezonta ware vase. It was made by the Cincinnati Art Pottery Company about 1895 and is marked with the word "Cincinnati" stenciled in a circle. (Smithsonian Institution)

*The Cincinnati Art Pottery Company made this pitcher marked "KEZONTA." It has a yellow crackle glaze with gold overglaze decorations. The interior is covered with a clear glaze. The pitcher is 12 inches high and 6 inches in diameter. The gold decoration is credited to Jesse Dean of New York, who worked from about 1870 to 1910. (Smithsonian Institution)*

# Clewell

*Canton, Ohio*

∾

Charles Walter Clewell of Canton, Ohio, made a unique pottery called "Clewell Ware." A leaflet given out with pieces of the pottery said:

> A number of years ago, while visiting the Wadsworth Atheneum in Hartford, I saw a small bronze wine jug in the J. Pierpont Morgan Memorial Collection. The bronze had been found at Boscoreale during the excavations* which led to the finding of the famous silver treasure of the Louvre, was accredited to the Romans and dated 200 B.C. It was blue; a wonderful blue varying from the very light tones through turquoise to almost black with flecks of green and rustlike brown and spots of bare darkened metal.
>
> Seeing this little jug cost me more than two years of experimenting and a number of trips to Hartford to compare results, but finally the perfect blue appeared. It was a long hunt and particularly difficult; textbooks gave me no help.

The blue-patinated bronze that Charles Clewell developed was used on Clewell Ware after 1923. Clewell also developed a method of bronze coating on pottery. He could then treat the bronze in various ways to make it turn different colors. At a specific moment during the process when he felt the effect was ideal, he chemically treated the piece to stop the coloring and permanently fix the design and color. This meant that Clewell Ware could be washed later and the colors would remain.

Clewell started his experiments in 1899. The studio was opened around 1906. Clewell Ware was made in very limited quantities from 1902 to 1955. Pottery blanks were bought from Ohio potteries such as Roseville; Weller; Owens; Rookwood; Cambridge; Knowles, Taylor and Knowles; and others. The pieces were covered with a thin coating of bronze and specially treated. Sometimes the bronze was made to look as if it had been hammered. Other pieces looked as if they had been made with metal rivets. A few pieces had incised line designs, and some were made with a silver finish. They were well suited for use as pitchers and vases because the pieces actually had metal on the outside and pottery on the inside. A Clewell advertisement that appeared in the 1908 Burr McIntosh Christmas Catalog suggested the purchase of a Holland Stein and Tankard set:

*A pair of 6½-inch Clewell vases, brown with green patina, flank a seed-form vase, 6 inches tall, in the same colors. (Wolf's)*

(Left to right) *Three Clewell vases: streaked green patina, 7½ inches tall; green patina, 5½ inches; and brown patina, green foot, 8½ inches. (Wolf's)*

*Incised.*

*Incised.*

*Impressed.*

**Clewell Metal Art Canton, O.**
*Impressed.*

* The excavations took place in southern Italy, at the foot of Mount Vesuvius, in the late 1800s.

*The Clewell mug was offered for sale in 1908 by the Clewell Studio, 1956 East 9th Street, Canton, Ohio, through a Christmas catalog. It is part of the Holland Stein and Tankard Set, handmade of hammered copper with a porcelain lining. The pieces could be furnished plain or marked with a monogram or inscription. The mug, which is 4½ inches high and 3 inches in diameter, is unmarked. The small souvenir piece (right) is 1½ inches high and 4 inches in diameter. The "brass" label "riveted" to the bowl says, "Compliments/Canton Bridge Co./Canton O." The bottom is marked with the circular "Clewell Canton, O" mark. (Private collection)*

These sets are faithful reproductions of the original old Holland Steins of four hundred years ago, made of hammered copper (brass or silver) with porcelain lining and hand made by a special process which we control. Sets furnished plain or quaintly marked with monogram or inscription.

After Charles Clewell died in 1965 at the age of eighty-nine, his daughter sold most of the remaining stock to nearby collectors and art institutes. It is said that fewer than three thousand pieces remained.

Pieces of Clewell were marked with an incised "Clewell," an impressed "Clewell Metal Art Canton, O.," "Clewell Coppers," "Clewell Canton, O.," or a *W* within a *C*.

Clewell also cast bronzes that can be found signed with his name. His formula for producing the blue patina on bronze was burned at his death and his method remains a secret.

## Clifton Pottery
### See Lonhuda Pottery
~

## Cowan Pottery
### Cleveland and Rocky River, Ohio
~

R. Guy Cowan* was born in East Liverpool, Ohio, on August 1, 1884. His father and grandfather had been potters and he started to help in his father's pottery at a young age. He studied art in high

*Cowan mark, stamped in black or impressed on the bottom.*

---

\* Reginald Guy Cowan was his given name, but Guy would not use it and was always known as R. Guy Cowan (from a letter dated March 20, 1965, from R. M. Hanna to The Western Reserve Historical Society).

COWAN

*Impressed.*

ℭℛ

*Incised.*

COWAN
POTTERY

*1913–1917, incised.*

Cowan Pottery

*1913–1917, incised.*

LAKEWARE

*After 1928, mark in mold.*

school, graduated, and moved to Cleveland, Ohio, where he taught ceramics classes at East Technical High School. He took a few years off from teaching and completed a course in ceramic engineering at Alfred University in New York State in 1911. He then returned to teaching in Cleveland, and in 1913 opened his own pottery studio. During his years of teaching and studying, he often visited the studio of Horace Potter at the Potter Studios, a popular gathering place for many Cleveland artists. Metalwork, jewelry, and ceramics were made there and sold in the retail shop.

In 1913, Guy Cowan built a kiln in his backyard at the corner of East Ninety-seventh Street and Euclid Avenue. His work was exhibited, and with the help of the City of Cleveland and the Cleveland Chamber of Commerce, he incorporated his business and built a larger studio at Nicholson Avenue in Lakewood, Ohio. Most of the early Cowan pieces were lead glazed and were made from terra-cotta and buff clays probably obtained near East Liverpool, Ohio.

During World War I, Guy Cowan closed his pottery studio, but the pottery received official recognition and first prize at the International Show at the Chicago Art Institute in 1917. Cowan served in the Chemical Warfare Service as a captain. After the war, he was offered several jobs. He decided to reopen the Cowan Pottery Studio, and Wendell G. Wilson, an army major with whom he had served, came to manage it.

Soon after the pottery reopened, the natural gas well at the plant ran out, so a new pottery was built at Lake Avenue and Linda Street in Rocky River, Ohio, in 1920. An old barn was used as the office and working plant. Nine gas kilns were built at the site.

*The elephant bookend with a lobster-red glaze is 7½ inches high. The stork flower frog is 12 inches high. (Wolf's)*

(Above) *A 1929 catalog of the Cowan Potters, Inc. shows the King and Queen decanters based on the characters in Lewis Carroll's "Alice Through the Looking Glass." Figures retailed at $5.00 each in ivory, black, or oriental. Waylande De Santis Gregory designed the set.*

(Left) *The Art Deco centerpiece and candleholder are glazed with silver luster. (Berenice Kent Collection)*

Pale green glaze was used on this plate with carved decorations of deer and dogs. It is 11½ inches in diameter. The Cowan Pottery made these dishes, which were designed by Thelma Frazier Winter. The line was soon dropped because so many were damaged in the kiln. (*Private collection*)

A blue-green Cowan dinner plate, decorated with carved fish and seaweed. Probably a factory sample. On the back, "$200/dozen" has been written in dark glaze. (*June Greenwald Antiques*)

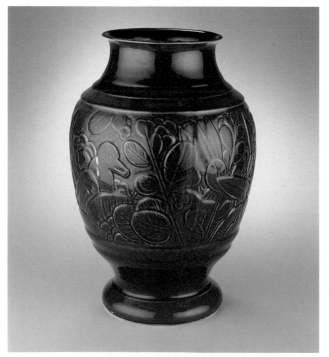

Ducks and foliage are carved on the sides of this large maroon-glazed vase. The 12-inch-high piece was made by the Cowan Pottery in the 1920s. It is marked with the incised name "Cowan" and the circular Cowan mark. (*Private collection*)

A brilliant yellow crackle glaze covers this Cowan vase. Irregularities on the lower half of the piece are caused by thicker glaze and are not part of the planned decoration. It is 7 inches high, 5 inches wide, and marked with the circular Cowan impressed mark. (*Private collection*)

The large camel bookends are 8½ inches high, 8¼ inches long, and 4¾ inches wide. (*June Greenwald Antiques*)

A Cowan elf flower holder. The bowl, 10½ inches wide, 17 inches long, and 4½ inches high, is marked with the circular Cowan impressed mark. (*Private collection*)

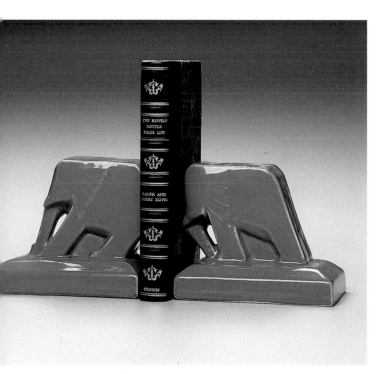

This pair of bookends, often called "Push me, Pull me," features carved elephants. Each measures 4¾ inches high, 5½ inches long, and 3¾ inches wide. Each is marked in ink, "Cowan Pottery, Rocky River." (*Private collection*)

A flower bowl has a removable flower holder in the bottom (unseen in the picture) and a removable carved top. Flower stems were poked through the hole and into the lower holder. The bowl measures 5¾ inches high, 10 inches long, and 8½ inches wide and carries the circular Cowan mark. (*Private collection*)

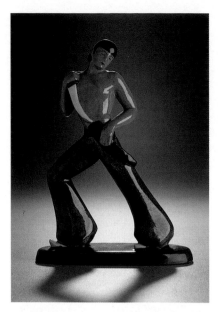

*The dancer was made in several different color combinations. This version had marooned yellow parts, other versions had green parts or were made in an undecorated cream color. There is a matching woman dancer. The figure by Elizabeth Seaver Ness is 9½ inches high. (Private collection)*

Cowan briefly returned to school around 1921 and took courses at the John Huntington Polytechnic Institute in Cleveland. In 1921 he began a large-scale commercial production, and more than twelve hundred dealers in the United States, including stores such as Marshall Field of Chicago, Wanamaker of Philadelphia, and Halle Brothers of Cleveland, sold his pottery. Instead of redware he used a high-fired porcelain body and colorful glazes. Almost all of the pieces were molded. He also made tiles: the floor of the Solarium of the Cleveland Museum of Art was paved with Cowan floor tile that remained until 1958, when the floor was replaced; the tiles were made from buff clay from eastern Ohio. The pottery also made doorknobs, fountains, wall panels, vases and figurines, flower holders, and other commercial wares. The firm had forty employees by 1925.

The Cleveland City Directory of 1927 notes that the Cowan Pottery Studio, Inc., was incorporated in 1927 with a capital of $100,000. It was formerly the Cleveland Pottery and Tile Company. Officers were R. Guy Cowan, president; Harry J. Thompson, vice president and treasurer; and Jerome Fiske, secretary.

The pottery's designs were usually by Cowan himself, but he often bought designs from other Cleveland artists and students at the former Cleveland School of Art, now the Cleveland Institute of Art. Cowan headed the Ceramic Department at the School of Art from 1928 through 1933, while Waylande Gregory was the "artist, sculptor in residence." Gregory, a highly paid Cowan Pottery employee, designed pieces for Cowan, and two student artists, Paul Bogatay and Thelma Frazier (Winter), were hired by Cowan on a permanent basis.

The Cowan Pottery Studio started having money problems in 1929, and Guy decided to reorganize it into an artists' colony. The firm was reorganized as Cowan Potters, Inc. Howard P. Eells, Jr., was chairman of the board, Guy Cowan was president, and Charles C. Berry was vice president and general manager. A group of wealthy civic-minded Clevelanders, including Mr. and Mrs. F. F. Prentice, William G. Mather, John L. Severance, H. G. Dalton, Mr. and Mrs. E. B. Greens, Mrs. Ben P. Bole, Lyman Treadway, and Mary Newberry, helped with the financing. The new company planned to move the factory to a modern building in a nearby suburb, where "spirit and physical beauty will be fitting and compatible with the artistic nature of its work" (*The Bystander of Cleveland*, September 1929).

Most of the company's money problems continued into the Depression, and in December 1931 Cowan Potters, Inc., was closed. The remaining stock was sold to the Bailey Company, a department store in Cleveland. Guy Cowan continued working in Cleveland as a research engineer for Ferro Enamel until 1933, when he moved to Syracuse, New York, to become a consultant to the Onondaga Pottery Company. He continued to work and teach there until he died in March 1957.

*This 9-inch candlestick with a groundhog was made for the Rowfant Club of Cleveland, Ohio, in 1925. It is signed in ink, "R.G. Cowan #64 of 156 copies." (Private collection)*

The first pottery made by Guy Cowan was of red clay covered with lead glaze that was hand-signed. When a new kiln was built in 1920, a real porcelain body was used. The body was made from English china clay, English ball clay, Maine feldspar, and Illinois flint. The English ball clay was shipped by boat to Philadelphia and brought to Cleveland one or two train carloads at a time.

The equipment at the plant was the most modern of its day. The clay was ground, searched by magnets for iron, and filter-pressed into slabs. Jiggered clay was used on the potter's wheel and for hand-modeling. Slip clay was used to pour into the molds. The artist made the original design using plaster or clay. A plaster cast was made and filled with plaster to form a new model, and the new model was then reworked. The perfected model was used to make a block and case that formed many molds. Some of the molds were made in as many as twenty pieces.

Most of the wares were made of porcelain and covered with a colored glaze. Tiles were made of tan clay from eastern Ohio.

The firm was making commercial wares and tiles in 1921. By 1925, Cowan had a full line of table settings, bowls, candlesticks, compotes, lamp bases, patterned dishes, teapots, cups and saucers, wares for the sickroom which included toast covers, and the usual figurines and vases.

The flower figurines were introduced in 1925. The table setting of bowl, flower holder, compotes, and candlestick became popular. Lakeware, an inexpensive line for flower shops, was introduced in 1928. It had the Cowan shapes, but different glazes. In later years, the Lakeware and Cowan glazes seem to have been interchanged. Cowan also made humidors, wine sets, Sunbonnet Girl bookends, and a variety of statuettes for radio cabinets. A 1930 contest that offered $10 for the best planting promoted the strawberry jars.

The range of products produced by the Cowan Potteries is far-reaching, from art pottery to commercial pottery. Limited-edition pieces were made to sell at high prices, while some ashtrays sold for as little as 50¢. Pieces were glazed in jade, la garda, daffodil, oriental red, basalt, apple blossom, larkspur, jet, delft blue, russet brown, plum, silver, feu rouge, May green, ivory, a light blue called "clair de lune," the famous Egyptian blue, and crystal. In the fall of 1928, verd antique, October, and fawn glazes were introduced. In 1930, new matrix glazes were azure, plum, peach, and fir green; each gave a two-colored mottled effect. Lusterware was colored fire blue, marigold, sea green, and larkspur blue. Crackleware was glazed guava, spruce, terra-cotta, parchment, or Egyptian blue. Some pieces were coated with black slip and had designs cut through to the white body. Glazes were low gloss or flat. Sometimes two glazes were used on the same piece and a new name was used in the catalog; for example, ivory and nasturtium green made April, ivory with pink was apple blossom, and ivory and orchid produced hyacinth. Many colors were given fanciful names.

The most famous piece of Cowan pottery is the Jazz bowl made by Viktor Schreckengost in 1931. It was a special order from Eleanor Roosevelt for use at the governor's mansion in Albany, New York. Her order was for a set of twenty "New Yorkish" punch bowls. After seeing the bowls, she ordered another for the White House even before her husband, Franklin Delano Roosevelt, was elected president. The bowl was then put into production at the pottery and about fifty were made. Some were turquoise

An 8-inch pink vase sits on a separate 1½-inch pottery base made to resemble an oriental-carved wooden stand. Each carries an impressed Cowan mark. Cowan made many different "wooden" stands to hold oriental-shaped vases, popular for flower arranging in the 1930s. (Private collection)

Moses is an 18½-inch-high brilliant blue figure designed by Alexander Blazys and made at the Cowan Pottery in 1930. (Courtesy of the Western Reserve Historical Society)

blue, some green. Early examples had a straight top edge; later ones had a flared edge due to sagging problems with the straight edge. Two sizes were made, the largest 11½ by 16½ inches. Schreckengost was an important figure in the American ceramics industry. He had trained in Vienna and studied and taught at the Cleveland School of Art. He worked at Cowan and several Sebring, Ohio, potteries. He was a designer for Murray Ohio Company, a toy firm, and is still working in ceramics.

Among Cowan marks are "Cowan Pottery" incised on early redware pieces, often in conjunction with the artist's initials or Cowan's monogram; "Cowan" stamped in black; "Cowan Pottery" stamped in black; and "Lakeware" impressed on that line from 1927 to 1931.

## ARTISTS AND DESIGNERS

*(The listing includes some of their known pieces;
dates other than birth and death dates
indicate a reference in catalogs.)*

*Russell Barnett Aiken.* (b. 1910).

*Elizabeth Anderson.* (Married Hugh Seaver; later married Eliot Ness) "Spanish Dancers," "Pierrot and Pierette," 1928.

*Whitney Atchley.* (b. 1908).

*Arthur E. Baggs.* (b. 1886, d. 1947) Potter and ceramist, crystalline glaze expert; owner, Marblehead Pottery, 1915–1936; headed Ceramic Department of Ohio State University, 1928–1935.

*Alexander Blazys.* (b. 1894, d. 1963) 1927–1929. Sculptor—most important piece is monumental sculpture in bronze, *City Fettering Nature,* Cleveland Museum of Art; also ceramic sculptures, "Moses," "Russian Dancers"; head of Sculpture Department, Cleveland School of Art.

*Paul Bogatay.* (b. 1905, d. 1972) 1929–1930. Designer, unique pottery in limited edition.

*R. Guy Cowan.* (b. 1884, d. 1957) 1912–1931. "Adam and Eve," "Margarita," "Madonna," 1929.

*Dalzee.*

*Edris Eckhardt.* (b. 1907) Designer, WPA potter; glass artist.

*Waylande De Santis Gregory.* (b. 1905, d. 1971) Artist, sculptor in residence, Cleveland School of Art. Beaten dog, relief decoration vase, 1929; "U-19," "Pan Sitting on a Toadstool Swan," "Salome," "Alice in Wonderland," 1930; "Burlesque Dancer," "Diana and the Two Fawns," "Tors," 1932. Later taught at Cranbrook Academy, Bloomfield Hills, Michigan. Opened own studio in Bound Brook, New Jersey, 1940–1945.

*Richard O. Hummel.* Ceramic technician, chemist; mixed glazes, made clay bodies.

*A. Drexel Jacobson.* (b. 1895, d. 1973) "Julia," "Antinea," 1928; "Introspection," 1932.

*Raoul Josset.* 1930. B-16 large bowl, relief decoration; sports figurines—football, polo, etc. French monumental terra-cottas with Chicago Terra-Cotta Company. Invited by Cowan to work in pottery.

*Jose Martin.* 1930. French woodcarver; did intricate carvings on plaster

*Thelma Frazier (Winter) and Paul Bogatay are shown in 1930 applying underglaze color and liquid body stains to Cowan Pottery vases before glazing. The Indian figures in the center of the table were designed by F. Luis Mora. Notice the Art Deco decorations on the vases and platter on the table.*

31

*Limited-edition figures of Adam and Eve, shown in a 1930 catalog of Cowan Potters, Inc.*

molds for lidded jars, etc. Art Deco style. Invited to pottery by Cowan.

*Mr. McDonald.*

*F. Luis Mora.* (b. 1874, d. 1940) Sculptor and painter of Southwest. Series of three ceramic mold figures: Indian Brave, 16 inches high; Seated Girl, 9 inches; Woman with Flower Basket, 16 inches.

*Elmer L. Novotny.* (b. 1909) Enamelist, portrait painter; headed Art Department at Kent State University until his retirement in 1974.

*Margaret Postgate.* 1929, 1932.

*Viktor Schreckengost.* (b. 1906) Arabesque plate, 1931; Jazz bowl, 1931.

*Elsa Shaw.* Design instructor, Cleveland School of Art. Tile mural of Grecian figures, Art Deco style.

*Walter A. Sinz.* (b. 1881) 1925–1930. Sculptor, Sculpture Department, Cleveland School of Art. "Me and My Shadow," relief plates. Central figurines for table settings with bowls and candlesticks.

*Jack Waugh.* Mold maker.

*Frank N. Wilcox.* (b. 1887) 1925. Designed Boy and Girl bookends.

*H. Edward Winter.* (b. 1908, d. 1976) 1930. Designer, limited-edition pottery.

*Thelma Frazier Winter.* (b. 1903, d. 1977) 1928–1930. Designer, limited editions of vases and plaques. Colorist in underglaze painting for F. Luis Mora's Indian Series (three figures, 9 to 16 inches high) and Elsa Shaw's large-scale tile murals. Service plates, limited edition, in pale blue-green (opalescent glaze with raised design) undersea design. Crackle plates, 1929–1930.

### LIMITED EDITIONS

*Partial list:* Antinea, 100, bust of a woman, 13⅞ inches high, Drexel Jacobson, 1928; Burlesque Dancer, 50, Waylande Gregory; Giulia, 500, bust of Italian girl, 10⅝ inches high, A. Drexel Jacobson, 1928; Mary, 50, Margaret Postgate, 1929; Madonna, 50, Margaret Postgate, 1929; Adam and Eve, 25, 13½ inches high, terra-cotta glaze, R. Guy Cowan, 1929; Margarita, 50, shell-green glaze, R. Guy Cowan, 1929; Diana and the Two Fawns, 100, Waylande Gregory, 1929; Torso, 1929, Waylande Gregory; Moses, blue glaze, Alexander Blazys, 1930; service plates, undersea designs, pale blue-green with raised white decorations, Thelma Frazier Winter, 1930.

## Paul E. Cox Pottery
### New Orleans, Louisiana
~

Paul E. Cox worked at the Newcomb Pottery in New Orleans, Louisiana, from 1910 to 1918. He taught at Iowa State College from 1920 to 1939, then opened a pottery in New Orleans in 1939. His main product was strawberry canning pots, but he also made art pottery, some of which closely resembled the Newcomb Pottery moss and moonlight (blue and green) wares. The pottery was sold in 1946.

We have seen a marked black-glazed vase with paper label, "The Paul E. Cox Pottery, New Orleans, Louisiana, 3(7)8 Pine Street, telephone 6401-W." The Newcomb-type pieces are marked with a circular mark, "The Paul E. Cox Pottery, New Orleans, La."

## Craven Art Pottery
### East Liverpool, Ohio
~

William Percival Jervis is a name known to pottery researchers because of his books: *A Book of Pottery Marks* and *Rough Notes on Pottery*, 1896; *The Encyclopedia of Ceramics*, 1902; and *A Pottery Primer*, 1911. He also had his own art pottery factory that created unusual pottery during the early 1900s.

Jervis came to the United States from England before 1896. In 1902, he became manager of the Avon Faience Company. He then worked at the Corona Pottery, and later at Rose Valley Pottery. In 1905, the Craven Art Pottery Company of East Liverpool, Ohio, was organized by W. P. Jervis and Albert Cusick. It is believed that others were also involved.

Jervis made faience with a matte glaze. His glazes were deliberately developed to produce a shaded effect because he felt that the shading was truer to nature. Glazes were in greens, blues, yellows, oranges, pinks, crimsons, and blacks. The body of the art pottery was Ohio yellowware clay and New Jersey marl. The pieces were made to be utilitarian and their shapes were determined by their use. Jervis would think of a flower for a vase and then design the vase to suit it.

Some Craven vases feature raised designs that look as if they were made from squeezed toothpaste. This squeeze-bag method had been used by Jervis and Frederick Rhead at Avon Works. Many other pieces had incised writing as part of the decoration. Cutout

*Olive and vermilion glaze covers this vase made about 1905 by the Craven Art Pottery. It is 5¼ inches high and 5 inches in diameter, and the bottom is marked with an impressed J. (Smithsonian Institution)*

J ERVIS

*Incised.*

CRAVEN

*Incised.*

JERVIS

*Incised.*

An Egyptian-inspired design is carved on this blue-glazed bowl marked "Jervis." It was made at the Craven Art Pottery, East Liverpool, Ohio. (Courtesy of the Western Reserve Historical Society)

This Craven bowl, 3½ by 8 inches, is marked both "Craven" and "Jervis." (Private collection)

**DALLAS**

Impressed.

sections and hand-painted flowers were used. Some of the pieces show the potters' lack of skill, with sagging bases and uneven walls. The pottery seemed highly experimental.

Jervis left Craven in 1908 and established the Jervis Pottery on Long Island, New York. (See Jervis Pottery.)

The exact date of the closing of the Craven factory is not known. A 1945 summary of the pottery industry of the East Liverpool district in the *Bulletin of the American Ceramic Society* lists the Corns Knob Works at Laura Avenue in East Liverpool in 1890. In about 1900, Corns Knob sold out to Benty Brothers, who made artware until 1906, when the firm became known as Craven. Craven discontinued business and suspended operations in about 1910.

Two incised marks, "Craven" and "Jervis," were used, sometimes on the same piece.

## Dallas Pottery
### Cincinnati, Ohio

Yellowware and brown-glazed wares were made at the Hamilton Road Pottery of Cincinnati, Ohio, beginning in 1856. Frederick Dallas bought the pottery and building in 1865, adding new equipment. By 1869 he was making cream-colored pottery and stone china. In 1879 he added two kilns to fire decorated wares, one for Maria Longworth Nichols (see Rookwood Pottery)—who, after her disagreement with the Pottery Club of Cincinnati, decided to work alone—and the other for Mary Louise McLaughlin and the Pottery Club. Nichols had experimented with glazes at the Dallas Pottery but found that the kilns were too hot for her purposes and had a special kiln built. The Pottery Club rented one studio at the Dallas Pottery, Nichols another.

By 1880 Dallas had his own staff and showroom and was making his own wares. Some of these pieces are very similar to the work done by Longworth and Nichols. Dallas died in June 1881. By early 1882 the decorated faience work was discontinued. The pottery closed in July that year.

# Dedham Pottery
## Chelsea and Dedham, Massachusetts

~

The Robertson family was involved in making pottery for many years before they established the Chelsea Keramic Art Works in Chelsea, Massachusetts, in 1872. James Robertson, born in 1810 in Edinburgh, Scotland, was the son of a potter at the Fife Pottery. James worked in the same pottery, but when he was about sixteen years old he went to Watsons Factory in Prestonpans, Scotland, where he married. He traveled with his wife to northern England and there he worked in several potteries. He managed a redware pottery, and worked in a blackware factory and in other firms that made luster and transfer wares.

In 1853 James Robertson immigrated to the United States, arriving in New Jersey with his family. They had planned to settle on a piece of land in Illinois that Robertson had purchased when he was in England, but it turned out to be a swamp and the family was forced to remain in New Jersey. James first worked in South River, then in the shop of James Carr in South Amboy. He next worked in New York City, but then returned to New Jersey to the firm of Speeler, Taylor and Bloor in Trenton. By 1859, the family had moved to Boston, Massachusetts.

Robertson had a daughter and three sons. According to a city directory, his son George was in business with him in Boston in 1859. Records of the day show that Robertson managed the "East Boston Pottery," a name that may have referred to the New England Pottery Company. In 1860 he joined Nathaniel Plympton to form the Plympton and Robertson Pottery, which won a prize for its work at an 1860 exhibition in Boston. By 1862 the firm had changed owners and the pottery was owned by a Mr. Homer. Robertson continued to work as company manager until his retirement in 1872. (*Early New England Potters and Their Wares* by Lura Watkins states that James Robertson worked for the East Boston Crockery Manufactory from 1865 to 1871. No mention is made of the Plympton and Robertson Pottery.)

(Left) *Olive green glaze covers this 7-inch-high teapot. It was made by the Chelsea Keramic Art Works about 1880–1888 and is marked "CKAW." It probably was made from a mold of the similar English Copeland teapot. (Smithsonian Institution)* (Right) *The metal cover on the Copeland teapot is slightly shorter than the ceramic cover used by Chelsea Keramic. (Private collection)*

(Opposite) *This 3¾-inch pitcher with raised decorations is marked with the CKAW mark of the Chelsea Keramic Art Works.* (*Private collection*)

Following a family tradition, the three Robertson sons, Hugh C., George W., and Alexander W., went into the pottery business. In 1866, in an old varnish shop at Willow and Marginal streets in Chelsea, Massachusetts, Alexander W. Robertson started a redware pottery. The pottery was located on the Chelsea marshes near a fine deposit of red clay on the Snake River near Powder Horn Hill. In 1867, Hugh Cornwall Robertson went to work with his brother making red clay flowerpots and vases. The pots were unglazed or coated with dark green paint. James Robertson joined his sons at the Chelsea Pottery on June 1, 1872. He made what is believed to be the first pressed clay tiles produced in the United States. The firm name became James Robertson and Sons.

From about 1875 until 1889 the company was known as the Chelsea Keramic Art Works. The Robertsons made red bisque ware that was a new, more sophisticated type of pottery. It was similar to the Grecian terra-cotta pieces that were first made in 1875. The urn-shaped pieces had red figures on a black ground in the ancient style. The red clay color showed through the undecorated sections and the black encaustic decoration filled in around the design. Each piece was polished with boiled linseed oil and had a smooth texture that was sometimes ornamented with engraved lines. Other redware pieces were made with high-relief modeled designs of children and birds. Franz Xavier Dengler, the sculptor, made these pieces before his death at the age of twenty-five. Other artists who worked with the firm were John G. Low (who later founded the Low Tile Works), Isaac Elwood Scott, William Rimmer, and George W. Fenety.

The public did not seem to want the art pottery produced by the Chelsea Keramic Art Works, so in 1877 the company introduced a new ware called "Chelsea Faience Floral." The decoration was either carved in relief or applied to the vase while it was damp. A soft glaze covered the entire piece. Some pieces were made of a buff-colored clay with a hammered effect or with cut designs filled in with a white clay that formed a mosaic effect under the glaze. This pottery was popular, but it was too expensive for the general public. Some of the pieces were modeled by Josephine Day, Hugh Robertson's sister-in-law, but Hugh did many of the pieces himself.

*A vase made by Hugh C. Robertson about 1875–1880 pictures low-relief horsemen in a landscape, and is glazed with speckled blue-green glaze. It is 8¾ inches high and marked with the impressed mark "Chelsea Keramic (Art W)or(ks), Robertson and Sons." In the lower right-hand corner of the front of the vase is the cipher "HCR," and on the side "after Keloy."* (*Smithsonian Institution*)

In 1878, a creamware was made that took colored glazes. Another type of pottery produced at this time was called "Bourg-la-Reine of Chelsea," a faience made by covering the piece with colored clays, often blue and white slip. Robertson used a painting technique and covered it with a transparent glaze in the same manner as Limoges faience.

John Low left the firm in 1878 to start his own tile works. George W. Robertson went to work for him. In 1890, after twelve years at the Low Tile Works, George W. Robertson founded his own fac-

*This brown-glazed Chelsea Keramic tile made about 1880 is 6 inches square and is marked "CKAW." (Smithsonian Institution)*

tory, the Chelsea Keramic Art Tile Works, in Morrisville, Pennsylvania (see Robertson Art Tile Company).

James Robertson died in 1880, but the company continued under the same name. Alexander W. Robertson retired in 1884 and the firm was then controlled by Hugh C. Robertson. Years before, Hugh had seen Chinese sang de boeuf glaze at the Philadelphia Centennial Exhibition. He decided to try to find the secret of this red glaze. During the years that he experimented with it, several other types of wares were made at the pottery, many of them the indirect result of his experiments. A full, satinlike glaze in a dull metallic color and shades of brown was developed. A brown and blue mottled glaze was used on many pieces.

Hugh C. Robertson made many engraved or carved high-relief stoneware plaques featuring designs taken from La Fontaine's fables or from the works of Charles Dickens, or pictures of celebrities such as Dickens, Oliver Wendell Holmes, Lord Byron, and Henry Wadsworth Longfellow.

The company made a stoneware that was somewhat similar to parian in appearance. They did experiments attempting to create a red glaze that produced sea green, peachblow-shaded, apple-green, mustard yellow, blue-green, purple, and maroon, all with a hard, brilliant finish. Other pieces were made with a Japanese-style crackle with a gray and blue underglaze. It was a technique with effects that often appeared in later products at the Dedham Pottery.

The discovery of the sang de boeuf glaze reads like a storybook drama. Robertson worked almost day and night in his pottery grinding the pigment and watching the kiln. He kept peering into the oven at fifteen-minute intervals for sixty hours at a time. He had to be sure that the temperature was perfect. He supposedly used every dry bit of wood in his pottery to keep the kiln going. His method was primitive by today's standards; chemical formulas and temperature gauges were not available. He had a piece of old oriental sang de boeuf which he broke into small pieces and used for experiments. Using this sample, he found that the ware could not be refired as he wished, so he kept making his own porcelain thimbles until he finally discovered the method. He named his red glaze "Robertson's blood."

Several other types of pottery were developed by Hugh C. Robertson during this period. He made large wall plaques that looked as though they were produced from carved wood. Figures were incised into the surface on some, while other types of plaques were made by carving bas-relief wet clay on a clay background. The figures were in high relief and some examples looked almost like sculpture work. A ware was also made by using raised-clay decorations on a flat surface. Some pieces were glazed to look like the blue and white jasperware of Wedgwood.

All the inventive and artistic achievements of the Chelsea

Keramic Art Works were acclaimed, but financial success never came because the pieces required too much time and handwork by the artists. Money problems closed the firm in 1889. Fortunately, the art patrons of the area did not want to see Robertson stop making pottery, so in 1891 they helped him form a new company called Chelsea Pottery U.S.

## CHELSEA POTTERY U.S.

### *(1891–1895)*

Hugh C. Robertson was the manager of the newly formed Chelsea Pottery U.S. Learning from the financial failure of his earlier company, Robertson and his directors decided that the firm should try making salable tablewares and avoid the expensive, time-consuming art wares. Robertson went back to the crackleware glaze he had achieved earlier on a few large vases. He worked on refining the process, and within a few months of the formation of the new firm, he developed what is now the famous crackleware. The pieces were made in gray with freehand blue decoration. One known piece is dated 1891 and has the initials "JTC" for J. Templeton Coolidge, one of the directors of the new firm. Several of these pieces were marked with the incised clover mark "C.P.U.S." In a letter dated November 17, 1947, Milton Robertson wrote:

> The plate you refer to has the letters in the Clover Leaf—CPUS, which stands for Chelsea Pottery, U.S. to identify it against Chelsea Potteries in England. It is the old mark used at the Chelsea, Massachusetts, plant before it was removed to Dedham. However, as the impression was made in the clay, and considerable of the bisque ware was brought to Dedham undecorated and unglazed, some of the early Dedham ware carried the Chelsea imprint. As a matter of fact, toward the closing days of Dedham Pottery, I came across some of the old Chelsea plates with the Chelsea mark on them, but they also had the mark like the one in the corner of this letter.

The company's products were selling, but the kiln had always been on damp ground and smoke from a nearby factory sometimes damaged the wares. In 1895, Arthur A. Carey, a director of the pottery, bought some land in East Dedham, Massachusetts, near a canal that ran from the Charles River to the Neponset. The water-power was useful for the crushing machinery and a nearby railroad made the delivery of goods convenient. A four-story brick building was built on the new parcel of land and the name of the firm was changed to the Dedham Pottery Company. The change in the name was partly to avoid confusion with the Chelsea Porcelain Company of England.

*1881–1895; CPUS mark.*

*1880–1899.*

*1893; CPUS inside the border, handwritten under the glaze.*

**CHELSEA KERAMIC ART WORKS ROBERTSON & SONS.**
*1872–1889.*

*This 11-inch-high oxblood vase was made about 1895. (Skinner, Inc.)*

*Slightly iridescent crimson, orange, red, gray, and green glazes were used on this Dedham Pottery vase made by Hugh C. Robertson about 1899–1908. The 8-inch-high piece is incised "Dedham Pottery" with the cipher "HCR." (Private collection; photograph from The Art Museum, Princeton University, Princeton, New Jersey)*

*Hugh Robertson designed this vase for the Dedham Pottery about 1900. It is 6½ inches high. (From the collections of Henry Ford Museum & Greenfield Village)*

*Thick green glaze over light gray covers this "Volcanic Ware" vase made by the Dedham Pottery. The 7¾-inch piece is incised "Dedham Pottery" and "H.R." (Smithsonian Institution)*

*This Dedham Pottery platter with wolves and owls is 12½ inches long and 7¾ inches wide. It has the typical white crackled glaze decorated with blue over the glaze, and has the rabbit mark with "Dedham Pottery Co., Dedham, Mass." stamped in blue. The pattern is not included in the list of tableware patterns of the factory. (Smithsonian Institution)*

*An unusual piece of Chelsea pottery. This plate has no crackle glaze. The blue decoration is similar to the designs made on the tableware of the Dedham Pottery. The 10-inch-diameter piece has a border design called "dolphin," but it is not the Dedham factory Dolphin, Jack o'Lantern, or Fish pattern. It must be an early attempt at the famous line of tableware. It is marked "CPUS." (Smithsonian Institution)*

## DEDHAM POTTERY
### *(1895–1943)*

When Hugh C. Robertson arrived in Dedham to start work in his new buildings, he brought most of the employees from the Chelsea Pottery U.S. The town of Dedham had no raw materials for the pottery, but the new firm's knowledge of the earlier designs made success possible. Most of the clay came from Maryland and New Jersey, the feldspar from Maine. Iowa clay, English clay, Kentucky clay, and green cobalt were also used.

The Dedham Pottery had two kilns. One was used to make the crackle-glazed dishes that have become the best known of its works. The ware was fired at a high temperature so that a true porcelain was made. It was hard, with "a soft gray glaze and curiously crackled with a blue in-glaze decoration and fired at a heat of from 2000 to 2500 degrees," said a Dedham Pottery brochure in 1896.

In the second kiln, the firm made what were called "accidental glazes" or "volcanic ware." The pieces were fired ten to twelve times to produce the desired changes in the thick paste glaze that was applied to the top of the vases. The glaze ran and created mottled and striped effects. This process required great skill because too much firing left unattractive bare spots on the red clay. The vases were made in crimson, green, yellow, blue, slate, gray, mahogany, and other colors.

Hugh C. Robertson suffered for many years from lead poisoning, the result of his glaze experiments. His death in 1908 may have caused problems for Dedham Pottery, as indicated by Edwin Barber in his 1909 edition of *The Pottery and Porcelain of the United States*. According to Barber, "At the present time, the Dedham Pottery is in course of reorganization, and all lovers of the beautiful in art will welcome its speedy reopening." Either the firm's problems were brief or Barber misunderstood the situation, because Hugh C. Robertson's son, William A. Robertson, succeeded Hugh as head of the pottery. Unfortunately, William had suffered burns in a 1905 kiln explosion that left him with only limited use of his hands. He was able to run the pottery, but he could not design or model pieces. Consequently, most of the work after 1908 was produced from Hugh C. Robertson's old designs. But some of the designers remained at the factory, and two of them did some important work. Maud Davenport, of Dedham, started working in 1904. She designed the pond lily border. She occasionally signed her initials on the plate back or put a small *o* into the border design. She worked until 1929. Her brother, Charles Davenport, joined the Dedham Pottery in 1914 and headed the decorating division. He made borders, and was also a sculptor and made some of the small animal pieces.

The factory continued to prosper until 1929, when William Robertson died. His son, J. Milton Robertson, continued operating the factory until April 17, 1943. The last remaining pottery was sold at a sale at Gimbel's department store in New York City in September

*1896–1932, impressed.*

*1896–1943, ink stamp, "registered" added, 1929–1943.*

*This Dedham Pottery 5-inch-high "Naughty Dutch Boy" ashtray was painted by Charles Davenport. Water poured into the boy's head reappears in an entertaining way. (Arman's Absentee Auctions)*

*Dedham Pottery plates with center designs: the lobster plate (top) is 6½ inches in diameter; the crab (above) is 7½ inches. (Smithsonian Institution)*

1943. The pottery buildings stood until 1946. In a letter to Mrs. William W. Fisher on October 21, 1943, J. Milton Robertson, then a navy lieutenant commander, added these facts:

> The manufacture of the ware in the clay state ceased in January 1942, and at that time we notified all our old customers, at the last known address. . . . We continued firing ghost kilns until last March and finally released the help on April 17, 1943. The pieces of crackleware were sent to the Society of Arts and Crafts, 32 Newbury St., Boston.
>
> It is not my intention to ever reopen the plant. It would be difficult getting artists and craftsmen and many repairs are necessary to the kilns. . . .
>
> Many people were disappointed but the threat of closing had been going on for so long, they rather thought that it was a sales talk. Actually I carried the load on that place over a period of years, when good business practice would definitely say close.

During the last five years the firm was in business, its sales averaged about $3,000 a year. More than 250,000 pieces of crackleware are believed to have been made by the factory.

Other members of the family remained in the pottery business. Hugh C. Robertson's brother Alexander had moved to California in 1884 and founded his own firm (see Roblin Pottery). Alexander's son, Fred H. Robertson, worked at Roblin before it closed following the San Francisco earthquake of 1906. Fred's son, George B. Robertson, formally organized the Robertson Pottery in Los Angeles in 1934 and kept it open until 1952.

### PRODUCT

The most important ware made at the Dedham Pottery was the famous crackleware. Its manufacture gives a few clues to its age. Plates and other similar pieces were made in hinged molds. Hugh Robertson decided that to keep the design uniform, the decorators should have some sort of guidelines. The molds for the rabbit plate, which was the first standard design, were made with a slightly engraved border that the decorators could follow. The decorators became so familiar with the pattern that the plates were finally made smooth. The pottery was fired, glazed, decorated freehand, and fired again. While the plates were still hot from the kiln, lampblack was rubbed on the piece so that it would darken the crackle of the glaze on the face of the piece.

Crackleware has several characteristics. The tablewares were made with repetitive borders with no pattern but the crackle lines in the center. The back of a dish has no crackle, but it does have an eggshell texture with black specks in the glaze. The foot rim of a plate is unglazed and there are almost always three fingerprints that can be seen where a hand held the plate while glazing. All the pieces are marked. The number of stamped rabbit marks on the back of a piece has no relation to the year when the piece was made.

There were more than sixty border designs, but only the rabbit design was kept in stock; the others had to be ordered. Thirteen designs were listed as standard in 1938. Special center designs could also be ordered. In

*The scotty dog design on this Dedham crackleware jar and plate is an unusual image for the pottery. The plate is 8½ inches across, the jar 6 inches high. (Skinner, Inc.)*

addition to plates, Dedham Pottery made mugs, cups and saucers, serving pieces, and some unusual creations, like the "Naughty Dutch Boy" ashtray (pour water into his hat and he relieves himself into the ashtray).

The first of the border designs was the rabbit. In 1891, a prize for the best design was offered to students at The Boston Museum of Fine Arts School. Joseph L. Smith, a teacher, and Alice Morse, a student, drew the winning design: the rabbits rest between what look like brussels sprouts. There are ten rabbits to a plate, with the rabbit border originally going counterclockwise (decorator Charles Mills soon reversed the direction). Smith also made the fish and poppy borders.

The pond lily border was designed by Maud Davenport after 1904. Her brother, Charles Davenport, made several borders after 1914, including the cat, dog, and chick, and designed a plate for the Republicans. He is said to have designed the GOP plate border with elephants, but when he got to tne end, there was not enough space for a whole elephant. To solve the problem, he drew a baby elephant, and the design remained that way.

Denman Ross made the tapestry lion and Charles Mills created the dolphin, magnolia, iris, and water-lily designs.

*Dedham Pottery border design plates: Birds in a Potted Orange Tree pattern, 8-inch plate, (upper right); Magnolia pattern (center bottom); and a 6-inch Horse Chestnut pattern plate (left). (Private collection)*

## PLATE BORDER PATTERNS

*Azalea.*

*Duck.*

*Magnolia.*

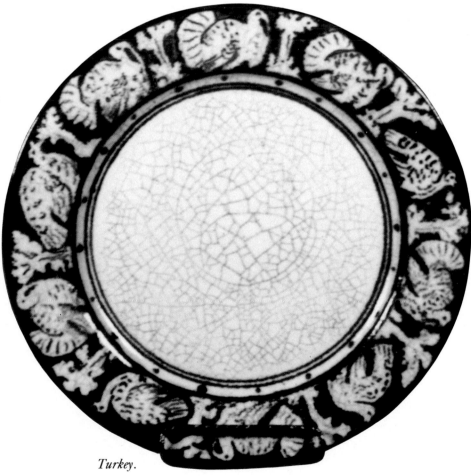

*Grape.*

## BORDER DESIGNS OF DEDHAM PLATES

Apple, Azalea, Birds in Potted Orange Tree, Butterfly, Cat, Cherry, Chick, Clover, Clover (raised), Cosmos, Crab, Dolphin, Dolphin (upside down), Duck, Duck (tufted), Elephant, Fish, Flower (five petals), Flower (seven petals), Grape, Grouse, Horse Chestnut (three styles), Horse Chestnut (raised), Iris (two styles), Jack o'Lantern, Lion (tapestry), Magnolia (two styles), Moth (three styles), Moth with Flower, Mushroom (three styles), Nasturtium, Owl (two styles), Peacock, Pineapple, Pineapple (raised), Polar Bear, Pond Lily, Quail (raised), Rabbit (raised counterclockwise), Rabbit (one ear), Rabbit (two ears), Rabbit (with monogram), Snowtree (three styles), Strawberry (two styles), Swan, Turkey (two styles), Turtles, Turtles Cavorting, Wild Rose, Wolf and Owl.

## SPECIAL CENTER DESIGNS OF DEDHAM PLATES

Fairbanks House, Fairbanks Coat of Arms, Set of Four Sailing Ships, Poppy, Lobster, Crab, Pair of Scotty Dogs, Avery Oak, Golden Gate, Rabbit, Day Lily.

The Dedham Pottery blue and white wares have remained popular, and reproductions are being made by the Potting Shed in Massachusetts. To avoid confusion with the originals, each piece is marked with a star and the year of manufacture.

*Turkey.*

*Pond Lily.*

*Snow Tree Plant.*

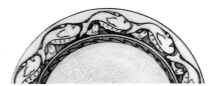

*Dolphin Upside Down.*

*Birds in Potted Orange Tree.*

*Iris.*

*Swan.*

*Horse Chestnut.*

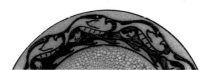

*Dolphin.*

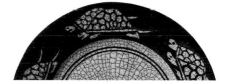

*Turtle.*

*Owl.*

*Polar Bear.*

*Stork (modern name for pattern).*

*Elephant.*

*Rabbit.*

*Moth.*

*only* the Dedham pottery ever reproduced the dragon's-blood color of priceless Ming porcelains

*only* the Dedham pottery ever reproduced the crackle-finish of priceless old Ming porcelains

# Gimbels sells entire remaining stock of the Dedham Pottery
## $70,000 *worth for* $35,000

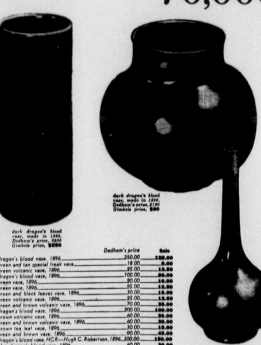

**GIMBELS SELLS THE LAST OF THE DEDHAM POTTERY**

Massachusetts workshop the only pottery in the world to reproduce dragon's blood color and blue crackle of Ming porcelains

The selling of the complete factory museum and showroom stock of the Dedham Potteries, beginning tomorrow on Gimbels Fifth Floor, brings to a close one of the most interesting stories in American crafts. Mr. J. Milton Robertson, the seventh generation of potters in his family, has closed the shop to accept a commission as Commander in the United States Navy, and Dedham pottery will no longer be made.

**7 Generations of Potters**

Three generations of Robertsons have been potters in America, and the firm goes back to 1853, when it was known as Plympton and Robertson. The product of the time was white and yellow crockery, which in 1860 won an exhibition award and a comment by the judges; the ware compared favorably with Bennington ware. In the late '60's the Robertson, inspired by early Greek, Roman, and Egyptian vases in the Cesnola collection, experimented with red bisque, producing many shapes of unusually pure beauty. They also applied some of the black decorations characteristic of Greek wares, and did some modeling in high relief.

Chelsea Faience was their next development; an unusually high rich glaze which they used with strong but subdued smoky colors of great beauty. This Chelsea Faience was applied to what are believed to be the first pressed tiles made in the United States. The tiles were of great interest, and were given an award at an exhibition.

**Find Dragon's Blood and Crackle Secrets**

The real climax in the Robertson history came, however, when Hugh Robertson, having seen the Oriental displays at the Centennial in Philadelphia in 1876, experimented for the lost secret of the wonderful deep dragon's blood color of old Ming porcelains and for the hairline fine blue crackle of the Ming period. He finally succeeded, and the workshop of course won a world-wide reputation among potters. Hugh Robertson is the only person ever known to have discovered the secret of the dragon's blood or sang de boeuf color and the secret of the blue crackleware of the Ming period. The secret has been handed down in the family, and it has been so carefully guarded that a few years ago when Mr. J. Milton Robertson's father died it was thought at first that he had not even passed the secret on to his son. Since the sang de boeuf was discovered the pottery has produced infinite variations of the color, including some unusual iridescent vases.

**Famous Artists Worked on Dedham**

Craftsmanship as fine as this naturally attracted a superior group of artists. Mr. Joseph Linden Smith, the prominent New England artist, designed the famous rabbit pattern which became so popular that it was chosen as the trade-mark of the pottery. He also did the fish pattern and the poppy pattern. Mr. Denman Ross did the lion pattern, and Mr. Charles E. Mills did the magnolia, iris, water lily and dolphin patterns. A soft cloudy blue is the only color used for decorating the crackleware, and while the designs are distinctly American, all the artists have attempted to keep some of the feeling of Ming designs. All Dedham pottery is, of course, hand made and decorated by hand.

**Gimbels Collection Largest**

The collection at Gimbels is the largest collection of Dedham pottery ever placed on sale. It includes pieces that go back almost to the beginning of the Robertsons' pottery-making days in this country, and it covers all the time down to the present. There are dozens of dragon's blood vases included; there are interesting volcanic vases, mixed color glazed vases, tea green vases. Most of the crackleware patterns are represented, some by only a piece or two, others by many pieces.

Why is this one of the most important sales of pottery in a decade? Because Dedham is one of the finest examples of American craftsmanship, because there has never been a collection of Dedham offered for sale to compare with this one, and because *no more Dedham will be made.* Mr. J. Milton Robertson, the present owner (and the seventh generation of Robertson potters) is now a Commander in the United States Navy. He is discontinuing the pottery.

Dedham pottery has always been comparatively rare. Its makers were much more interested in technical and artistic problems than in selling. Back in 1867 the Robertsons were experimenting with red bisque with black decorations inspired by Greek and Egyptian vases (there are many pieces of red bisque in our collection). Later they developed highly glazed Chelsea faience (we have over 600 Chelsea faience tiles in deep smoky wonderful colors). But the pottery's world-wide reputation came in 1886, when Hugh Robertson produced the first smouldering dragon's-blood reds since the secret was lost in China 500 years ago—reds that range from the flame color of burning coals to a deep blackish glow and even into blue reds. *No other potters in the world have ever found the secret of the Ming sang-de-boeuf or the spider-web fine blue crackle of priceless Ming porcelains.*

Tomorrow morning the entire showroom collection, accumulated since the pottery opening 90 years ago, goes on sale at Gimbels. There are dragon's-blood vases that were $100 (they're going for $50); there are tiny little bowls of cloudy blue crackleware going for 75c. There are plates and cups and bowls in the famous rabbit pattern (designed by John Linden Smith, at one time a director of the Boston Museum of Fine Arts). There are crackleware demi-tasses, platters, coffee pots, teapots. There are hundreds of jars, legions of vases. Here's a bare sample of the list. Mail and phone orders accepted. All items subject to prior sale. Use our easy payment plan on $20 or more (service charge). 5th FL.

| | Dedham's price | Sale |
|---|---|---|
| dragon's blood vase, 1896 | 250.00 | 125.00 |
| green and tan special freak vase | 18.00 | 9.00 |
| green volcanic vase, 1896 | 95.00 | 12.50 |
| dragon's blood vase, 1896 | 100.00 | 50.00 |
| green vase, 1896 | 90.00 | 15.00 |
| green vase, 1896 | 95.00 | 12.50 |
| green and black leaves vase, 1896 | 30.00 | 15.00 |
| green volcanic vase, 1896 | 25.00 | 12.50 |
| green and brown volcanic vase, 1896 | 70.00 | 35.00 |
| dragon's blood vase, 1896 | 200.00 | 100.00 |
| brown volcanic vase, 1896 | 60.00 | 30.00 |
| green and brown volcanic vase, 1896 | 60.00 | 30.00 |
| brown tea leaf vase, 1896 | 30.00 | 15.00 |
| green and brown vase, 1896 | 90.00 | 45.00 |
| dragon's blood vase, HCR—Hugh C. Robertson, 1896 | 300.00 | 150.00 |
| blue dragon's blood vase, 1896 | 60.00 | 30.00 |
| hard paste glaze vase, Paris Exhibition collection, green, 1896 | 40.00 | 20.00 |
| red clay ware made in 1872 | 1.00 to 2.00 | 50c to 1.00 |
| red clay ware ashtray, 1872 | 3.00 | 1.50 |
| red clay ware urn, 1872 | 3.00 | 1.50 |
| brown faience candle holder, ca 1872 | 5.00 | 2.50 |
| yellow faience vase, ca 1872 | 10.00 | 5.00 |
| vase, ca 1888—dragon's blood vase | 1000.00 | 500.00 |
| vase, ca 1888—dragon's blood trail piece | 5.00 | 2.50 |
| bowl, Chelsea faience made 1880 | 10.00 | 5.00 |
| lamp vase, Chelsea faience made 1880 | 8.00 | 4.00 |
| cocoa pot, Chelsea faience made 1880 | 8.00 | 4.00 |
| cracker jar, Chelsea faience made 1880 | 20.00 | 10.00 |
| umbrella stand, 1879 | 10.00 | 5.00 |
| vase, volcanic tea leaf design HCR—Hugh C. Robertson, 1896 | 25.00 | 12.50 |
| volcanic tea leaf vase | 20.00 | 10.00 |
| silver green vase | 20.00 | 10.00 |
| hard paste glaze vase, Boston Museum Fine Arts Collection, 1898 | 25.00 | 12.50 |
| mixed red and slate iridescent vase, 1878 | 55.00 | 27.50 |
| volcanic tea leaf vase, 1878 | 15.00 | 7.50 |
| iris red and green vase, 1878 | 50.00 | 25.00 |
| light volcanic hard paste glaze hand thrown by HCR—Hugh C. Robertson, 1896 | 45.00 | 22.50 |
| red and green vase, 1896 | 25.00 | 12.50 |
| volcanic vase, 1896 | 40.00 | 20.00 |
| volcanic tea leaf vase, 1896 | 20.00 | 10.00 |
| green vase dated 11-16-96, HCR—Hugh C. Robertson | 70.00 | 35.00 |
| green vase, 1896 | 45.00 | 22.50 |
| green and red vase, 1896 | 50.00 | 25.00 |
| green and dragon hand thrown vase, 1896 | 40.00 | 20.00 |
| Chinese tea leaf vase, 1896 | 60.00 | 30.00 |
| slate and dragon blood vase, 1896 | 20.00 | 10.00 |
| green and black vase, 1896 | 25.00 | 12.50 |
| brown special letter Z vase, 1896 | 20.00 | 10.00 |
| brown and green vase, HCR, Hugh C. Robertson, 1896 | 30.00 | 15.00 |
| brown and slate yellow vase, 1878 | 45.00 | 22.50 |
| Chelsea faience tiles | 2.00 | 1.00 |

*dark dragon's blood vase, made in 1896, Dedham's price, $100 Gimbels price, $50*

*dark dragon's blood vase, made in 1888, Dedham's price, $500 Gimbels price, $250*

*Chelsea faience vase, made in 1880, Dedham's price, $10 Gimbels price, $5*

*green and red glaze vase, made in 1896, Dedham's price, $32 Gimbels price, $16*

*blue crackleware swan pattern mug, Dedham's price, $3 Gimbels price, $1.50*

*green volcanic vase, made in 1896, Dedham's price, $36 Gimbels price, $18*

*blue crackleware iris pattern plate, Dedham's price, $4 Gimbels price, $2*

*red bisque clay vase, made in 1872, Dedham's price, $1 Gimbels price, 50c*

*blue crackleware rabbit pattern bowl, Dedham's price, $4 Gimbels price, $2*

*red bisque, black decoration, 1872, Dedham's price, $2 Gimbels price, $1*

**GIMBELS OPEN MONDAY NIGHT till 9**

33rd & Bway New York 1, N.Y. PEnn 6-5100

**BUY POTTERY AFTER YOU BUY WAR BONDS**

202 Columns Height

On September 19, 1943, this advertisement appeared in the New York Times. Notice the sale included dragon's blood, volcanic, redware, and other pieces made in the early days of the Chelsea factory.

## William Dell Pottery
*Cincinnati, Ohio*

~

William Dell was the superintendent and manager of the Cincinnati Art Pottery. When the pottery went out of business in 1891, Dell obtained the molds and glaze formulas and continued making the "Hungarian" faience that had been made there. Pieces were signed with his name. He died in January 1892.

## Denver China and Pottery
*See Lonhuda Pottery*

~

## Durant Kilns
*Bedford Village, New York*

~

Leon Volkmar and his father, Charles, established the Volkmar Kilns in Metuchen, New Jersey, in 1903 (see Volkmar Pottery). In the summer of 1910, Jean Durant (Mrs. Clarence) Rice, who had studied with the Volkmars, made some pottery that was glazed by Leon Volkmar. She obtained orders for her pieces, and in the fall of 1910 asked Volkmar to supervise the technical aspects of the production at her pottery building. The firm was named the Durant Kilns. Pieces were produced beginning in 1911, and by 1913 the firm had rented a gallery in New York City. Pottery was sold there until 1918. Rice died in 1919, leaving Volkmar the rights to the business and the land. He bought the assets in 1924. Another New York City firm, Arden Studios, sold Durant Kilns pottery until 1925.

Durant Kilns favored simple oriental forms and monochromatic glazes. Blue, red, yellow, and purple glazes were used. The thick glaze was often allowed to run thinner in sections to vary the color. From 1913 to 1920, Volkmar did the creative design and finishing work while other workers helped with production. After 1930, only the Volkmar name was used as a mark. Volkmar taught at the Pennsylvania Museum school, Columbia University, and the University of Cincinnati. He died in California in 1959.

Pottery marks include the name Durant, the letter *V*, or the name Volkmar.

*Cream-colored earthenware is covered with an apple-green glaze to decorate this 9⅞-inch vase by Durant Kilns. (Courtesy of the Brooklyn Museum, Brooklyn, New York, gift of Mrs. Luke Vincent Lockwood)*

## Edgerton Art Clay Works
*See Pauline Pottery*

~

## Edwin Bennett Pottery
*See Bennett*

~

*Incised.*

FM C°

*Printed.*

*Printed.*

# Enfield Pottery and Tile Works
### See Tile Companies

~

# Faience Manufacturing Company
### Greenpoint, New York

~

In 1880 the Faience Manufacturing Company opened in the Greenpoint section of Brooklyn, New York. The company was in operation until 1892. At first the firm made earthenware vases, jardinieres, and baskets. Hand-modeled flowers, colored slip decoration, and colorful glazes were used to adorn the pieces. Edward Lycett (1833–1910) joined the company in 1884.

Lycett was one of the most famous china decorators in the United States. He was born in Newcastle, England, and had worked at the Copeland Garrett Pottery, where he studied art and decorated vases. He was also a painter whose work was exhibited several times. After moving to New York in 1861, he opened a shop where he decorated porcelains and porcelain panels for furniture manufacturers. The panels were decorated with painted figures and heavy gold. In 1865, Lycett was commissioned to decorate the second set of Lincoln china for the White House in Washington, D.C.

Records show that Edward Lycett also decorated for the Jersey City Pottery in New Jersey and the Union Porcelain Works in Greenpoint. His work ranged from six-foot panels made for the front of a New York building to roses on chamber pots and reproductions of royal services. He made a special type of plate called "anamorphosis" for children: a distorted group of fine lines was drawn so that if held at the proper angle it appeared as an animal.

By the 1870s, china painting had become a popular pastime for wealthy women. Lycett and his staff welcomed prominent women as students and taught them the art of decorating porcelains. Maria Longworth Nichols of the Rookwood factory was believed to have sent some of her early works to be fired at the Lycett kilns.

In 1877, Lycett was invited to teach china painting at the St. Louis, Missouri, School of Design. He took the job and left his business under the direction of his son William, who had formed a company called Warren and Lycett with George Warren. After one year, Edward Lycett moved to Cincinnati for a few months and taught china painting. Then he moved to East Liverpool, Ohio, where he opened a decorating business and made plans to establish his own ceramics manufacturing company in Philadelphia. While in East Liverpool in 1879, he decorated some underglaze stoneware cups and saucers that were made by Homer Laughlin.

Lycett's Philadelphia factory had just opened when Shakespeare Laughlin, the main force behind the project, died. Lycett decided to return to New York City and resume the china-painting business, this time with John Bennett as his partner.

*A 7-inch vase with raised flowers and leaves made by Faience Manufacturing Company is marked with an incised "FM Co" and the numbers 8 and 216. (Private collection)*

Lycett joined the Faience Manufacturing Company in 1884. As director of the factory, he managed more than twenty-five decorators and students. Hand-painted pottery and some porcelain wares were made. It was at Faience Manufacturing that Lycett experimented with glazes, bodies, and new shapes. The company made a fine grade of porcelain, including large vases with elaborate decorations. While experimenting with glazes, Lycett developed a special gold, a mazarine blue, and an iridescent glaze he called "reflet metallique" that was said to resemble the ancient Persian glazes. Some tiles were also made using this special glaze.

In 1890, Lycett retired and moved to Atlanta, Georgia. His three sons, Joe, Frank, and William, were also china decorators. William had a china-decorating firm in Atlanta, and Edward did some of the work there.

Early pieces were marked "F M Co." Later a monogram of the letters was used. The crown over an *R* in a circle, for Royal Crown ware, was used during Lycett's early period with Faience Manufacturing.

*Raised figures are part of the decoration on this gilt and painted Faience Manufacturing Company covered vase made about 1886–1892. The vase is 15⅜ inches high, 10⅝ inches wide (including the handles), and 7¾ inches long. (High Museum of Art, Atlanta, Georgia; Virginia Carroll Crawford Collection)*

## Faience Pottery Co.
### Zanesville, Ohio
~

The Faience Pottery Company, a small firm that made artware, worked in Zanesville, Ohio, from 1902 to 1905. In 1906 it closed because of financial problems, and although there were attempts to reestablish it, the pottery building was acquired by the Fisher Veneer Tile Manufacturing Company in 1907.

## Florentine Pottery Co.
### Chillicothe, Ohio
~

The Florentine Pottery Company in Chillicothe, Ohio, was founded in 1900 for "the purpose of making faience ware." The first manager was George Bradshaw, an English potter, who had been managing potteries in the Ohio area. Upon Bradshaw's death in 1902, F. J. A. Arbenz, his assistant, took charge. After much study, Arbenz produced a bronze glaze. Vases and other pieces using this metallic glaze were sold under the name of "Effecto" ware. The company discontinued the artwares in 1905 and began the manufacture of sanitary ware. In 1919, the factory moved to Cambridge, Ohio.

*Printed.*

## Fort Hays
### Hays, Kansas
~

Pottery was made at Fort Hays State College in Hays, Kansas, from 1935 to 1948 under the supervision of the Department of Art. John Strange was the instructor. The students used local clay.

**Fort Hays
Kansas State
College**

*Incised.*

*This 5-inch-high dark blue–glazed vase has an allover decoration of raised leaves carved from the vase. It is marked with the impressed words "Fort Hays, Kansas State College." (Private collection)*

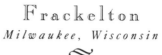

# Frackelton
## Milwaukee, Wisconsin

*Incised.*

*An olive jar made from stoneware by Susan S. Frackelton. (The Pottery and Porcelain of the United States by Edwin Barber, 1909)*

Susan Stuart Goodrich Frackelton was a writer, decorator of china and pottery, and founder of a pottery. She was born in Milwaukee, Wisconsin, in 1848, the daughter of a banker who later ran a brickyard. She went to a New York finishing school, and studied art with Heinrich Vianden of Milwaukee. From 1867 to 1891 she operated a china, glassware, and stoneware shop and also taught china decorating. Her invention of a gas-fired kiln to be used at home made it possible for women to make pottery as a hobby. She developed new, odorless china-paint colors, wrote a guide for china painters, and won awards at the international competitions. Her pottery was often salt-glazed stoneware decorated with cobalt blue.

In 1882 she helped design a big brick house at Case Street and Ogden Avenue in Milwaukee. It was in this house that she continued to hold classes in china decoration, made pottery and stoneware, and carried on other artistic pursuits. In 1896 she married Richard Frackelton, who later became a dealer in chinaware.

Mrs. Frackelton's pottery was made from Milwaukee brick clay or of gray and blue stoneware with relief and underglaze blue decorations. She did the molding, firing, and decorating herself. In 1902 she moved to Chicago, lectured, and did book illuminations. She died in 1932.

Pieces are marked with her initials in a cipher and sometimes have the date and her signature.

# Fulper Pottery
## Flemington, New Jersey

Drain tiles were being made by 1805 in Flemington, New Jersey. Samuel Hill (1793–1858), who made earthenware and drain tiles, came to Flemington from New Brunswick, New Jersey, in 1814 to work as a potter. One of his workmen, Abraham Fulper, bought the firm in 1858 when Hill died. At first, Fulper made only drain tiles, but he soon produced earthenware and stoneware. Vinegar jugs, pickling jars, bottles, beer mugs, butter churns, bowls, and "drinking foundations for poultry" were also produced at the pottery.

*Ink stamp, before 1920; 1917 patent claimed use from 1840.*

FULPER
*1920–1925,
incised.*

*"Potter at Wheel"
mark, 1909–1914.*

*Ink stamp, before 1920;
"Chinese"-style letters.*

*Incised mark, after
1915 to early 1920s.*

*Paper label, 1915.*

*Cipher for
Martin Stangl.*

The firm was under the direction of William H. Fulper II, Abraham's grandson, by the early 1900s. The pottery introduced its artware line, Vasekraft, in 1909. Martin Stangl became Fulper's ceramics engineer in 1911, and helped invent a group of famille rose glazes, including ashes of roses, deep rose, peach bloom, old rose, and true rose. Stangl left in 1914 or 1915 to work for Haeger in Dundee, Illinois. The Fulper Pottery won several awards at the 1915 San Francisco Panama Pacific International Exposition.

The Vasekraft line was produced using classical and oriental shapes. The line included the expensive famille rose, a copy of the famous Chinese glazes; "Mirror Glaze," a high-gloss, crystalline glaze; and "Mission Matte," a brown-black glaze with shaded greens. According to the catalogs, other colors were "cat's-eye, rouge, mustard matte, bronze, elephant's breath (gray), cucumber green, blue wisteria, plum, yellow, café au lait, mulberry, verte antique, mission matte, and violet wisteria." Crystal, or what is now

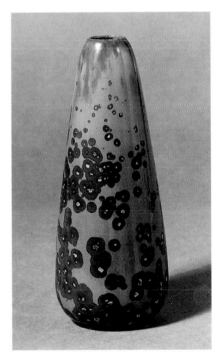

*Dark green and black glazes with silver crystalline formations are on this 8½-inch vase. It has the printed Fulper mark in the vertical rectangle and the original paper label: "Vasekraft, med. double ori., form Cucumber Green, $4.40 Vasekraft, Fulper 1805" and the potter's emblem. (Collection of the Newark Museum)*

*This 6⅞-inch-high vase has a green crystalline glaze. It is marked with the Fulper stamp in a vertical rectangle, and an original paper label: "Vasekraft, med. Globular Bottle, Leopard Skin, crystal $4.40, Vasekraft, Fulper 1805" and the emblem of a potter. (Collection of the Newark Museum)*

*Brown to olive glazes cover this Fulper vase, which is 5½ inches high. The piece is marked with the original rectangular paper label: "Vasekraft, Slender Ovoid, Leopard Skin $1.00, Vasekraft, Fulper 1805" (1805 is the year the pottery chose to date its founding; the date was used on its registered trademark). The Vasekraft line was introduced in 1909, and the Newark Museum acquired this piece in 1914. (Collection of the Newark Museum)*

(Left to right) *This unusual vase, 5 inches high and 7 inches in diameter, has a center holder for flowers. The green glaze with some crystalline formations was dripped over a dark tan. The piece is marked with the Fulper printed mark, a paper label for Fulper, and the paper label for the Panama Pacific International Exposition, 1915. A footed bowl, 8 inches in diameter, with three swirling supports for the flower holder, is similar to No. 504 in the Vasekraft catalog and is glazed with the green known as "verte antique." (Private collection)*

*The name "Fulper" is stamped in a vertical rectangle on the vase at left. The glaze of the 8½-inch-high vase is light to dark green iridescent. The factory name is incised on the vase at right, which stands 9 inches high. (Private collection)*

(Left to right) *A small Fulper ewer, 4½ inches high; on the bottom is a paper label printed with the name "Fulper" in a vertical rectangle; written in pen is "38C Dipstick, Ashes of Roses, $1.00." An 8-inch vase with golden glaze poured over dark blue, marked with the Roman numeral VI and the incised Fulper rectangle mark. A bulbous light blue vase with gold trim, marked with the Fulper rectangle in relief. And an unmarked lily pad flower frog, catalog no. 424. (Private collection)*

No. 498 Heraldic Bowl, café au lait with green and mahogany flambé, dia. 8¼ inches. $4.50

No. 501 Handled Bowl, Venetian blue, dia. 7 inches, $2.00

No. 500 Iris Bowl, mustard matte with green flambé or blue wistaria with green flambé, diameter 10 inches, $6.00

No. 503 Modeled Bowl, verte antique with mahogany and white flambé, diameter 9 inches, $4.00

No. 504 Bowl with flower holder, verte antique with Chinese blue and white flambé, diameter 8 inches, $3.50

No. 484S Bowl with flower holder, verte antique with white flambé, dia. 8 in. $3.00
No. 484L Blue wistaria with white flambé, diameter, 10½ inches, $4.50

No. 456 Penguin Self-contained Flower Holder, naturalistic, height 7 inches, $1.75

No. 424 Lily Pad, naturalistic glaze, $ .50

No. 451 English Castle Flower Holder, naturalistic glazes, height 5 inches, $1.50

No. 438 Flower Bowl with effigy feet, blue matte, with blue of the sky lining, or mustard and mission matte with yellow flambé 10½ in. diameter, $6.00

No. 58 Ovoid Bowl, mustard matte with brown and black flambé, $4.50

No. 443 Cat-tail Vase, café au lait or verte antique, height 12½ inches, $4.00

No. 468 Peacock Bowl, Chinese blue and white flambé, diameter 10 inches, $5.00

No. 50 Modeled Square Vase, height 8 inches, blue matte or verte antique, $1.50

No. 76 Fernery and insert, café au lait, height 4 inches, $1.70

No. 26 Fool's Cap Vase, tall, height 10½ inches, green flambé or cucumber green, $2.50
Fool's Cap Vase, medium, height 7½ ins., green mirrored, $1.50
Fool's Cap Vase, Small, height 5½ inches, mulberry flambé $1.00

No. 20 Tall Ovoid with neck, Chinese blue or green flambé, height 13 inches, $6.00

No. 489 Urn Vase, mahogany and Chinese blue flambé, height 8 inches, $3.00

*Two pages from the Vasekraft catalog, dates unknown. (Hunterdon County Historical Society)*

*Fulper made many table lamps, some with glass shades, others with pottery shades. This mottled glazed vase is topped by a leaded glass shade with colored glass inserts. The lamp is 20½ inches high. (David Rago Arts & Crafts Gallery)*

*A Fulper vase glazed in greenish browns. The vase is 11 inches high and 2¾ inches in diameter. It is stamped Fulper and has the Pan Pacific sticker. (Smithsonian Institution)*

*The hammered olive green over light green glaze used on this centerpiece is rare. The 10½-inch-high vase was made about 1915. (Skinner, Inc.)*

*The "Iris bowl," no. 500 in the Vasekraft catalog. The piece is not marked. (Private collection)*

*A Fulper advertisement printed on paper, 11½ by 7½ inches. Notice the vases that are pictured.*

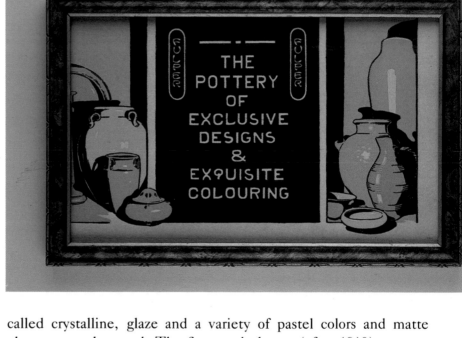

*An 8¾-inch vase with glossy glaze in shades of blue poured over the off-white, blue-speckled body. A Fulper paper label is glued to the base.*

called crystalline, glaze and a variety of pastel colors and matte glazes were also used. The firm made lamps (after 1910), pottery lampshades (often set with glass), ashtrays, cigarette boxes, vases, bowls, and other giftwares. The shapes were made of "clay wrought into odd—sometimes too odd forms," stated *The American Magazine of Art* in 1916.

John Kunsman, who started working at Fulper in 1889, was Fulper Pottery's master potter. He experimented with art pottery forms before 1909, and was depicted on the company's logo. His signature is found on several pieces. Edward Wyckoff and John Ogden Winner Kugler were other Fulper potters who worked on the art line. At the same time, the firm was making the "Fulper Germ-Proof Filter," a set of jars that held cold drinking water. They even made dolls' heads for a short time. In 1920, the firm introduced the first solid-colored glazed dinnerware produced in the United States;

green was the only color used for the dinnerwares until 1930, when other colors were added.

The Fulper Pottery continued to expand, and in 1926 acquired the Anchor Pottery Company of Trenton, New Jersey. A fire in 1929 destroyed the Fulper Pottery buildings in Flemington, and the firm decided to move most of its operations to the Trenton plant. Artware was still made on a small scale in Flemington until 1935.

J. Martin Stangl acquired the firm in 1929 and the name Stangl was used on dinnerwares by 1935. The corporate name was changed in 1955. In June 1972 the company was purchased by Frank H. Wheaton, Jr., of Wheaton Industries. The pottery in Trenton was closed in 1978, and the firm was purchased by Pfaltzgraff Company.

It is difficult to date marks used by Fulper. Marks were raised, incised, or stamped in ink. Early pieces made from 1909 to about 1914 were marked with a paper label "Vasekraft" and often a vertical ink-stamped mark "Fulper" enclosed in a rectangle. A mark with oriental-looking letters spelling Fulper was used about 1915 to 1920. After 1915 the mark was incised or raised, the letters in an oval. From about 1920 to 1925 the horizontal form of the mark was used. A three- or four-digit number was used on the same pieces. These were factory-style numbers. Other marks used are "Flemington" in impressed horizontal block letters, "Prang" in vertical printed block letters, and "Rafco" in horizontal impressed letters.

*A pale beige semigloss glaze covers this 12-inch-high Fulper vase. (David Rago Arts & Crafts Gallery)*

## Gay Head Pottery
### *Martha's Vineyard, Massachusetts*

Gay Head Pottery was made on Martha's Vineyard at Cottage City, Massachusetts, around 1879. W. F. Willard made vases using the multicolored clays found on the island. Red, blue, slate, and buff-colored clays were mixed to give a marbleized effect to the finished vase. The pieces were dried in the sun and not baked because firing would destroy the color. The pottery was impressed "Gay Head" on the side of each piece.

## Graham Pottery
### *Brooklyn, New York*

Charles Graham Chemical Pottery Works in Brooklyn, New York, started making chemical stonewares in 1880. Graham soon began experimenting with more artistic products, and in 1884 he received a patent for his method of decorating stoneware by using hydrofluoric acid. Charles Benham, who carved designs on stoneware made at the Graham Pottery, cut designs into the unbaked clay. The piece would then be salt-glazed. The pottery stopped making artwares about 1900 and returned to making pieces used to hold chemicals.

*Impressed.*

*Impressed.*

GRAND FEU
POTTERY

L. A.. CAL.

*Impressed in mold.*

Cornelius Brauckman (1863–1951) was born in Missouri and moved to Los Angeles, California, in 1909. He started Grand Feu Pottery around 1913 and began to make a high-fired white stoneware known as grès, a *grand feu* ware. The same type of ceramic was made at University City Pottery in St. Louis, Missouri. While there are technical differences between porcelain and grès, both *grand feu* wares, each is fired at high temperatures. Pieces were made with glazes of many types. Green, blue, yellow, and red in dull or glossy finish, drip glazes, and mottled colors were used. The pottery is unlisted after 1916. Pieces were marked "Grand Feu Pottery L.A., Cal." (about 1912–1916), or "Brauckman Art Pottery" (about 1916–1918).

*This mottled green, brown, and violet* grand feu *vase with "Moss Agate" glaze is 11¾ inches high. (Smithsonian Institution)*

*(Left) A dark chocolate brown glaze covers this* Grand Feu *vase. (Smithsonian Institution)*

*(Below) These* Grand Feu *"Sunray" vases are glazed buff, green, and pale green. They were made before 1913. The bulbous vase is 7½ by 4⅛ inches, the cylindrical vase is 2⅛ by 4⅜ inches high. (Smithsonian Institution)*

# Grueby Faience Co.

### Boston, Massachusetts

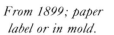

*From 1899; paper
label or in mold.*

*Before 1899–c.
1905.*

William Henry Grueby was born in 1867. As a boy of thirteen he began to work at the Low Art Tile Works in Chelsea, Massachusetts, where he remained for about ten years. In 1890, Grueby started making architectural faience at a plant in Revere, Massachusetts. Early in 1891 he leased space from Fiske, Coleman and Company, where he and Eugene R. Atwood worked as Atwood & Grueby. Atwood & Grueby made and installed tile in several Boston locations before the firm closed. In 1894, Grueby founded a pottery, Grueby Faience Company, still using the facilities of Fiske, Coleman. ("Grueby Faience Co., glazed brick" is listed in the Boston City Directory of 1895.) According to a November 1, 1910, reference in *Arts and Decoration,* Coleman sent Grueby to work at the larger company's exhibit of tile at the Chicago World's Fair in 1893. It was at the fair that Grueby first saw examples of foreign art pottery work. He probably met Charles F. Binns of Royal Worcester and saw the French pottery of Delaherche and Chaplet.

Grueby decided to develop his own glazes. He experimented and soon had a glaze that was similar to the French *grès flammé* (earthenware dipped in opaque enamel and fired until vitrification). It had a matte finish rather than the gloss popular with other potteries of the time. The glaze was given a dull finish, not by sandblasting or acid treatment as had been done before, but by a special method of firing in the kiln. In 1897 he reorganized and incorporated the Grueby Faience Company, and added George Prentice Kendrick, a designer and craftsman, and William Hagerman Graves, an architect, to the board. The designs by Kendrick were used through all of the Grueby company's years and were the primary designs until 1902. Circulars for the company for 1899–1900 mention the designs as being done entirely by Kendrick. A 1902 article in *Scribner's Magazine* commented that "there is no change in the arrangement yet known." After 1902 other designs were made by Addison B. LeBoutillier, a French architect.

The pottery was made by hand, although a few examples such as a scarab paperweight may have been molded. The pieces were thrown on a foot-powered wheel, after which the modeling was done by one of the young women or men hired by the firm. Most of these artists were graduates of the Museum of Fine Arts School in Boston, the Normal Art School, or the Cowles Art School. The initials of some of the artists can be found on pieces of Grueby ware.

At the Paris Exposition in 1900, Grueby won two gold medals and one silver, competing against some pieces of Rookwood pottery. Grueby's work achieved renown in America a year later at the Pan American Exposition in Buffalo, New York.

The work at the company was divided into two types, architectural tiles and art pottery. In 1907, Grueby Pottery Company, a

**GRUEBY**

*In use by 1904, incised.*

**GRUEBY
BOSTON.MASS**

*In use by 1904, incised.*

**GRUEBY POTTERY
BOSTON.U.S.A.**

*In use by 1904, incised.*

**HAUTEVILLE**

*c. 1913–c. 1920.*

*c. 1921–1926.*

**GRUEBY**

*1928 patent; claimed use since 1888.*

*A Grueby tile, 13 inches square, made in 1906. (Smithsonian Institution)*

(Above) *Grueby mark.* (Right) *Paper label.*

*Marks on backs of Grueby tiles.*

The Craftsman *magazine of December 1914 pictured this Grueby tile bathroom wall. The floor is a dull green tile with a pond lily border, and the wall tiles picture fleur-de-lis in natural colors.*

(Below) *Part of a set of four tiles made with the emblems of the four Gospels. One 7½-inch tile of blue with green relief that shows a winged ox holding a book is the emblem of Saint Luke. The other tile, of orange with green relief, that shows an eagle holding a book is the emblem of Saint John. (Smithsonian Institution)*

marketing division of Grueby Faience created around 1898, was incorporated in Massachusetts. Grueby himself was president. Shortly afterward, in 1908, Augustus A. Carpenter of Chicago became president of Grueby Faience, probably because he offered new capital to the firm. By 1909, however, Grueby Faience went bankrupt. Grueby then started a new company for the production of architectural tiles, the Grueby Faience and Tile Company.

Too much success seemed to doom the art pottery firm. The Grueby style of pottery with its simple lines and dull finish became a popular national style, and dozens of cheaper copies were made at other factories. Grueby offered few new designs and this lack of creativity may have led to the problems in marketing. The firm had to close the art pottery about 1910. The tile and architectural pottery firm burned in 1913 but was rebuilt and continued to work until 1920, the last year it is listed in the Boston City Directory. It was purchased by the C. Pardee Works of Perth Amboy, New Jersey.

**GRUEBY FAIENCE**
*Artists' Names, Marks, and the Years They Worked*

Julia H. Bradley. 1926.

Florence S. Liley.

Gertrude Priest.

Ruth Erickson. 1899–1910.

Annie V. Lingley. 1899–1910.

Marie A. Seaman.

Ellen R. Farrington.

Lillian Newman.

Gertrude Standwood.

George Prentiss Kendrick. 1898–1901. b. 1850, d. 1919.

Norma Pierce.

E. T. (tiles). 1900–1905.

Addison B. LeBoutillier. 1901–1906.

Wilhelmina Post. c. 1898–1907.

Kiichi Yamada.

*A yellow Grueby vase. (Robert Koch)*

*Five modeled leaves form the decoration on this light green matte-glazed vase. The 8³/₄-inch piece has a paper label. A similar but taller Grueby vase was exhibited at the Paris World's Fair in 1900. (June Greenwald Antiques)*

*A 5¹/₂-inch Grueby vase with incised stems, leaves, and buds. The vase is marked with the impressed circular mark with the lotus flower, "Grueby Pottery, Boston, USA," and the number "400" and cipher "RE" for Ruth Erickson. (Private collection)*

## PRODUCT

The most important type of art pottery made by the Grueby Faience Company was the matte glaze ware developed by William Grueby. These pieces were modeled by hand. The veining of the leaf was added to the vase as a thin piece of clay. The additions were tooled onto the wall of the vase. Some incised lines were also used.

The designs featured natural shapes such as the mullein leaf, acanthus leaf, lotus, tulip, marsh grasses, and the plantain. The hand-tooling on the clay gives a surface that appears rough but is really smooth to the touch.

The glaze was applied about ¹/₃₂-inch thick. Most pieces were of a single color or a blended monotone. Green was favored, but the firm also made pieces glazed with pink, yellow, brown, blue, gray, grayish purple, or creamy white. Some pieces were made with a flower motif glazed in a different color, such as yellow on a green or blue ground. One writer describing the ware in *Pottery and Glass* in 1909 wrote:

> The surface of Grueby enamels has much the character of a watermelon or cucumber, or the warm brown of a russet apple, and is full of delicate veining and mottling which give it an individuality of its own. The forms, of which there are several hundred, run from small cabinet bits to great jars three feet high and new ones are constantly added.

*Seven red buds and seven green leaves form the decoration on this 6¹/₂-by-8¹/₄-inch Grueby vase. It is impressed with the circular "Faience" mark and "43." (David Rago Arts & Crafts Gallery)*

*A realistic daffodil is carved on the side of this green Grueby vase. (Courtesy of the Strong Museum, Rochester, New York)*

Grueby Faience Company made this dark green 8-inch-high earthenware vase about 1897. It is 3³/₈ inches in diameter at the base. (Courtesy of the Brooklyn Museum, Brooklyn, New York, gift of Arthur W. Clement)

Tan stippled glaze appears on a gray stoneware vase made by the Grueby Pottery about 1905. It is 3¹/₂ inches high. (Smithsonian Institution)

Two-color Grueby vases are prized today. This tall thin example is decorated with narcissus on a green ground. (Skinner, Inc.)

(Below left) Yellow water lilies and green lily pads decorate this Grueby 6-inch tile. It is impressed "Grueby, Boston, 1914." (Below right) Green, blue, and brown trees decorate this Grueby tile made about 1900. It is marked "Grueby Faience and Tile Co., Boston, Mass." The tile is 6 inches square. (Christie's)

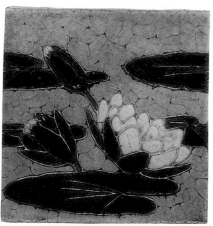

Wilhelmina Post made this tobacco jar for the Grueby Pottery about 1907. The 7³/₄-inch jar decorated with modeled tobacco flowers has a light green and white matte glaze. It is marked with the impressed "Grueby Pottery, Boston, USA" circular mark. The incised letters "WP" and the symbols "1/4/7, X" also appear on the bottom of the jar. (Private collection; photograph from The Art Museum, Princeton University)

Grueby also made lamp bases for Tiffany; Duffner & Kimberly; and Bigelow & Kennard, and many types of tiles. Grueby tiles were decorated with floral and geometric patterns, flowers, medieval knights, illustrations from Lewis Carroll or Rudyard Kipling, and specially ordered designs. Some tiles were cloisonné-type with walls of clay to hold colored glazes in a stylized design. This technique is occasionally found on the art pottery. One ware that created great comment in the early 1900s was a white crackleware of a quality claimed to be equal to that of old Korean pottery.

Of course, the method of manufacture and the handwork of the potters

*This tile with a tan border shows a deer on a blue-green background. It is 4 inches square. (Smithsonian Institution)*

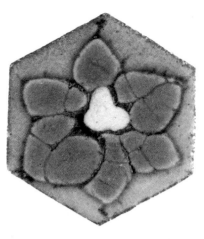

*A hexagonal tile is yellow with green and white floral decoration. Each edge of the tile is 3 inches long. (Smithsonian Institution)*

*A stylized flower of dull yellow decorates this blue tile. Each edge is 4 inches long. (Smithsonian Institution)*

*An unusual color scheme of pale blue drip glaze on a sand-colored bisque ground was used on this experimental Grueby vase. The impressed mark indicates it was made about 1905. The vase is 11¼ inches high. (Skinner, Inc.)*

*Dark green glaze was used on this Grueby earthenware vase made about 1910. It measures 9 inches high by 2⅜ inches in diameter at the base. (Courtesy of the Brooklyn Museum, Brooklyn, New York, gift from the collection of Edward A. Behr)*

*Geometric patterns of yellow, ocher, and white matte glazes appear on this 7½-inch-high vase. It was made about 1892–1902. The vase has the impressed circular mark "Grueby Faience Co., Boston, USA." It also has an original paper label with a lotus flower (as on Grueby tiles) and the notation "price $18, No. B." (Collection of the Newark Museum)*

and artists meant no two pieces of Grueby ware were exactly alike.

According to the *American Pottery Gazette* of August 10, 1907, the clays for all Grueby products were American, coming from deposits in New Jersey and on Martha's Vineyard. And *Keramic Studio* said in February 1905 that "the business of the Grueby pottery, everyone knows, was originally the making of drain and sanitary piping, etc. The artware necessarily must have been of the same materials to avoid too great complexity of production."

This scarab pottery paperweight was made by Grueby for the St. Louis World's Fair in 1904. It has a green semimatte glaze. The scarab is 4 inches long by 2¾ inches wide by 1¼ inches high. It is marked with the impressed circle and lotus mark, "Grueby Faience Co., Boston, USA." (Smithsonian Institution)

Molded leaves and flower buds of dark green and yellow matte glaze decorate this Grueby pottery vase. It is 12 inches high and marked with the impressed circle, lotus mark, and the symbols "20, AL." It was probably made by Annie V. Lingley about 1899–1910. (David Hanks)

Yellow daffodils are modeled against a green background on this 12¼-inch-high Grueby vase. It is marked with the impressed mark "Grueby Pottery, Boston, USA" and the number "170." The vase was made about 1891–1901.

Green leaves fold over a yellow base on this 9¼-inch vase made by Grueby about 1905. (Skinner, Inc.)

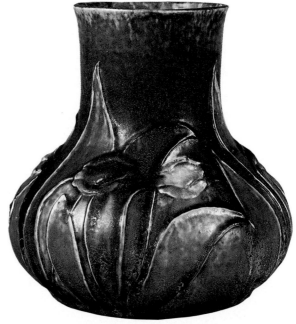

Grueby made many large vases. This 21-inch-high 1905 example has brownish green glaze. (Skinner, Inc.)

Modeled tulip leaves and flowers of green and yellow matte glaze decorate this 8⅝-inch vase. The piece is marked with the "Grueby Pottery, Boston, USA" impressed circular mark. It is also marked with the cipher "MJC"(?), "36," and the painted notation "X." (Private collection; photograph from The Art Museum, Princeton University, Princeton, New Jersey)

# Halcyon

### *Halcyon, California*

~

The Temple of the People was a utopian colony set up in Halcyon, California, in 1904. A sanatorium was founded there the same year, and in 1910 a pottery was set up to provide therapy for patients. The pottery was under the direction of Alexander W. Robertson. Local San Luis Obispo red clay was used from which pieces were modeled and carved. The pottery often depicted natural forms and many pieces were decorated with lizards. The pottery closed from 1913 until the 1930s, when Gertrude Wall of Walrich Pottery gave classes there. White clay was used, with glazes from the Walrich Pottery. The pottery was closed permanently in 1940.

Pieces were marked with the words "Halcyon, California." Sometimes an artist's initials or the date was added. The 1930s pieces were marked "HP."

# Hampshire Pottery

### *Keene, New Hampshire*

~

James Scollay Taft was born in Nelson, New Hampshire, in 1844. He began working in 1863. His first job was in a mill, then he worked in a grocery, and finally, in 1871, he purchased an old clothespin factory in Keene, New Hampshire, where he started making pottery. This was the first year of operation of the Hampshire Pottery Company. Taft's uncle, James Burnap, joined him in the business.

Keene was an ideal location for a pottery because of the large deposits of feldspar and clay in the area. At first the firm made redware, mainly flowerpots; later it added stoneware. In 1874 Taft acquired another pottery factory to produce the company's redware. The original works made the stoneware. A majolica-type glazed line was soon added. The majolica ware was evidently the result of the expertise of Thomas Stanley, an English potter who began working in Keene in 1879. The pieces were made with green, yellow, brown, and blue glazes on a white body.

The new line of pottery was a success and other types were added. The firm was enlarged and a new kiln was built in 1883. Wallace L. King was the artist in charge of all the decorative work made in the new kiln. The most famous new product was the Royal Worcester–type glaze. It had a creamy yellow-pink tone and was used on all types of baskets, jugs, jars, cuspidors, rose bowls, tea sets, and the like. The colored glazed souvenir wares, decorated with transfer-printed scenes or designs, sold well.

The green matte finish used by the pottery was also popular. It is interesting that while the Grueby Faience Co. was credited with making the first popular matte-finished art pottery in America, the Hampshire Pottery used this glaze in 1883, four years before Grueby.

*Impressed.*

*1930s, incised.*

HALCYON
CALIF.

*Impressed.*

J.S.T. & CO.
KEENE, NH

*Incised.*

J.S. TAFT & CO.
KEENE, N.H.

*Incised.*

*Printed red, used before 1904.*

*Printed red, used before 1904.*

*Printed red, used before 1904.*

J.S. TAFT & COMPANY
KEENE, N.H.

*Incised.*

Hampshire
Pottery

*Incised.*

Cadmon Robertson designed this vase for Hampshire Pottery about 1904–1914. The vase, made of white clay covered with a matte green glaze, is 7¹/₈ inches high, 3³/₈ inches in diameter at the base, and 3⁷/₁₆ inches at the top. The incised marks on the base include "Hampshire Pottery" and M in a circle. The M is said to be a tribute from Robertson to his wife, Emoretta. (Gift of Dr. Joseph H. Boyer, 1971.448; photograph c. 1991, The Art Institute of Chicago, Chicago, Illinois. All rights reserved.)

By about 1883, approximately forty employees worked at the plant, roughly half of them decorators. Many of the pieces were made to be left undecorated and sold to amateur home decorators.

The firm continued to grow and made many types of specialties and souvenir pieces, plus a new decorative line designed by a Japanese artist employed by the pottery.

Cadmon Robertson, Taft's brother-in-law, joined the firm in 1904 and soon afterward was in charge of all the manufacturing. Robertson (no relation to the other famous art pottery Robertsons or to Chelsea Keramic Art Works) was born in Chesterfield, New Hampshire, where he was educated as a chemist. While at the Hampshire Pottery, he developed more than nine hundred glaze formulas, including the famous colored matte glazes, and was also responsible for many designs. His death in 1914 created problems for the firm. Wallace King, the artist in charge of decoration, had retired in 1908, so the firm's only important remaining executive was James Taft.

In 1916, Taft sold the Hampshire Pottery to George Morton, a Bostonian who had worked at the Grueby Pottery. Morton made

This green-glazed bowl, 9¹/₂ inches in diameter and 3 inches high, has a white glaze on the bottom. The plant decoration is in high relief. (Smithsonian Institution)

Dark orange-brown glaze and brown flowers cover this Hampshire ewer. It is 6¹/₄ inches high and marked "J.S.T. & Co., Keene, NH." (Private collection)

more than a thousand items, but stayed with the firm for only one year before returning to Grueby. The factory closed during World War I because the demand for pottery was limited.

Morton reopened the firm after the war and added some machinery for the manufacture of white hotel china. He also added presses for making mosaic floor tiles, and from 1919 to 1921 the tiles became the main product of the Hampshire Pottery.

The plant closed permanently in 1923 when competition from Ohio and New Jersey potteries made it impossible to continue at a profit. The New England plant had to import coal, while many of its competitors were using the less expensive natural gas.

### PRODUCT

Redware and stoneware were the earliest products of the firm. Majolica ware was started in 1879. It was glazed in a variety of colors on a white body. Some pieces were cast in molds, giving the appearance of relief designs. Mugs with a dark green glaze shading to red that had a relief border near the rim were common. Brown glaze pitchers and tea sets shaped like ears of corn were among the more unusual forms, as were marmalade dishes shaped and colored like oranges. Many vases were made in brown, yellow, orange, blue, or green with white.

The 1883 Royal Worcester glaze was made on a semiporcelain body with a dull pale cream finish with pink overtones. The glaze took five firings and the ware was decorated with black transfer designs, often pictures of local views. Two of the most popular pieces made with this glaze were the famous Longfellow jug and the witch jug made to be sold in Salem, Massachusetts. Souvenir items were a very important part of the firm's production and were such a success that a new line of colored glazed wares of blue, mahogany, and olive green was added. The finish on these pieces had a grained effect caused during firing. Most of the shapes for the souvenirs were copied from early Greek and Egyptian styles. The name of the resort, college, or locality was put on the souvenir pieces with gilt.

The factory made baskets, jugs, cracker jars, chocolate sets, cuspidors, comb and brush trays, bonbon dishes, powder boxes, rose bowls, pitchers, tea sets, and umbrella stands. White ware was either decorated or left plain.

All of the numerous glazes developed by Cadmon Robertson were used after 1904. He created matte glazes in green, blue, gray, bronze, yellow, and peacock blue, which shaded from green to blue. The semiporcelain body was fired at a high temperature. Foreign clay (often English) was used, although New Jersey and Florida clays were the most popular. The firing created minute white crystals in the glaze, giving each piece a soft appearance. The interiors of many of the pieces were brightly glazed, which made them practical for daily use. The pottery also made an extensive line of artwares that included candlesticks, vases, lamps, bowls, and dishes.

After the war the firm continued producing many of the old shapes and colors, and added some new colors. Many types of lamps, candlesticks, jars, vases, and tea sets were made. During its later years of operation, the Hampshire Pottery shifted its manufacturing from art pottery to hotel china and mosaic floor tile.

*Dark blue glaze covers this 7½-inch vase. An incised border of wavelike scrolls circles the top. It is marked with the incised words "Hampshire Pottery." (Private collection)*

*Dark green matte glaze was used on this 3½-inch-high vase with raised leaves. It has two marks placed over each other, the incised word "Hampshire" and the gold overglaze mark "Mt. Washington." (Private collection)*

## ARTISTS

Eliza Adams, Blanche Andrews, Mrs. John Dennison, F. L. Gillride, Marion Grinnel, Ida Jefts, Wallace King, and Emma Mercure.

## MARKS

Among the Hampshire marks are "HAMPSHIRE KEENE N. H." printed in red; "J. S. T. & CO. KEENE N. H." impressed; "JAMES S. TAFT & CO. KEENE, N. H."; "HAMPSHIRE"; "HAMPSHIRE POTTERY, KEENE N. H."; "KEENE, N. H."; "J. S. TAFT, KEENE, N. H."; and "HAMPSHIRE POTTERY." A paper label was also used, and Wallace King, the head artist, sometimes signed his work.

# D. F. Haynes
*See Chesapeake Pottery*

# Herold China and Pottery Co.
*Golden, Colorado*

John J. Herold emigrated from Austria in 1891. He worked in New York, then in a Pittsburgh glass factory, and by 1898 was employed in Zanesville, Ohio. He became a pottery decorator working at the Weller pottery and then at J. B. Owens. By 1900, he was employed at the Roseville Pottery and five years later was superintendent of the Roseville plant.

Herold became sick with tuberculosis and left Zanesville in 1908, for a healthier climate. He founded the Herold China and Pottery Company in Golden, Colorado, in 1910. Art pottery was probably not made at Herold China and Pottery, but Herold was familiar with the art pottery tradition from his years in Ohio. He made porcelains and ornamental pieces, then sold the firm and returned to Ohio in 1914. The Colorado plant became Coors Porcelain in 1921.

Herold became superintendent of the Ohio Pottery in Zanesville, Ohio, in the early 1920s. He died in 1923.

# Hull House
*Chicago, Illinois*

*Rubber stamp.*

*Incised.*

Hull House, a famous social settlement house in Chicago, Illinois, was founded in 1889 by Jane Addams and Ellen Gates Starr. During the late 1890s, the settlement established a pottery where immigrants from the surrounding neighborhoods could learn all aspects of pottery production. By 1898, vases, jars, and bowls were being made by William Bulger, one of the Hull House residential staff members, and Frank Hazenplug, a settlement resident.

*Hull House plate. (University of Illinois at Chicago Circle)*

*Arts and Crafts style pitcher, cup, and saucer. (University of Illinois at Chicago Circle)*

Hull House Kilns began operations in 1927 with Myrtle French as instructor. Pieces produced there were glazed green, blue, yellow, orange, or red. Some had incised or hand-painted designs. Bowls, tea sets, plates, and some animals and figurines were also made there. Pieces were rubber-stamped "Hull House Kilns, Chicago." By the late 1930s, Hull House had moved on to other social programs and away from pottery production. However, neighborhood centers associated with Hull House continue to offer craft classes around Chicago.

## Hull Pottery
### *Crooksville, Ohio*

The Acme Pottery Company was formed in Crooksville, Ohio, in 1903. It had been in existence for only two years when it changed ownership and became the A. E. Hull Pottery Company. In 1917 the factory began making pottery that was sold to florists and gift shops in all parts of the country. Hull Pottery was selling so well by 1921 that Addis E. Hull traveled to Europe to buy pottery in France, England, and Germany to be sold through the Hull Pottery outlets. In 1923 the pottery built a continuous kiln 310 feet long at a cost of $75,000, and by 1925 the firm was credited with making more than 3 million pieces of pottery a year. One Hull plant was converted to making tile in 1927, but by 1929 that plant closed and the importation of pottery ended.

In 1937 Hull contracted to make 11 million pieces for the Shulton Company of New York, and the A. E. Hull Pottery expanded to

*Paper label.*

*Hull*
USA

*Stamp.*

hull
u.s.a.

*Mark in mold.*

450 employees. The pottery continued to produce until it burned to the ground in 1950. By 1952, the firm was restored and headed by J. Brandon Hull, Addis Hull's son. The company name was changed to the Hull Pottery Company. The firm closed in 1986.

A. E. Hull Pottery made many types of wares, including artware, lamp bases, novelties, blue band kitchenware, and Zane Grey kitchenware and stoneware. Pieces of the pottery are marked "Hull Art U.S." or "Hull U.S.A." and some were marked with a paper label. Pieces made after 1952 are marked "hull" (with a small *h*). The artware includes pattern numbers stamped on the pieces: 100 is the double rose pattern; 300, orchid; 400, iris; 500, dogwood; 600, poppy. Figurines shaped like butterflies, people, birds, and animals were also made.

## Iowa State Pottery
### *Ames, Iowa*

*Impressed.*

*Impressed.*

Iowa State College in Ames, Iowa, founded a ceramic engineering department in 1906. Students were trained to work in manufacturing companies making sparkplugs, electrical porcelains, and other commercial clay products. In 1915 the college added a modeled pottery class for engineering students and for women in the home economics courses.

Paul Cox of the Newcomb Pottery became head of ceramic engineering in 1920. To keep state political leaders interested in the school, he started to make products from Iowa clay deposits. Cox promoted the department by throwing pots on a wheel at Iowa state fairs and by writing for magazines. The classes grew and in 1924 Cox established a commercial art pottery and hired Mary Yancey, a Newcomb graduate, to design pottery and to teach.

Pieces made at the pottery were handcrafted and decorated with plants or prairie-inspired designs. Among the designs pictured were clover, lilies, poppies, jonquils, tulips, berries, maple trees, and pinecones. Vases, pitchers, and tiles were made of Iowa clay covered with tin enamel glaze in a glossy finish. Blue, brown, gray, green, white, yellow, pink, and red glazes were used. Cox, or occasionally Yancey, threw the pottery on a wheel, then Yancey carved or incised a design and decorated it. The students did the rest of the production, firing the kiln and mixing the glaze. Pieces were marked "ISC Ames" in a circle, or with a *Y* for Yancey, or with the name Cox. Iowa State pottery was made commercially for only six years. It is thought that about eight hundred pieces were produced. Mary Yancey left the pottery in 1930 when she married a ceramic engineer, Frank Hodgdon, and moved to Boston. In 1931 she joined three other women to start a studio pottery, Clay Craft Studios. She later taught at Fullerton Junior College near Los Angeles. Paul Cox left Iowa State in 1939 but continued to work as a potter at his own studio in Baton Rouge, Louisiana. He died in 1968.

## Jalan Pottery
### San Francisco, California

~

Manuel E. Jalanivich and Ingvardt Olsen formed the Jalan Pottery about 1920 in San Francisco. Jalanivich had worked under George Ohr and Leon Volkmar. Olsen had worked in Denmark. At Jalan Pottery they used native California clays decorated with Egyptian, Chinese, and Persian-inspired designs. Yellow, green, purple, red, and blue were favored colors. They made vases, jardinieres, and figurines. The San Francisco pottery closed in 1938, but the firm moved to Belmont, California, and continued to operate for a few years in the early 1940s. Jalanivich died in 1944. Pieces are marked "Jalan" in incised letters.

## Jervis Pottery
### Oyster Bay, New York

~

William Percival Jervis was an English author and potter. In 1902 he was working as manager of the Avon Faience Company in Tiltonsville, Ohio. He changed jobs often. In 1903 he was at the Corona Pottery, in 1904 at Rose Valley, and in 1905 at Craven Art Pottery. In 1908 he established his own pottery, the Jervis Pottery, in Oyster Bay, New York. There he worked with Frederick Hürten Rhead, who had previously been at Roseville and had worked with Jervis at Avon. But Rhead soon left to join the University City Pottery. Jervis Pottery made several different types of pottery, including sgraffito designs on redware covered with white slip. Glazes were in grayed, not bright, tones. Metallic glazes were also used. Vases, pitchers, flowerpots, and steins were the primary products made at the pottery. It closed about 1912.

The mark used was the name Jervis in a hexagonal block with the initials *O* and *B*, for Oyster Bay, on each side of the larger mark.

JALAN

*Incised.*

*Incised.*

*This tall incised and carved vase, signed "Jervis," may have been made after William Jervis left Craven and was working with Frederick Rhead at Jervis Pottery. The anonymous poem inscribed on the vase reads (on the vase front): "Cupid as he lay among/Roses by a bee was stung/Whereupon in anger flying/To his mother said he was dying." It continues (on the back of the vase): " 'Alas!' said she my lad if you/ . . . a pernicious torment is/Can tell me how great's . . ./. . . those thou woundest with thy dart." (Collection of Ann Koepke)*

The tradition of pottery in North Carolina goes back to the 1750s. Household wares and whiskey jugs were made by many potteries throughout the eighteenth and nineteenth centuries. Pottery was made in the ancient potters' tradition known around the world and the results were simple utilitarian shapes and glazes.

In 1915, Juliana and Jacques Busbee became interested in what by then had become a dying art in North Carolina. They searched the state and either bought or photographed many examples of the folk pottery. They also encouraged any potter they could locate, and soon set up a training and sales organization for what they named "Jugtown Pottery." (The term *jugtown* originally had unflattering connotations, as it meant any town where jugs for whiskey were made, especially during Prohibition.)

The Busbees opened a tearoom at Sixty Washington Square in Greenwich Village, New York City, to sell their pottery. By 1919 the tearoom was popular for both its pottery and the caliber of its guests from the art and literary worlds. During these years, Mrs. Busbee remained in New York at the tearoom while Mr. Busbee worked with the potters in North Carolina.

By 1921, Jacques Busbee decided that it was time to build a shop at Jugtown, North Carolina. And because the older potters were unable or unwilling to learn to make new shapes or to produce pottery on a schedule, he hired eighteen-year-old Ben Owen as a potter in 1923. Busbee determined the shapes, Owen turned the pieces, then Busbee did the glazing. Several other local men were hired to help mix clay, cut wood, and tend the kilns.

The pottery sold well and soon the New York City tearoom, known as the Village Store, was moved to 37 East Sixtieth Street. Sales increased as the pottery received publicity from many magazines, including *Country Life*, *House Beautiful*, and *The New Yorker*.

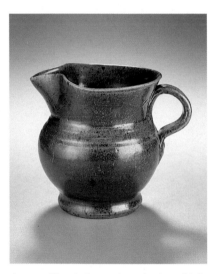

*A small pitcher, 4¾ inches high, marked "Jugtown Ware." (Private collection)*

*Two Jugtown pieces. The bowl is 4 inches in diameter and 2 inches high, and the vase is 4½ inches high. Both have the impressed circular Jugtown Ware mark. (Private collection)*

As a market grew, other potters near the Jugtown Pottery began developing their wares and keeping up with the new shapes and glazes, and soon an industry was established in North Carolina. Juliana Busbee sold the New York store in 1926 and moved into a log cabin near the Jugtown Pottery.

The Busbees were eccentric, interesting people, and they attracted visitors from all over the world. Mrs. Busbee wore clothes made only of handwoven fabrics from North Carolina. She always asked her guests to help with the dishes and paid no attention to what people said about her. Mr. Busbee wore the first Bermuda shorts seen in the area.

During the Depression, the potters kept working and the Jugtown Pottery continued to prosper. Jacques Busbee died in 1947, but Juliana Busbee and Ben Owen continued to run the pottery. Juliana became ill in 1958, and at about the same time the pottery began having financial problems. Juliana said she had willed the Jugtown Pottery to Ben Owen, but no will could be found and Juliana was apparently not mentally competent to make one. The state of North Carolina considered taking over the property.

Friends of the pottery organized to save it as a nonprofit organization for the state. In 1958, corporate papers were signed to form Jugtown Incorporated, but during the period of Juliana's illness another corporation was also formed, with John Mare as principal. Juliana signed two separate deeds turning the pottery's property over to the two different corporations. Legal problems arose that led to the pottery's closing in 1959. By April 1960 the legal matters had been resolved and the business reopened. Busbee died in March 1962, and Ben Owen left the company to start his own pottery. He died in October 1983.

Nancy Sweezy, a potter, operated the Jugtown Pottery for Country Roads, Inc., from 1968 to 1983. The old marks were kept in use. In 1983 the pottery was sold to Vernon Owens, principal potter at Jugtown since 1960 and a second cousin of Ben Owen. In 1985, Nancy Sweezy helped organize a permanent collection of Jugtown pottery dating from 1923 to 1983 and arranged for the sale of any remaining wares produced during those years.

*Two green-blue vases made by the Jugtown Pottery. The vase on the left is 10 inches high; the vase on the right, 5⅝ inches high. (North Carolina Museum of Art)*

### PRODUCT

The Jugtown wares were all simple shapes. The early pieces were utilitarian adaptations of early pottery. Jugs, crocks, pie plates, sugar and cream dishes, plates, candlesticks, bean pots, tea sets, stew pans, pickle jars, and preserve jars were the primary forms. Later the company produced oriental-inspired pottery and decorative pieces for the New York market. All the Jugtown wares were glazed.

The pottery used Rockingham ware and the stoneware of past centuries as early design inspirations. A local red clay was used to make their orange-colored ware. A local buff-colored clay was used for the gray stoneware with blue or white decorations. Black, white, dark brown, Chinese blue and green, or "frogskin" glazes were used on the Chinese-style pieces. A few pieces were decorated with flowers, incised designs, or impressed patterns such as thumbprints.

The pottery was handmade, thrown on a kick wheel, and then glazed and fired. Pieces were marked "Jugtown Ware" impressed in a circle from the early days of the factory, probably about 1922 or 1923. The name was not registered until 1959.

# Kenton Hills
## *Erlanger, Kentucky*

*Showroom label; not used on pottery.*

*Impressed.*

*Label.*

*Incised.*

The failing Rookwood Pottery of Cincinnati, Ohio, laid off many skilled potters and decorators during the Depression. In 1937, a group of former Rookwood employees headed by chemist Harold Bopp founded the Harold Bopp Pottery in Erlanger, Kentucky. In 1939 the company was refinanced by George Seyler, father of the artist David Seyler who had worked at the Rookwood Pottery. In addition to Seyler, who was named art director, Bopp hired William Hentschel and Arthur Conant as designers, Rosemary Dickman and Alza Stratton as decorators, John Reichart as moldman, and Mayo Taylor as kilnman. The company was renamed Kenton Hills Porcelains, Inc., or, unofficially, Kenton Hills Pottery.

The company's lines resembled Rookwood pottery. Its wares included a high-fired soft-paste porcelain, glazed with either underglaze brown slip or colorful hand decorations. The glazes used included Spanish red, cat's-eye green or blue, Danish blue, and oxblood; also celadon, mossy green, poplar green, morning blue, dusty pink, Persian blue, mandarin yellow, jungle black, hard white, decorator white, shell white, and savage coral. Pieces were made from native clays.

In 1941, the workmen left for war jobs and the company sold its stock and rented its property. The business itself was sold to the Crestline Lamp Company in 1945. All molds were destroyed. David Seyler, who headed the Department of Sculpture at the University of Nebraska after 1948, stated that the pieces were marked as follows: Every Kenton Hills piece was impressed on the base with either the experimental "HB" lotus blossom or the "KH" tulip blossom. Neither mark dates a piece. An impressed number is the mold shape number, while impressed initials or a signature designates the designer or sculptor who created the form or added slip decoration to the clay shape. An impressed circle in the base center was always used on some molds as a lamp drill guide if required. Underglaze painted initials are those of the decorator. The word "Unica" or "Serica" added on decorated pieces implies a unique piece or one of a limited edition (usually lamp bases). The letter *S* (for special) indicates an experimental shape, usually one of a kind for a test kiln.

*Julian Bechtold. Made very few pieces.*

**ℬ**

*Harold Bopp. Made very few pieces.*

*Experimental Harold Bopp pottery mark.*

*Paul Chidaw. Part-time.*

**C**

*Arthur Conant. Made very few pieces.*

**RBD**

*Rose Brunner Dickman.*

**RD**

*Rosemary Dickman.*

*Charlotte Haupt. Made very few pieces.*

*William Hentschel.*

*Leo Murphy. Part-time.*

*Harold Nash. Part-time.*

**DS**

*David Seyler.*

*Alza Stratton.*

*Unknown.*

*A selection of pieces in the 1941 Kenton Hills catalog: Three pieces designed by David Seyler; sculpture of sitting woman by Charlotte Haupt.*

# Knowles, Taylor and Knowles
### East Liverpool, Ohio
~

The Knowles, Taylor and Knowles Company of East Liverpool, Ohio, made many types of ceramics. Knowles, Taylor and Knowles did make one rare form of art pottery, Lotus ware, so a short history of the company is included here.

Isaac W. Knowles founded a pottery in East Liverpool in 1853 to make Rockingham ware and yellowware. In 1870, John N. Taylor and Homer S. Knowles, Isaac's son, joined the firm, which then became known as Knowles, Taylor and Knowles. Joseph G. Lee and Willis A. Knowles were added as partners in 1888, but the business's name was not changed. The firm incorporated in January 1891 and added the word *Company* to its name.

The company made ironstone ware beginning in 1872, the first such ware made in Ohio. The firm specialized in hotel china, which was usually thicker than home-use china. Pieces were marked "K. T. & K."

Lotus ware was made commercially from about 1891 to 1896 and was displayed at the World's Columbian Exposition in 1893. It was named by Will Rhodes, one of the company's salesmen, who thought one piece resembled a lotus leaf. Homer Knowles, one of the partners, and Joshua Poole, plant superintendent, developed the formula for Lotus ware. Some writers have called Lotus ware a type of

*These two Lotus ware vases with olive bodies and white flowers are 6 inches and 7½ inches high. Both are marked with the Lotus ware stamp. (Private collection)*

An assortment of Knowles, Taylor and Knowles Lotus ware pieces. Lotus is made of porcelain, but the dark green vases at left are made of pottery with porcelain decoration. (Wolf's)

belleek porcelain ware, but belleek, unlike the Lotus ware, is a very thin porcelain with a creamy yellow glaze that appears wet.

Poole, who had been a manager of the Belleek Pottery in Ireland, also helped develop a true belleek ware for Knowles, Taylor and Knowles by 1889. This was not Lotus ware, but a true belleek, which today is even rarer than Lotus. It was marked with the round Knowles, Taylor and Knowles mark and the word "Belleek." In November 1889, the pottery's factory was destroyed by fire and the belleek ware was discontinued.

The first set of experimented Lotus ware dishes was made in 1889 from a bone china that was actually made with animal bones. George and William Morley, from England, and Henry Schmidt, from Germany, were brought to the firm to assist in the production. Kenneth Beattie was the chief modeler at the pottery.

Schmidt worked in secrecy in a small workshop, where he personally applied the leaves, flowers, "jewels," and filigree to the pieces of Lotus ware. He worked with the pieces in the hard green (unbaked) state. After the decorations were applied, the Lotus ware was baked in the same kilns as the commercial hotel wares. There was much breakage in the kilns both during the firing for the bisque state and after the decorating. Eventually the line was discontinued because of the high cost of producing it.

A few pieces of undecorated Lotus ware were made from molds taken from commercial objects. One dish shaped like a fan behind a reclining woman was molded from an identical brass dish. Pieces were made and decorated at the factory, but the ware was also sold plain to be decorated by amateur china painters. The ladies of East Liverpool returned their decorated pieces to the kiln to be baked, so these colored decorations have remained intact. Some pieces, ap-

A Lotus ware vase painted and gilded in East Liverpool about 1890. Notice that the body of this vase is very similar to another Lotus ware vase pictured here. The decorations, however, were often "one of a kind." (From the collections of Henry Ford Museum & Greenfield Village)

*A page from the Knowles, Taylor and Knowles Company catalog, circa 1890, showing examples of "white flowers on olive body." Also pictured are "white flowers on a celadon body" and the more common white Lotus ware. (East Liverpool Historical Society)*

parently decorated out of town and not properly baked, have been found with the color peeling.

Although the name Lotus ware is synonymous with a very white bone china to most collectors, a limited amount of art pottery was made and marked "Lotus." Lotus ware pottery had a dark green glaze on a chocolate pottery body with applied white porcelain decorations of leaves, branches, and flower tendrils.

Most Lotus ware was marked with the round Knowles, Taylor and Knowles emblem and the words "LOTUS WARE."

## Lessell Art Ware
### Parkersburg, West Virginia

*Stamped.*

Lessell Art Ware Company was started in Parkersburg, West Virginia, in 1911 and was owned by John Lessell, who had worked at Arc-en-Ciel Pottery and Owens Pottery Company. He made a line of art pottery that resembled pieces of copper and bronze with rivets. He may also have made gold- and silver-colored pieces. The company closed in 1912 and Lessell then worked with other potteries, including Weller.

Few pieces are known. One existing vase shows an oval mark with the words "Lessell Ware, Parkersburg."

# Lonhuda Pottery
### *Steubenville, Ohio*
∾

William Long of Steubenville, Ohio, founded the Lonhuda Pottery Company in 1892. Long was born in Ohio on July 18, 1844. After serving in the Civil War, he was discharged in 1865 and married a nurse he met in a military hospital. The Longs eventually moved to Steubenville, where he became a druggist. They had two sons, Charles and Albert.

Long discovered a new vocation when he saw a display of pottery at the Philadelphia Exposition of 1876. He set up a laboratory in the back of his drugstore and began experimenting with glazes. He made his first successful piece in 1889.

In 1892 he decided to form a pottery company with W. H. Hunter, editor of the Steubenville *Daily Gazette*, and Alfred Day, secretary of the U.S. Potters Association. The first letters of each man's name were used to form the company name, Lonhuda. Though the records are confused, William Long either developed a brown underglaze of the type used by Rookwood or was licensed to use a process apparently developed by Laura Fry in 1883. Contemporary records show that both Long and Rookwood bought licenses from Laura Fry, as reported in *China Glass and Pottery Review*, August 15, 1897.

The Lonhuda Pottery hired Fry (who stayed until 1894), Sarah R. McLaughlin, Helen M. Harper, and Jessie R. Spaulding as artists. Other artists who may have worked at the factory are Elizabeth Ayers, Charles John Dibowski, and Mary Taylor. The company made underglaze pieces with slip decoration and the familiar brown background. The pottery was sold in all parts of the United States and was also shipped to Europe. Lonhuda pottery was exhibited at the Chicago World's Fair in 1893.

Samuel A. Weller (see Weller) was attracted to the pottery and immediately decided that it would fit into his future plans. He had a plant in Zanesville, Ohio, and was able to convince Long to make Lonhuda there. A new firm, known as the Lonhuda Faience Company, was formed by Long and Weller in January 1895. The factory had been making Lonhuda for less than a year when fire destroyed much of the building. By that time, Weller no longer needed Long and his secrets, and Long may have wanted to move on.

After the two separated, Weller quickly rebuilt his factory, and made an underglaze pottery similar to Lonhuda called "Louwelsa."

*"Denaura Denver" is marked on this 1903 green vase made by the Denver China and Pottery Company. It was made with a relief design of a tulip. The vase is 8½ inches high by 4¾ inches wide. (Smithsonian Institution)*

*Incised.*

*Impressed, c. 1893.*

*Impressed, c. 1892, c. 1895–1896; also used later with Denver mark.*

*Impressed, c. 1896, 1901–1905.*

*Impressed, 1901–1905.*

*Impressed, 1901–1905.*

*Laura A. Fry.*

*Helen M. Harper.*

*W. A. Long.*

*Sarah R. McLaughlin.*

*Jessie R. Spaulding.*

*Yellow violets decorate this chocolate brown–glazed Lonhuda vase. It is marked with "Lonhuda, 1893, 115" and other symbols. (The Benjamin Collection, Smithsonian Institution)*

Long went to work for the J. B. Owens Company of Zanesville, where he stayed four years. Even after Long left, Owens continued to make pottery glazed by the (Laura) Fry method, marketing it under the name "Utopian."

Long moved to Denver, Colorado, in 1900. The following year, he organized the Denver China and Pottery Company, which should not be confused with the Denver Art Pottery founded by Frederick J. and Francis George White. Long's Denver China and Pottery Company worked until 1905, when Long moved to Clifton, New Jersey, and founded the Clifton Pottery. He worked there from 1905 to 1908, making a line called "Crystal Patina." In need of work in 1909, Long moved back to Zanesville and worked for Weller again until 1912. A short time later he went to the Roseville Pottery, and by 1914 he was working with the American Encaustic Tiling Company. He was hospitalized soon after and died in 1918.

## PRODUCT

The Lonhuda Pottery was inspired by the forms of American Indian pottery. William Long admired the shapes of this pottery and even used an Indian head as part of his mark. His pieces were made of colored clay with a slip decoration added to the unfired pieces. He used red, brown, yellow, and gray colors. The clay itself was usually an imported yellow. The high-gloss brown glaze was his most famous and he also used a clear glaze and a matte glaze. Pieces were made with decorations picturing Indians, famous people, dogs, seascapes, landscapes, fish, birds, and flowers.

The art pottery at the Denver China and Pottery Company was covered with a matte glaze, often green. It was slightly iridescent, with molded relief designs of Colorado flowers or Art Nouveau geometric patterns. The line was called "Denaura." The firm also made a general line of pottery.

The Clifton Art Pottery made several types of white clay pieces covered with crystalline glaze. The line, called "Crystal Patina," resembled old bronzes. They also made Clifton Indian ware, a line of pottery made from red New Jersey clay and resembling early Indian pieces. The interiors of these pieces were often glazed black. In addition, Clifton Art Pottery

*A small vase made by Clifton Pottery. The piece stands 4½ inches high and is marked "Clifton 1906." (Private collection)*

made a matte-glazed ware in pale robin's-egg blue. Tirrube ware had a matte ground with floral slip decorations. Art Nouveau–inspired pieces were also produced at the pottery.

### MARKS

The Lonhuda mark with a monogram was used about 1892. The impressed solid Indian mark was first used in 1893 and is usually found on pieces that were inspired by Indian pottery shapes. The Indian profile was used later. "LF" (for Lonhuda Faience) in a shield was used about 1896. It is also found with the Denver mark used about 1901–1905. Dates were put on many early pieces. Impressed numbers to indicate shape were also used.

Clifton wares were marked with the name Clifton or a cypher.

## Low Art Tile
### *See Tile Companies*
~

## Marblehead Pottery
### *Marblehead, Massachusetts*
~

Marblehead Pottery was established in 1904 by Dr. Herbert J. Hall in connection with Devereux Mansion, a sanatorium he ran in Marblehead, Massachusetts. Dr. Hall thought that work would be beneficial to his patients, so he developed a series of craft classes for them that included woodcarving, weaving, metalwork, and pottery. The pottery installed in the sanatorium had a kick wheel, a turning lathe, and a six-burner kerosene kiln. Local clay was used. By 1908 there were three designers, a decorator, a thrower, and a kilnman. The pottery's output averaged two hundred pieces per week.

During the first few years, the patients were instructed by Jessie Luther of Providence, Rhode Island, and Arthur E. Baggs of Alfred, New York. Around 1908, the pottery was separated from the sanatorium and Baggs was made director of the pottery. He had previously worked under Professor Charles F. Binns of the New York State School of Clay-working and Ceramics. Baggs was an artist and designer, and he used experimental glazes and methods of decoration to make an artistic product.

Arthur Baggs became the owner of the pottery in 1915 and continued its work. When more space was required, the pottery moved to 111 Front Street in Marblehead. It was always a small operation; only six people worked at the factory in 1916. The factory continued operating until 1936. Baggs worked only summers after 1920. From 1925 to 1928, he worked for the Cowan Pottery and taught at the Cleveland School of Art. Then in 1928 he became a professor of ceramics at Ohio State University. Baggs died in 1947.

Many artists were associated with the pottery. Arthur Irwin Hennessey and Maude Milner were designers there, working before 1912. Annie Aldrich and Rachel Grinwell, though not on the staff, created designs. Mrs. E. D. (Hannah) Tutt was a decorator and E. J.

*Stamped.*

*αEB*

*Incised; initials of A. E. Baggs.*

*Photograph of paper label and mark on bottom of mustard-colored vase at top center on page 82.*

*Hannah Tutt executed this Marblehead vase about 1908–1910. It is modeled and painted with decorations of conventionalized flowers of green, brown, black, and yellow matte glaze. It is 7 inches high and marked with the Marblehead ship mark, an incised "HT," and an original paper label, "Marblehead, A-5, Pottery." (Collection of the Newark Museum)*

*This vase with dark mustard–colored background is decorated with brown, green, orange, and blue geometric designs. The interior is glazed glossy blue-green. The vase is marked with the Marblehead ship mark. (Smithsonian Institution)*

*A 1908 vase by the Marblehead Pottery decorated with ships and waves in tones of gray and blue. It was designed by Arthur E. Baggs and Arthur I. Hennessey. (Keramic Studio, June 1908)*

*In 1908, Keramic Studio published an article about Marblehead Pottery. This vase, with peacock feather design in blue and green, was designed by A. E. Baggs. (Keramic Studio, June 1908)*

Lewis was a kilnman. John Swallow, an English thrower, worked there in 1916 and before, and his wife sometimes helped. John Selmer-Larsen was a designer and Benjamin Tutt was a workman at the factory.

## PRODUCT

At first, the pottery produced at Marblehead was made with shapes and decorations that avoided realistic natural designs and favored conventional geometric designs. There were no realistic flowers or scenes on the early pottery. Conventionalized marine forms such as seaweed, ships, sea horses, and fish were used. Later pieces, particularly plates and tiles, did include flowers in a more realistic style. Conventionalized birds, fruit, and animals were also used.

The body was a mixture of New Jersey and Massachusetts clay. Colors were chiefly metallic oxides with matte glaze and stippling. Many of the bowls were enameled on the inside with a different color on the exterior. The most famous glaze used was Marblehead blue, which was a deep gray-blue matte glaze. Black was often added to incised lines. Pieces were also made of gray, yellow, green, brown, rose, or lavender (wisteria) colors. A few pieces with red glaze and experimental pieces of tin-enameled majolica and luster were also made. Special colors could be ordered from the pottery. Designs were worked in three or four colors. Sometimes the design was incised but most pieces were decorated with subtly colored decorations or solid colors.

The pottery offered a special new ware about 1912 that consisted of a tin-enameled faience with a cream-colored background. The new ware evidently was not a success, as it does not appear in any later records. Arthur Baggs mentions a body type he developed that looked like porcelain

although it was fired at a low heat. Using this material, he made bowls which were perforated and glazed as was the rice-pattern china of the Chinese.

The pottery made a variety of items, including tiles, pitchers, cider sets, lamps, jars, garden sculpture, ornaments, tableware, vases, bookends, and candlesticks. Marblehead pottery is marked with the stylized picture of a ship flanked with the letters *M* and *P*.

## Markham Pottery
### Ann Arbor, Michigan and National City, California

The Markham Pottery was founded by Herman C. Markham of Ann Arbor, Michigan. His son Kenneth worked with him. Herman was a wood engraver and watercolorist. He worked in the Department of Archaeology of the University of Michigan. About 1885 he started experimenting with pottery at his home, and by 1905 was making commercial pots using local clay.

Most of the Markham pottery was made by hand and very little machinery was used. The pottery's glazes were very unusual. At first Markham tried to develop vases that would keep water cool. These pieces were called "utile," a name he later discontinued. He made the original models on a wheel, then copied them in a mold. He then treated the pieces to create unique surface decorations that gave an aged appearance. One style called "reseau" and another called "arabesque" were described as follows:

> There are two general styles of surface, reseau and arabesque. On both the matte glaze is used. In the reseau the texture is fine, the traceries more delicate and slightly raised so that they seem nutbrown and russet; while the traceries, wandering at will and yet with a seeming purpose, are of ochre. Here and there is an elusive tone of green, mysteriously appearing and disappearing.
>
> "Wind-swept-by-the-Sea," we say, as we look at the largest vase. . . . It is as if the wind, catching up a swirl of green sea water

*First mark: UP cipher, incised.*

*Incised.*

had cast it down upon this stately piece, over mottlings of vari-colored sands and seaweeds.

The arabesque pattern . . . has a background of rough, unfinished texture, while the surface of the relief is smooth. The original color of the vase appears to have been yellow-brown with tones of wine, but back of the raised pattern is an under surface of rich green. It is as if the vase were formed of strata of different colors, and the eating away of the upper surface had revealed the green beneath. [One] vase . . . has a background of metallic black, the pattern being in tones of deep orange, red and brown. [Another] is in green and neutral brown, while [a third] resembles nothing so much as deeply marked tree bark. ["Our American Potteries," in *Sketch Book,* October 1905.]

Specimens from the Markham kilns at Ann Arbor, Michigan, were of bowls and vases covered with curious forest and autumn leaf effects. The colours were soft, yet brilliant, and artistically mingled. There were copper bronzes, greens, browns and olive greens, combined with reds, yellows and oranges. The suggestions of patterns through the colour are most tantalizing, and one might trace the veins of leaves and forest vistas. ["Fifteenth Annual Exhibition of the New York Society of Keramic Arts" in *International Studio,* June 1907.]

The Markham Pottery moved to National City, California, in 1913, and continued making the same type of art pottery until 1921. Herman Markham died in 1922.

Pieces were marked with the name Markham and were often numbered. It is thought that pieces numbered below 6000 are from the Ann Arbor pottery and that those above 6000 were made in California.

## Matt Morgan Pottery
### Cincinnati, Ohio
~

*Impressed.*

*Impressed.*

Matt Morgan was a cartoonist in London, England. He came to Cincinnati, Ohio, in the 1870s, and by 1887 headed the lithography department of Strobridge and Company. He continued doing work for Strobridge even after he opened an art pottery in 1883.

The art pottery was founded after Morgan met and became friendly with George Ligowsky, the inventor of the clay pigeon. How or why the two decided to open a pottery is unknown, but the artist and the maker of sportsman's targets joined forces. Ligowsky made the clay and Morgan decorated the pieces to resemble Moorish ware. Their pieces were covered with incised designs, and colors were applied to the raised portions. Shiny and matte glaze finishes were used. Some wares resemble Rookwood, probably because some of the artists worked at both the Rookwood and Matt Morgan potteries.

Several decorators worked for the firm and put their initials on the bottom of the pieces they made. The firm's principal designer,

## N.J.H.

*Initials of decorator,*
*N. J. Hirschfeld.*

*Unknown artist.*

*The paper label used by Matt Morgan and found on one of the blue vases shown at bottom left on this page.*

*Incised.*

aside from Matt Morgan himself, was Herman Carl Mueller (apparently no relation to Karl Mueller of Union Porcelain Works). Herman Mueller trained in Nuremberg and Munich, Germany, and in 1875 arrived in Cincinnati. He worked for the Kensington Art Tile Company of Newport, Kentucky, and for Matt Morgan. Later he worked for the American Encaustic Tiling Company and the Mosaic Tile Company in Zanesville, Ohio. He founded his own company, the Mueller Tile Co., in 1908 in Trenton, New Jersey.

Matthew Andrew Daly worked for Matt Morgan, but he soon left to join the Rookwood Pottery. N. J. Hirschfeld, another decorator, also left Morgan to go to Rookwood.

Matt Morgan Pottery was in business for only a year; it closed because of financial problems. Matt Morgan died in Casino, New York, in 1890. He had married twice and had sixteen children.

The firm used several impressed marks and paper labels.

*Each of these Matt Morgan vases with dark blue glaze and gold trim is 4⅜ inches high and 2⅝ inches wide. The vases are of slightly different colors. Each is marked with the "Matt Morgan" impressed mark and the number "323." One has a paper label from the factory. (Private collection)*

*This Matt Morgan vase is brown and turquoise. (Sotheby's)*

*Matt Morgan plaque, 14 inches in diameter, marked with a paper label. It has a green iridescent glaze.*

# J. W. McCoy Pottery Co.

## *Roseville and Zanesville, Ohio*

~

LOY-NEL-ART
McCOY

*Impressed.*

The J. W. McCoy Pottery was founded in 1899 by James McCoy. More than one hundred workers were busy at the Roseville, Ohio, factory making commercial wares and a line of art pottery that included such items as mugs, jardinieres, pedestals, and tankards. The factory was destroyed by fire in 1903 but was soon rebuilt, and in January 1905 the firm was incorporated and had new working capital.

George S. Brush became manager of the firm in 1909. Brush had worked for the Owens Pottery from 1901 to 1905 but left to organize the Brush Pottery Company in 1907. He made stoneware and art pottery until a fire in 1908 destroyed the pottery. Although the Brush Pottery continued as a corporation until 1912, Brush began working for McCoy in 1909. In August 1911, Brush purchased a former Owens Pottery plant in Zanesville, and in November of that year sold his plant, molds, and equipment to McCoy. The next month, the McCoy Pottery became the Brush-McCoy Pottery Company. The firm kept several of the old Owens molds and made those pieces too. The Zanesville offices and plant were at Brush-McCoy Plant No. 1, and the Roseville plant was called Plant No. 2.

In 1912 Brush-McCoy bought the A. Radford Pottery of Clarksburg, West Virginia, and continued several Radford lines. The Zanesville plant burned to the ground in 1918.

The pottery changed its name to the Brush Pottery Company in 1925 (not the same firm as the Brush Pottery that worked in Roseville from 1907 to 1912). After George Brush died in 1934, the firm continued, making florist pottery, cookie jars, red flowerpots, and novelties. In 1978 Brush Pottery was sold to C.S.C. Inc., and then to Virgil Cole and John O. Everhart in 1979. The name became Brush Line Inc., and its products included garden items and lamp bases. In January 1982 the plant closed, then reopened with non-union labor, and then closed again near the end of the year.

### BRUSH-McCOY AND BRUSH LINES 1902–1957
*(Dates are of the first mention in the catalog or from other sources.)*

*Aegean Inlaid:* green vase with white Greek key design, 1915.

*Amaryllis:* molded amaryllis flowers form panels on vase, glazed in colors of Kolorkraft, Majolica, etc., 1926.

*Art Vellum:* mottled ware, blue, beige, green, rose, 1923.

*Athenian:* bronze-colored glaze, many shapes from other lines, 1928.

*Basket:* basketweave border with top border of grapevines, 1915.

*Beautirose:* raised decorative border of roses, center design of roses, green, pink, 1915.

*Bittersweet:* ivory decorated with bittersweet vines, natural colors, 1945.

*Blended Glaze:* green, brown, yellow, orange, pink, and other colors blended together on a variety of shapes used in other lines, 1910.

*Blue Bird:* ivory with flying blue birds, rose trim, 1915.

*Bon-ton:* ivory matte glaze, blue, brown, or green tint, some have tulips, others grape clusters, 1916.

*Bristol:* white and blue kitchen ware, sponged band, 1910.

*Bruco:* white, green, and red flowers, semiporcelain, toilet set, 1918.

*Cameo:* garlands and cameo medallion, twisted fluting at base and rim, yellow, green, brown, 1933.

*Chromart:* scene of trees, mountains, and road, blended blue, tan, browns, 1920.

*Cleo:* geometric or floral designs in bright colors on ivory background, 1914.

*Colonial Mat:* paneled shapes with green, blue, or beige matte glaze, 1925.

*Colorcraft:* brown and blue decoration on white Bristol ware, 1922.

*Columbian:* blue-banded yellow bowls, 1915–1918.

*Corn:* realistic corn design, green, yellow, before 1910 (later made by Shawnee Pottery).

*Dandy-line:* standard yellow cooking ware, 1915–1918.

*Decorated Autumn Oak Leaf:* overall raised decoration of oak leaves, acorns, and a squirrel, cream, brown, orange, 1915.

*Dresden:* cream, raised background pattern of vertical pointed panels and border, pink and green roses, 1915.

*Egyptian:* brown glaze with green antique finish, 1923.

*Empress:* high-gloss blue, green, rose, yellow, lavender, brown, yellow-green, urn-shaped modeled vases, 1933.

*Fawn:* blue, green, maroon, brown vellum glaze, 1933.

*Flora:* pink, maroon, green, yellow, brown-yellow background, stylized flowers, 1915.

*Floradora:* modeled flowers and leaves on loglike pieces, natural colors, 1928.

*Florastone:* high-fired gray stoneware body, high-gloss glaze of blue, rose, green, stylized flowers, dots, 1924.

*This 4½-inch vase is glazed dark brown with yellow flowers. It is marked with the incised words "Loy-Nel-Art McCoy." (Private collection)*

*Glo-art:* swirled shapes, ruffled rims, 1939.

*Grape:* white lattice background, blue grapes, green leaves, brown trim, utility wares, 1912.

*Grecian:* Nuglaze shape, green or brown stonecraft finish, 1916.

*Green-on-ivory:* sponged mixing bowls, utility wares, raised pineapple designs, 1904.

*Green Rust:* jardinieres, greens shaded to browns, 1930.

*Green Woodland (High-gloss):* same pattern as Woodland, but solid-colored high-gloss glaze, jardinieres, 1913.

*Ivotint:* ivory glaze with green or brown accents on molded shapes from many lines, sometimes other colors were added, 1929.

*Jetwood:* black tree designs on shaded background, 1923.

*Jewel:* high-gloss jewel design, border of triangles and dots, raised decoration, matte body, 1923.

*King Tut:* Egyptian figures on band of beige, green-colored stoneware body, c. 1923.

*Kolorkraft:* kitchen wares, vases, various colors, high gloss, 1928.

*Krakle-Kraft:* blue crackle glaze on plain forms, 1924.

*Lotus:* pointed vertical panels, ivory on green or gray, black trim, 1918.

*Loy-Nel-Art line:* standard brown glaze similar to Weller Louwelsa or matte green, hand-decorated with embossed and incised decoration, c. 1906 (designed by J. W. McCoy, named for McCoy's sons, Lloyd, Nelson, and Arthur).

*Lucile:* toilet wares, white body, pink roses on ribbon bow design, 1908.

*Majolica:* high glaze on amaryllis shapes, variegated glaze of browns and blues resembling majolica pottery, 1926.

*Marble:* Greek columns, Greek key design, ivory marbleized glaze, 1910.

*Mat-Glaze:* green, brown, cream glaze on modeled shapes, 1920.

*Mat Green line:* dull green glazed ware similar to Grueby glaze, vases, jardinieres, dishes, umbrella stands, cuspidors, 1908.

*Moderne Kolorkraft:* high-gloss solid or mottled rose, blue, orchid, green, or ivory glaze on modern shapes, 1928.

*Monochrome:* raised design of doves and clouds, stylized flowers, gray and white, 1918.

*Moss Green:* line similar to Silken Mat Green, darker green glaze, 1916.

*Mount Pelee:* dull black lava-type pottery with some iridescence, inspired by pottery found in ancient ruins, first made in 1902, much destroyed in 1903 fire.

*Navarre Faience:* matte green and white, made from Owens molds for Henri Deux line, 1912.

*Newmat:* green, dark blue, orange, or cream, 1921.

*Nuglaze:* jardinieres embossed with roses, masks, grapes, tricolor, 1923.

*Nurock:* brown kitchen ware, similar to English Rockingham, 1915–1918.

*Nymph:* matte glaze, green, blue, rose, brown drip, plain shapes, 1933.

*Oakwood:* stenciled border with Greek-inspired design, vase decorated to look like wood with raised pottery resembling metal holder, 1914.

*Old Egypt:* Egyptian beetle decoration, 1915.

*Old Ivory:* creamy glaze on ivory body, brown glaze highlighting incised decoration, 1910.

*Olympia:* leaves, berries, flowers in relief, natural colors, 1900.

*Onyx:* green, brown, or blue, high glaze, simple shapes, 1912.

*Oriental:* shaded blue, tan, brown glaze, similar to Landsun by Peters & Reed, 1920.

*Oriental Pottery:* cream to red shading on creamware, black embossed garden scenes, 1912.

*Panelart:* shapes with alternating panels of design, stylized flowers, natural flower sprays, orange-yellow or dark green, 1924.

*Pastel:* green, blue, roses, fluted shapes, some with tulip design, kitchen ware, 1927.

*Peach Bloom Ivotint:* amaryllis shape, ivory with pink and green shading, 1933.

*Peacock:* embossed peacock on brown or blue and white pieces, 1916.

*Perfection:* brown cooking wares, 1920.

*Pompeian:* modeled, brown semimatte finish, inlaid with green, 1920.

*Poppy:* dark green background, pink poppies, matte glaze, 1914.

*Radford's Radura:* matte glaze, green, blended colors, 1912.

*Radford's Ruko:* similar to jasperware, 1912.

*Radford's Thera:* matte glaze with slip decoration, 1912.

*Radio Bug:* ceramic bug with a crystal radio enclosed, 1927.

*Red Onyx:* light and dark brown high-gloss glaze, drip decoration, jardinieres, 1910.

*Renaissance:* brown-glazed ware, after 1905.

*Rockraft:* modeled from rocks, moss green or natural color, 1933.

*Roman:* green or brown low-priced ware decorated with fluted effects, lion's heads, flower festoons, 1927.

*Roman Decorated:* green, red, and gold bands, panels of scenes of Roman chariots and lions, 1915.

*Rosewood:* similar to Olympia, 1900.

*Silken Mat Green:* Greek key design, matte green glaze, 1915.

*Stardust:* matte gray in high-gloss black with white streaks, 1957.

*Stonecraft:* gray-white body, fluted sides, decorated top, 1920.

*Sylvan:* relief trees, green, brown, ivory, similar to Weller Forest ware, 1915; later Sylvan pattern featured hollyhocks, tan, green, white, pink, c. 1930.

*Venetian (Venitian):* cream and gold or brown on beige bands of decoration, sometimes with center design of stylized flowers, 1912.

*Vestal:* garlands and cameos, relief decoration, matte green, rose, tan, 1933.

*Vista:* green and brown trees, beige or green grass, blue sky, white ducks, 1918.

*Vogue:* white column with green, black, or gold in recessed areas, 1916.

*Whitestone Bristol:* cooking and toilet wares, blue, green tint, raised decoration, 1912–1918.

*Woodland:* tree and fences embossed on center panel, beige, ivory with green trim, 1912.

*Zuniart:* high-gloss Zuni Indian–type decoration, red, blue, or beige, 1923.

See also Brush Pottery; Nelson McCoy Pottery.

# Nelson McCoy Pottery
### Roseville, Ohio

James McCoy of the J. W. McCoy Pottery backed his son Nelson in the formation of a pottery in Roseville, Ohio, in 1910. At first, the Nelson McCoy Sanitary and Stoneware Company made stoneware kitchen utensils, but by 1926 it began making artware. The company's name was changed to the Nelson McCoy Pottery in 1933.

When Nelson McCoy died in 1945, his nephew Nelson McCoy Melick, who had worked for the company since 1924, became president. Following Melick's death in 1954, Nelson McCoy, Jr., became president. At the same time, Nelson was also president of the Mount Clemens Pottery of Mount Clemens, Michigan, which purchased the Nelson McCoy Pottery in 1967.

The Roseville plant became the Nelson McCoy Division of D. T. Chase Enterprises of Hartford, Connecticut, in 1972, then

*Impressed, 1940s; same mark, embossed, used 1940s–1960s.*

*Impressed, 1940s.*

*Late 1940s–1966.*

*1972–1990.*

became part of the Lancaster Colony Corporation two years later. Nelson McCoy, Jr., left the company in 1981, and in 1986 the plant became a subsidiary of Designer Accents of Sebring, Ohio, and Montville, New Jersey. Nelson McCoy Pottery, which had been renamed Nelson McCoy Ceramics, then the McCoy Company, closed in December 1990 and was heavily damaged by a fire on June 23, 1991.

The Nelson McCoy Pottery did not make very much art pottery. Some early pieces resemble Weller, Roseville, or other popular pottery of the time.

## Merrimac Pottery
### Newburyport, Massachusetts

T. S. Nickerson founded the Merrimac Ceramic Company in Newburyport, Massachusetts, in 1897. The company made inexpensive drainpipes, florists' containers, and enameled tiles. Nickerson started making art pottery when the business reorganized in 1902 as the Merrimac Pottery Company.

Nickerson had studied colors and glazes in London, England, with Sir William Crookes, the English chemist and physicist. Later Nickerson worked alone in Massachusetts developing the glazes that characterize the best of the Merrimac work. At first Merrimac Pottery made small vases and ornamental pieces to be used in the home, but realizing the demand, Nickerson began to make quantities of decorative garden pottery.

In 1908 Nickerson sold the pottery and the existing inventory to Frank A. Bray. The pottery building burned later that year and most of the plant and stock was destroyed. There was a liquidation sale in November and the pottery was permanently closed.

### PRODUCT

The art pottery vases for home use made by Merrimac Pottery were glazed in tones of green, violet, dull grape, dull rose, brownish red, dull black, yellow, orange, or metallic glazes of blue or purple that slightly resembled polished iron. The colors were sometimes applied as a crackled glaze. The

*Paper label.*

*Impressed.*

(Above and below) *A selection of Merrimac pottery from* The Craftsman, *a magazine published in 1903.*

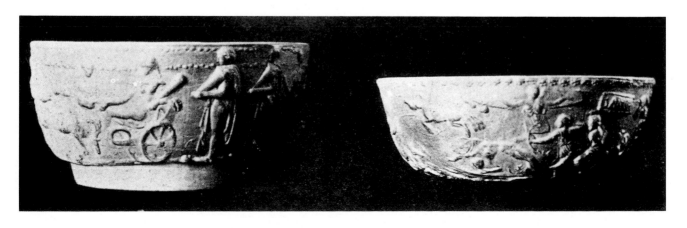

crackleware ranks as the best line made by Merrimac.

The garden pottery was made of white clay or a natural terra-cotta. One of Merrimac's most famous lines was their Etruscan pottery, reproductions of ancient Roman Arretine pieces displayed in the Boston Museum of Art. The pieces were made of terra-cotta with decorations in low relief.

### MARKS

A paper label appeared on all pieces of Merrimac Ceramic Co. work made from September 1900 to August 1901. After that, an impressed mark of a sturgeon was used.

The name Merrimac, which is the Indian word for sturgeon, derives from the river that flows through Newburyport.

## Middle Lane
*See Brouwer and Middle Lane*
~

## Moravian Pottery and Tile
*See Tile Companies*
~

## Mosaic Tile Co.
*See Tile Companies*
~

## Mueller Mosaic Tile Co.
*See Tile Companies*
~

## Nashville Art Pottery
*Nashville, Tennessee*
~

*Incised.*

Elizabeth (Bettie) J. Scovel (Scoville) founded the Nashville Art Pottery about 1884. She had visited Cincinnati to study the facilities and products of the Rookwood Pottery and other potteries, and returned to Nashville to open her own art studio and pottery. Drawing and painting, then modeling, and finally pottery were done at the studio. She hired a potter and fireman to do the heavy work, but made her own molds and modeled the forms. Early pieces were made of red earthenware, later pieces with white or native clays.

"Goldstone" and "Pomegranate" wares were first produced in 1888. Goldstone, made on a red body, had a rich, dark brown glaze with golden highlights. Pomegranate ware, named for its beautiful red color, was the result of an accident: All of the ware in an over-fired kiln had been destroyed, with the exception of a single piece at the bottom—a white clay body with a mottled pink and blue glaze and red veining. The pottery closed in 1889. Only a few marked pieces are known.

Black and gold leaves decorate this brown-glazed redware vase, 9½ inches high, attributed to the Nashville Art Pottery. (The Art Museum, Princeton University, New Jersey)

The Nashville Art Pottery made this 8-inch-high brown-glazed redware pitcher. (The Art Museum, Princeton University, New Jersey)

Green leaves edged in gold and curved gold lines decorate the surface of this repainted vase by Nashville Art Pottery. It has a yellow-glazed interior and is 5¾ inches high. (The Art Museum, Princeton University, New Jersey)

# Newcomb Pottery/New Orleans Art Pottery

### New Orleans, Louisiana

New Orleans was a center of culture and industry when Ellsworth Woodward arrived there from Massachusetts in 1885. Woodward believed in vocational education for women and felt that, with training, some young women would continue working as a career. Others, of course, would marry, but because of their training they would appreciate the fine arts and help create a market for many of the items made at arts and crafts schools.

The first school organized by Woodward offered classes in brasswork, stenciling, wood carving, and clay modeling. The thirty students who joined the clay modeling group soon formed the Ladies Decorative Art League (called the Art League for Women in some sources), meeting at 249 Baronne Street.

In 1886, with his brother William, Ellsworth organized the New Orleans Art Pottery Company. The firm had one hundred subscribers at $10 per share of stock. The thirty young women from the League joined the firm and took shares in exchange for their labor. The pottery company rented a building at 224 Baronne Street, built a kiln, outfitted the room with the $1,000 that was subscribed, and hired two potters to produce the clay bodies the women decorated.

*Stamped.*

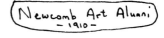

*Incised.*

*Impressed.*

**NEWCOMB COLLEGE**

*Incised.*

*a1 - a2 - etc.*

*Code marks.*

**Q**

*Buff clay body, before 1910.*

[W]

*White clay body, before 1910.*

**R**

*Clay mixture.*

**U**

*Clay mixture.*

(Above) *Lamp pictured in* The Craftsman *magazine, October 1903, in an article about the Newcomb Pottery. Notice the leaded glass shade.*

(Right) *Vases and bowls made by the New Orleans Art Pottery club.* (Ceramic Age, *April 1935*)

Joseph Fortune Meyer, the first of the potters, had extensive training before he came to work for the New Orleans Art Pottery Company. His father had been a potter, and Meyer and a partner had made and sold "peasant" pottery produced from local clays. They knew every process in making pottery: They located the clay, built the kilns, fired them with wood, made the glaze from private formulas, and then sold the pieces at the French Market.

Meyer had come to the United States from his native France when his father moved to Biloxi, Mississippi, before the Civil War. Joseph was nine when he made the three-month ocean trip, and the experience left him with a love of the sea and sailing that influenced some of his later works. He had no formal education, but he read incessantly and is credited with almost total recall. As a youngster, he had no religious beliefs, but he married a Catholic. The marriage produced no children, but he and his wife raised a servant girl's child as their own. Joseph Meyer was a shrewd businessman and was very careful about money. An active potter through much of the Newcomb period, Meyer died in 1931.

The other potter hired by the New Orleans Art Pottery Company was George Ohr, an eccentric but gifted potter who had already started his own pottery firm in Biloxi. He married a New Orleans woman in 1886.

The New Orleans Art Pottery Company, with the help of the two potters and thirty young women, made jardinieres, lawn pots, and a few other items that were sold in large cities such as Boston and Chicago. The firm closed after a year and was replaced by the Art League Pottery Club, a group with many of the same members, plus students from Tulane University and Sophie Newcomb College. The group, also known as the Baronne Street Pottery, dissolved in 1891 because of financial problems.

William Woodward became a professor of art at Tulane University in 1890. He had been in charge of drawing and design at Tulane's School of Architecture in 1883, and became a professor of

*Leona Nicholson made this vase for the Newcomb Pottery about 1900–1910. It is decorated with designs of stylized flowers in blue, green, yellow, and white. The 5½-inch glossy-glazed vase is marked with the impressed cipher "NC," the cipher "JM, LN," painted numbers "BZ-72," and an original paper sticker "BZ-72, $3.50." (Collection of the Newark Museum)*

*Stylized flowers of blue and green glossy glaze decorate this 6½-inch Newcomb Pottery vase. The artist is C. Payne, the potter Joseph Meyer. The vase is marked with the impressed cipher "NC," the cipher "JM," the incised mark "C. Payne," and the painted cipher "CP." (Private collection; photograph from The Art Museum, Princeton University, Princeton, New Jersey)*

*Green and blue glossy-glazed water lilies decorate this 9¼-inch-high vase made about 1904. It is marked with a Newcomb Pottery paper label, the impressed cipher "NC, ZZ71," and the artist's name, "S.E. Wells" (for Sabina Elliot Wells). (Photograph courtesy of Newcomb College, Tulane University, New Orleans, Louisiana)*

painting at Newcomb College's School of Art in 1890. Ellsworth Woodward supervised fine arts at Sophie Newcomb College, the women's college of Tulane University, from the college's founding in 1886. The two brothers each held two jobs for a year or so, since the college was just a few blocks from the New Orleans Art Pottery.

In 1895 the Woodward brothers, particularly Ellsworth, convinced the college to start a pottery class and to sell the product made by the students. The board of trustees of Sophie Newcomb College agreed to support the novel experiment of an art course in which the developed product could be sold. They approved funds and Ellsworth Woodward began teaching the class in October 1895. The money raised selling the class's product was used to furnish a room in an abandoned chemistry laboratory. Woodward installed a round kiln with four fireboxes, a kick wheel, drying shelves, tubs for clay, decorators' smocks, glaze pots, and a hand mill for grinding. Some of the saggers and perhaps other equipment came from earlier New Orleans potteries, such as the Hernandez pottery and the Saloy porcelain factory.

Mary G. Sheerer, who had studied at the Cincinnati Art Academy and the Art Students League in Cincinnati, was hired in 1894 to teach classes in pottery decoration. Like the Rookwood decorators she knew, Sheerer favored slip-painted decoration, but when slip painting was found too difficult to control in the warm, drafty New Orleans building, she switched to biscuit painting. After the biscuit method also failed, she started using a type of cut or carved design. Joseph Meyer threw the body shapes designed by Sheerer.

*Sadie Irvine decorated this blue vase with yellow jonquils on long stems. The 7¼-inch vase is marked with the impressed "CN" cipher, "JM JB70," "253," and the artist's mark. (Christie's)*

To date pieces of Newcomb Pottery, it helps to know not only the dating systems, but also the dates when some of the artists worked. The following is an alphabetical list of artists and potters who worked at the Newcomb Pottery. (The listing is incomplete, since no record of the artists was kept.) Immediately following the artist's name are the dates she was a student—undergraduate or graduate—at the college. Other dates of service to the pottery are explained, and a date in parentheses is the year an article was published mentioning the artist's name. If known, the mark is shown with the artist's name.

Aurelia Arbo. c. 1931. Art craftsman, 1931–1940.

Lucia Cecelia Arena. c. 1921–1922. Art craftsman, 1922–1928.

Leontine Esther Augustine (Godat). c. 1920.

Mrs. Avery. c. 1895–1897.

Vincent Axford. Ceramic engineer, 1922–1927.

Eunice Baccich. c. 1913–1919. Art craftsman, 1921–1929.

Henrietta Davidson Bailey. 1901–1905. Pottery design, 1905–1909; art craftsman, 1909–1926; teacher, 1926–1938. (1905)

Mary Frances Baker. 1905–1906. (1905)

Emma Claire Bancroft. 1918–1919.

G·BARTLETT

Gladys Bartlett. 1908–1911, 1918–1919.

Eunice Lea Bate (Coleman). 1917–1919.

Alice Toutant Beauregard. 1909–1912, 1914–1916. Art craftsman, 1916–1917.

Mrs. C. F. Belden. 1885–1887, 1890–1891.

Marie (Maria) Levering Benson. 1904–1906. Pottery worker, 1906–1908.

Alix Bettison. 1908–1911.

G.B.

Grace Blethen (Dunn). 1900–1908. Art craftsman, 1908–1909.

Frances Ware Blocker. 1896–1902.

Selina E. Bres. See Selina E. Bres Gregory.

M.W.B.

Mary W. Butler. 1899–1904. Pottery design, 1903–1908; teacher, 1907–1934. (1904)

CMC
CMC

Corinne Chalaron. c. 1920. Art craftsman, 1922–1926.

Frances Lawrence Howe Cocke. c. 1889–1894. Pottery design, 1906–1907. (1904)

Browning Colemann. 1901–1903.

COX

Paul Ernest Cox. Director, 1910–1918.

Ruth Forbes Cramer. Art craftsman, 1921–1924.

Sophie Quinette Cramer. Art craftsman, 1922–1925.

Ethel Canney Crumb. c. 1913–1917.

Elizabeth (Betty) Davis. c. 1924. Art craftsman, 1924–1926.

M.D.

Marie Odelle Delavigne. c. 1892–1899. Pottery design, 1901–1904; art craftsman, 1908–1925.

Olive W. Dodd. c. 1898–1903. Pottery design, 1903–1919. (1904)

*Georgia Bertha Drennan.*
*1902–1907.*

# A.C.D.

*Adele Ida Duggan. 1904–1906,*
*1912–1913.*

*May Louise Dunn. 1906–1910.*

*Esther Huger Elliott. 1890–1891,*
*1896–1905. (1904)*

*Bessie A. Ficklin. 1889–1891,*
*1896–1899, 1902–1904.*

*Evangeline Magruder Folse. c. 1919.*
*Art craftsman, 1922–1924.*

# F
# FF

*Francis A. Ford. Pottery, ceramic*
*technician, c. 1930–1948.*

# G

*Jules Gabry. Potter, 1895.*

*Ethel Ruby Gastrell. 1925–1926.*

*Jane Gibbs. c. 1905.*

*Adele Godchaux. c. 1926.*

*Juanita Louise Gonzalez.*
*1921–1925. Teacher, 1931–1934.*

# HSG

*Hannah Seymour Graham.*
*c. 1910–1914.*

---

# Rai R

*Rosa Rainold Gra(i)ner. c. 1926.*
*Art craftsman, 1917–1929.*

*Matilda Geddings Gray. c. 1908.*

*Angela Gregory. Teacher, c. 1925.*

# SEBG S.E.B. S.E.B.G.

*Selina E. Bres Gregory. c.*
*1896–1901. Art craftsman,*
*1908–1909. (1904)*

# L.A.G.

*Lillian (Lily) Ann Guedry.*
*1899–1905.*

*Mrs. C. C. Hawthorne. 1889–1893,*
*1896–1898.*

*Cecile Mathilde Heller. c. 1911.*

*Sarah Henderson. 1890–1891,*
*1900–1902.*

*Julia Michel Hoerner. 1913–1916.*

*Edith Hohn. c. 1921–1925.*

*Sally Shephard Holt. 1902–1905,*
*1907–1909. Art craftsman,*
*1910–1929.*

*Emily Hamilton Huger.*
*1897–1902. (1904)*

---

*Helen Elizabeth Hughes. c. 1925. Art*
*craftsman, c. 1928–1929.*

*Jonathan Browne Hunt. Potter,*
*1928–1933.*

*Sarah Agnes Estelle (Sadie) Irvine.*
*1902–1906. Art craftsman,*
*1908–1929; decorator and teacher,*
*1929–1952.*

*Lois Janvier. c. 1910.*

*Florence M. Jardet. c. 1905–1908.*

*Frances Devereaux Jones.*
*1889–1894. Teacher, 1895–1901.*

# H.J.
# H.C.Joor

*Harriet (Hattie) Coulter Joor.*
*1896–1901. Pottery design,*
*1901–1906. (1904)*

*Lucia Jordan. 1904–1907.*

*Mable Paul Jordan. c. 1905, 1932.*
*Art craftsman, 1914–1915.*

# I.B.K.

*Irene Keep. 1889–1902. Pottery*
*worker, 1903–1904.*

*Roberta Beverly Kennon.*
*1896–1901. Pottery design,*
*1901–1905.*

*Nina Ansley King. Art craftsman,*
*1917–1920.*

K K

Katherine Kopman. 1894–1898.
Teacher, 1898–1905, 1907–1913.

M

Marguerite (Margot) Labarre.
1905–1906. Pottery worker,
1905–1906.

Catherine Priestly Labouisse.
1910–1913. Art craftsman, c.
1915–1917, 1922–1923.

J Le B

Jeanne Louise LeBeuf. c. 1925,
c. 1941.

Louise LeBeuf. 1901–1906.

E.M.H.L.

$\frac{E | M}{H | L}$

E He B

EML

Emilie de Hoa LeBlanc. c.
1897–1901. Pottery worker,
1901–1905.

M Le B

M He B

M.H.L.

Marie de Hoa LeBlanc. c.
1897–1902. Pottery worker,
1901–1908; art craftsman,
1908–1914.

Daisy Leonard. 1895–1897.

Sarah Bloom Levy. 1896–1900.
Pottery design, 1901–1908; art
craftsman, 1908–1909.

---

 G/F E

Emily Frances Lines (Gensler).
c. 1897–1898, 1901–1903,
1919–1920. Art craftsman,
1920–1922. (1904)

c L CE

Cynthia Pugh Littlejohn. c.
1905–1908. Art craftsman,
1909–1910, 1914–1920.

Roberta Lonegan (?).

Lenw

A Ln

Lonnegon

Lonnegan

LONNEGAN

Ada Wilt Lonnegan. 1896–1901. Art
craftsman, 1909–1910, 1914–1920.

C.L.

Corinna Morgiana Luria. c.
1910–1915. Art craftsman,
1915–1916. May have been
watercolorist only.

Floy Maddox. c. 1927–1929.

Ruth Maddox. c. 1930.

Gertrude Maes. c. 1904–1905,
1922–1924. Art craftsman,
1925–1929.

AM

Alma Florence Mason (Burke). c.
1904–1909. Art craftsman,
1910–1921.

Gerald Mauberret. c. 1904. Pottery
design, 1905–1906.

---

Juanita Marie Mauras.
c. 1905–1908. Art craftsman,
1908–1929; assistant in pottery,
1925–1937.

Marie Marcia Mayfield. c. 1926.

Anna Laura McDonald. c. 1924.

Ida Florence McDonald.
c. 1908–1911.

J M  M  M
J M

Joseph Fortune Meyer. Potter,
c. 1893–1928.

Julia Michel. See Julia Michel
Hoerner.

James Miller. Potter, c. 1903–1905.

Robert Miller. Potter, c. 1900–1910.

C. Sliger Millspaugh (?).

Hilda Modinger. c. 1917–1922.

M M  MM

May Sydney (Sydnor) Morel.
c. 1910–1917.

LN

Leona Fischer Nicholson.
1896–1897, 1899–1903. Pottery
design, 1903–1908; art craftsman,
intermittently 1908–1929.

Helen Hughes Ogden. Art craftsman,
1928–1929.

George Ohr. Potter, c. 1893–1898.

Ellen Theresa Hughes Garic Oliver.
c. 1910–1916. Art craftsman,
1916–1917.

MP

Mary Harrison Palfrey. c.
1909–1912. Art craftsman,
1912–1913, 1915–1916.

C. Payne

*Charlotte Payne. c. 1895,
1902–1905.*

**BR**

*Beverly Randolph.
1900–1902. (1904)*

*Gladys Randolph. c. 1906.*

*Mary Reinfort. c. 1891–1894.
Pottery design, 1901–1902.*

DAR

*Dagmar Adelaide Renshaw.
c. 1908–1912.*

*Mary Walcot Richardson.
1897–1902.*

*Maude Robinson. c. 1905–1907. Art
craftsman, 1909–1910.*

*Elizabeth Goelet Rogers.
1895–1901. (1904)*

*Harry Rogers. Potter, 1926–1929.*

*Amelie Roman. 1895–1901. Teacher,
1900–1939. (1904, 1905)*

D.R.

*Desiree Roman. c. 1889–1891.
Pottery design, 1901–1905; clerk of
pottery and sales agent,
1903–1939. (1904)*

MR

*Mary Lillian Rosenblatt.
c. 1924–1928.*

 MRoss

*Marie Medora Ross. c. 1889–1893.
Pottery design, 1896–1906.*

*Mazie Teresa Ryan. c. 1896–1901.
Pottery design, 1901–1906; art
craftsman, 1910–1914. b. 1880,
d. 1946.*

*Alice Raymond Scudder. c.
1899–1903, 1905–1911,
1914–1915.*

*Mary Given Sheerer. Teacher,
1894–1931.*

*Margaret Shelby. 1904–1907.*

ⒺⓈ

*Erin E. (Effie) Shepard.
1900–1909. Art craftsman,
1910–1913. d. 1917.*

FS    AES

AES    AES

AES    A FS

*Anna Frances Connor Simpson.
1902–1908. Art craftsman,
1908–1929. b. 1880, d. 1930.*

C
B
S

*Carrie Bell Sliger (Millspaugh).
c. 1891–1900.*

GRS Ⓢ

*Gertrude Roberts Smith. Teacher,
1889–1934.*

KS  KS

*Kenneth Eugene Smith. Manager,
1931–1945; teacher, ceramic
engineer, potter, 1929–1945.*

*Lillian Jeanne Smith. 1911–1914.*

MWS

*Mary Williamson Summey (Smith).
c. 1906–1909. Art craftsman,
1909–1913, 1918–1920.*

*Alice Rosalie Urquhart. c.
1886–1887, 1890–1893,
1896–1897. Pottery design,
1903–1908; art craftsman,
1908–1917.*

*Emma J. Urquhart. 1901 1909. Art
craftsman, 1912–1914.*

*Elizabeth M. Villere. 1895–1896,
1902–1904.*

*Katherine (Kate) Walker.
1887–1892.*

*Fred E. Walrath. Potter,
c. 1918–1921.*

*Ethel Gastrel Warren. c. 1923. Art
craftsman, 1924–1925.*

*George Wasmuth. Potter,
c. 1895–1896.*

LWATKINS

*Lynne Watkins. c. 1905–1908.*

HWEIL

*Hermoine Weil. c. 1917.*

*Sabina Elliot Wells. c. 1902–1903. Pottery design, 1903–1904. (1905)*

*Jane Randolph Whipple. c. 1931.*

*Katherine (Katie) Louise Wood. 1885–1886, 1891–1898, 1902–1903.*

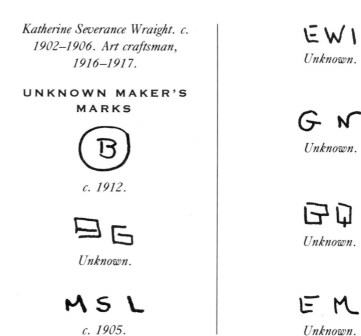

*Katherine Severance Wraight. c. 1902–1906. Art craftsman, 1916–1917.*

## UNKNOWN MAKER'S MARKS

*c. 1912.*

*Unknown.*

*c. 1905.*

*Unknown.*

*Unknown.*

*Unknown.*

*Unknown.*

*This lidded jar is 4¾ inches high and is glazed green with a pinecone motif. The piece is marked with the "NC" mark, "EHE, JM, Q, KK3." It is the work of Esther Huger Elliott, and was made before 1910. The jar was stolen from the Art Department of Newcomb College on December 24, 1976. (Photograph courtesy of Newcomb College, Tulane University, New Orleans, Louisiana)*

In Sheerer's accounts of the school, she mentions that M. Gabry, a Frenchman who had worked at the Hernandez porcelain factory in New Orleans and at the Golfe-Juan Pottery in Cannes, France, was hired to make the forms on the wheel and to supervise the glazing and firing. Gabry committed suicide in December 1895, and another potter, George Wasmuth, was hired for a few months. In 1896 Joseph Fortune Meyer, who had earlier worked for Woodward and the New Orleans Pottery Company, was hired. He remained at the school as chief potter until 1925, throwing almost every piece that was decorated at the factory. George Ohr also worked at Newcomb in 1896 or 1897, but he was fired by 1898 because he was "not fit" to instruct young ladies. Robert Miller, another potter, worked at the school from 1909 to 1910.

In 1910 a new technician, Paul E. Cox, was brought in to assure a more uniform product. In 1904 he had been the second graduate of the New York State College of Clay-working and Ceramics. Cox was concerned with the technical problems of glaze, clay body, and control of the product in a way his predecessors could not be. Early potters worked by trial and error, and rarely had written records to guide them. Glaze and clay formulas were carefully guarded family secrets.

Cox improved the quality of the Mississippi clay used at Newcomb by adding feldspar and flint. He developed a raw lead glaze with a semimatte texture as underglaze. He found that three firings were needed to get the best effect from this new glaze. The first coat was dipped, the next two sprayed. His blue and green matte glazes were so popular that the shiny glazes used earlier were rarely seen on pieces after 1910. Later he discovered a clay in New Orleans that could be used at the pottery. During his years at the school, Cox

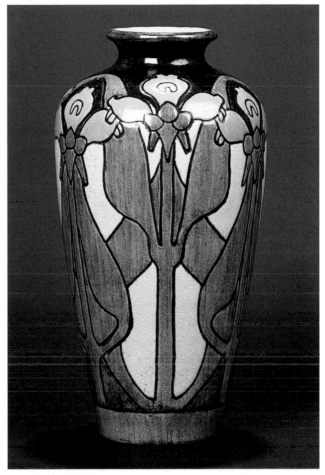

A vase decorated by Anna Frances Simpson has Spanish moss–covered trees and a moon, the most popular design at the Newcomb pottery. It is marked "NC," "AFS," "150," "QC," and "35." The vase is 10¾ inches high. (David Rago Arts & Crafts Gallery)

This high-glaze vase with iris blossoms and green leaves is marked "S.E.W." (Sabina Elliot Wells), "NC," and "FF9." The vase is 10¼ inches high. (David Rago Arts & Crafts Gallery)

An early Newcomb high-glaze pitcher decorated with paper-white narcissus and green leaves. Marked "AR" (Amelie Roman), "NC," and "JM," it is 6¾ by 4½ inches. (David Rago Arts & Crafts Gallery)

This Newcomb bowl is of light blue matte glaze with a band of raised lilies of the valley. It is 6 inches in diameter and 4½ inches high. The vase is marked with the impressed cipher "NC," the artist cipher "AFS" (for Anna Frances Simpson), and "CM, 288." (Private collection)

Fish swim around the border of this 9¼-inch plate by Marie de Hoa Le-Blanc, 1906. (Neal Auction Company)

(Left) Newcomb Pottery vase, 11¾ inches high, signed "Mazie T Ryan," dating from about 1897–1910. (Right) An 8¼-inch-high vase with matte glaze, signed "Henrietta Bailey," about 1910. (Smithsonian Institution)

built a modern kiln that mechanized production so that all of the decorators were able to make a better wage. Cox remained with the school until 1918, then in 1920 became director of ceramic engineering at Iowa State College. He returned to New Orleans in 1939 to open his own pottery, but the business was not successful and closed within a short time.

By 1929, Kenneth E. Smith was manager of the Newcomb Pottery and Professor Lota Lee Troy was in charge of all the activities at the Newcomb School of Art, where young women continued to decorate the pottery. Under their direction, the pottery earned about $20,000 per year through the 1930s. In 1931, Ellsworth Woodward and Mary Sheerer returned to the pottery for a short time. Robert Feild and John Canady headed the art school after Troy. Sadie Irvine, one of Newcomb's foremost decorators since 1908, retired in 1952, and Kathrine Choi became head of the pottery department.

Styles of Newcomb pottery varied with changes in potters or chief designers. It is possible to classify the pottery pieces in five main chronological divisions.

### FIRST PERIOD (TO 1899)

From the start of the factory until about 1910, the main influences on the design and quality of the work were those of Mary Sheerer and Joseph Meyer. The basic rules had been set by the trustees of the university and the faculty of the Sophie Newcomb Art Department. All of the finished products had to be approved by Miss Sheerer to maintain quality. The designs used by the young women reflected the natural environment of the New Orleans area. Plants were popular as design motifs, although the very early pieces sometimes had geometric patterns. Typical subjects were tall pines, palm trees, jasmine, wild rose, syringa, fleur-de-lis, orange, plum, magnolia, lotus leaves and flowers, water lily, moss-draped cypress, snowdrop, spiderwort, iris, alyssum, marsh maple, and the popular live oak and moon design. Floral designs were always kept simple. The whole plant was shown, not just a flower or a detail.

The clay was taken from Bayou Tchulakabaufa in Mississippi and St. Tammany Parish (county), Louisiana. Both a white clay and a buff clay body were used before 1910. Sheerer also mentions a red clay that was used for the undecorated terra-cotta pieces.

Every piece had to be original and never duplicated. It had to be marked with the initials of the college, the designer, and the potter. Each woman was given half of the sale price of her pieces. If a decorator showed promise, she was given two years of free study plus a free studio after graduation. Many of the decorators needed the money they obtained through the sale of the pottery, so they continued to work after leaving school.

Color selection was the choice of the decorator, but the blue-green tones seem to have become a Newcomb Pottery characteristic, and the women preferred those shades. The shapes of the pieces were determined by Sheerer and later by Sadie Irvine. The women selected the pottery shapes from a book, the potter threw them on a wheel, and the clay vases were stored in a damp room until they were needed for decorating.

From about 1895 to 1900 the designs were slip-painted on the bisque, with a transparent glaze over the decorations. The designs were usually green, blue, or yellow with the cream color of the body showing. Some buff clay pieces were decorated with white slip.

## SECOND PERIOD (1900–1910)

Because slip-painting proved unreliable, the women used incised carving on the unfired clay. The damp clay vase was smoothed and stored until a decorator scratched a design on the surface. The scratches were then worked into deeper cuts. After the incised decoration was finished, the piece was sponged to remove any marks. The sponging also brought fine silica to the surface of the clay and added to the misty effect that is prized in this period of Newcomb pottery. The piece was then tinted with underglaze colors that were heavier in the deeper cuts. Black underglaze was occasionally used in the incised lines. The entire piece was then dipped into transparent glossy glaze. All these pieces have colored outsides and cream-colored interiors. Some early pieces, however, were glazed with

*Two different designs on candlesticks by Anna Frances Simpson, made in 1917. One pictures lilies of the valley, the other rice plants. (Neal Auction Company)*

*Newcomb made special dinnerware services. This 7-inch-high chocolate pot belongs to one of the sets. Erin E. Shepard decorated it with incised flowers in 1906. (Neal Auction Company)*

*This jardiniere, 7 inches high, was decorated in 1912 by Anna Frances Simpson. She pictured palmetto palm trees. (Neal Auction Company)*

*A rare high-glaze Newcomb pot, 5 inches high, by Desiree Roman. Its underglaze painting depicts cypress trees. (Neal Auction Company)*

*This yellow, blue, green, and ivory jar decorated with lemons and foliage is 6 inches high. (Wolf's)*

*This 8-inch jardiniere was decorated with a band of trees by Leona Nichol-son in 1907. (Neal Auction Company)*

*A Newcomb tile showing Joseph Meyer at the potter's wheel. The undated tile was decorated by Leona Nicholson. (Neal Auction Company)*

*Anna Frances Simpson created this covered jar, about 1910–1915, decorated with live oaks. (Neal Auction Company)*

colors that were the result of accidental blendings in the kiln.

Although the pottery was described as artistic and well made by many of the magazines of the day, at least one (*Scribner's*, March 1903) seemed to disagree:

> The characteristic look of the larger pieces is peculiar and not pleasing to all persons as the surface is streaked and spotted with pale gray in a way that suggests inadequate technical treatment, the patterns being very dark blue or in the light gray relieved on the dark blue, the darker color itself being applied in the same streaky way.

Most of the wares from the second period had the characteristic blue-green color with incised decoration, often emphasized with black. A few experimental luster pieces were made during this period.

### THIRD PERIOD (1910–1930)

A new design technique, used from 1910 to about 1930, was developed under the guidance of Paul Cox. The low molded relief designs were carved into the pottery while it was damp, and a matte glaze intended to resemble that used at the Rookwood Pottery was added. Color was the result of applied underglaze on the bisque ware and a dip in a semitransparent matte glaze, so the finished glaze had underglaze decoration and the soft misty effect remained. The inside was glazed without color.

### FOURTH AND FIFTH PERIODS (1930–1945)

Design elements and glaze techniques overlapped from period to period because making pottery was an ongoing business. When a particularly popular design was developed, it remained in the line for a while. The favorite Newcomb pottery design, from about 1920 to 1930, was probably the pale blue and green tree dripping with Spanish moss reflected in the moonlight. The motif was supposedly first used by Sadie Irvine in one of the early periods, and the design remained popular.

The Newcomb Pottery made many types of vases, mugs, and other salable items, such as tea sets, candlesticks, and lamps. Leaded glass, bead, and metal shades were also made at the art school. See the bibliography for a very comprehensive paper by Paul Cox on the technical aspects of making glaze, firing, etc.

### MARKS

One of the rules of Newcomb Pottery required that every piece be marked. This practice was continued at least through the 1920s. The artist's initials, "NC" for the pottery, code numbers for the type of clay body and glaze formula, and the inventory number were incised by hand in the bottom of each piece. The cut-in lines were sometimes filled with color to make them more legible.

Before 1910, the clay bodies were marked "Q" for buff clay and "W" for white clay body. A scratch through the pottery mark means the piece is a second. If the mark is obliterated, it means the piece is unendorsed by the pottery. The pottery symbol, an *N* within a *C*, was used on almost all pieces. A few pieces are known by the incised words "NEWCOMB COLLEGE." Some pieces were also marked with a paper label that said: "Newcomb

Pottery, New Orleans, Designs are not duplicated." The matte-finished pieces made after 1910 had impressed, unglazed marks made by dies.

Newcomb Pottery was considered an artistic success in its day. Proof of this is the numerous awards that were given to the pottery at exhibitions and fairs: 1900, Paris; 1901, Buffalo Pan American Exposition; 1902, Charleston West Indian Exposition; 1904, St. Louis Fair; 1905, Portland, Oregon, Lewis and Clark Centennial Exposition; 1907, Jamestown Tercentenary Exposition; 1913, Knoxville, Tennessee; and 1915, San Francisco, California, Panama Pacific International Exposition.

A tyg, or three-handled mug, dating from 1908. (Neal Auction Company)

## Niloak Pottery
### Benton, Arkansas

Niloak (pronounced Nigh-loak) pottery was made in Benton, Arkansas, from 1910 to 1947. Niloak's special marbleized art pottery line is of great interest to collectors, but the factory also made other hand-thrown, cast, and molded wares.

J. H. Hyten had a pottery in Boonsboro, Iowa, during the mid-1800s, but moved to Arkansas for his health. In Benton, Arkansas, Hyten worked at a stoneware pottery, which he bought about 1885 and renamed the Eagle Pottery. The hills in the area provided good potting clay of many colors and a natural gas supply to heat the kiln. Hyten died shortly after his purchase of the pottery, but his widow married a potter who ran the factory until 1895, when the couple moved to Ohio.

Hyten's son, Charles D. "Bullet" Hyten, who worked in the stoneware pottery and was eighteen at the time of his father's death, decided to stay in Arkansas and run the pottery. His two brothers joined him, and the firm became known as Hyten Bros. Pottery.

In 1909, Arthur Dovey, who had already introduced a swirl ware at Ouachita Pottery, joined Charles Hyten's pottery. In early 1910, the firm began making a swirl ware using colored clays. A mixture of several colors of clay was put on the potter's wheel and a multicolored spiral design of the natural-colored clays was formed. Some of the first pieces were glazed inside and out, but Hyten soon decided that only the inside of the pieces had to be glazed so they could hold water. The exterior remained in the natural matte finish of the multicolored clays and was finished with a sandpapering process. The end result was ware with an almost satin finish.

Manufacturing this marbleized pottery required several special processes, since different clays shrink at different rates. To avoid uneven shrinkage, Hyten developed his own process. He added whiting, ground flint, and, when needed, coloring pigments to the

NILOAK

*Impressed die stamp, 1910–1947.*

**NILOAK**

*Impressed die stamp, used until 1910.*

**Niloak**

*Raised or incised, late 1930s–1947.*

Hywood
BY
Niloak

*Stamped in black or raised letters, early 1930s.*

*Black ink stamp, early 1930s.*

NILOAK

*Impressed, mid-1930s; raised or incised mold mark, late 1930s–1947.*

*Paper label of store.*

*Paper label.*

HYWOOD

*Incised, early 1930s.*

*Black or green ink stamp, 1931–1932.*

A 7½-inch Niloak swirl vase made in the mid-1930s. The brightness of the colors is due to the availability of better commercial dyes. (*Collection of David Edwin Gifford; photograph by Gene Taylor, courtesy of the Old State House Museum, Little Rock, Arkansas*)

This tubular vase made of a marbleized mixture of blue, cream, and terra-cotta colored clays is 9 inches high. (*Private collection*)

The 5½-inch-high Niloak vase on the left is marked with a paper label: "The Gift Shop, Biggs Art Store, of Hot Springs, National Park, Ark" that is pasted over the incised Niloak mark. The vase is made from blue, cream, brown, and terra-cotta clays. On the right is an 8-inch-high vase marked "Niloak." It is made from blue, gray, cream, and terra-cotta colored clays. (*Private collection*)

liquid clay. Though the clay was then worked in the more usual ways, the baking process was unorthodox. The pottery was fired for thirty-six to forty-eight hours in a steadily increasing heat, until the temperature finally reached 2,100° F. Charles Hyten applied for a patent on this process in June 1924, and received it January 31, 1928. Patent 1657997 states that "the invention, more specifically speaking, has to do with the production of clay pottery of a decorative character by virtue of the use of clay of different colors." It explains the process and also the coloring agents added to the clay.

The company catalogs offered pottery pieces made of "natural shades of the colorful clays found only in the foothills of the Ozark Mountains." Blue, red, white, gray, brown, and beige clays were found there. When unavailable colors were needed, oxides were added to white clay: cobalt oxide for blue, ferric oxide for red, and chromic oxide for gray, as stated in the patent.

In 1910, Hyten decided to market the art pottery under the name Niloak, which is "kaolin" spelled backward. Kaolin, a fine white clay, had been used to make ceramics for centuries since its introduction in the Orient.

Niloak pottery was offered for sale in a local jeweler's window. Business was so good that in 1911, the same year Dovey left the business, the Niloak Pottery Company was formed. The owners sold company stock and used the money to build a two-story plant with modern equipment. Hyten was superintendent. The new pottery still made the stoneware line of the earlier Eagle Pottery and some decorated glazed wares, but the colored-clay, marbleized pieces accounted for a growing percentage of the pottery's output.

By 1912, the sales force had been increased and Niloak pottery was selling well in all parts of the country. In 1918 Hyten bought total control of the company. During each of its most productive years, the firm made about fifty thousand pieces. Up to six potters were employed at various times to throw swirl Niloak. Niloak was displayed at the 1934 Chicago World's Fair and was sold in stores in all parts of the United States and in Cuba, Europe, and the Far East.

Niloak pottery was expensive, and sales fell drastically during the Depression. By 1932 the firm began to make castwares in several types of high-gloss and semimatte finishes. Some hand-turned pieces were also made in later years. The castware line included both solid and multicolored pieces. At first, the new line was stamped "Hywood Art Pottery," then "Hywood by Niloak, Benton, Arkansas," then "Hywood by Niloak," but was soon marked simply "Niloak."

During the Depression years, the building and properties were mortgaged and Hyten lost control of the business. He continued as a salesman until 1941, when he joined Camark Pottery, Camden, Arkansas, as a salesman. Marbleized Niloak was made intermittently after 1930 up to 1946, and the pottery continued operating until 1947 when it was converted into the Winburn Tile Company. Charles Hyten died in 1944.

*This Hywood Art Pottery "Ozark Dawn" vase, 7½ inches high, dates from 1931–1932. (Collection of David Edwin Gifford; photograph by Gene Taylor, courtesy of the Old State House Museum, Little Rock, Arkansas)*

*This swan vase is marked with the raised word "Niloak." It is a molded vase, 7½ inches high, with a green and pink matte glaze. (Private collection)*

## PRODUCT

The swirled mixed clay pottery apparently developed by Arthur Dovey and perfected by Charles Hyten is the most popular of Niloak's wares collected today. This pottery was called "Mission" to suggest it would be appropriate for a house furnished with Mission-style furniture. Although a few of these early pieces were glazed both inside and out, most of the marbleized wares were glazed only on the inside. The pieces with glazing on the outside are the earlier type, since the soft, sandpapered, satiny finish of the natural clay was preferred.

The colors of the pieces depended on the supply of clay on hand and the skill of the potter. Two or more colors were used, usually blue and brown. It is unusual to find a piece that is predominantly white, although white was sometimes included in the mixture. It is thought that the earlier pieces were of dark brown, cream, and blue. Later pieces show green, blue, and pink mixtures. Early pieces are possibly a bit less colorful. The clays used were of natural color whenever possible, but some of the pieces were made with tinted clay.

All types of pottery shapes were made: vases, candlesticks, tobacco humidors with lids, wine and ale bottles with corks, fruit bowls, lamps, mugs, tiles, umbrella stands, ashtrays, pitchers, clock cases, fern dishes, smoking sets, steins, tankards, match holders, jardinieres, and lamps.

The Hywood line was entirely different from the other ware. At first it consisted of hand-thrown vases, but it soon became a cast or molded pottery and was marketed as Niloak. The cast pieces were small animals such as squirrels or frogs, small vases, pitchers, and other inexpensive novelty items. The Hywood line was made from 1931 to 1947.

### MARKS

Both impressed marks and paper labels were used. Although it is often claimed that all Niloak was marked, unmarked pieces are known. This may be because a paper label was put on the piece at the factory and the label has disappeared.

The impressed marks included the name of the factory, "NILOAK," in either art style or printed form. The word "Niloak" was sometimes part of the mold and appears in raised letters under the glaze. The date also sometimes appears on pieces made after the patent was granted in 1928. The name NILOAK was registered November 3, 1924, as No. 195889.

The paper labels were of several types, either "Niloak Pottery" in a circle or "From the Niloak potteries at Benton, Arkansas" on a jug. Often a model number and price were included in the center of the circle. A vase-shaped metallic label was used in the 1930s. The Hywood pieces were marked with the words "Hywood by Niloak," and later with the word "Niloak." These were stamped on the piece in black or in raised letters. Sometimes a patent number was included.

## Norse Pottery
### *Edgerton, Wisconsin and Rockford, Illinois*

The Norse Pottery Company of Rockford, Illinois, offered Norse ware for sale in 1909. The pottery was made to resemble ancient Norse bronze vessels and was coated with a dull metallic glaze. The company produced replicas of ancient relics—pottery copies of stone, iron, or bronze vases. The pieces were made of red clay with colored, oil-painted finish.

*Impressed.*

*This black Norse Pottery vase was made about 1909. It is 7⅝ inches high and 12⅛ inches wide. The original advertisement labeled this bowl "from the bronze era." It is a copy of a piece from Bornholm, Denmark. (Smithsonian Institution)*

*The footed jardiniere is an example from one of the Norse lines that has the "semblance to the bronze originals preserved in a dull metallic glaze with the effect of verdigris preserved in the corners and crevices and the sunken lines of the etching." The jardiniere shows the Greek influences on Norse Pottery. (Pottery and Glass II, March 1909)*

*Norse Pottery examples include: (above left) a copy of a jardiniere from the Middle Bronze Age, the original found at Bornholm; (left) a vase from the Iron Age, the original found at Jutland; (above) a tankard copied from one of the Late Bronze Age. (Pottery and Glass II, March 1909)*

The company was originally established in Edgerton, Wisconsin, in 1903, when two employees of the Pauline Pottery, Thorwald P. A. Samson and Louis Ipson, decided to make a variety of wares. One of their customers was a wholesale house in Rockford, Illinois. The owner, A. W. Wheelock, bought the Norse Pottery in 1904 and moved it to Rockford. Norse wares were sold in many parts of the country. The firm closed in 1913.

## North Dakota School of Mines
### Grand Forks, North Dakota
⌒

**U.N.D.**

GRAND FORKS, N.D.

*Incised.*

*Ink-stamped.*

The North Dakota School of Mines was established in 1898 at the University of North Dakota in Grand Forks, with Earle J. Babcock as director. Babcock, previously a chemistry instructor at the university, had already been making summer surveys by buckboard or bicycle in search of the state's mineral resources. He found good clay and asked a number of working pottery firms, such as Roseville and Owens, to use the North Dakota clay to make pieces for display at the 1904 St. Louis World's Fair. Marcia Bisbee, another chemistry instructor at the university, also modeled a small leaf-shaped ashtray from some of the clay that Babcock had discovered. When a collection of pottery made from this clay was exhibited at the St. Louis fair, many people were surprised at the high quality of the North Dakota clay.

By 1909 the university started offering a ceramics course. A year

later the university hired a trained potter, Margaret Kelly Cable, who offered instruction in working with North Dakota clay and ceramic materials, and taught methods of forming clay wares, glazing, and firing.

Cable had been trained at the Handicraft Guild in Minneapolis and at the potteries of East Liverpool, Ohio, and had studied with both Charles Binns of the New York State College of Clay-working and Ceramics and Frederick Rhead, art director of the Homer Laughlin Pottery and other potteries. One of her students, Charles Grantier, designed Dickota pottery for the Dickinson Clay Pottery Company in Dickinson, North Dakota, from 1935 to 1937. Cable remained at the University of North Dakota until her retirement in 1949. She died in 1960.

In 1937, Cable worked with Indians at the Pine Ridge Reservation in western South Dakota. Pieces made there were decorated with Sioux designs but glazed and fired at the university pottery. These pieces were usually marked "Pine Ridge, Sioux Indian."

Julia Edna Mattson of Kensington, Minnesota, taught at the

university from 1924 to 1963. She trained at the Kansas Art Institute, North Texas Agricultural College, and Alfred University's New York State College of Clay-working and Ceramics. She also taught at Alfred and in 1948 at the Kalamazoo Institute of Arts. She died in 1967.

Flora Cable Huckfield, Margaret Cable's sister, worked at the school from 1924 to 1949. She made pottery of her own design and pieces, such as souvenirs, to special order. She died in 1960.

Other artists were Hildegarde Fried, who worked from 1918 to 1924; Frieda Hammers, 1926–1939; William H. McKenney, 1949–1952; and Margaret Pachl, 1949–1970.

All of the pieces produced at the University of North Dakota were made from local clays. The design of the work varied through the years from strongly colored Art Nouveau and Art Deco designs to simpler modern, utilitarian styles. Some of the pieces were produced by a cutaway technique that made the finished work resemble the acid-cut cameo glass of Frederick Carder. Others had borders or overall designs of an intaglio type. Many were plain, solid-colored glazed pieces. The flowers and animals of North Dakota were common subjects depicted in the designs. Favored glazes were green, brown, blue, orange, pink, lavender, and other matte colors. Pieces stamped with the university name were made until 1963. Since

*Margaret Cable posing at work in 1926. (Photograph courtesy of Barbara Wamelink)*

*Flora Cable in front of shelves of North Dakota State pottery. The photograph is dated 1926. (Photograph courtesy of Barbara Wamelink)*

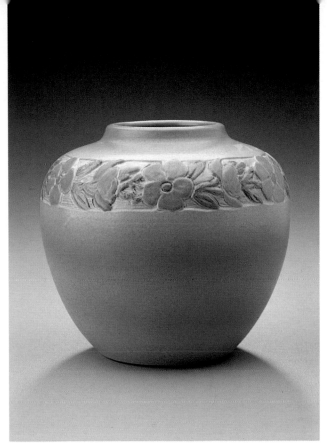

*This pink vase with carved floral decorations has the circular mark of the University of North Dakota and is incised "Millard-Huck-2557, Prairie Rose." It is 6¼ inches high by 6¾ inches wide. Huck is the artist Flora Huckfield. (Private collection)*

*Carved foliage decorates this 11-inch vase marked "Dorothy-Xmas, 1928." The piece also has the university circular stamp. (Barbara Wamelink)*

then, only the students' names have appeared on the pottery.

Each piece has an incised mark in a circle in cobalt blue under the glaze: "University of North Dakota Grand Forks, N.D. Made at School of Mines N.D. Clay." A few are marked "U.N.D. Grand Forks, N.D." Records exist making it possible to date pieces of the pottery from the glaze number and form. The university used consecutive numbers until 1927 (number 722), then unfortunately started again with number 1. The chairman of the Ceramics Department at the university has had success dating pieces, however, and the university has an almost complete set of records of the glazes. Some of the mold shapes have also been dated.

### ARTISTS

*Margaret Kelly Cable.* 1910–1949. Signed pieces "M. Cable," "Cable," "MKC," "MC," "Maggie," "Maggie Mud."

*Agnes Dollahan.* c. 1946.

*Frieda L. Hammers.* 1926–1939. Signed pieces "Hammers," "FLH."

*Flora Cable Huckfield.* 1923–1949. Signed pieces "Huck," "Huckie," "Huck" in an oval, "FCH," "H," "H" in a circle.

*Julia Edna Mattson.* 1924–1963. Signed pieces "JM," "JEM," "Mattson."

*Margaret Pachl.* 1949–1970.

**ERIC**

*Incised.*

**MKC.**
**1917**

*Margaret Kelly Cable, incised, c. 1935.*

**HUCK**

*Flora Cable Huckfield, incised, c. 1935.*

## Odell & Booth Brothers
### *Tarrytown, New York*

**O&BB**

*Incised.*

Charles Mortimer Odell and Walter and Henry Booth of Staffordshire, England, started a pottery about 1880 in Tarrytown, New York named Odell & Booth Brothers. They made majolica and faience decorated under the glaze in the style of the French Limoges/barbotine wares, the same glaze styles used at the early Cincinnati art potteries.

Odell & Booth Brothers made three types of pottery: "Limoges" glazed in the manner of the French wares decorated with slip; "Barbotine" pieces decorated with applied, molded flowers and foliage; and "Faience," a cream-colored earthenware with designs outlined by dark lines on a sponged background. The pottery made umbrella stands, lamp bases, plaques, vases, and parts of chandeliers, as well as pieces that were sold to amateur decorators.

The company became Odell & Booth in 1884, when Walter Booth returned to England. They began making fewer pieces of art pottery, and in 1885 the company closed. Pieces were marked "O & BB."

## George E. Ohr
### *Biloxi, Mississippi*

**G. E. OHR,
BILOXI.**

*Impressed,
1883–1898.*

*1899–1906:
"A visitor asked me for my
autograph and since then [1898] my
creations are marked like a check. The
previous 19 years' mark is like
any old newspaper type . . ."
G. E. Ohr/Biloxi, Miss.*

Eccentric artists are a part of the art pottery tradition, but none can claim a stranger career than the American potter George E. Ohr. Ohr worked as a potter for many years in Biloxi, Mississippi, and was considered an artist in his own time, yet he thought his talent was unappreciated. He purportedly thought his designs were so advanced they would only be fully appreciated in the future. He was right. In the late 1970s, his rediscovered pottery attracted the interest of museums, famous modern artists, and collectors.

Even as early as 1902, W. P. Jervis in *Encyclopedia of Ceramics* expressed Ohr's feelings about his pottery:

> Mr. Ohr with an unbounded confidence in his own genius is laying up at Biloxi a vast store of ware in the hopes that it may be purchased entire by the nation as an example of his prowess. Did we but accept him at his own estimate he is not only the foremost potter in America, but the whole world. He said so and he ought to know.

In 1969 we wrote an article about George Ohr that was published in *The Western Collector* in May 1972, the first major article about Ohr since he stopped making pottery in 1909. Later that year the Ohr family collection of about eight thousand pieces, which had remained in storage, was purchased for resale by Jim W. Carpenter, an antiques dealer. The collection included not only pottery, but also molds, records, and family photographs. To help sell the pottery, Carpenter commissioned a monograph written in 1973 about Ohr

and his work. For the first time, collectors and curators saw a quantity of work by this innovative potter, and within a few years Ohr was recognized as one of America's most important art potters. Dozens of books, articles, and exhibitions featuring Ohr's work appeared.

George Ohr was a far from modest man. In the autobiography he wrote for an art magazine in 1901, Ohr's language and choice of incidents reveal his eccentricity. It is an almost allegorical tale; he says of his birth: "I came on the second schooner and knocked the

This is probably the barrel-shaped water cooler seen in the picture of Ohr's pottery building. It is made of bisque, 29 by 15½ inches. The clay was carved and incised to look like a barrel. There are even a few "repairs," screw heads, and a name tag on the side that says "Biloxi Art Pottery G.E. Ohr." The piece is marked "OHR" on the bottom. (David Rago Arts & Crafts Gallery)

An 1895 photograph of George Ohr's pottery on display. Notice the reticulated ewers on the right. (Photograph courtesy of J. W. Carpenter)

*Two examples of Ohr's creative crimped designs. (David Rago Arts & Crafts Gallery)*

*This crimped and ruffled vase is an example of the complex shapes created by George Ohr. (J. W. Carpenter)*

nose out of joint of the first one, and kept it so, as the other three storks that came in town were nothing to brag about and that completed the programme (3 hens, 1 rooster and a duck, I'm that duck . . .)."

George Ohr, who was born in 1857 to a Biloxi blacksmith and a German woman from Wurtemberg, evidently felt he was always in trouble—or, as he says, "in very hot aqua and evaporated liquified air." His family lived in Biloxi, but when he was old enough, probably eighteen, he ran away to New Orleans. There he worked at a ship chandler's store, where he was given free room and board plus

*George Ohr's booth at the Atlanta exhibit of 1895 should have attracted attention. He modestly claims to be the "greatest art potter on earth." Note the puzzle mugs on the table at right and the art pottery pieces on the ground in front of Ohr. (Photograph courtesy of J. W. Carpenter)*

soap for washing. By the third year, he was paid $15 a month and still given free soap. He felt he was entitled to $1.50 a day for the fifteen hours of daily work he was doing, so he went back to Biloxi. Over the years, he also worked as an apprentice in a file cutter's shop and in a tinker's shop.

Around 1879 Ohr received a letter from an old friend, Joseph F. Meyer, who was later a potter at Sophie Newcomb College. Meyer offered Ohr $10 a month plus the chance to learn a trade. Ohr hopped a ride on a freight train and went back to New Orleans to become a potter. Meyer was then making simple pottery on a wheel. Ohr worked as a potter long enough to gain some skill and then spent two years traveling across sixteen states to see other potters and their potteries. He returned to Biloxi with $26.80 and equipped his own pottery. Ohr was able to make much of the pottery's equipment himself because of his earlier training in ironwork, so most of his money was spent on bricks for the kiln. The less than humble Ohr in his autobiography details how he made the mortar, built the kiln, sawed the pine trees, floated them to town, built the shop, and did all the other necessary jobs.

The first year Ohr claims to have worked alone as a potter is 1883. He made more than six hundred pieces of his unique pottery and then exhibited them at the 1885 New Orleans Cotton Centennial Exposition, where the pottery apparently was stolen. But he kept making his "mud fixings" and kept displaying them at fairs. He also worked for a while at the New Orleans Pottery Company in the late 1880s. A pot exists with the names "George Ohr" and "Crescent City Pottery" marked on it, although nothing further is known about Crescent City Pottery.

Although Ohr's second pottery shop, built in 1888, burned in 1894, he rebuilt it by 1895. The building was well known in the area and was even pictured on souvenir plates made in Europe. George Ohr continued to make pottery in Biloxi and spent a brief time in the mid-1890s at the Newcomb Pottery working under Joseph Meyer. He was fired because he was "not fit to teach young ladies," according to a thesis prepared at Sophie Newcomb College (date, title, and author unknown).

By 1906, when he was almost fifty, Ohr was doing little pottery, and by 1909 he had closed his pottery and stored thousands of pieces in the pottery shed as his legacy to his children. He and his family believed this pottery would be purchased someday by the United States government. He donated about twelve pieces to the Smithsonian Institution, where they were kept in storage and almost completely ignored until the 1970s.

About 1909 Ohr's son had bought a Cadillac dealership and the family went into this new business. George Ohr died in 1918, still convinced he was the greatest potter who ever lived.

Ohr's eccentricities are well known. He was sometimes called the "Mad Potter of Biloxi," partly because of his appearance. He

*Grover Cleveland is shown on one side of this 8-inch-high molded pitcher, his wife on the reverse. It is covered with mottled green and navy glaze. (Skinner, Inc.)*

*George Ohr decorated many pieces with folded, ruffled clay snakes. Pieces with these decorations are among the most prized pieces of Ohr pottery. Bowls, vases, and pitchers in varied colors were made with snakes. This example is from the original Ohr storage group rediscovered in the 1970s. Many fake snake pieces have been made and are a problem for collectors. (J. W. Carpenter)*

( Left ) *Puzzle mugs, shown at center and right, were made in quantity by Mr. Ohr. The bottom of the mugs are signed "G.E. Ohr" in script. To drink from the mugs, you held a finger over a hole in the handle, then sipped on the handle as if it were a straw. The mug at left is a small, filled chamber pot. Below is the same miniature chamber pot, viewed from above, with Mr. Ohr's pottery embellishments. It was a risqué joke of the early 1900s that he sold at fairs. (Private collection)*

had long hair that he knotted on top of his head with a brass pin. His beard, very long, was tucked around his ears or into his shirt to keep it from interfering with the clay on the potter's wheel. And his amazing mustache was so long that he kept it out of the clay by placing the ends behind his ears. A cast of his muscular arm is said to be among the sculpted models used by drawing students at the Newcomb School of Art.

Ohr often played practical jokes. He once scandalized the townfolk when he appeared in a Mardi Gras float in a nightshirt, leaning against a large cross. He left his family a collection of trick photographs showing him as twins, making faces, and in other comical poses. Perhaps his most interesting eccentricity was to name his seven children Leo, Lio, Zio, Oto, Clo, Ojo, and Geo so their initials would also be their first names.

*This 6½-inch-high vase has an orange glaze that is slightly iridescent. It is decorated on the side with the inscription "Mr. J. R. Alexander, Biloxi, 1898." The impressed typeset-style mark "G.E. Ohr, Biloxi Miss" is on the bottom. (Private collection)*

*The Ohr pottery made some early pieces in molds, like these 7½-inch-high paneled pitchers decorated with women wearing flowing draperies. The word "Biloxi" is scratched on the bottom of the pitcher on the left, but the other is unmarked. The original mold for the pitchers was found with the collection of pottery discovered in 1972. (Private collection)*

*(Opposite page) This vase has a folded, crimped top. It is 7 inches high and signed "G.E. Ohr" in script. Notice the bubbles in the pink glaze. Many Ohr pieces have blemishes in the glaze. (Private collection)*

A yellowish beige glaze with green mottling covers the outside of this folded vase. The interior is glazed with a lighter color. Ohr always glazed the interior of his vases. It is 3½ inches high and 6 inches wide. The piece is incised with the typeset-style mark "G.E. Ohr, Biloxi, Miss." (*Private collection*)

This free-form vase is 3 inches high and 4 inches across. Collectors sometimes call these "vaginal vases" and this shape brings a premium price. The piece is glazed light and dark green with red mottling and is marked with the typeset-style mark "G.E. Ohr, Biloxi, Miss." (*Private collection*)

A speckled glaze was favored by Ohr for a time. This 5½-inch folded vase is covered with a yellow glaze speckled with green. The interior is yellow. The piece is marked with a typeset-style mark "G.E. Ohr, Biloxi, Miss." (*Private collection*)

This free-form bowl has remarkably thin edges. The glaze is orange and brown. The height at the highest point is 3¼ inches. It is marked with the typeset style "G.E. Ohr, Biloxi, Miss." (*Private collection*)

Mottled yellow and green glaze was used on this bowl with folded edges. It is 5 inches by 3 inches wide and 3 inches high and is marked "G.E. Ohr, Biloxi, Miss." in typeset style. (*Private collection*)

Two snakes decorate this glossy bowl found in the Ohr collection discovered in 1972. (*J. W. Carpenter*)

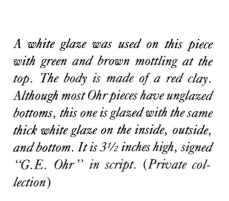

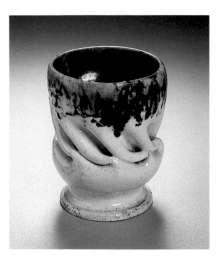

A white glaze was used on this piece with green and brown mottling at the top. The body is made of a red clay. Although most Ohr pieces have unglazed bottoms, this one is glazed with the same thick white glaze on the inside, outside, and bottom. It is 3½ inches high, signed "G.E. Ohr" in script. (*Private collection*)

A gray and mottled green bubbled glaze was used on this scalloped-top vase. It is 3¾ inches high, marked "G.E. Ohr, Biloxi, Miss." in typeset style. (*Private collection*)

## PRODUCT

Some of the pottery pieces made by George Ohr were unlike any other American art pottery forms. Pieces varied in size from the height of a thimble to that of a man. He usually used a local clay, often red or yellow, fired at low temperature in the wood-burning kiln. Sometimes he would try clay from other cities such as New Orleans or Mobile, Alabama. Pieces made from these strange clays were sometimes marked to explain where the mud had been found.

Ohr made molded wares early in his career. Pieces were decorated with Art Nouveau–style girls, fishermen, a girl on a bicycle, President Grover Cleveland, and a steamboat. Some of the molds still exist, and in the mid-1980s a few pieces were recast. Some of the hand-thrown pieces have molded handles and spouts.

Ohr produced hand-formed pieces to sell at fairs, including a large variety of hats, inkwells shaped like houses, artists' palettes, cannons, mule heads, busts of presidents, banks, chamber pots, and puzzle mugs. These were small souvenir-type items with varied glazes in yellow to brown tones.

The most unusual of the Ohr pieces were made of what appears to be twisted clay. It was very thin clay that he twisted, crushed, folded, or dented into odd shapes. Some pieces were pleated before they were twisted, and some were made with edges that had been pinched to their thinnest or chipped before glazing. Each piece was different in both shape and glaze. Some were made from marbleized clay. Ohr decorated vases with modeled snakes and lizards with bodies that resembled a looped ribbon. Sometimes a vase had added ruffles of clay or applied looped handles.

Edwin Barber, in his *Pottery and Porcelain Development Since 1893*, mentions seeing modeled designs of crabs, seashells, wildcats, lizards, serpents, and dragons. Incised decorations of flowers or inscriptions are on some pieces. Some Ohr teapots have surface dents that resemble hammer marks on metal. He made a statue of a potato, numerous puzzle jugs and Cadogan-type pots, and 3-inch souvenir chamber pots complete with excrement. A group of "fun tokens," small pieces of pottery stamped with sayings such as "I love you," are said to be made by Ohr. He also made small, irregularly shaped ceramic pieces that could be tied on as labels.

*Inkwells of many shapes were modeled and molded, by Ohr. (Upper left) This dark brown inkwell is shaped like a log cabin. It is 3 inches long, 2½ inches high, and marked "G.E. Ohr, Biloxi" in typeset style. (Upper right) The donkey head inkwell has a hole at the top for a pen. This 5½-inch piece is marked "Geo. E. Ohr, Biloxi, Miss." (Lower right) Ohr shaped this inkwell like an artist's palette, with pen, tubes of paint, and an ink pot. The palette is 6¼ inches long. It is marked "Geo. E. Ohr, Biloxi, Miss." in typeset style. These pieces were all found in the Ohr storage area and have been in a private collection since the 1970s. Beware: this type of Ohr inkwell is being copied and given a fake Ohr mark today. (Lower left) Ohr made a realistic printer's type holder of brown-glazed pottery for the wooden parts, and dark metallic glaze for the type. Notice the "screw." The "wood" is inscribed in script "Jackson News 5-10-95." The type says:*

> *The poet sings in dainty rhyme*
> *Of summer days and sunny clime*
> *Of beauteous maideens passing fair*
> *With witching eyes and waving hair*
> *Till near the end you're apt to C*
> *A welcome to the pot-Ohr-E.*
> *Resp'Y*
> *GEO E OHR*
> *Biloxi, Miss. 5-12-95*

*The back of the piece is marked "G.E. OHR, BILOXI" in capital letters and with the inscribed letter H. The piece is 5½ inches long. (Private collection)*

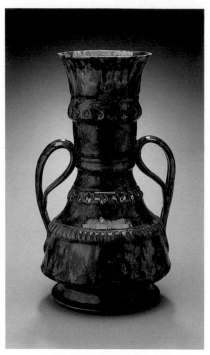

*Snake decorations were used on this 7-inch vase. It has a green-speckled, slightly iridescent glaze. The handle is applied. The piece is marked with the script signature "G.E. Ohr" and "Biloxi, Miss." (Private collection)*

*A scroll-handled pitcher, 8 inches high. Notice the pleated borders. (David Rago Arts & Crafts Gallery)*

*A pink vase, 9 inches high, is marked with the typeset-impressed mark. (Private collection)*

*(Right) George Ohr evidently took the edge of the wet clay of this bowl between his fingers and pinched it, drawing the clay as thin as possible as he pulled the edge. The glaze is an iridescent brown. The metallic-finish vase is about 5 inches in diameter and is marked "G.E. Ohr, Biloxi, Miss." in typeset style. (Private collection)*

*(Above) This inkwell is 7¾ inches long. The artist's palette is yellow with spots of colored "paint," and the inkwell is metallic black. (J. W. Carpenter)*

The glazes Ohr used are as varied as his pottery shapes. Brown, purple, blue, yellow, green lusters and black and other metallic glazes were included in his palette. A bright pink with drip designs of another color and a mottled speckled effect are found on some wares. Many of the glazes are flawed or even burned. Most of the pieces found in storage were of brown to yellow coloring. Many unglazed pieces were also found. Most of these were made of marbleized beige to orange-red clays. It is not known whether many of these were unfinished when put away or if Ohr planned to sell

George Ohr modeled many styles of hats. The finished piece had no special use but to be decorative. This green and brown hat is 4½ inches long and is marked on the crown with the impressed mark "G.E. Ohr, Biloxi." (Private collection)

A snake curls around the handle of this Ohr jug, which is ruffled at the top and indented around the base. (J. W. Carpenter)

Not every artist would make a statue of a potato, but George Ohr did. This green-glazed figure is 10 inches high. It is marked "G.E. Ohr" in script. (Private collection)

This 6-inch-high blue vase with snake decoration has a cleverly crimped center. The typeset mark is impressed on the bottom. (Private collection)

A mottled yellow Ohr puzzle jug, 9¼ inches tall. When water is poured into a hole in the bottom, it will then pour from the holes in the side or the top of the spout. To avoid getting wet, you must cover the properly sized holes. Notice the snake climbing around the top. The unmarked piece was found in the 1970s collection. (Private collection)

A 5-inch-high unglazed crumpled vase. Notice the mixture of colored clays used to make it. It is marked with the script mark. Hundreds of these unglazed pieces were in the rediscovered storage area; unfortunately, many have been reglazed and sold in an altered state. (Private collection)

*The clay for this vase was pleated like material, then the entire vase was formed and bent into its irregular shape. The brown glaze has brown speckling. It is 2½ inches high, 5 inches in diameter, and marked "G.E. Ohr, Biloxi" in typeset style. (Private collection)*

them without glaze, but by the end of the century, Ohr was turning away from glazing his wares.

Collectors seek the unusual and Ohr pottery has become popular and expensive. Unfortunately, some of the unglazed pieces have been "clobbered" with modern glaze. Glossy red glaze, large polka-dot decorations, and bright colors are suspect. Some pieces have also been embellished with recently added snakes or dragons. Again unfortunately, a few of the reglazed, embellished pieces have been exhibited and pictured in catalogs and books. Beware of pieces with round stilt marks on the bottom. Most Ohr pieces have three lines from Y-shaped stilts on the bottom. Beware also of glazed pieces with unglazed bottoms. Figural inkwells are being copied.

The main source of Ohr pottery found by today's collectors was a group of nearly eight thousand pieces stored over Ohr's garage. The pieces were covered with dirt and dust that clung to crevices. A totally clean piece may be new or reglazed. Ohr marked almost all of his pottery, so unmarked pieces may be fakes. Pieces were marked in many ways. The hand script signature "G. E. Ohr" was used from 1899 to 1906, according to a letter by Ohr. Before that he used a printed mark: "G. E. Ohr, Biloxi Miss." or "Geo. E. Ohr, Biloxi, Miss." Some pieces had poems, inscriptions, dates, and other marks. J. H. P. are the initials of J. Harry Portman, a foster brother of Ohr. He worked at the pottery and sometimes his initials appear with an Ohr mark.

## Ouachita Pottery
### Hot Springs, Arkansas
~

**OUACHITA
HOT SPRINGS, ARK**
*Impressed.*

In 1906 the Ouachita Pottery, successor to the Mountain Valley Pottery Co., was organized in Hot Springs, Arkansas. Arthur Dovey, a potter from the Rookwood Pottery of Cincinnati, came to work at the pottery, which was named for the nearby Ouachita Mountains.

*This covered sugar bowl glazed in matte green has an incised design of geometric shapes. It is 3¾ inches high by 7 inches wide. The piece is marked on the bottom in impressed letters "Ouachita, Hot Springs, Ark." (Private collection)*

The art pottery was made from white clay found nine miles away from Hot Springs. Pieces were glazed in both matte and glossy finish. The green matte glazed pieces with carved decoration closely resemble the Rookwood designs of the time. The company also made a swirled clay pottery, apparently introduced by Dovey. Art pottery was made at Ouachita only until 1908, when the firm incorporated as the Hot Springs Clay Products Company.

Dovey went to St. Louis in 1908 to work for the Ouachita Coal and Clay Products Company, then a year later moved to Benton, Arkansas, and helped start the Niloak Pottery.

Pieces are marked "Ouachita, Hot Springs, Ark." and "H.S.C.P.Co., Hot Springs" (Hot Springs Clay Products Company). The initials S.E.S., for artist Sara Elizabeth Smith, and M.D., probably another artist mark, have also been found.

*A hand-thrown Ouachita vase, 6 inches high. (Collection of David Edwin Gifford; photograph by Gene Taylor, courtesy of Old State House Museum, Little Rock, Arkansas)*

# Overbeck Pottery
### Cambridge City, Iowa

Four sisters founded the Overbeck Pottery in their family home in Cambridge City, Indiana, about 1910. All of the work was done by four of six sisters, who were all daughters of John Overpeck. (The four girls changed their name to Overbeck in 1911, after their parents died.)

Margaret, the oldest, was on the art faculty at DePauw University in Greencastle, Indiana. She taught drawing, watercolors, and china painting. She had previously worked at a pottery in Zanesville, Ohio, and had studied art under Arthur W. Dow at Columbia University in New York City. Hannah, the principal designer, was also a photographer and teacher. Many of her china-painting designs were published in *Keramic Studio*. Elizabeth studied with Margaret and with Charles F. Binns at Alfred, New York, in 1909 and 1910. She became well known as a teacher and lecturer on pottery and won many national awards. Mary, the youngest, studied with Margaret and with Arthur Dow and Marshall Fry at Columbia, and taught in Boulder, Colorado, and in Indiana. She was a bookplate designer and did many other designs that were published in *Keramic Studio*.

All of the sisters except Elizabeth studied at the Art Academy in Cincinnati, Ohio. They all worked in many forms of art, including oil paintings and watercolors. They even built furniture, did enamels on copper, and made jewelry.

Margaret, the guiding spirit in the founding of the pottery, died shortly after it opened. The work at the studio was divided more or less equally among the three surviving sisters. Hannah was a decorator and created most of the designs. Elizabeth, the technician, worked with the clay and glazes and executed the designs. Mary designed and glazed. All the sisters were capable of filling any of the jobs required in making pottery. After Hannah's death, the others

**MARKS**

*Impressed.*

*Elizabeth.*

*Mary F.*

*Hannah.*

*The iridescent gold decoration on this pottery vase is similar to that on the Weller LaSa line. This vase is clearly marked on the bottom with the Swastika Keramos logo. (Private collection)*

kept working, and when Elizabeth died, Mary continued to make the pottery alone until her death in 1955.

The pottery was made from a mixture of feldspar from Pennsylvania, kaolin from Delaware, and ball clay from Tennessee. Some pieces were made with local red clay. The wares were glazed in raspberry, turquoise, lavender, creamy yellow, dark gray, pink, blue, green, and a wide range of other colors. Commercial and art pottery were made there at the same time. The pots were made on a wheel. With the exception of the molded cups and saucers and a few small figurines, all the pieces were one of a kind. The glaze was either matte or glossy. Designs were incised, carved, or glazed in patterns. Most designs were based on nature and pictured flowers or insects. The pottery also produced dinner sets, figurines, vases, and bowls. The figurines, single or group, were often humorous caricatures of people at work or play.

After 1911 the pottery was marked with the Overbeck monogram. The initials of the designer and potter were added. Earlier pieces were marked with the incised name of the artist.

## Owen China Company
### Minerva, Ohio

The Owen China Company of Minerva, Ohio, made art pottery marked "Swastika Keramos," named for the ancient decorative symbol and the Greek word for "pottery," from 1906 to about 1908. The company was founded in 1902 by Ted Owen. John Lessell of J. B. Owens Pottery (not related to Owen China Company) may have worked on this line.

Local clays were used to make semiporcelain hotel china and some art pottery. Swastika pieces were made with metallic bronze, brass, or copper glazes. Other colors were sometimes used with the metallic glazes.

The Owen China Company went out of business in 1931.

# Owens Pottery Company
## Zanesville, Ohio

~

J. B. Owens was born near Roseville, Ohio, in 1859. He discovered at an early age that he was a good salesman, and while in his twenties became a traveling salesman for a line of stoneware. By 1885, he was making pottery and stoneware at his own plant in Roseville. State records indicate he may have had a factory in Zanesville even before he moved there in 1891 and built a new plant to make stoneware.

Art pottery was made at the J. B. Owens Pottery Company from 1896 until 1907. Owens employed many potters and artists, including Karl Langenbeck, who was hired as head chemist in 1891. Langenbeck, an experienced potter, had worked with Maria Longworth Nichols of Rookwood fame and had founded the Avon Pottery Company. Samuel Geijsbeek was brought in as manager of the art department in 1896 and eventually became superintendent of the pottery. He later moved to Golden, Colorado, to manage the Geijsbeek Pottery, then to Seattle to work for Gladding, McBean & Co.

John Lessell, the foreman of J. B. Owens Pottery in 1905, developed iridescent glazes. Hugo Herb (1907), Guido Howarth, and Frank L. (Di)Ferrel(1) were also employed. W. A. Long, who designed the Lonhuda line at Weller, worked for the J. B. Owens Pottery from 1896 to about 1900. Long had also developed Weller's Louwelsa line, which is similar to the Utopian line designed by Geijsbeek for Owens.

The Owens Pottery burned in March 1902, but Owens bought

*Raised.*

*Impressed.*

*Owens
Utopian
Impressed.*

*Impressed.*     *Impressed.*

**OWENSART**
*Impressed, after 1906.*

HENRI          OWENS
DEUX           UTOPIAN

*Impressed.*     *Impressed.*

**OWENS**
*Impressed.*

*Experimental marks used internally at factories.*

*This Owens vase, meant to look like an American Indian pottery vessel, is 6½ inches long, 5 inches high, and 4 inches wide. Its color is terra-cotta with black and brown designs. (Smithsonian Institution)*

*This 10½-inch bottle-shaped Owens vase has a brown to green to gold glaze. The lifelike daffodils were painted by Delores Harvey, whose initials appear at the base of the vase. The impressed mark "J.B. Owens, Utopian, 1010B" appears on the bottom.*

*Owens Pottery made a variety of artware. Blue flowers in relief decorate this 10¼-inch-high vase marked "Owens." (Smithsonian Institution)*

*A matte lavender glaze was used on this 4-inch-high vase with dragonfly decoration. It was made about 1905. (Smithsonian Institution)*

the Corona Pottery plant in Corona, New York, in July and also rebuilt his Zanesville plant, which was open again by August. The company made many types of art pottery using Ohio and Tennessee clay. The size and output of the New York plant is not known.

Owens Pottery's 1904 catalog lists eight hundred items. The pottery was awarded four gold medals at the Lewis and Clark Exposition in Portland, Oregon, in 1905, the same year Owens started manufacturing tiles.

The art pottery made by J. B. Owens Pottery was of high quality, with a special type of glaze for each line. No general characteristic identifies all Owens pottery, though some of the lines can be easily recognized even if unmarked.

In 1907, the J. B. Owens Pottery Company in Zanesville was closed and its production of art pottery apparently ceased. Production at the Corona plant may have continued for another year, and Owens himself may have continued producing some art pottery in Zanesville for a year or two.

By 1909, Owens had started a new business producing tiles in Zanesville. He had a successful tile operation, the J. B. Owens Floor & Wall Tile Company, until 1928, when the plant again burned. (The plant was sometimes referred to as the Empire Floor & Wall Tile Co. The Zanesville Chamber of Commerce booklet of 1918 has a picture of the J. B. Owens Floor & Wall Tile Co. and says it is six years old.) Ignoring the advice of others, Owens rebuilt the plant and lost everything during the Depression. He moved to Homestead, Florida, where he died in 1934.

*An Owens pitcher, 6 inches high, with brown glaze.*

\* An asterisk indicates an artist listed in Edwin Barber's *Marks of American Potters.*

*Virginia Adams. Also worked at Roseville; Weller.*

\* *Estelle Beardsley.*

\* *Edith Bell.*

\* *Fanny Bell.*

\* *Anna Fulton Best. Also worked at Roseville; Weller.*

\* *Cecilia Bloomer.*

\* *Lillian Bloomer.*

*John Butterworth. Also worked at Roseville; Weller.*

*C. M. C. Unknown.*

*Charles W. Chilcote. Also worked at Weller; Zane.*

*Chilectsi.*

*Daniel Cook. Also worked at Rookwood.*

\* *Cora Davis.*

\* *Walter I. Denny.*

*E. Unknown.*

\* *Harrie (Harry?) Eberlein.*

\* *Hattie Eberlein. Also worked at Roseville.*

\* *Cecil Excel.*

*J. F. Unknown.*

*Frank Ferrell. Designer, 1907. Also worked at Peters & Reed; Roseville; Weller.*

*Charles Fouts. Also worked at Weller.*

\* *Charles Gray. Also worked at Weller.*

\* *Martha E. Gray.*

\* *Delores Harvey.*

\* *Albert Haubrich. Also worked at Weller.*

*Hugo Herb. Modeler, 1906. Also worked at Weller.*

*John Herold. Also worked at Roseville; Weller.*

\* *H. Hoskins.*

*Roy Hook. Also worked at Roseville; Weller.*

*H. I. Unknown.*

*Guido Howarth.*

*Karl Langenbeck. Chemist.*

*Harry Larzelere. Also worked at Roseville.*

John Lessell (Lassell). Foreman, 1905. Also worked at Weller.

*A. V. Lewis. Also worked at Weller.*

William A. Long. Also worked at Lonhuda; Weller.

Mc. Unknown.

R. M. Unknown.

*Cora McCandless.*

*Carrie McDonald.*

B. Mallen. Also worked at Roseville.

Hattie Mitchell. Also worked at Owens; Roseville.

*Miss Oshe.*

Bert Owens. Pottery mark B. 01.

*Mary L. Pierce. Also worked at Weller.*

Albert Radford. Also worked at Radford; Weller.

Marie Rauchfuss. Also worked at Rookwood; Weller.

*Harry Robinson. Also worked at Weller.*

*Hattie M. Ross. Also worked at Weller.*

*R. Lillian Shoemaker. Also worked at Roseville.*

Helen Smith. Also worked at Roseville; Weller.

*Ida Steele.*

Tot Steele. Also worked at Roseville; Weller.

*William H. Stemm. Also worked at Weller.*

*Mary Fauntleroy Stevens.*

C. Minnie Terry (?) Also worked at Roseville; Weller.

*Mae Timberlake. Also worked at Roseville; Weller.*

*Sarah Timberlake. Also worked at Roseville; Weller.*

*Arthur Williams. Also worked at Roseville.*

*Aborigine:* matte glaze finish, crude, American Indian–inspired designs, 1907.

*Alpine:* matte glaze, shaded gray or brown background, artist freehand slip decoration in blue, green, others usually flowers, fruit, c. 1905 (example marked "Steele").

*Aqua Verde:* slightly iridescent glaze, usually green, embossed stylized Art Nouveau decoration, 1907.

*Art Jasper:* Similar to English jasperware, small molded pieces of clay attached to main body, probably Radford's work, 1903.

*Art Nouveau:* high-gloss glaze, decorated under glaze with swirls on green to dark brown background, marked "JB Owens/Art Nouveau," date of introduction unknown.

*Art Vellum:* orange, brown, other earth-tone colors, vellum finish, underglaze decoration, 1905.

*Brushmodel Lotus:* similar to Lotus, matte glaze, 1907.

*Corona:* bronze colored, 1902.

*Corona Animals:* animal figures in natural colors, from life-sized garden figures to small indoor decorative pieces under 5 inches, unglazed, 1904.

*Cyrano:* blue, red, black, or dark brown background with raised white lacy decorations, glossy glaze, sometimes mistaken for Weller's Turada, 1898.

*Delft:* bucket-shaped blue and white ware with Dutch scenes, 1904.

*Feroza Faience:* metallic lustre ware with iridescent effects, pieces appear bronzelike, 1901.

*Gunmetal:* unglazed, resembles dull gunmetal, engraved decoration, 1905.

*Henri Deux:* Art Nouveau designs cut into clay, filled with color, 1900.

*Lotus:* underglaze decoration, natural subjects, light shaded background, high-gloss glaze, similar to Rookwood's iris glaze, 1907.

*Matt Green:* matte green molded bodies, some with raised designs, 1905.

*Matt Lotus:* matte pieces in Lotus line, 1907.

*Matt Soudaneze:* matte pieces in Soudaneze line, date unknown.

*Matt Utopian:* light color matte finish, 1905.

*Mission:* matte glaze, slip-painted designs of old California missions, landscapes, etc.; each came with a weathered-oak stand, 1903.

*Onyx:* high-glaze mottled finish, dark brown to cream, 1898.

*Opalesce Inlaid:* solid-colored background of light color, overglaze irregularly spaced wavy lines of olive green or light color on copper, gold, or silver, floral decorations inlaid and outlined in black, 1905.

*Opalesce Utopian:* coated with gold and overlaid with small coralinelike beads, underglaze slip decoration similar to Utopian line on one area of a piece, 1905.

*Parchment Lotus:* similar to Lotus, 1906.

*A rare Owens vase covered with copper and gold metallic-colored finish. The incised iris decoration was evidently part of the work done at Owens, with a thin sheet of copper overlay made by Clewell pottery of Canton, Ohio. The 12½-inch-high vase has the impressed Owens mark and a Clewell paper label. (Private collection)*

*A 12½-inch vase marked with the Owens Art flame. (Private collection)*

*An Owens Cyrano jardiniere, 7½ inches tall and 8 inches in diameter. It is unmarked. Cyrano is sometimes mistaken for Weller Turada, but Turada pieces are almost always marked and the shape of the center band is slightly different. (Private collection)*

*Poster:* brown tones of background like Utopian, Greek actors, musicians, 1900.

*Red Flame:* red glazed background, embossed floral decorations, 1905.

*Rustic:* imitation tree trunks, stumps, matte glaze, 1904.

*Soudanese:* ebony black background glaze, inlaid decoration of flowers, animals, birds in shades of lavender, white, etc., high-gloss glaze, 1906–1907.

*Sunburst:* similar to Utopian, high-gloss glaze, 1906.

*Utopian:* high-gloss dark brown background, underglaze slip-painting of flowers, portraits, Indians, animals, also made in light shades of blue, pink, and brown, similar to Rookwood's standard glaze, 1896 (first line made, developed by Samuel Geijsbeek).

*Venetian:* iridescent metallic glaze on indented surface, 1904.

*Wedgwood Jasper:* resembles English Wedgwood pottery, 1903. Probably by Radford.

Other lines named by collectors include Black Lotus, Creamware, Etruscan Incised, Jeweled, Light, Matt Incised, Opalesce Beaded, Opalesce Beaded Plain, Silverplate, and Transfer. The name "Oriental" appears on a piece that looks like Cyrano. Lamp bases marked with *A* and "AS" numbers may have been produced at Owens.

## Park Lane Pottery
### See Wannopee Pottery
~

## Pauline Pottery
### Chicago, Illinois and Edgerton, Wisconsin
~

Pauline (Mrs. Oscar I.) Jacobus (1840–1930) was one of the many women who became interested in painting china during the last quarter of the nineteenth century. She not only painted china, but also gave lessons in the art. While studying at the Chicago Art Institute in the early 1880s, Mrs. Jacobus saw an exhibit of pottery with raised decorations. A few years later, she met the actress Sarah Bernhardt, who showed Mrs. Jacobus her experiments in modeling sculpture. China painting had been interesting, but here was an art Mrs. Jacobus could apply to pottery. A short time later, she opened her own studio to make and decorate art pottery.

Her kiln, which had been sufficient for hardening china paints, was not adequate to fire pottery and she set out to learn the proper techniques. She enrolled at the Rookwood School for Pottery Decoration held at the home and studio of Maria Longworth Nichols of Cincinnati, Ohio, where she began to learn all the techniques of the pottery business, including mixing clay, shaping, throwing, molding, glazing, and firing.

Oscar Jacobus was a member of the Chicago Board of Trade. While Pauline was studying in Cincinnati, Oscar wrote to her about a group of women who were planning to open an art pottery studio in Chicago. Mrs. Jacobus was determined to be the first to make art pottery in her hometown, so she rushed back with John Sargent, a qualified kiln maker. Laura Fry, also from Rookwood, helped her outfit the workshop. In 1883, she sent out invitations for her first exhibit of art pottery in Chicago. The entire pottery staff consisted of Mrs. Jacobus, one presser, and two student decorators. One of her original decorators was a woman named Springer (one of her pieces is in the Wisconsin State Historical Society Collection marked with her name and the date, 1883).

Mrs. Jacobus's pottery was named "Pauline" by her husband, and a few pieces were marked with the script name "Pauline Pottery." At the first exhibit, some Pauline Pottery was purchased by Tiffany of New York, where it continued to be sold for many years. Marshall Field of Chicago and Kimball's of Boston were two other early retailers of Pauline Pottery.

The early Pauline Pottery pieces were made of a dense Ohio clay that had to be shipped to the Chicago pottery. The glazes were primarily matte and there was much incised and gilded work on buff or red-colored wares.

The Pauline Pottery Company operated from a small, overcrowded Chicago shop from 1883 to 1888. When the student decorators were replaced by a staff of artists, it became apparent that the operation would have to move to larger quarters.

Mr. Jacobus had heard about a bed of superior pottery clay 125 miles from Chicago near Edgerton, Wisconsin, that had been used since the 1850s to make building bricks. Mr. and Mrs. Jacobus were most interested in a layer of cream-colored clay that had been discovered beneath the brick clay. The advantage of building a pottery near the clay and not having to ship it from Ohio was obvious to both of them.

In November 1887, Mr. Jacobus met with several men from Edgerton and convinced them of the economic soundness of making pottery. To sweeten the pie, he showed them a contract he held with the Bell Telephone Company to make porous battery cups, an enterprise that would provide employment to about thirty local men. Since the fame and the sales of Pauline Pottery were known, many of Edgerton's businessmen were interested. Three of them, W. W. Babcock, F. W. Coon, and Andrew Jenson, went to Chicago and reported back that it seemed a worthwhile business venture. In two weeks $11,000 was raised and a final $8,000 was soon added, probably by Mr. Jacobus.

The pottery corporation was formed with W. W. Babcock as president, C. F. Mabbett as vice president, and Thomas Hutson as treasurer, plus five directors: O. I. Jacobus, J. P. Towne, Andrew Jenson, Henry Marsden, and M. L. Pelton. The Pauline Pottery was incorporated on February 14, 1888, with capital stock of $20,000 (when the extra $1,000 was raised is unknown). The stock was divided into 400 shares of $50 each. The E. C. Hopkins Warehouse

*Incised, probably used before 1891.*

*Incised.*

*Incised.*

*Incised, used after 1891.*

*Pauline Pottery*
*1883*

*Incised.*

PAULINE
POTTERY

*Incised.*

PAULINE
POTTERY

*Incised.*

*Unknown.*

m.B

*Unknown.*

ΛΣØ

*Unknown.*

*Unknown, 1883.*

*Unknown.*

E A H

*Eugenia A. Hutchinson.*

Fannie

*Unknown.*

*Pauline Pottery made this gray covered jar and plate. The jar is 7⅛ inches in diameter. Both bear the crown mark over "136." (Smithsonian Institution)*

was purchased by the end of March, and John Sargent was hired from Cincinnati to build the kiln. He built four three-cone–shaped kilns for the battery cups and one square kiln for firing the art pottery at a different temperature. The company purchased clay washers, pressers, lathes, a 40-horsepower engine, and all the other needed machinery. Mr. Jacobus was the superintendent of the battery cup works on the first and second floors, and Mrs. Jacobus continued to make her art pottery on the third floor.

Thirteen women were hired to decorate the art pottery. All of the decoration was underglaze and the painting was done in mineral colors with a brush in what contemporary artists called the "Japanese style."

Twenty-two other people were employed at the firm. Two more were added in 1891, when Thorwald P. A. Samson and Louis Ipson arrived from Denmark. Samson was an artist and modeler, Ipson a molder. Most of the Pauline pottery at the time was made in molds. The two Danes worked only a year and then formed the American Art Clay Works in Edgerton, Wisconsin, making terra-cotta figures and busts from local red clay. Their pottery worked from 1892 to 1895, when the American Art Clay Works was renamed the Edgerton Art Clay Works. These pieces are marked "Edgerton Art Clay" or "ECW."

An interesting sidelight to the history of the Pauline Pottery is the part played by Wilder Pickard of Pickard China. Pickard saw some Pauline pottery in Marshall Field's. He contacted the pottery and in March 1889 was given a contract to sell the decorated ware in Indiana, Michigan, Illinois, Missouri, Iowa, Wisconsin, and Minnesota. Before he became Pauline Pottery's sales agent, the art pottery had been sold to order only and sales were restricted to a few of the larger cities. A note in the *Wisconsin Tobacco Reporter*, Edgerton, Wisconsin, November 20, 1891, states that in November 1891, "Mr. Pickard has sold more goods for the Pottery this season, than all other years put together."

In May 1893, Oscar Jacobus died and the business ran into problems. The battery cup part of the business lost money because the dry cell battery had been invented and the demand for cups fell. There were also some legal problems regarding a patent infringement. Pauline Jacobus lost control of the business, and in May 1894 five of the stockholders of the original Pauline Pottery of Edgerton incorporated as the Edgerton Pottery Company. The new pottery continued to use the plant, making an artware of a lower quality. (The various Edgerton potteries should not be confused. In addition to Edgerton Pottery, there was Edgerton Art Clay Works, successor to American Art Clay Works, and the china-decorating business founded in 1893 by Willard Pickard, Pauline Pottery's former sales agent.)

The business failed, and by 1902 the original plant was sold for scrap value. The Edgerton businessmen who had financed the factory lost all of their investment. At the sale, Mrs. Jacobus bought the kiln and remaining clay. When she could not find a kiln builder, she marked each brick of the kiln and with the help of a local brickmason rebuilt it in the backyard of "The Bogert," her family home. She put the clay and potter's wheel in the basement of the house and continued working. She did her decorating and glazing in a low building at the back of the yard. It is said that she dug some of the clay from the flower beds behind her house.

Mrs. Jacobus was able to do every job connected with making art pottery. She hired student decorators and in the summer ran a type of boardinghouse. Volume 5 of *Sketch Book*, in 1906, announced the "PAULINE POTTERY, near Edgerton, Wisconsin, study and re-creation combined, summer school during July for practical instruction in art of Pottery. Number of pupils limited, for rates and further particulars address Mrs. Pauline Jacobus." The course cost $20 for four weeks plus $7 for room and board. The boardinghouse-pottery was well run and had many Chicago guests. Jacobus made the pottery forms in the summer and did the decorating, firing, and glazing during the winter. This small studio version of the Pauline Pottery continued from 1902 to 1909, when Mrs. Jacobus closed her operation.

During the years she worked making pottery, Pauline Jacobus washed, molded, threw, cast, glazed, and decorated the clay, and filled and fired the kiln. Heavy manual labor was required to fill and lift the saggers and to seal and brick the kiln, and Pauline did it all if no assistants were available.

She was such a proper Chicago lady, with such formal manners, that the locals rather feared her. When her house caught fire on July 19, 1911, a young man pounded on her door to tell her. But by the time he overcame his timidity and told her his story, the fire had soared out of control. The house was totally destroyed, leaving only the kiln and the log cabin where Pauline had sold some of the seconds.

Pauline then went to live with her daughter and son-in-law, Jenny and John Coons. When the Coons family moved to Texas, Pauline went with them, only briefly returning to Edgerton in 1927. The last few years of her life were spent in the Masonic Home at Dousman, Wisconsin. She died in 1930, and is buried in Oak Woods Cemetery, Chicago, in the Dow Bogert vault.

### PRODUCT

The variety of wares produced at the Pauline Pottery in Chicago as well as at Edgerton makes it difficult to cite one or two types as characteristic. The early pieces made from Ohio clay were heavy and grayish in body color. Matte glazes were preferred. At the same time, the pottery made a redware that was decorated with incised designs, then gilded over the glaze.

The clay from the beds at Edgerton was considered a yellow clay, but it fired to a near-white color. Many of the pieces appeared light yellow

*A Pauline Pottery squat vase, 3 inches high and 7½ inches in diameter, white with brown leaves. (State Historical Society of Wisconsin)*

*This Pauline Pottery vase of deep blue is 9 inches high and 4 inches in diameter. It is marked with the crown trademark and the words "Made for M.F. & Co.," indicating that it was sold by Marshall Field, the Chicago department store. (State Historical Society of Wisconsin)*

*A Pauline Pottery plate, 5½ inches in diameter. (State Historical Society of Wisconsin)*

because of a transparent lead glaze that was applied over the painted decoration. The decoration was always underglaze. The clay body was soft, as the pottery was fired at a low temperature. A chip shows a chalk-colored base with a pale honey-yellow glaze. The glaze was very often "crazed." The fine network of lines on the glaze was caused by what a potter would call a poor "fit"; the glaze and the clay expanded at different rates, causing the crazed surface. These lines have often allowed water to seep into the clay body. Some pieces are badly discolored because water has remained too long in a bowl.

The pale yellow pieces decorated with colors reminded some early contemporary experts of old Italian faience. Designs of garlands and scrolls, griffins and dragons, flowers and fruits, add to this effect. Bertha Jaques in *Sketch Book*, June 1906, features a picture of such a pitcher, numbered 18.

A dark blue to green glaze was another popular finish until about 1906. The color seems to have been sprayed onto the pieces. Other pieces were of brown into yellow, yellow into dull green, olive green into rose pink, or dark blue into rose pink.

The underglaze decorations were of many types. Floral patterns were done with freehand brush painting. The flowers were outlined with a thin black line. Often designs seemed to "bleed," which was the result of unintentional glaze flooding. Nearly all Pauline decorations have a "pattern book" quality, although some are drawn with more freedom. Most pieces were made with the yellow-toned glaze and decorated with flowers in muted tones, with everything outlined in black. Some wares had raised leaves or heads that protruded from the sides of the vases in high relief. Another type of ware reminded purchasers in the early 1900s of the majolica ware of the 1880 period. Sponged or brushed gilding was often used on the edges or around the decorations. The gilding was put on over the glaze. A red-brown band that shades from the rim into the base was also popular.

Pauline Pottery was made with two firings. The body clay was first fired to bisque, then decorated, glazed, and fired a second time. Because each piece was decorated by hand, no two are exactly alike, even though some designs were repeated over and over.

### MARKS

The most familiar mark on Pauline Pottery is the crown made from two *P*'s, one of them reversed. The mark was not recorded with the federal copyrights office prior to 1891, but it was probably used before that date. The mark was originally inscribed by hand. It may have been used in Chicago, but so far no records have appeared to prove this. The crown mark appears either with *o*, *p*, or *c* in the center. The words "trade mark" appear with the crown after 1891.

The frustrating aspect of dating by mark is that a piece occasionally appears to confuse the records. The State Historical Society of Wisconsin at Madison owns a bowl with a high-relief band of oak leaves and a matte glaze. It is marked with the printed crown and a shape number 166, but it is not made from Edgerton clay. Some Ohio clay may have been sent to Edgerton, although there is no record that this was done. It may even be an Ohio clay piece from the Chicago period.

Early pieces had the name of the pottery stamped or incised by hand. Later ones were sometimes in blue or green underglaze. There were model numbers (the smaller the number, the older the piece) as well as decora-

*A globular Pauline Pottery vase, 4¼ inches high and 6¼ inches in diameter, white with yellow flowers. (State Historical Society of Wisconsin)*

tors' symbols or initials on some pieces. A few pieces were made with the name Pauline Pottery and a date. One known piece is marked in this manner and dated 1883. A large covered vase at the State Historical Society of Wisconsin and a rose jar with lid at the Neville Public Museum are marked with the crown and the words "trade mark" and "made for M. F. & Co," meaning made for Marshall Field of Chicago.

Some sources have erroneously listed a different crown with the letter *G* in the center. There is no evidence that this was a Pauline Pottery mark.

Artists' signature marks are, in most cases, unidentified. Many of the artists and students were trained at the Chicago Art Institute.

## Paul Revere Pottery

*Boston and Brighton, Massachusetts*

〜

The Paul Revere Pottery was formed for a group of girls working to learn a trade and to keep "occupied." Their pottery was made in several locations in or near Boston from 1906 to 1942.

Edith Guerrier, a librarian in Boston, and her friend Edith Brown suggested in 1906 that members of The Saturday Evening Girls Club make pottery. The club met weekly at the North End Branch of the Boston Public Library. Miss Guerrier and Miss Brown had recently visited a pottery in Switzerland and thought the teenage girls in the club would find the work interesting, cultural, and financially rewarding. The two women studied potting and glazing, and in about a year bought a kiln and hired a pottery chemist from the Merrimac Pottery.

By 1907, Italian and Jewish immigrant girls were being trained in pottery making at their two teachers' Chestnut Hill home and at a summer camp near West Gloucester, Massachusetts. The camp's location was soon found impractical, however, and in 1908 the group moved its operation to a four-story brick house at 18 Hull Street, near the Old North Church where Paul Revere had seen his famous signal lanterns. The house, known as the Library Club House, was financed by Mrs. James J. Storrow, one of the original backers of North End settlement house projects that were designed to provide occupation for the unemployed or idle. The group began using the name Paul Revere for its pottery after the move to Hull Street.

The girls were daughters of immigrant families in the Boston area, and the hope was that the new settlement house project would "keep them off the streets." The Library Club House, sponsored by wealthy Bostonians, offered many activities, including lectures, readings, classes in music and dancing, six glee clubs, and other entertainments. Glee club concerts and theater productions raised money to help support the pottery project.

By 1912, the Paul Revere Pottery was an important activity at the house. Pottery made by The Saturday Evening Girls Club was very popular and sold well. More than two hundred girls worked on the pottery, although only about fifteen to twenty were active at any one given time.

**S.E.G.**

*Incised.*

**P.R.P**

*Incised.*

*Paper label.*

*Paper label.*

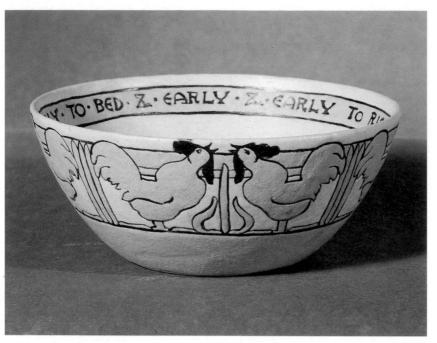

*Incised and painted roosters decorate the outside of this bowl. Note the incised and painted motto on the inside. Yellow, black, and white matte glazes were used. The bowl, 5½ inches in diameter, was made about 1910. On the bottom of the bowl are the marks "1.10," the artist's initials "CG" in a vertical rectangle, part of the original paper label with an "SEG" within a sketch of a bowl, and the price, $2.50. (Collection of the Newark Museum)*

*Pine tree vase. (House Beautiful, 1914)*

*These dishes marked "S.E.G." are all decorated in beige and yellow. The plate is 8½ inches in diameter. (Skinner, Inc.)*

This chrysanthemum vase was offered in an undated catalog as "VCCd vase, 9 in., blue green and cream, $50.00 less 40%." The catalog also states that "any item displayed may be obtained in any of the colors shown in the center color plate." (The catalog also shows some pieces that were pictured in an article about the pottery in 1914; the cover picture of the catalog appeared in a 1922 article.)

This Saturday Evening Girls bowl, 11½ inches in diameter, has white geese outlined in black against a blue and green background. It is signed and dated 1914. (Skinner, Inc.)

Working conditions were excellent. The pottery rooms were decorated with flowers and someone read aloud to the girls while they worked. They had an eight-hour day with a half day off on Saturday and two weeks' paid vacation. The group worked with a potter, a designer, and a kiln operator. New girls sat next to the more experienced so they could learn the trade quickly. Some of the girls planned to earn a living as potters, while others joined the group just to keep busy.

The popularity of the pottery made expansion necessary, and in 1915 the firm built its own building on Nottingham Hill in Brighton, Massachusetts. There is some confusion in the records, but it seems that Storrow still supported the group at this time. Edith Brown was the main designer of the pottery. She added the cost of the clean, attractive factory plus a living wage to the price of the pottery. She felt that many people preferred to buy products made under good working conditions even if the cost was higher.

Brown died in 1932 and the Paul Revere Pottery continued without her, but finally closed in 1942. Mrs. Storrow, the financial angel for the firm, died in 1944.

### PRODUCT

The Paul Revere Pottery made a wide variety of art pottery, but the main lines offered for sale were children's dishes and tiles. Their glazes were solid colors with a matte or glossy finish. Decorations were outlined in black and filled with color. Yellow, green, blue, tan, and a metallic gunmetal

This 9-inch-high vase is glazed in powder blue. It was made before 1916. (Smithsonian Institution)

*Sara Galner decorated this 13-inch bowl in 1913. The daffodil border is incised and painted. The bottom has the painted marks "S.E.G. 7-13" and the artist's initials "S.G." (Skinner, Inc.)*

*The decorative band on this rose ground vase is a landscape. (Skinner, Inc.)*

*The Paul Revere Pottery offered this vase about 1910. It is 5¹¹/₁₆ inches high and has incised and painted decorations of yellow daffodils and green leaves on a blue background. The vase is marked with the initials "AM" (for Albina Mangini?). (Private collection; photograph from The Art Museum, Princeton University, Princeton, New Jersey)*

shade were used. Pale cream lined with green or blue and gunmetal lined with red, blue, yellow, maroon, green, or brown were featured in many of the dishwares. Most pieces were hand-thrown, except for the figural pieces such as inkwells, paperweights, and bookends.

The pottery made childrens' bread and milk sets, consisting of a plate, bowl, and pitcher using chickens, rabbits, nursery rhymes, ducks, roosters, boats, flowers, trees, cats, windmills, and even special-order pieces with the owner's name and birth date or initials as designs. Their flower vases were decorated with large flowers, especially chrysanthemums, iris, nasturtiums, wild roses, and clover. Some pieces were decorated with a high-gloss glaze in dark colors from green to black. All types of bowls were made, from salad bowls to individual open salt dishes. Also in the line were plates, coffee cups, saucers, cream pitchers, sugar bowls, egg cups, platters, milk or water pitchers, mugs, honey jars, salt and peppers, toilet sets for children, flower vases, lamps, desk sets, candlesticks, and paperweights. Full luncheon and dinner sets were sold in stock patterns and to special order. If a piece broke, a replacement could be purchased to match.

Tiles were made in great variety. Some were molded, and most were decorated with designs incised in the wet clay, then colored with soft colors. The most interesting were those that pictured Boston street scenes, Paul Revere's house, the Old South Church, the Schoolmaster's House, the Mather and Eliot houses and others, made to be used on fireplace mantels. Other tile sets showed the three ships of Columbus and there was a thirteen-tile set of the ride of Paul Revere. The tiles were 4 or 5 inches square with matte surfaces.

The factory also made bisque doll heads for a short period during World War I. They were made with socket necks to fit either a bisque doll shoulder or a papier-mâché torso. But even after the heads were fired, the wigs and eyes never arrived from Europe, and no heads were ever completed for sale. Some of these heads were found in 1950 in a river near the old factory.

Pottery pieces were marked with a paper label, "Bowl Shop, S.E.G." and the address, or with a round stamped mark picturing a man on horseback with the words "Paul Revere Pottery." Some pieces had incised initials indicating the decorator.

## Peters and Reed
### Zanesville, Ohio
~

John D. Peters and Adam Reed founded the Peters and Reed Pottery Company in Zanesville, Ohio, in 1898. The two men had been working for Sam Weller at the Weller Pottery and decided to open their own pottery company. They started in an old building that had been used by the Clark Stoneware Company. The building was rented from a bank with a "buy later" option, but Peters and Reed could not raise the money, so Roseville Pottery bought the plant.

Peters and Reed Pottery was incorporated in 1901, however, with Adam Reed as president and J. D. Peters as treasurer, and the firm was established at a new location in South Zanesville. There the partners made flowerpots because there was a ready market. The Weller factory had stopped making flowerpots about 1897 when that firm began to concentrate on art pottery. After a short while, Peters and Reed added cuspidors and jardinieres with painted decorations to its lines. About 1903, they added cooking ware.

During these early years, Peters and Reed apparently made some pieces of dark brown glazed artware decorated with light-colored sprigging. This early artware is believed to be the work of Reed and Albert Radford, who lived in Zanesville at the time.

To improve the quality of their pottery, Peters and Reed asked Frank Ferrel, one of the designers at Weller, to sell them some

*Hand-painted jardiniere by Peters and Reed Pottery Company as shown in* Pottery and Glass, *June 1909.*

*A selection of pieces from an undated Peters and Reed Pottery Company catalog, circa 1910. (Left to right)* Moss Aztec, Pereco Ware, *and* Chromal Ware. (Courtesy of Ohio Historical Society Library)

*Three Peters and Reed vases:* (left) *light green wreath appliqué on dark green ground, 9 inches high, 4 inches wide;* (center) *red and green cherry sprig on dark brown ground, 9 inches high, 4 inches wide;* (right) *yellow lion's head and red and green appliqué on dark brown ground, 14 inches high, 8 inches wide.*

ideas. In 1905, after he left Weller and before he started working at the J. B. Owens Pottery, Ferrel did some designing for Peters and Reed, later becoming a full-time salesman and designer for them. In 1918, Ferrel went to work for Roseville Pottery.

Moss Aztec was the most famous line that Ferrel designed for Peters and Reed. Ferrel's design for the line had been rejected by Weller, but Peters and Reed began producing it sometime between 1905 and 1912. The pottery had a red clay body that was glazed and then dipped in a mixture of paraffin and coal oil, which gave the piece a green cast. The 1921 catalog describes it as having "the quiet effect of the rich red brown tones of the Historic Aztec Indians coupled with the apparent mossy deposit of nature." Peters and Reed became Zane Pottery in 1921, and after 1926 the pieces were made of white clay rather than red.

The firm made many other lines that also sold well. The kitchen wares started in 1903 were discontinued about 1906. The description in the catalog of some of the wares reads:

*Chromal.* The Chromal ware resembles the Landsun line with the exception that beautiful scenic effects are portrayed in a very effective manner.

*Landsun.* The Landsun ware is finished in blended effects of different colors, which makes many very beautiful pieces, each piece being different.

*Montene.* The Montene ware is made in two decorations. The rich copper bronze iridescent and the green variegated semi-matte finish.

*Pereco.* The Pereco ware has a semi-matte finish, in plain green, orange, and blue colors, which harmonize with any scheme of decorations.

*Persian.* The Persian ware is made in blue and brown, plain semi-matte finish.

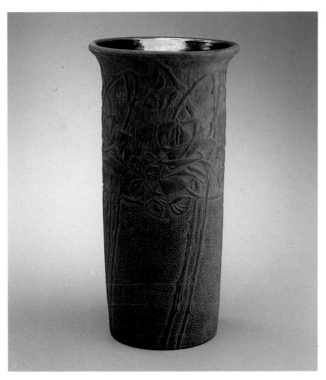

A "sewer tile" vase from the Moss Aztec line is brick red with green glaze and raised roses as decoration. The piece is 12 inches high. Although the bottom is unmarked, the name "Ferrell" is part of the design on the front of the vase. (Private collection)

Light green sprig appliqués decorate this 5½-inch vase by Peters and Reed. (Private collection)

After Peters retired in 1920, Adam Reed and Harry S. McClelland, then the company secretary, bought the plant. The following year, they changed the company's name to the Zane Pottery Company. See Zane Pottery.

## Pewabic Pottery
### Detroit, Michigan

Many of the famous American art potteries, such as the Pewabic Pottery of Detroit, Michigan, were started by talented women. Pewabic Pottery was founded by Mary Chase Perry (Stratton). She was born in Hancock, Michigan, in 1868. After her father was killed (murdered by a man who mistook him for someone else), her mother moved the family to Ann Arbor, Michigan, and then to Detroit.

Miss Perry went to art school in Cincinnati and New York, where she worked in clay sculpture and china painting. In 1903 she decided to join her next-door neighbor, Horace James Caulkins, in making pottery. Horace Caulkins was in the dental supply business and had developed a kiln for making dental enamel. It was in this kiln that their tiles and vases were fired. Their first shop was built in a coach house at the back of a mansion located at John R. and Alfred streets in Detroit. Pewabic was the Indian name for a nearby river

Impressed, 1906–1910; may have been used earlier.

PEWABIC

Paper label, 1906–1910.

PEWABIC

Inked rubber stamp, used as early as 1910.

Impressed "curved mark," used with or without maple leaves, 1906–1913.

Impressed "circular mark,"
1909–1918.

Impressed, 1910–1967. Most
common Pewabic mark; notice shape
of C and O.

Paper labels, 1908–1967.

Impressed "medallion mark," used
after 1930.

The initials "WBS" for William
B. Stratton were sometimes added
to the marks on pieces he worked on
between 1920 and 1938.

and it was only after many years that Miss Perry learned that the word meant "copper color in clay."

Perry stated in an article in the *American Ceramic Society Bulletin* in 1946 that at first she had no training and just experimented with the glazes. The first items made at the pottery were bowls and jars characterized by a dark green matte glaze. These were ordered by a Chicago dealer named Burleigh for $1,000. Perry also sold an architect some 3-by-6-inch tiles with rounded edges and uneven surfaces. She also made small square jars with covers in a tile machine using the clay dust method. The machine was operated by hand. Varying shrinkages made the fit of the covers an unsure thing and it was often hard to find the right lid for a jar. The jars were made with a shiny dark blue glaze, filled with cosmetics, then sent to South America.

By 1904 Mary Chase Perry was making vases with brown, buff, and yellow matte glaze. In 1907 a new pottery was built, designed as an English-type studio and laboratory building. She and Caulkins bought a miniature Crossley clay outfit from the Chicago Fair and set it up in the basement. Three years later, they had a full-size blunger, filter press, and pug mill. Perry designed and glazed pieces and hired others to throw the pots. The pottery's famous Persian or Egyptian blue glaze was used by 1911. Early pieces were sometimes decorated with applied modeled leaf forms. Orange, yellow, brown, blue, purple, and white glazes, crystalline glazes, heavy volcanic-type glazes, and lusters were used.

Two marked Pewabic pieces with hand-made metal covers. The bowl on the left is 3 inches high by 7 inches in diameter; the pewter cover has an ivory handle and is marked "Potter Studio." (June Greenwald Antiques) The dish on the right is 4½ inches high by 6½ inches in diameter; its brass cover is marked "Potter & Mellen." (Private collection). The Potter Studio (1909–1929) of Cleveland, Ohio became Potter & Mellen in 1933. The company often made special covers for antique pottery, porcelain, and art pottery bowls.

*This 1925 Pewabic vase is 8⁵/₁₆ inches high. (From the collections of Henry Ford Museum & Greenfield Village)*

*A 1930 Pewabic vase, height 4⁹/₁₆ inches. (From the collections of Henry Ford Museum & Greenfield Village)*

Pewabic Pottery gained fame throughout the world, especially for its tiles. The company produced building friezes and panels of colored mosaic with matte glaze for Ford buildings in Detroit, New York City, Omaha, and San Francisco. It made tiles for St. Paul's Cathedral in Detroit, and floors and decorations for churches in Pittsburgh, Evanston, St. Paul, Philadelphia, and Washington, D.C. An irregular tesserae ceiling was created for the Oberlin College Art Gallery in Ohio; fountains, alcoves, and stair risers for the Detroit Institute of Art; and faience tiles and trim for the Union Guardian Building in Detroit. The pottery also made elaborate bathroom, fireplace, and floor tiles, and fountains, friezes, and entrance doorways for shops, church altars, and even swimming pools. The architectural features and tiles made by Miss Perry were always specially designed to order; architects knew her designs would be suitable.

*This 10½-inch vase with modeled decorations of tulips and leaves is covered with a green matte glaze. Made by Mary Chase Perry about 1903–1905, it is marked with the impressed "Pewabic" in an arc surmounted by five maple leaves. (Private collection; photograph from The Art Museum, Princeton University, Princeton, New Jersey)*

*Bas-relief of a lunette in the Della Robbia manner made for the Church of the Most Holy Redeemer, Detroit, Michigan. (The American Magazine of Art, January 1926)*

This fountain can still be seen at Stan Hywet Hall, Akron, Ohio. It was ordered from the Pewabic Pottery of Detroit on August 4, 1915: "Frank Seiberling, Akron, Ohio, porch floor and fountain at about $1,350.00." The design was based on the poem "Well of St. Keyne," by Robert Southey (1774–1843). The fountain was designed by Pewabic's founder, Mary Chase Perry, and records still exist to show her notes and thoughts. It is believed that Ms. Perry also designed the floor tiling for the Powder Room and the Della Robbia Room, and decorative tiles for some of the fireplaces in the house. (Stan Hywet Hall and Gardens)

Detail of the fountain above. (Stan Hywet Hall and Gardens)

*Gold iridescent glaze over blue glaze decorates this 18¾-inch vase made about 1910–1912. (The Detroit Institute of Arts, Detroit, Michigan, gift of Charles L. Freer)*

*Pewabic tile in the wall decoration of the shrine of the Immaculate Conception, Washington, D.C. (The American Magazine of Art, January 1926)*

*Veined leaves decorate this green matte vase. The 12½-inch piece has the early Pewabic maple leaf mark. (David Rago Arts & Crafts Gallery)*

Mary Perry married William Buck Stratton in 1918. She continued her work at the pottery and decorated her own home with tiles. Horace Caulkins died in 1923 and Mrs. Stratton ran the Pewabic Pottery alone. Several of the most important orders for tile for building interiors came after 1923. The Depression affected the pottery and in 1931 orders were scarce, but through Mrs. Stratton's efforts the pottery continued. The Strattons moved from their large home to a small one in 1937 and a year later Mr. Stratton died in a streetcar accident.

Ira Peters, Stratton's secretary, and his wife, Ella, worked with Mary Stratton at the pottery until Mrs. Stratton's death in 1961 at age ninety-three. In their home studio, Ira and Ella Peters continued making a similar ware using Pewabic glazes until 1971. Their pieces are marked with a circle, the letters "PP," and the word "Detroit." The mark is the old Pewabic mark with the factory name removed.

The Pewabic Pottery itself became the property of Michigan State University about 1966 and reopened in 1968 as an adult ceramic center, museum, studio, and school. The Pewabic Society, a nonprofit organization, was founded in 1981 to resume the production of tiles and to continue the pottery's educational programs.

### PRODUCT

About 1903, Mary Perry developed an iridescent glaze that was one of the most famous glazes used by the Pewabic Pottery. It was still being used when she died.

The pottery has a hard white body covered with heavy opaque enamels of many colors. The clay was fired at a high temperature and is so hard, the *American Pottery Gazette* claimed in 1907, that it is "neither earthenware nor

*Pewabic tile, 6¹/₁₆ inches square, dated 1930. (From the collections of Henry Ford Museum & Greenfield Village)*

Porcelain.'' It was made of clay from Florida, Michigan, North Carolina, Virginia, and England. Ivory, brown, blue, and gray glazes were used, usually in matte finish. Other pieces were green, purple, yellow, or white. On some pieces light-colored crystalline spots can be found. Some examples have a heavy glaze that trickled down the side of the vase. Other early wares were decorated with relief forms of leaves and plants, using a dull matte glaze.

In the early days of the Pewabic Pottery when these glazes were first being used, Miss Perry and Mr. Caulkins employed a man to throw the forms on a wheel and an errand boy who did much of the other routine work. Perry was the artist and did all of the high-relief decorations and designs.

She continued experimenting with glazes through the years and kept some of the best pieces for collector Charles Lang Freer. Many of these examples were eventually given to museums. Her famed blue jar in the Peacock Room of the Freer Gallery in Washington, D.C., was one of these special pieces.

Although vases were made through all the years of the pottery, the only dishes produced were a set for Teachers College at Columbia University in

New York. The Pewabic Pottery made sixty dozen plates, cups, and saucers, with a broad blue band to signify the New Jersey Palisades bluffs across the Hudson River from the college and a green wavy line below to symbolize the river.

Pewabic mosaics were made in a unique manner. According to *American Magazine*, January 1926:

> The Pewabic mosaic is made with a clay body, with or without sand or grog, and comes out of the kiln in long strips, in an unglazed, bright glazed and an iridescent glazed state. The long strips, about three-eighths of an inch wide, are broken into little squares which are pasted face up (an improvement on the old method of pasting them face down) on the design, and are arranged and rearranged by the artist until the desired color effect is obtained. When the design is perfected, a paper is pasted on the face, the first paper sponged off and the sheet pressed into cement.

### MARKS

Paper labels and impressed marks were used on the pottery. Some of the paper labels have the name of the pottery and a number. The meaning of the numbers is not yet determined but they do not seem to refer to shape or glaze.

*A Pewabic "Crocus" vase made about 1900 is 3⁵/₁₆ inches high. (From the collections of Henry Ford Museum & Greenfield Village)*

## Pisgah Forest Pottery
### Pisgah Forest, North Carolina

Walter Benjamin Stephen was born in Clinton, Iowa, on October 3, 1876. His family moved to Chadron, Nebraska, when he was ten. Both of his parents were artistic; his father was a stonecutter and his mother an artist. After ten years in Nebraska, the family moved to western Tennessee. There Walter and his father, Andrew, were stonemasons.

In 1901, when they dug a new well, the Stephens found a clay that was an unusual color. Walter and his mother made boxes and figures from the clay. The family built a kiln and a kick wheel and Walter and his mother experimented with pottery making.

They called their firm the Nonconnah Pottery. Mrs. Stephen decorated the pieces with raised designs of light clay. Her decorations included covered wagons, Indians, buffalo hunts, and other early American scenes.

Walter Stephen's parents died in 1910, and by the summer of 1913 he moved near the foot of Mount Pisgah in North Carolina. C. P. Ryman became his partner and the two men built a shop and kiln. They dissolved the partnership in 1916.

Stephen began to experiment with pottery again in 1920 and by 1926 he had founded Pisgah Forest Pottery, which housed equipment to make his fire-vitrified ware. The company name was changed to Stephen Pottery for a few years in the 1940s. Walter Stephen died in 1961, but the Pisgah Forest Pottery continued in

*Raised.*

*Raised.*

*Raised.*

*Raised.*

*Raised.*

*Raised.*

*Raised,
after 1961.*

*Raised.*

*Raised.*

*Raised.*

This mottled vase, 6½ inches in diameter, has green and maroon specks in the glaze. The impressed mark shows the man at the potter's wheel and "Pisgah, 1937." (Private collection)

A 5½-inch-high pitcher with relief decoration. The piece has the Pisgah Forest potter at the wheel mark and is also signed in ink "W.B. Stephen." (Private collection)

Pisgah Forest vases. The vase on the left is 4 inches high and is dated 1934. It bears the potter at the wheel mark and is signed "W. Stephen." The handled vase on the right is 6 inches high and also has the potter at the wheel mark. It is dated 1939. (Private collection)

One of Stephen's favorite designs was the covered wagon. It appears on this 14½-inch-high vase. (Smithsonian Institution)

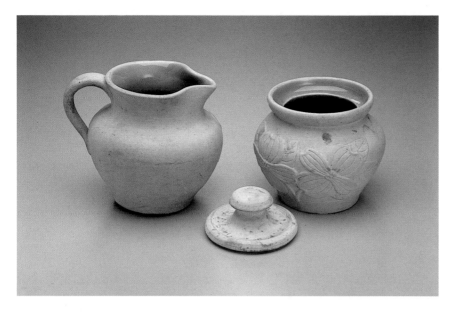

A *creamer and covered sugar bowl by Pisgah Forest, both 3½ inches tall and decorated on one side with flowers in relief. They have a glazed interior and an unglazed exterior. Both pieces are marked with the potter at the wheel mark. (Private collection)*

business under the direction of J. Thomas Case and Grady G. Ledbetter. The firm is open during the summer and still makes pottery. The salesroom in Arden, North Carolina, is open year-round.

### PRODUCT

The early pieces made by Walter Stephen were dark glazed pots with cameolike decorations. Dark green, light blue, and later bronze or black were used as background glazes for the white decorations. One type of Pisgah Forest Pottery was made with a crystalline glaze in ivory, silver, or other shades. The general line of pottery was glazed turquoise or wine, the most popular colors, or ivory, pink, green, yellow, or brown. Black was used in the early 1950s.

The pottery made vases, teapots, jugs, candlesticks, tea sets, mugs, bowls, and even miniature cream and sugar sets.

Early pieces were marked "Stephen" or "W.B. Stephen." After 1926, the Pisgah pieces were marked "Pisgah Forest." Some were marked with the year, date, and the picture of a potter at his wheel. All of the marks were raised on the pieces.

(A source of confusion for the pottery collector may be other potters who worked in the Pisgah Mountain area. O. L. Bachelder's Omar Khayyam Pottery made pottery during the same years and in the same area.)

An *oversized cup and saucer marked with the Pisgah Forest potter at the wheel mark and the year 1940. The cup is 2½ inches high and 5 inches in diameter; the saucer measures 6¾ inches in diameter. (Private collection)*

## Poillon Pottery
### *Woodbridge, New Jersey*
~

The Poillon Pottery was founded in Woodbridge, New Jersey, about 1904. Clara L. Poillon and H. A. Poillon ran the pottery, which made a variety of ware similar to majolica, with blue, green, or yellow glazes. Gold luster, orange luster, and matte glazes were also used. Pottery garden tubs were made in red or cream terra-cotta with

*Raised figures of men seated at a table decorate this Poillon Pottery vase. The piece is 12½ inches high. It has a yellowish brown–crackled glaze. (Smithsonian Institution)*

**Losanti**

*Mark on porcelain.*

*Mark used by Mary Louise McLaughlin.*

*Laura A. Fry made this pitcher in 1881 while with the Cincinnati Pottery Club. The pitcher has blue decorations and is incised with the cipher "LAF, 1881, Cin. Pottery Club." (Cincinnati Art Museum, gift of the Women's Art Museum Association)*

bold relief carvings. The firm also produced breakfast and luncheon sets, lamps, and vases.

The Poillon Pottery exhibited pieces at the Art Palace of the St. Louis Exposition in 1904. They showed a vase by Joseph Insco and a jardiniere by T. H. Pond.

## Pottery Club of Cincinnati
### Cincinnati, Ohio

The birth of art pottery in America probably took place in Cincinnati, Ohio, at a ladies' china-painting meeting in 1874. Benn Pitman of the Cincinnati School of Design started a class for women. His school did not include china painting, so he hired Marie Eggers as a teacher and convened a class in his office. The original class members were Jane Porter Hart Dodd (Mrs. William), Minerva Engart Dominick (Mrs. George), Henrietta D. Leonard (Mrs. E. G.), Charlotte Keenan, Florence Leonard, Clara Chipman Newton, Georgie Woollard, and Mary Louise McLaughlin. Eventually, more than twenty-four women were involved in the class, including Maria Longworth Nichols and Clara Fletcher.

The painting was an overglaze decoration on porcelain. Edwin Griffith began his own class in overglaze painting in 1877. He had a room with an oven to fire the work in a building on Fifth and Race streets. That same year, Mary Louise McLaughlin published a book about china painting on porcelain. She also began to make pottery similar to some she had seen at the Centennial Exhibition of 1876 in Philadelphia. The French pottery she saw was made by artists at the Haviland factory as one-of-a-kind pieces. McLaughlin had some success and made a few pieces in 1877. She worked at the firm of P. L. Coultry and Co., whose staff helped her, as did Joseph Bailey and his son Joseph of the Dallas Pottery Co.

McLaughlin obtained some colored glazes from Paris but also tried some of the glazes from Coultry and Co. Her clay came from Ohio. She eventually made some pottery of a quality shown at the Paris Exposition of 1878. A deep blue–colored faience vase with underglaze decoration was given an honorable mention, although it has been said that the vase earned a higher award before the judges learned the maker was a woman.

Encouraged by her success, McLaughlin founded the Pottery Club of Cincinnati in 1879. Composed of fifteen women, the club later increased its membership to twenty-five. Two kilns were built at the Frederick Dallas Pottery in 1879. The cost of building the kilns and other expenses were paid by McLaughlin and Maria Longworth Nichols. Nichols was not a member of the Pottery Club, but she later became the founder of the Rookwood factory (see Rookwood Pottery). It was the work of the club that led to the founding of many of the other art pottery factories in the Cincinnati area.

The members of the Pottery Club often signed their names or initials to their work. The fifteen original members were McLaughlin, Clara Chipman Newton, Alice B. Holabird, Henrietta D. Leonard (Mrs. E. G.), Florence Leonard Kebler (Mrs. Charles A.), Minerva Engart Dominick (Mrs. George), Abbie Taylor Field (Mrs. Walter), Florence Carlisle, Agnes Pitman, Fannie M. Banks, L. M. Merriam (Mrs. Andrew B.), Mary Rhodes Ellis (Mrs. Frank R.), Mary Virginia Keenan, Clara Fletcher, and one vacancy believed to have been for Mrs. Nichols, whose invitation to the club was apparently lost before she received it. Honorary members included Laura A. Fry, Caroline A. Lord, and Elizabeth Nourse. Other women who exhibited Cincinnati art pottery of the same type and either worked in the same building or may have been later members of the club were Mrs. W. P. Hulbert, Mrs. C. A. Plimpton, Adelaide Nourse, Mrs. D. Meredith, Mrs. William Dodd, and K. deGolter.

*Mrs. Cordelia A. Plimpton made this 16½-inch vase in 1881 while a member of the Cincinnati Pottery Club. Her husband designed the Arabian scene. The design was made by inlaying colored clays into the body of the piece. The clays in tones of cream, brown, and terra-cotta came from Ohio; the black clay, from Indiana. (Cincinnati Art Museum, gift of the Women's Art Museum Association)*

Each of the artists worked in a unique style. Pottery pieces by members of the Pottery Club of Cincinnati are usually without any mark to indicate their group affiliation. All the pieces were made of either red, yellow, or cream-colored Ohio clay. Incised work, relief modeling, and glaze designs were used in all colors, including gold. The slip, a mixture of fine clay and water, was applied with a brush to a damp clay pot. This was a very different method from that used in France, although the effect was similar. The use of red clay by these women was not significant at first, since the clay was completely covered with slip. (Rookwood artists went back to the red clay and left it exposed, thus establishing the brown-red color of Ohio art pottery.) After the club's eviction in 1883 from the studio it had rented at the Rookwood Pottery since 1881, member-artists were limited to using only overglaze decoration. The club disbanded in 1890 for lack of money.

McLaughlin, an artist of many interests, decided to try to develop a true porcelain from Ohio clay. She built a kiln on her suburban Cincinnati property and began experimenting despite her neighbors' complaints about the smoke. The clay came from the Ohio River Valley near the Kentucky state line. She tried many different clay bodies before making the first pieces of what she called "Losanti" ware in 1900. (L'Osantiville was an early name for Cincinnati.) Losanti is not an art pottery, but a true porcelain. It was marked with the name Losanti or the initials "L Mᶜ L." The porcelain was decorated with relief carving and slip painting under the glaze. Some pieces were made with the colored clay inlay that was known as "grain of rice." The ware had a cutout space that was filled with a translucent glaze. Losanti ware was discontinued in 1906.

McLaughlin continued her varied interests. She did wood carving, portrait painting, landscape painting, lace making, embroidery, and weaving, and she made a variety of art jewelry of metal and stones. She died in 1939.

*The 10¼-inch-high pilgrim jar is decorated with painted underglaze decorations of the "French style." The flowers are in shades of pink, black, and gray. It was made by Mary Louise McLaughlin about 1877. (Cincinnati Art Museum, gift of the Women's Art Museum Association)*

*This Radford Pottery vase with gray and white raised decorations is 7 inches high. A profile of Abraham Lincoln appears on one side and an eagle on the other. The vase is unmarked except for the number 12 incised on the bottom. (Private collection)*

## A. Radford Pottery
### Tiffin and Zanesville, Ohio and Clarksburg, West Virginia

Albert Radford was born in Staffordshire, England, in 1862. He was one of a family of potters dating back generations. Some of the Radford family worked at the Wedgwood factory in England, but it is uncertain whether Albert ever worked there or at any other English pottery.

Radford moved to the United States in 1885 and took a job at the Haynes Pottery Company in Baltimore, Maryland. There he met and married Ellen Hackney, another employee of the pottery. A year later, the couple moved to Trenton, New Jersey, where Albert worked for the Eagle Pottery Company. While there, he received an award for his work from the Pennsylvania Museum and School of Industrial Art.

About 1890 Radford and his family moved to Broadway, Virginia, where he started his own firm, A. Radford Pottery Company. His first pieces came from the kiln in 1891, but the records do not reveal what type of pottery was made at this plant.

The Radfords moved to Tiffin, Ohio, about 1893 and Albert began working at the Sanitary Pottery of Tiffin. At the same time, he built a kiln on his own property where he made Radford Tiffin jasperware, which resembled Wedgwood jasperware. The Sanitary Pottery of Tiffin closed about 1898 and Radford moved to Zanesville, Ohio.

The city directory of Zanesville first lists Albert Radford in 1901. Radford worked as a modeler at the S. A. Weller Pottery in Zanesville until he left to go to work as the general manager of the Zanesville Art Pottery. When the Zanesville Art Pottery plant was destroyed by fire in 1901, Radford moved on to the J. B. Owens Pottery as superintendent and modeler. He was probably the originator of the Owens Pottery's Wedgwood Jasper line.

In 1903 Radford again founded his own firm, A. Radford Pottery Company of Zanesville, Ohio. According to Fred W. Radford, Albert Radford's grandson, Albert never worked at this pottery; the work was done by Albert's father, Edward Thomas Radford. The firm started early in 1903 and by August was sold to the Arc-en-Ciel Pottery. It is unclear whether the sale had been planned or the Radford Pottery was forced to sell. A trustee handled the sale.

The A. Radford Pottery made Zanesville jasperware. A piece of glazed pottery marked "A. Radford" has been located, but it may

RUKO

*Impressed.*

[THERA]

*Incised.*

RADFORD
JASPER

*Impressed.*

**A. RADFORD**
        **POTTERY CO.**                **RADURA**
     *Impressed.*                    *Impressed.*

have been a test piece and not part of the commercial production.

In 1904 Albert Radford left Zanesville for Clarksburg, West Virginia, where he reestablished his pottery. This firm, also called A. Radford Pottery Company, made the Ruko, Radura, and Thera pottery lines. Radford died suddenly of a heart attack in August 1904. The pottery remained in business after his death until 1912. Albert Haubrich, who had worked for the Weller and Owens potteries, was manager of the decorating department.

### PRODUCT

The first Radford product was the Radford Tiffin jasperware made about 1893. The body of the ware was made from English china clay, English ball clay, silica, barium, and other chemicals. Color was added to the clay. Tiffin jasperware was made in royal blue, light blue, olive green, and two shades of gray. The body of the ware was fine-grained and was either cast or turned. Radford modeled the cameos by hand. A mold was made of clay and plaster and the cameos were cast and put on the jasperware body. Some of the cameos were apparently molded from Wedgwood cameos, but most were designed by Radford.

Tiffin jasperware was sometimes impressed "Radford Jasper" with die-cut letters. Radford made bonbon dishes, jewel boxes, nut bowls, flowerpots, cracker jars, card receivers, plaques, comb trays, pitchers, pin trays, fern dishes, butter dishes, cheese covers, cookie jars, sugar bowls and creamers, and ring stands of jasperware. All of these items were listed in the Tiffin Pottery price list.

Zanesville jasperware was made in 1903 at the plant that became the Arc-en-Ciel Pottery. It was made from ball clay, feldspar, and silica and required less heat in the firing than the Tiffin jasperware. Most of the cameos were molded with the vase. The cameo was then painted with solid-colored slip. A few pieces were made with separately cast cameos. These were probably made by Albert's father, Edward Thomas Radford.

*Albert Radford's letterhead.*

*Each of these Radford Pottery vases is 9 inches high and has a classical relief design on the front and back. Both are marked only with the incised number 22. (Private collection)*

Some of these pieces were painted inside with slip to give the finished piece a different interior finish, called "bark" or "orange peel."

Zanesville jasperware was made in royal blue, light blue, olive green, and two shades of gray, and was sometimes trimmed with pink or light yellow-brown. The jasperware was marked with an incised number.

Other wares were made at the Zanesville pottery, possibly as experiments to determine the production for the Clarksburg plant. Listed in the ledgers of 1903 are jasperware, glazed jardinieres, etched vases, blended vases printed with black figures, and light green pitchers dipped in enamel.

The Clarksburg factory made several different lines under the direction of Albert Radford. One was Ruko, an art pottery similar to Weller's Louwelsa line. The name Ruko is impressed on the base of most pieces. Another, Radura, was a matte-glazed line in green, dark blue, black, light blue, red, pink, yellow, brown, lilac, light lavender, or tan. The glaze was developed by Radford's son, Albert E. Radford. Thera was another of the lines from the Clarksburg plant. It too has a matte glaze, similar to Lonhuda. One reference lists Velvety Art Ware as a product—a colored ware with hand-painted designs. Records show it was made in pink, green, purple, light blue, and yellow-green.

In 1971, Fred Radford, grandson of Albert Radford, reproduced some of the Zanesville jasperware. He used the original molds and original clay formulas and made six different vases. All of these pieces are marked as reproductions, dated, and numbered.

# Redlands
## *Redlands, California*
~

*Relief tadpole mark.*

Wesley H. Trippett, a self-taught potter, worked in Redlands, California, from about 1902 to 1908. His pottery was made from local clay naturally colored from cream to red. He left many pieces unglazed. Trippett's work included vases, covered jars, bowls, bonbon dishes, plaques, and tiles. Some were plain, while others were decorated with relief-carved designs picturing lizards, rabbits, toads, crabs, and frogs.

Pieces are marked with a circle enclosing a tadpolelike figure. Around the edge of the circle are the words "Redlands Pottery."

# Red Wing
### Red Wing, Minnesota

The Red Wing Stoneware Company was started in 1878 in Red Wing, Minnesota. The company went through cycles of competition and mergers with other potteries in the area, and by the 1920s the resulting Red Wing Union Stoneware Company began making pottery. At first the firm made pottery flowerpots and vases decorated with cattails, leaves, flowers, and cranes. The pieces had a green stain over a tan background.

As sales climbed, the firm expanded its art pottery line and made ashtrays, cookie jars, jardinieres, mugs, candlesticks, trays, bowls, and other items. From about 1930 to 1938 or 1939, Red Wing made pottery for George Rumrill, who sold the pieces as Rum Rill pottery.

The firm began making dinnerware during the 1930s. In 1936 its name was changed from Red Wing Union Stoneware Company to Red Wing Potteries, Inc. Red Wing dinnerware was made using imported clays from several other states. Local clays had been suitable for stoneware, but they were too impure for dinnerware.

Red Wing Potteries closed in 1967. One cause was labor trouble, but the many imported dinnerwares had usurped a great share of Red Wing's business.

*Other marks using the words "Red Wing" were used by the pottery.*

*Stamped, black ink.*

*Stamped, black ink.*

*Incised.*

*Impressed, used after 1936.*

*Silver paper label, used after 1936.*

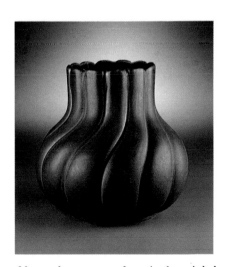

*A Red Wing paper label used after 1936.*

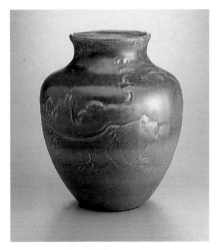

An olive green glaze with yellow highlights covers the raised designs of lions and foliage on this 8-inch-high vase, which bears a stamped mark, "Red Wing, Union So———." (*Private collection*)

This 12-inch glossy-glazed vase is marked "RumRill 166" in a circular ink stamp. The number 166 is also incised on the bottom of the piece. (*Private collection*)

Matte glaze covers the raised, swirled ribbing of this Rum Rill vase. The piece is incised with a handwritten mark, "RumRill 451." (*Private collection*)

# Rhead Pottery

*Santa Barbara, California*

Frederick Hürten Rhead was an important part of the American art pottery industry. Born in England in 1880, he was the son of Frederick Alfred Rhead, who was well known in the ceramics industry. Frederick Hürten Rhead worked with his father before moving to the United States in 1902.

In America, Rhead worked at the Vance/Avon Faience Pottery with William Jervis (1902–1903), the Weller Pottery (1904), Roseville Pottery (1904–1908), Jervis Pottery (1908–1909), University City Pottery (1909–1911), and Arequipa Pottery (1911–1913). From Arequipa in San Francisco, Rhead moved to Santa Barbara, where he set up his own studio pottery. At first it was known as the Pottery of Camarata, but it was incorporated as Rhead Pottery in 1914.

*Impressed.*

*Impressed.*

*A Rhead Pottery jardiniere, 8³/₄ inches high by 10³/₄ inches in diameter, is marked on the bottom with the potter at the wheel mark and the number 567. (Photograph by Robert Lowry, from the Erie Art Museum, Erie, Pennsylvania)*

Although he was a talented potter, Rhead was a poor business-man and his pottery closed in 1917. Rhead then went to work as director of research for the American Encaustic Tiling Company. In 1927, he went to Homer Laughlin China Company. Perhaps his best known design was Fiesta dinnerware. He died in 1942.

## PRODUCT

Pieces were made of clay from several sites in California. Many designs were Egyptian-inspired, and decorations were incised and inlaid. The favored glazes used by Rhead were high-gloss "Mirror Black" and a matte black glaze called "Elephant's Breath." He also used some new glazes, including a metallic brown and white.

Rhead had studied ceramics in England and also had the opportunity to examine many pieces of Ming and Ch'ien Lung ceramics, part of a collection that belonged to the owner of the Santa Barbara store where some of Rhead's works were sold. The oriental influence was obvious in the shapes of Rhead's pieces. But during his long career in the pottery industry, Rhead's work included many types of designs. He used Egyptian, Art Nouveau, Doulton, and other sources for ideas. He also reworked some of his own designs from other factories.

Rhead made vases, tiles, ceramic lighting fixtures, bowls, and some pieces of dinnerware, including creamers and sugars and plates. He hired an Italian potter to throw the large pieces, an Englishwoman to throw the small pieces, and young girls to decorate the small ones. He designed the pieces and determined the glazes. He finished many of the pieces himself, sometimes with the help of his wife, Agnes, or Lois Whitcomb (who in 1917 became the second Mrs. Rhead) or some of the high school girls he hired. Pieces were marked with an impressed mark showing a potter at the wheel and often the words "Rhead Pottery, Santa Barbara." He also used a paper label.

# Robineau Pottery
## *Syracuse, New York*

Adelaide Alsop Robineau was a major influence in the American art pottery movement. She was born in Middletown, Connecticut, and as a girl became interested in china painting. She attended St. Mary's Hall, a school in Faribault, Minnesota, and later taught there until about 1899, when she left to study painting under William Merritt Chase in New York City.

While in New York, Adelaide Alsop met and married Samuel Edouard Robineau, who was also interested in ceramics. With George H. Clark, they bought the magazine *China Decorator*, publishing it in 1900 under the name *Keramic Studio*. The Robineaus studied the work and writing of Taxile Doat, the French ceramicist who was making high-fire porcelains. They translated his French manuscript for *Keramic Studio*. In 1905 the series of Doat articles was compiled into a book, *Grand Feu Ceramics*.

During the early 1900s, Mrs. Robineau began to experiment

*Incised.*

*Incised.*

*The turquoise blue Robineau vase with crackled glaze is 7³⁄₈ by 3³⁄₄ inches. The other vase has a crystalline glaze. (David Rago Arts & Crafts Gallery)*

**ROBLIN**

*Impressed.*

**ROBLIN**

*Impressed.*

with porcelains made from American clay. She also developed matte and crystalline glazes. Colors ranged from light brown to blue, green, and yellow. Some pieces were carved and pierced with intricate designs. She threw all of her own work. She worked with Professor Charles Binns at Alfred University in New York State during the summer of 1903, and in 1904 she displayed some of her porcelains at the Louisiana Purchase Exposition in St. Louis, Missouri.

Mrs. Robineau made many decorative porcelain vases and even produced doorknobs from 1905 to 1910. The doorknobs were colored with some of the earlier glazes, plus dark blue, dark green, red, white, and black. She also tried several other types of ceramics, including eggshell porcelain and a type of stoneware.

From 1909 to 1911, Mrs. Robineau worked at the University City Pottery in Missouri. When it closed, she returned to her home in Syracuse, New York, and started the Four Winds Summer School, offering classes in pottery making, china painting, and other skills. She continued to make pottery even after Four Winds closed in 1914. By 1920 Mrs. Robineau was on the staff at Syracuse University and continued to work on the campus until she retired in 1928.

## Roblin Pottery
### San Francisco, California

While visiting friends in Cincinnati in the late 1890s, Linna Irelan saw the work of the Cincinnati Pottery Club and thought that a similar project would be worthwhile for some women in San Francisco, her hometown. At first she could not find anyone to help her establish a pottery club, but around 1898 Alexander W. Robertson (see Dedham Pottery) joined her in forming the A. W. Roblin Pottery. The name was a combination of Robertson and Linna.

One type of Roblin Pottery was a faience with glazes of green, tan, dull blue, or gray. The pieces resembled the works of the Chelsea Keramic Co. of Massachusetts. Another type was made of red clay that was found in Monterey County, California. The pieces were fired once and sometimes decorated with white slip in engobe style. The finish was satin. Decorations were usually animal shapes, such as lizards, frogs, horned toads, and birds, or flowers, mushrooms, and toadstools.

Robertson threw all of the pieces on a wheel. Irelan decorated the pieces without the use of molds. She used only wooden tools to do the modeling, relief, and incised work. Incised pieces were often covered with a transparent colored glaze. All the clay and glaze material came from California.

The Roblin Pottery was almost completely destroyed in the San Francisco earthquake of 1906, and went out of business in April of that year. Mrs. Irelan continued working as an artist in leather. Robertson continued as a potter in California, working for Halcyon

*(Above left) Roblin vase, 2½ inches high. (Above right) Matte glaze and somber colors were often used on Roblin pottery. This vase is only 2½ inches high. (Smithsonian Institution)*

Art Pottery (1910–1912) and Alberhill Pottery (1912–1914).

Robertson's son, Fred H. Robertson, worked at Roblin in 1903, then at The Los Angeles Pressed Brick Company, and later at Claycraft Potteries Company of Los Angeles. Fred's son, George Robertson, founded the Robertson Pottery in California in 1934. Fred worked with George until 1952, the year the pottery closed. Fred died later the same year.

Pieces of Roblin pottery were marked with the word "Roblin" and an impressed figure of a bear. Sometimes Robertson's name and some numbers were also impressed.

*Roblin redware vase, 2½ inches high. (Smithsonian Institution)*

*An assortment of Roblin ware as shown in* Keramic Studio, *January 1902.*

# Rookwood Pottery
## *Cincinnati, Ohio*

The Rookwood Pottery was founded in 1880, but to completely understand the history of the pottery it is necessary to go back a few years to discover some of the artistic influences on Maria Longworth Nichols, Rookwood's founder.

Maria Longworth was born in 1849 to a wealthy Cincinnati family. She attended a private school and received the usual education for a young lady of her day. She married Colonel George Ward Nichols in 1867 and they later had a son and a daughter. It has been said that the marriage was "not a happy one."

Mrs. Nichols first started decorating china in 1873. A neighbor, Karl Langenbeck, had been given a set of china decorating paints, and he, Nichols, and another neighbor, Mrs. Learner Harrison, began practicing with the paints. When Marie Eggers started a china decorating class in Cincinnati in 1874, Nichols and others joined the group. Nichols found artistic inspiration in some Japanese design books that were given to her by a friend in 1875. It was the first time she had seen this style of design, and after viewing the Japanese exhibit at the Philadelphia Centennial Exposition in 1876, she decided to form an American pottery company to make similar wares. The same exhibition also included some fine examples of French Haviland art pottery, which inspired the glazing techniques later used by Nichols.

At first Nichols considered hiring Japanese workmen and planned to set up a pseudo-Japanese pottery, but she later dismissed the idea. She and her friends continued to experiment with underglaze decoration, trying to adapt the methods seen on the Haviland works from Auteuil, France.

China decorating was becoming both an industry and a mania among people of means. Mary Louise McLaughlin (see Pottery Club of Cincinnati) published several books about china painting and glazing techniques. Her pieces were probably the first underglaze art pottery wares made in the United States. McLaughlin founded the Women's Pottery Club in 1879, but for some reason (perhaps her invitation was lost), Mrs. Nichols was not a member. McLaughlin originally worked at the Coultry Pottery and used yellowware, but she soon moved to the Frederick Dallas Pottery.

Using a kiln with a high heat, Mrs. Nichols began her own experiments at the Dallas Pottery. Because the Dallas kiln was too hot, McLaughlin had a special one built for her pieces. Nichols heard about the new kiln, so she too had a special kiln built for her work. McLaughlin sent work to Thomas C. Smith and Sons of Greenpoint, New York, to be fired; Nichols sent her pieces to Lycett's in New York City for firing. The working arrangements at the Dallas Pottery seem odd: McLaughlin and her group worked in one room and Nichols and her group in another. The two rooms at the

*Painted or incised, before 1882.*

*Painted or incised, before 1882.*

*Printed in black under glaze, 1880–1882.*

*Stamped or in relief, before 1883.*

*Impressed, 1883*

*Found on Garfield memorial pitcher, 1881–1882.*

*Stamped, c. 1883.*

*Stamped, c. 1883.*

*Incised mark, rare.*

*Blue underglaze mark.*

**ROOKWOOD
1882**

*Impressed name and date,
1882–1886.*

*Paper label used at World's
Columbian Exposition, 1883.*

*Rare mark written in blue
underglaze, found on blue stein.*

*Impressed monogram, 1886.*

*Flame added each year from 1887 to
1900. Pieces made in 1900 have
fourteen flame marks.*

*Roman numeral indicating last two
digits of year after 1900; this mark
indicates 1901.*

Dallas Pottery were entered through the same yard, but each group remained completely independent.

Mrs. Nichols at first used graniteware that was made at the Dallas Pottery, but it would not take the colors desired. She tried Rockingham clays, and was able to make pieces decorated in cobalt blue and black. Later, with the help of Joseph Bailey, the pottery's superintendent, she developed dark green, claret brown and, at last, light blue and light green. This limited palette was discouraging to Nichols, but in 1880 her father suggested that if she really wanted to have a pottery, she could use an old schoolhouse he had purchased at a sheriff's sale.

The schoolhouse pottery was a solution to many of the problems at the Dallas Pottery. Mrs. Nichols could make her own clay mixtures, colors, and glazes, and could even control the heat of the kiln. Bailey helped her decide what equipment she needed. She tried to hire him but he would not desert his employer of fifteen years, so instead she hired his son, Joseph Bailey, Jr.

The schoolhouse was transformed into a working pottery and named "Rookwood" after the name of her childhood home in Cincinnati. Henry Farny, a Cincinnati artist, designed the firm's trademark, a kiln and a spray of fruit blossoms with two rooks.

Just as the pottery was nearing completion in October 1880, legal problems with T. J. Wheatley (see T. J. Wheatley & Company) erupted over rights to the underglaze process, and the unfinished factory was threatened with closure. Mrs. Nichols pushed on with her project, however, and continued to hire workmen and artists. By November 1880 Wheatley had dropped his legal action against Rookwood, and the first pieces were fired.

The Rookwood Pottery made several types of wares from the very beginning. Commercial tableware for household use was white graniteware and had a cream-colored body. Some yellow clay wares were also made. Both Nichols's art pottery and some artwork made by outside amateurs were fired at the Rookwood Pottery. Nichols furnished the biscuit pottery to the amateurs for their decoration, and she also fired the finished pieces. Although there was no working space at the factory for the artists, Nichols was happy to help them in other ways.

In 1881, Nichols hired Clara Chipman Newton to manage the office details. Edward Cranch worked part-time for the pottery handling administrative problems. Both also worked part-time as deco-

*Special pieces fired for 50th
anniversary, printed on ware.*

*75th anniversary, printed on ware.*

**ROOKWOOD
CINTI,O**

*After 1942.*

**ROOKWOOD
FAIENCE**

*Mark on tile, 1958.*

ROOKWOOD POTTERY
STARKVILLE MISS

*Impressed paper label, 1962–1967.*

rators. Although not officially Rookwood employees, James Broomfield, Henry Farny, and Ferdinand Mersman (see Cambridge Art Tile Works) also worked as artists.

By 1881 the Rookwood Pottery was making quantities of dinnerware, often decorated with underglaze blue or brown prints of birds, fish, or other animals. High-relief decorated vases, such as the Garfield Vase, were created by Ferdinand Mersman, while Mrs. Nichols made Japanese-inspired artware. The pottery even produced some "printed ware."

In June 1881, after the death of Frederick Dallas and the closing of the Dallas Pottery, Joseph Bailey, Sr., became the superintendent of the Rookwood Pottery. He stayed until 1883, when he left for Chicago, then returned in 1885.

In the summer of 1881, the pottery was enlarged and space was provided for the Rookwood School for Pottery Decoration. Mrs. Nichols hoped the school would be financially successful and thought it would furnish more decorators for the pottery. Space was also provided to the Pottery Club.

| | | | |
|---|---|---|---|
| *Ginger.* | **G** | *Sage green.* | **S** |
| *Olive.* | **O** | *White.* | **W** |
| *Red.* | **R** | *Red.* | **Y** |

*Impressed in pieces made after 1914 to indicate soft porcelain.*

*Trial for new glaze.*

*Stanley Burt trial mark.*

**X15X**

*Trial mark for new decorating technique.*

*Joseph Bailey, Sr., trial mark.*

*Other process marks.*

*Birds fly on this blue and beige vase with gold highlights. It is marked "Rookwood, 1884." Although the piece has no artist's signature, the bird design was used by Albert Valentien on other pieces. (Private collection)*

*Birds and rushes decorate this cream to orange 9-inch-high vase. It is signed with the incised initials "ARV" (Albert R. Valentien), the incised name "Rookwood," and the date 1885. (Private collection)*

*Clara Chipman Newton decorated this stein with blue decorations on a cream body. It was made in 1881 and is marked with the script words "Rookwood Pottery."*

| | |
|---|---|
| K1 and K3 | *Used on matching teacup and saucer c. 1922.* |
| M | *Used on ship pattern tableware.* |
| 2800 | *Used on ship pattern tableware.* |
| S | *A piece not in the regular line, usually a demonstration piece.* |
| SC | *Cream and sugar set, 1946–1950.* |
| T | *Impressed with a number on a trial piece.* |
| V | *Impressed to show vellum finish after 1904.* |
| Y | *With a number, used on architectural pieces to indicate shape and with a letter to indicate size.* |
| Z | *After a number indicates the shape used for matte glaze pieces from 1900 to 1904.* |
| X | *Cut on the base to show the piece was considered imperfect or of second quality.* |
| * | *Cut on the base to show that articles did not sell as seconds and could be given away to employees.* |

That same year, a decorating department was formally organized. Albert R. Valentien, Laura A. Fry, Harriet Wenderoth, W. H. Breuer, Alfred Brennan, and Fanny Auckland (then twelve years old) worked in the department. William P. McDonald and Matthew A. Daly joined the decorators in 1882, and Martin Rettig, Albert Humphreys, and N. J. Hirshfeld were hired a short time later.

Even though the Rookwood Pottery was expanding, and selling

*(Left) This unglazed pitcher has incised decorations made with tools similar to those used to tool leather. The piece is marked with the very rare and early script mark, incised on the bottom, "Rookwood Pottery Cin." (Right) This plain 3-inch-high, gray unglazed pitcher has the rare kiln mark used in 1881 and 1882. (Wolf's)*

A pitcher, 6½ inches high, 3¾ inches wide, and 2⅛ inches long, with Limoges-type glaze, 1882, marked "C.C.N." for Clara Chipman Newton. (Courtesy of the Brooklyn Museum, Brooklyn, New York, gift of Mrs. J. Ethel Brown)

This 6-inch-diameter vase has an orange-brown glaze that in some spots shows flecks of gold. It was designed by Artus Van Briggle and is dated 1887. The swastika and spider decorations are Indian inspired. Van Briggle used the same motif in work he did at his own pottery.

Albert Valentien signed this Rookwood vase with his initials, "A.R.V.," and the date "Dec. 15, 1881" in script. Valentien worked at Rookwood, then later moved to San Diego to found his own pottery. The 10-inch vase has white flowers on a gray background. (Early Antiques)

as much pottery as it was producing, the firm was not financially successful. Mrs. Nichols's father, who had paid for the original equipment and the building, continued backing the pottery until his death in December 1883.

That same year, William Watts Taylor joined the pottery as administrator and partner. He had no previous knowledge of pottery production and his only concern was running the factory in a businesslike way. One of his first changes in the Rookwood operation was to close the Rookwood School for Pottery Decoration. The Pottery Club continued to use the space for a short time, but because club members and local amateurs bought Rookwood pieces to be decorated at home and then had them fired at the Rookwood Pottery, there is some confusion about the early wares. The biscuit wares were stamped with the name Rookwood plus the date. The staff decorators usually signed the pieces. So some of the marked Rookwood pieces dating from 1882 to 1885 were decorated by artists who were not part of the pottery staff.

William Taylor analyzed the problems of the firm and changed some of its marketing methods. He started keeping records showing the types of Rookwood that sold quickly, and unpopular items were discontinued.

A discovery by Laura Fry in 1883 led to the "Rookwood Standard Glaze." She used an atomizer to apply color to the green clay body. This made more even glazing and more delicate shading possible. (Mrs. Nichols later claimed that the discovery had been her own and that the method was actually based on an ancient process;

Vase with fish decoration by Matthew Andrew Daly, 1887, marked "M.A.D." It is 14¼ inches high and 2⅝ inches in diameter. (Courtesy of the Brooklyn Museum, Brooklyn, New York, gift of Mrs. Carl H. DeSilver)

\* An asterisk indicates an artist listed in Edwin Barber's *Marks of American Potters*. Birth and death dates are given in parentheses after the name.

*E.A*

\* *Edward Abel (1868–1937). 1890–1895.*

\* *Louise Abel (1894–1981). 1919–1932.*

*HA*

\* *Howard Altman. 1899–1904.*

*LA*

\* *Lenore Asbury (1866–1933). 1894–1931; did occasional work in other years.*

*FA*

\* *Fanny Auckland (1868–1945). c. 1881–c. 1884; did incised decoration. Daughter of William Auckland.*

*WA*
*WA*

*William Auckland (1840–1888). c. 1881–c. 1887, first thrower at Rookwood. Previously at Dallas Pottery.*

*D. B. Unknown. 1882.*

*M.B.*

*M. B. Unknown. 1884–?.*

*Joseph Bailey. Superintendent, 1881–1885, 1886–1898.*

*CAB*

\* *Constance Amelia Baker. 1892–1904.*

*C. J. Barnhorn. Name on garden fountain, 1914.*

*EB*

\* *Elizabeth Barrett. 1924–1948. Married Jens Jensen 1931.*

*J.B*   *I.B.*

\* *Irene Bishop (1881–1925). 1900–1909. Married Edward Hurley 1907.*

*CFB*

\* *Caroline F. Bonsall. 1901–1905.*

*AMB*
*AMB*

\* *Anna Marie Bookprinter (1862–1947). 1884–1905. Married Albert Valentien 1887. Signed work "A.M.V." after marriage.*

*EWB*   *E.W.B.*

\* *Elizabeth Weldon Brain (1870–1960). 1898–1899.*

*AB*   *EB*
*B*

\* *Alfred Laurens Brennan (1853–1921). 1881–1885. Recorded as designer of a few early shapes.*

*WHB*   *YB*

\* *W. H. Breuer (1860–1932). 1881–1883.*

*C.P.C.*

*C. P. C. Unknown. 1882.*

*K. C. Unknown. 1916.*

*Q. C. C. Unknown. 1881.*

\* *Alice E. Caven (Craven) (d. 1980). 1916–1919.*

\* *Arthur P. Conant (1889–1966). 1915–1939. Husband of Patti M. Conant.*

*Patti M. Conant (b. 1888). 1914–1923. Wife of Arthur P. Conant.*

*D•C•*   *D•C•*

\* *Daniel Cook (1872–1950s?). 1893–1895. Also worked at Owens.*

*CL*   *CL*   *CC*

*Catherine Pissoreff Covalenco (1896–1932). 1925–1928.*

*S.E.C.*   *SE*

\* *Sara Elizabeth (Sallie) Coyne (1876–1939). 1891–1936.*

*Catherine Calhoun Crabtree.
1923–1924.*

**E.B.I.C.**

\* *Ellen Bertha I. Cranch. Relative of
Edward Cranch. 1894–1895.*

**E P C     E P C**

## C R A N C H

\* *Edward Pope Cranch
(1809–1892). Part-time decorator
1880–1892. Used black etched lines
on light clay body.*

\* *Cora Crofton. 1886–c. 1892.*

*Kate Curry. 1917–1918.*

**A. D.**

*A. D. Unknown. 1916.*

\* *Matthew Andrew Daly
(1860–1937). 1882–1903. Also
worked at Matt Morgan. Married
Olga Reed Pinney 1928.*

**V B A**

**V B D**

\* *Virginia B. Demarest. 1900–1903.*

*Mary Grace Denzler (b. 1892).
1913–1917.*

\* *Charles John Dibowski
(1875–1923). 1892–1895. Also may
have worked at Lonhuda.*

**E D.          E O**

\* *Edward George Diers
(1871–1947). 1896–1931.*

**C A D**

*Cecil A. Duell (1889–1946).
1907–1915. His wife, Cathryn A.
Duell, worked at Rookwood but was
not a decorator.*

*J. E. Unknown. 1882.*

*T. E. Unknown. 1892.*

**L          LE**

*Lorinda Epply (1874–1951).
1904–1948.*

**H ·F.**

*H. F. Unknown.*

**M. L. F.**

*M. L. F. Unknown. 1900.*

*Henry François Farny. c. 1880.*

\* *Rose Fechheimer (1874–1961).
1896–1906.*

\* *Edith Regina Felten (Felton)
(b. 1876). 1896–1908.*

**K. F.**

*Kate Field. c. 1880.*

**E·D·F**

\* *Emma D. Foertmeyer
(1866–1895). 1887–1895.*

**MF**

*Mattie Foglesong. 1897–1902.*

**F          F.**

\* *Laura A. Fry (Frey)
(1857–1943). Part-time,
1881–1887. Also worked at
Lonhuda, 1892.*

**L F**

*Lois Furukawa (b. 1912).
1944–1948.*

**WG**

*William T. Glass (b. 1930).
1959–1963.*

**AG**

\* *Arthur Goetting (1874–1968).
Summer, 1896.*

**K. G**

*Katherine deGolter. c. 1880. Not an
artist at Rookwood, but member of
Women's Pottery Club. Decorated
Rookwood blanks.*

*M. Haigo. 1885.*

**G.H.**

\* *Grace M. Hall. c. 1902–1905,
1910–1912.*

**LEH**

*Lena E. Hanscom. c. 1902–1907.*

*JH*

Janet Harris. (b. 1907).
1929–1932.

VEH WEH

William E. Hentschel (1892–1962).
1907–1939. Also worked at
Kenton Hills.

*KH*

* Katharine Leslie Hickman.
(b. 1873). 1895–1900.

/ticks

Orville B. Hicks. 1906–1907.

*BH* N.J.H.

* Nicholas Joseph Hirschfeld
(1860–1927). c. 1882–1883. Also
worked at Matt Morgan.

A.BJH.

Alice Belle Holabird. c. 1880. Not
an artist at Rookwood, but member
of Women's Pottery Club. Decorated
Rookwood blanks.

LH

Loretta Holtkamp (b. 1894).
1920–1954.

HB.

* Robert Bruce Horsfall
(1869–1948). 1893–1896.

HH

H.H

* Hattie Horton. 1882–1884.

---

A.H.

* Albert Humphreys (1864–1926).
c. 1882–1884.

E.J.H.

* Edward Timothy Hurley
(1869–1950). 1896–1948. Married
Irene Bishop 1907.

Joseph Jefferson. Before 1905. Actor
who visited frequently,
decorated plaques.

Jens Jacob Herring Krug Jensen.
(d. 1978). 1928–1948. Married
Elizabeth Barrett 1931.

KJ

Katherine Jones. 1924–1931.

ETK

E. T. K. Unknown. 1882.

F.E.K.

Florence Kebler. c. 1880.
Not an employee.

MJ Keenan

Mary Virginia Keenan. c. 1880. Not
an employee but member of
Women's Pottery Club.

F.K.

Flora R. King. (b. 1918).
1945–1946. Twin sister of Ora King.

OK

Ora King. (b. 1918). 1945–1948.
Twin sister of Flora King.

---

WK.

* William Klemm. 1900, 1902.

Charles Klinger. 1925.

* Mrs. F. D. Koehler. 1895–1897.

Anton Lang. Bohemian potter who
visited Rookwood, where he made a
few pieces he signed in script.

SL

* Frederick Sturgis Laurence. Artist,
1895–1904; manager of New York
sales office, 1904–1923.

ECL

* Eliza C. Lawrence. (d. 1903).
1900–1903.

Henrietta D. Leonard. 1882.
Women's Pottery Club.

LEY

Katherine (Kay) Elizabeth Ley.
(b. 1919). 1944–1947.

l N.L

Elizabeth Neave Lingenfelter Lincoln
(1876–1957). 1892–1931.

CCL

* Clara Christiana Lindeman
(1871–1966). 1898–after 1907.
Sister of Laura E. Lindeman.

L.E.L. (mark)

* Laura E. Lindeman (1873–1967). 1899–after 1905. Sister of Clara C. Lindeman.

* Elizabeth Neave Lingenfelter. See Elizabeth Neave Lingenfelter Lincoln.

TOM  LUNT

* Thomas (Tom) Lunt. 1892–1895.

HML.

Helen M. Lyons, 1913–1916.

E. M. M. Unknown. 1882.

J. M. Unknown. 1918.

S. N. M.

S. N. M. Unknown. 1882.

EM

Elizabeth F. McDermott. 1912–1919.

CHM.  MHM  EHM

Margaret Helen McDonald (1893–1964). 1913–1948.

W.P.M'D.

* William Purcell McDonald (1864–1931). 1882–1931.

M

Charles Jasper McLaughlin (1890–1964). 1913–1920.

S. M.

* Sadie Markland. (d. 1899). 1892–1899.

K.C.M.

* Kate C. Matchette (1875–1953). 1893.

ÆM

Ruben Earl Menzel. (1882–1971). Clay department, 1896; began decorating and signing his work, c. 1950–1959.

Ferdinand Mersman. Garfield vase and pitchers.

M

* Marianne Mitchell. 1901–1905.

M

Herman Milton Moos. 1925–1926.

FM  AM

Albert Cyrus Munson. 1890–1944.

C.N  C.CN

* Clara Chipman Newton (1848–1936). 1881–1884.

MLN

Maria Longworth Nichols (1849–1932). 1880–1889, freelance until 1906.

E.N.

Edith Noonan (1881–1982). 1904–1910. Married Stanley Burt 1910.

E. N.

Elizabeth Nourse. Not an employee.

M.N.

* Mary Madeline Nourse (1870–1959). 1891–1905.

M. E. Owen. 1883.

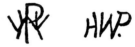

A. F. P. Unknown. c. 1907.

YRP  HWP

Helen W. Peachey. 1882–1883. Women's Pottery Club.

MP  MLP  MLP

* Mary Louella Perkins. 1886–1898.

PB

* Pauline Peters-Baurer. c. 1893–1894.

* O. Geneva Reed Pinney. See Olga Geneva Reed.

AP

Agnes Pitman. c. 1880. Not an employee.

AP

Albert Frank Pons (1888–1972). 1904–1911.

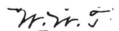

John Wesley Pullman (1887–1931).
1926–1931.

HR

H. R. Unknown. 1899.

H. A. R. Unknown. 1925–1926.

ĦR·

\* Marie Rauchfuss (b. 1879).
1899–1903. Also worked at
Owens; Weller.

O.G.R.

\* Olga Geneva Reed (b. 1873).
1890–1909. Married Mr. Pinney
in 1890s. Married
Matthew Daly, 1928.

Wilhelmine Rehm (1899–1967).
1927–1935, 1943–1948.

MR   M·R·

\* Martin Rettig (1869–1956).
1882–1885.

Jean Rich. 1942.

R.

\* Frederick Daniel Henry
Rothenbusch. 1896–1931.

I. C. S. Unknown. 1882.

Jane Sacksteder (b. 1924).
1945–1948.

\* Sara Sax (1870–1949).
1896–1931.

---

V·S.   V͞S

Virginia Scalf. 1944–1960.

\* Charles (Carl) Schmidt
(1875–1959). 1896–1927.

A.D.S.

Adeliza Drake Sehon (d. 1902).
1896–1902.

OWS   D·S

David W. Seyler (b. 1917). Not an
employee; sculptor who used the
pottery summers, 1934–1939.

   ⅩS

\* Kataro Shirayamadani
(1865–1948). 1887–1911,
1921–1948.

M·H·S

\* Marian Frances Hastings Smalley
(1886–1957). 1899–1902. Married
Francis Vreeland 1903.

ABS   A·BS

a₃s

\* Amelia Browne Sprague
(1870–1951). 1887–1903. Also
worked at Lonhuda.

\* Carolyn Stegner (b. 1923).
1945–1947.

---

S   C.F.S.   C.S.   C.S.

\* Caroline Frances Steinle
(1871–1944). 1866–1925. Also
worked at Roseville.

\* Maria Longworth Nichols Storer.
See Maria Longworth Nichols.

H·R·S·

\* Harriette Rosemary Strafer
(1873–1935). 1890–1899.

\* Helen Pabodie Stuntz
(1871–1949). 1892–1896.

$

\* Jeannette Swing (1866–1942).
1900–1904.

\* Mary Aldis Taylor (1859–1929).
1883–1885.

W·W·T

William Watts Taylor (d. 1913).
Administrator and partner,
1883–1913.

V.T.

Vera Tischler (b. 1900).
1920–1926.

CST   C.S.T.

Charles Stewart Todd (1886–1950).
1910–1922.

\* Sara Alice (Sallie) Toohey
(1872–1941). 1887–1931.

**A.R.V.**

* Albert Robert Valentien
(1862–1925). 1881–1905. Married
Anna Bookprinter 1887.

**a.m.v.**

* Anna Marie Valentien. See Anna
Marie Bookprinter.

**AVB   A.V.B.   A.V.B.**

* Artus Van Briggle (1869–1904).
1887–1901. Also worked at Avon
Pottery, until 1887; Van Briggle,
1901–1904. Married 1903.

**L.V.B**

* Leona Van Briggle (d. 1953).
1899–1901. Younger sister of Artus
Van Briggle.

**K.H.   K.V**

Katherine Van Horne (d. 1918).
c. 1907–1918.

**F.V.**

* Francis William Vreeland
(1879–1954). 1900–1902. Married
Marian Smalley 1903.

**L.E.W**

L. E. W. Unknown. 1882.

**M.H.W.**

M. H. W. Unknown. 1882.

**M.R.W.**

M. R. W. Unknown. 1886.

* John Hamilton Delaney ("Dee")
Wareham (1871–1954). 1893–1954.

---

**N.W.**

**H.W.**

* Harriet (Nettie) Wenderoth
(d. 1954). 1881–1885.
Previously attributed to
Henrietta (Nettie) Wilson.

**H.E.W.**

* Harriet (Hattie) Elizabeth Wilcox
(Willcox). 1886–1907, ?–1930.

**E L W**

Edith Lavette Wildman
(1888–1981). 1910–1912.

Alice Willitts. 1906–1907.

Henrietta (Nettie) Wilson. 1882.

Delia Workum (1904–1966).
1927–1929.

K. Y. Unknown. 1905–1906.

* Grace Young (1869–1947).
1886–1891, 1896–1903. Also
worked at Roseville.

**C Z**

Clotilda Marie Zanetta
(1890–1970). 1943–1948. Designed
religious figures; also worked at
Roseville; Weller.

---

* Josephine Ella Zettel (1874–1954).
1892–1904.

Unknown. 1889.

Unknown. 1906.

Unknown. 1907.

Unknown. 1909.

Unknown. 1917.

Unknown. 1925.

Unknown. 1943.

Unknown.

Unknown.

*This aquamarine vase in pilgrim-bottle shape is 11 inches high and 9 inches wide. The piece is marked "Rookwood, 1882 A.R.V." and has the anchor mark. (Private collection)*

*A pair of pilgrim bottles, each marked "Cranch, Rookwood, 1884," flank an 8-inch covered jar with vellum glaze dating from 1922. At the bottom front of the 7¾-inch bottles a phrase is printed, "Three wise men of Gotham went to sea in a bowl," a line from an old nursery rhyme. (Wolf's)*

*Few pieces of Rookwood were decorated with full figures. This standard-glaze vase shows the full figure of a Samurai warrior. It is signed "M.A.D." for Matthew A. Daly, and has the factory marks for 1889. The 13¼-inch-high vase sold for $10,250 in 1979, setting the record price for Rookwood at that time. (Skinner, Inc.)*

yet contemporary accounts mention that Rookwood and William Long paid license fees to Fry.)

An accident in the kiln produced another glaze, the "Tiger Eye" glaze that had gold streaks beneath the colored glaze. When the result was less dramatic and gold flecks appeared, it was called "Goldstone." The search for the reason why some pieces glazed as Tiger Eye led management to realize that a chemist was needed. Nichols's old neighbor, Karl Langenbeck, was hired around January 1885.

After her husband died in 1885, Mrs. Nichols spent less time at the pottery, and Joseph Bailey, Sr., returned to his job as superintendent. Mrs. Nichols married Bellamy Storer in March 1886 and left for a lengthy honeymoon in Europe. The firm continued to produce new types of wares and new designs, and a Japanese artist, Kataro Shirayamadani, joined the decorating staff. By the end of 1888, the firm was making enough money to pay back the losses of earlier years.

In 1889, the Rookwood Pottery gained international renown with a gold medal at the Exposition Universelle in Paris and the first prize gold medal at the Exhibition of American Art Industry in Philadelphia. Maria Nichols, now Mrs. Storer, retired from the Rookwood Pottery in 1890 and transferred her interests to Taylor. He organized a stock company called the Rookwood Pottery Company. New buildings were constructed and the firm moved to a new location on the summit of Mount Adams, overlooking Cincinnati.

Rookwood had several displays in the World Columbian Exposition held in Chicago in 1893 and won a "highest award" medal. Although only one level of awards was given, the resulting publicity helped the sales of Rookwood and many European museums bought examples.

This 1883 vase was decorated by Albert Valentien. White beetles and leaves are shown against an oatmeal background. The edges are touched with gold, an early decorating technique. The vase is 8 inches high. (Wolf's)

A Limoges-type glazed ewer decorated by N. J. Hirschfeld in 1882. The 6-inch piece has edges touched with gilding. (Wolf's)

Vase with gilding, butterflies, and bamboo decoration, 12 inches high, 1883. (Wolf's)

The pottery introduced electrodeposit silver on pottery, or silver overlay, in 1892. Rookwood continued to make new lines of pottery, and in 1894 Sea Green, Aerial Blue, and Iris were put into production. Some of these pieces were made with silver overlay by Gorham Manufacturing Co. Many of the new shapes were based on antique forms from Japan, Turkey, Greece, and Persia, or were copies of contemporary vases from Royal Worcester, Haviland, or Gallé.

The decorating department began to make portraits in 1897. Dogs and other animals, historical figures, actors, and birds, as well as flowers and Indians, appeared on the Standard Glaze vases.

The Indian portraits were copied from contemporary photographs circulating in stores and from photographs published in at least two books, *Indians of Today* by George Bird Frinnell (1900) and *North American Indian* by Edward S. Curtis. Both of these books were also inspirations for pieces decorated at the Weller Pottery. Portraits did not sell well and were discontinued by about 1903.

The pottery expanded its building in 1899. Stanley Burt, who had been hired as a chemist in 1892, took over as superintendent in 1898 when Joseph Bailey, Sr., died.

Once again, in 1900, an international exhibition helped the sales of Rookwood. The Paris Exposition awarded Rookwood several medals, including one gold. In 1901 the Pan American Exposition in Buffalo, New York, awarded more prizes to the firm.

Rookwood made decorative architectural tiles for the first time in 1901, and by 1903 these tiles had been ordered for use in the New York City subways. (Rookwood decorations can still be seen in some subway stations.) Once again, the factory had to expand and a New York office was opened to sell tiles. Garden pottery was added to its lines in 1906.

Taylor died in November 1913. His will provided that the Rook-

Lamps were often made from Rookwood vases. This lamp was originally made for kerosene. (Skinner, Inc.)

*A 6-inch vase with silver overlay, 1895. (Wolf's)*

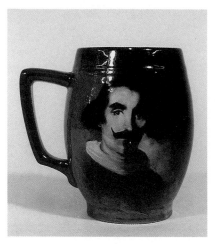

*Portrait mug by William P. McDonald, 1894. (Early Antiques)*

*William P. McDonald decorated this 14½-inch vase in 1897. (Christie's)*

*This Shirayamadani decorated vase with brown glaze and silver overlay was made in 1896. It is 7½ inches high. (Sotheby's)*

wood Pottery stock be given to a board of twelve trustees to hold until twenty-one years after the death of the last of the original trustees, when the stock would be given to the Cincinnati Museum Association. The trustees were to use all of the profits to improve the company, and they could sell stock only to Rookwood employees. Taylor also left money to be distributed to the employees who had worked there for more than five years.

The Rookwood Pottery Company continued under the direction of the board of trustees, with Joseph Henry Gest as president. Beginning in 1902, Gest had worked part-time for both Rookwood and the Cincinnati Art Museum, where he was a director.

*This large, 16½-inch-high earthenware vase was decorated by Matthew A. Daly. It sold at auction for $32,000 in 1980, to set the record price for that time. (Christie's)*

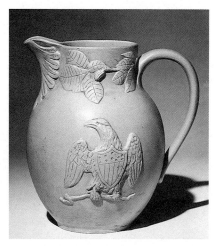

*This unglazed gray pitcher has a portrait bust of President James Garfield on one side and an eagle on the other. It is 10 inches high. The piece is marked with the "RP" flame mark with 9 flames (1895) and the impressed letter S. (Smithsonian Institution)*

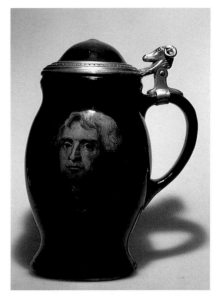

This Limoges-style 10-inch vase was signed by Valentien in 1892. It bears the rare "Rookwood Pottery Cin. O." mark. (Courtesy of the Western Reserve Historical Society)

This vase marked with eight flames and the Japanese signature of Shirayamadani is 14 inches high and 11 inches in diameter. (Courtesy of the Western Reserve Historical Society)

A Rookwood stein picturing Thomas Jefferson is signed "M.A. Daly, 1896."

The general pottery lines continued, with many new designs and additions to the architectural lines. In 1915, Rookwood Soft Porcelain was introduced. It had a semitranslucent body glazed with rich color; crackle-type glazes were also used. Jewel Porcelain, a series of new, less expensive, glazes, appeared about five years later.

In 1920 Rookwood filled a special order for a dozen service plates. This order led to the production of Rookwood's blue and white ship dinnerware sets. During that same year, Tiger Eye glaze was revived in several new colors, even a yellow-green crystalline glaze that was not the same as the original Tiger Eye. It was discontinued about 1950. The firm also made garden pottery, fountains, tiles, lamp bases, sculpture, and mass-produced pieces.

In 1928 a decision by the U.S. Board of Tax Appeals ruled that the Rookwood Pottery owed $19,873 in back income taxes. This, in addition to the Depression, left Rookwood Pottery in trouble with little cash reserve. The architectural tile department closed in the 1930s. Art pottery was a luxury that only a few could afford, so the expensive artist-decorated lines were discontinued in 1937. Some lower-cost pieces with flowing glazes were still made.

Henry Gest resigned as president in 1934, and was succeeded by John D. Wareham, who had worked for Rookwood for forty-one years as a decorator and vice president. The pottery was no longer a leader in design, and the financial problems grew until the firm went into receivership in 1941. A series of liquidation sales followed.

The Rookwood Pottery was sold for $60,500 to a group headed by Walter E. Schott, a Cincinnati auto dealer. Wareham continued

"Rushing Eagle, Sioux," a 13⅞-inch vase signed "Sturgis Laurence, 1899."

*Iris glaze vase by Albert R. Valentien, 1905, 15 inches high. (Wolf's)*

(Left) *A 1904 vase by Rose Fechheimer. Iris glaze is used with a design of crocuses on the 7-inch-high piece.* (Center) *Handled and footed bowl with Tiger Eye glaze and three-leaf clovers. Anna Marie Bookprinter made the bowl in 1886.* (Right) *A 6-inch-high vase with pansies on brown glaze by Harriet E. Wilcox, 1890.*

as director, and plans were made to reopen the plant. In November 1941 production resumed. But by the end of 1942, the pottery was turned over to the Institutum Divi Thomae, a nonprofit organization. It sold the operation of the pottery to Sperti, Inc., and in 1943 production again resumed on a small scale. Part of the plant was reserved for the manufacture of wooden blocks for water conduits used in army camps. The decorating staff was reassembled and John W. Milet was appointed to manage the pottery for Sperti.

When World War II ended, Rookwood production continued. Artist-decorated pottery was made from 1944 to 1949. Some changes had been made in the glazes, however, because many of the chemicals originally used were unavailable during and immediately after the war. The quality of the glazes consequently declined, and by

*Sea-green glaze was used on this 11½-inch-high vase by Sturgis Laurence, 1901. The sailboats and scene are pictured in blues and greens. (Wolf's)*

(Left) *An 8½-inch vase with crows and Iris glaze by Edward T. Hurley, 1903.* (Center) *An Iris-glazed cachepot with pendant blossoms by Anna Marie Valentien, 1889, stands 5½ inches tall.* (Right) *An 8½-inch-high brown-glazed vase with stylized blossoms by Olga Geneva Reed, 1900. (Sotheby's)*

F. Sturgis Laurence decorated this 10¾-inch sea green-glazed vase. (Skinner, Inc.)

The Japanese artist Kataro Shirayamadani decorated this Rookwood vase in 1906. (Sotheby's)

This ad appeared in the Sketch Book in the early 1900s. The same vase was offered in a 1904 mail-order catalog for the Rookwood Pottery. It was described as 8½ inches high and for sale at $40.

1947 the decorated pieces were noticeably inferior.

The staff of artists was discontinued in 1949, and less and less of Rookwood's plant was used for making pottery. For a time, only unglazed bisque pieces were made for amateurs to decorate. These pieces are marked with the Rookwood mark and the date.

James M. Smith bought the property in 1956 and tried to rebuild Rookwood's reputation, but failed. Late in 1959 the pottery was sold to the Herschede Hall Clock Company, and in 1960 pottery operations moved to Starkville, Mississippi. About twelve hundred molds

An 11½-inch vase is decorated with fish in a vellum blue-green sea, 1909. (Wolf's)

An example of the silver overlay used on pieces of Rookwood in the early 1900s. This vase is signed by Matthew A. Daly.

Silver overlay was used on this Rookwood vase decorated with apple blossoms on an olive green and orange ground. The vase is 6½ inches high. (Skinner, Inc.)

*Toadstools decorate this Iris glaze vase made by Charles Schmidt in 1908. It is 10½ by 5½ inches. (David Rago Arts & Crafts Gallery)*

*Rookwood plaque by Frederick Rothenbusch, 8¾ by 14 inches. (David Rago Arts & Crafts Gallery)*

*A bittersweet vine decorates this 1903 vase by Clara C. Lindeman. It is marked with the Rookwood flame mark and "III 922 D. C.C.L." (Courtesy of the Western Reserve Historical Society)*

*(Opposite page) This standard-glaze vase decorated by Kataro Shirayamadani in 1900 has swirling oriental designs and a three-dimensional carved and electroplated copper dragon climbing up the side and resting on the shoulder. Marks on the base include the Rookwood logo, the date, shape number 787 C, and the artist's cipher. The vase is 11½ inches high. (Courtesy of the Cincinnati Art Galleries)*

dating back to 1882 were shipped to the Starkville plant, and pieces marked "Rookwood" were made until 1966. The pottery manufactured at the new plant did not sell well, and the plant closed in 1967.

In 1971, Briarwood Lamps Inc. of Starkville bought the assets of the Rookwood Pottery Company, including three thousand block molds, five thousand glaze and clay formulas, the trademark, and the medals won by the company. Arnold Industries of Starkville purchased the molds, formulas, and awards in 1973, and Arthur Townley of Michigan Center, Michigan, bought Rookwood's assets in 1982. A limited number of clearly marked pieces have been made from the old molds since 1984.

Fake Rookwood can be a problem for unwary collectors. Modern copies of the Rookwood Standard Glaze were made during the late 1960s. These pieces are marked with impressed dates ranging from 1880 to 1886. Some have the "RP" symbol and a year in the 1890s indicated by the flames on the mark. A few 1897 Indian head–decorated mugs and some other popular late items were also made during the 1960s. Artists' signatures, such as "Maria Longworth Nichols," "MAD," "MR," and others, have been appearing. The collector should be careful when buying Rookwood or any other art pottery. Forgeries are not too difficult to recognize if you are familiar with the authentic pieces.

## SPECIAL ITEMS

The Rookwood Pottery made decorative vases, tiles, and plaques throughout most of its operating years. In addition, some specialty items were made.

(Left to right) *Rookwood pottery vases dating from 1894, 1903, 1905, 1907 (5½ inches high), and 1910. (Smithsonian Institution)*

*An Iris glaze vase by Albert Valentien, decorated with blue irises and green leaves. Signed by the artist on the side near the base, the 20½-inch vase is marked on the bottom with the Rookwood logo, the date 1903, and the shape number 901XX. (Courtesy of the Cincinnati Art Galleries)*

*Vase, 18⅜ inches high, by Shirayamadani made in 1900 with electroplated copper fish swimming over a sea-green glaze. Two large carp move among Art Nouveau currents and sea grasses with carved grasses on the upper half of the vase. Marks on the base include the Rookwood logo, the date, shape number 804 A, and the artist's cipher. (Courtesy of the Cincinnati Art Galleries)*

This 14¼-inch Rookwood vase showing a full-length figure of an Indian is called "Pablino Diaz Kiowa." Grace Young decorated the piece in 1901. It carries the Rookwood mark, the artist's impressed initials, and is inscribed with the vase's name and the shape number 907 C. This same vase was pictured on page 479 in The Pottery and Porcelain of the United States (2d ed., 1901) by Edwin Barber. The piece was a gift from Grace Young to Mr. Barber. (Wolf's)

*Architectural Faience:* Architectural faience was part of the business at the Rookwood Pottery from 1903 to the 1940s. The most important years for production of tiles were 1907 to 1913. Rookwood tiles included mantels, mantel facings, wall panels, drinking fountains, architectural reliefs for building exteriors, and plain and decorated tiles. The tiles were made in sizes from 2 by 3 inches to 12 by 18 inches. During a peak year, thirty colored glazes were made, 145 different decorative tiles, and hundreds of special tiles for borders and other uses. The tiles were made with matte finish.

*Lamps:* The lamps made at Rookwood were an important part of the early lines and included kerosene and electric types. The firm made the pottery bases and the metal mounts. They were still making lamps from their vases in the 1920s. The customer could choose a vase, then the pottery would drill and mount it. These lamps were marked "Rookwood Pottery" on the metal base. Later a paper label was used.

*Metal Mounts:* During the years 1894 to 1897, the Rookwood Pottery had its own staff to make and attach the metal mounts to lamps and other pieces. The pottery produced pewter mounts for jug and lamp fittings.

*Silver Deposit:* Rookwood hired E. H. Asano, a Japanese metalworker, and in 1899 formed a new metal-mounting department to do metal overlays by the electrodeposit method; both copper and silver were used. In 1902, after

This carved gesso advertising plaque was made in 1900. It is 31 by 19½ inches, and is colored with pastel and gouache by John D. Wareham and William McDonald. (Courtesy of the Cincinnati Art Galleries)

*Each of these green bookends pictures a girl seated on a bench. The 5½-inch-high pieces have the 1919 flame mark. (Private collection)*

*This vase, decorated with flowers and a vellum glaze, was made in 1909. It is 8 inches high. (Wolf's)*

an absence, Mr. Asano returned to Rookwood to resume his work, but he soon left for Japan. Some of the silver overlay made from 1892 to 1895 was made by Gorham Silver Company and the Gorham mark was used. A catalog dated about 1900 states:

> Metals applied appropriately to reliefs modeled by artists in connection with painted decorations characterize another type of Rookwood. This method gives the piece a variety and richness of texture and color, while retaining the unity of design usually lost in metal mounting.

*Novelties:* Many novelty items were sold by Rookwood beginning in the early 1900s. Bookends first appeared in 1908. A few new designs were added each year until eighty-five bookend designs were made. Other novelties made by the pottery included candlesticks, flower holders, figurines, candy boxes, ashtrays, inkwells, and wall sconces. Design ideas were taken from any source. One early bowl was actually molded from a melon. In the 1940s, a bust of a woman was made by making a mold of an old Italian majolica bust.

*Wall Plaques:* Wall plaques were made as early as 1896. At first these plaques were part of the experimental work for the architectural faience department. Some of the earliest ones (c. 1899) were decorated with copies of well-known oil paintings by masters such as Van Dyck, Rembrandt, Hogarth, and Franz Hals. One is decorated with an Indian head, and another, marked "Sturgis Laurence, 1903," has a landscape with a glossy finish.

In 1904 the vellum glaze was perfected. Vellum scenic tiles were an important product of the Rookwood Pottery until about 1950. Most of the vellum plaques show landscape scenes.

The plaques were almost always sold in oak frames and were expensive to make. The sizes ranged (without frame) from 4 by 8 inches to 14 by 16 inches. Some round and oval plaques were also made.

A word of warning to the collector: Reproductions of these vellum

*A 16-inch vellum vase dated 1915. It is 7 inches in diameter. (Courtesy of the Western Reserve Historical Society)*

(Opposite page) *This vase is 16½ inches high and was made in 1907 by the Japanese artist Kataro Shirayamadani. (Courtesy of the Western Reserve Historical Society)*

(Left to right) *A floral vellum vase, 7³/₄ inches high, with pink and white peonies on a shaded blue ground, by Margaret H. McDonald, 1919. A 1917 jar by Edward Hurley, with vellum glaze, decorated with oriental-style prunus on the shoulder of the celadon green body, 7¹/₂-inch diameter. And a scenic vellum vase with a pink setting sun behind wispy trees, by Frederick Rothenbusch, 1908, 7¹/₂ inches high. (Wolf's)*

plaques were made about 1970 by transferring an etched design in black or blue to a white tile. A little pink color was added and the result appeared to be a winter landscape. The entire plaque was then sprayed with a vellumlike matte overglaze and fired. These can be detected if they are compared with the originals.

## PRODUCT

*Clay, Glaze, Design:* The local Ohio clays used in the early years came from a variety of sources. Various colors of clay and even artificially tinted clays were tried. Red clay from Buena Vista, Ohio, chocolate-colored clay from Ripley, Ohio, yellow clay from Hanging Rock, Ohio, and white or cream clay from Chattanooga, Tennessee, were used by 1902. Most of the clays tended to be in the red to yellow color range, making the dark brown shade of the Standard Glaze a logical choice. The clays used in the 1960s were from Georgia, Tennessee, and Florida.

The sea-green glaze was used on a mixture of clay said to be from Chattanooga and Virginia. The mixture was a dull but not dark green. A method of creating pink was discovered about 1898 when the copper in the clay reacted with the tin in the glaze.

*A 1919 gray-blue matte-glazed vase with rooks, 7¹/₂ inches high by 2¹/₂ inches in diameter. (Courtesy of the Brooklyn Museum, Brooklyn, New York, gift of Susan J. Reed)*

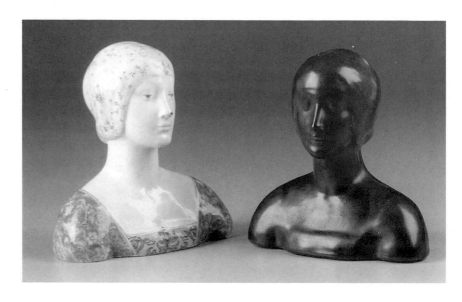

*Rookwood potters took inspiration from many sources. (Left) The flower-decorated bust, used as a model, was once in the office of the secretary of the Rookwood factory. It is Italian faience. (Right) The bronze-glazed bust has the 1912 flame mark and the symbols "II 2026." (Wolf's)*

*This 9¼-by-7-inch Rookwood vellum-glazed plaque was decorated by Charles "Carl" Schmidt in 1918. The river and trees are pictured in pastel shades of blue and gray. (Wolf's)*

*Another Carl Schmidt plaque made in 1919. The sailboats and water are in pastel shades of blue, gray, and white. The plaque is 9 by 7 inches. (Wolf's)*

In 1910, William Watts Taylor, head of the Rookwood Pottery, wrote a description of the process of making some of the artware that is worth quoting in full (it appeared in a quarterly of the University of the South—see the bibliography):

To start with the raw materials: these consist, for the body, of various plastic clays combined with flint and spar. These clays are mainly drawn from mines in the Ohio Valley. Clays even from the same mine vary more or less. This fact and their constantly varying adjustment to the glaze require the continual vigilance of the chemist. When these mixtures are decided, they are weighed with water into a great churnlike mixer, out of which they pass to the sifter of fine silk bolting cloth, and are pumped into vats where they settle to the consistency of very thick cream. This cream is what potters know as "slip" and if vases are to be made from clay in that state, it is done in plaster molds by a process known as "casting." The other process is to form them on the potter's wheel. For this, enough water must be taken from the slip to stiffen it to the consistency of dough. This is done in presses worked by a steam pump. The operation of the potter's wheel is what is known as "throwing," and the process was used, essentially as it is today, at least twenty-two hundred years before the Christian era. It is a simple application of the laws of centrifugal and centripetal force, which swing the planets in their courses, and I know of no mechanical operation which is so immediately creative, or so full of poetic suggestion. It has the added interest that no other material than clay can be worked in this way. Unfortunately, the continuance of so beautiful a craft is threatened by the very quality which recommends it to the artist. So responsive is the clay upon the wheel to the lightest touch of the thrower's hand, that no two

*Rookwood also made outdoor pottery. This garden fountain, 35 inches high, is marked with the 1914 flame mark. It is impressed with the factory mark and "C.J. Barnhorn."*

*Dark bands at the top and bottom frame the scene of flowers and birds on this 1916 vase signed with the cipher for Sara Sax. It is 14½ inches high. (Early Antiques)*

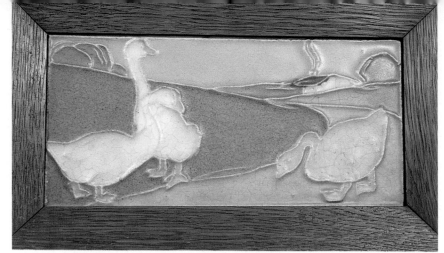

*A Rookwood tile in an oak frame is marked "RP." The tile was made about 1915–1925. (Western Reserve Historical Society)*

*Bathroom with Rookwood tiles made in 1925.*

*Queen Anne's lace is represented on the iris glaze vase with pink to gray coloring. The 10-inch-high vase has the flame mark for 1906 and the symbols "821 C W." It is marked with the initials "L.A." for artist Lenore Asbury. (Private collection)*

pieces can be made precisely alike, and this is fatal to that uniformity of shape which seems the sad necessity for commercial work. In the use of this process, and in the treatment afterward of the clay pieces, made either in this way or by casting, Rookwood departs from the methods of commercial production. Here, instead of drying the pieces at once for the kiln, they must be kept moist in what are known as damp rooms until needed for the decorator. We will follow them next to the studios where you will see them placed on whirlers ready for the artist. The palette consists of a glass plate on which the colored slips look much the same as oil colors. The design is first sketched on the piece with India ink, which, being a vegetable color, subsequently fires out and can therefore be freely used and the outlines followed or not as the artist thinks best. He then proceeds with the painting, mixing his slips and laying them on the pieces. They are all, of course, in slight relief, and during the painting or when it is finished, are gone over more or less with modeling tools. Ready at hand is an atomizing cup which must be constantly used to keep the piece itself and the color palette at the right point of moisture. The colors in the clay are very different from what they appear after firing. To allow for this transposition of color, as it were, into another key; to use the slip so that they may not crack or peel off, requires long practice and constant vigilance. The failures are frequent even with the most experienced, and often disheartening. For the raw material, so to speak, of the design, there must be available thousands of drawings and photographs from nature, either made by the artists themselves, or carefully selected from other sources. These are never literally copied, but serve only as authentic records of details and characteristics of the subject, which may be conventionalized wholly, or in part, or rendered much as in nature. After the piece is finished, which may take only a few hours or many days of time, it is slowly dried and is then ready for the firing. The pieces are placed in fire clay boxes called saggers, and these are piled in the kiln one upon the other with lutings of soft clay between to firm flame-tight joints. The door of the kiln, when full, is bricked up, and the firing proceeds for from twenty-four to thirty-six hours, after which the kiln is allowed three or four days to cool. The pieces are then taken out and dipped in the various glazes.

When the raw glaze has been thus applied to a piece and you see it slowly drying for the kiln, the color and decoration disappear, except as the latter may be traced through the slight reliefs. They look exactly as though they had received a heavy coat of ordinary whitewash. But what happens when they go back again into the fire is the transmutation of this whitewash into a glass or glaze, through which you can see again all the colors and decorations. This is true of all the varieties of Rookwood except the mat glazes. In these you do not see through the glaze at all, and therefore when they are used, no painting or coloring in clay is done. You will observe how radically this difference in method distinguishes the mat glazes from the others. The decorations, if any, on the clay pieces are entirely plastic, consisting of incised lines or modeled reliefs. Apart from these the artistic interest is now transferred entirely to the glaze itself, and the body, instead of being an integral part of the decorative medium, becomes merely a support for the glaze surface. The painting is done on the biscuit pieces with the various colored mat glazes in their raw state. When fired, these glazes are crystalline in structure, and though not the least transparent, admit of a certain interpenetration of light upon which much of its effect depends. The charm of texture is the highest quality of a fine mat glaze, and through this the colors play delightfully.

*This high-shouldered vase by Charles S. Todd in mottled blue matte glaze dates from 1920 and is 10 inches high. (Wolf's)*

More than forty thousand glaze formulas were listed at the factory and more than 500 glazes were in daily use during the mid-1930s. Rookwood pottery changed with the times in clay, glaze, and design.

## LINES

*(The dates given are the earliest known for the line. The quotations are from Rookwood catalogs of 1896, c. 1902, 1904, c. 1915, and from advertisements.)*

*Aerial Blue:* "Mono-chromatic ware with a quiet decoration in celestial blue on a cool, grayish white ground," 1894.

*Aurora Orange:* Textured surface like an orange peel, vellum finish in shades of yellow and orange, c. 1943.

*Aventurine:* A rich red, 1930.

*Bisque:* Unglazed finish, mainly found on early pieces.

*Brilliant:* A glaze name referred to in an article by Susan Frackelton, *Sketch Book,* July 1906.

*In 1924, this pottery sign was made to be placed in jewelry store windows. It is glazed tan and black.*

*Yellow vase with flowers and wax matte glaze, 17¼ inches high, 1927. (Wolf's)*

*This Rookwood tile with raised decoration has a yellow ground with blue and green relief areas. It is 6 by 6 inches. (Smithsonian Institution)*

*Butterfat:* A matte glaze with a greasy look made in shades of yellow, c. 1930.

*Cameo:* Slip-painted decoration under a clear glaze, c. 1893.

*Celadon Glaze:* Rich green glaze, c. 1930.

*Cirrus Glaze:* Thick white matte glaze resembling clouds, 1950s.

*Conventional Mat Glaze:* "This type is a mat glaze with flat, conventional decoration in colors. This new type of Rookwood appeals to a taste for simple, flat decorations rather than naturalistic treatment, and reflects an important movement in modern art," 1904.

*Coramundel:* Glaze to copy Tiger Eye, 1930s.

*Crystal Glaze:* Transparent glaze over incised designs or colored clay, developed 1943.

*Crystalline:* Another glaze name referred to in the article by Frackelton in *Sketch Book:* 1906; also mentioned as a new glaze in a booklet put out by the factory c. 1930.

*Flambé:* Red glaze of the Chinese type, c. 1920; mentioned in a Starkville, Mississippi, leaflet of the late 1960s.

*Flowing Glaze:* "This deep and heavy glaze has a quality resembling in many respects some of the old Chinese. It has a similar luminosity and at the same time a peculiar richness of texture. The decoration is painted upon the piece in slight relief, in forms and colors so simple that the glaze may flow pleasantly over them." c. 1907.

*Goldstone:* "Resembling the glistening of golden particles in aventurine, but rather more limpid [than Tiger Eye] by reason of the glaze. Both the Tiger Eye and Goldstone are seen on dark grounds," 1896.

*Incised Mat Glaze:* "Derives its name from the incised decoration. This type is made in reds, blues, yellows, greens, etc. in a multitude of shapes; sometimes in single colors, sometimes in a combination of two or more colors," 1904.

*Iris:* "Designates a large class of effects with a considerable range of color based upon a warm gray tone. Delicate pinks, soft blues, and greens, creamy whites and yellows, play tenderly into the gray scheme. In these lighter wares a more crisp decoration is used," 1904 (first made in 1894); Dark Iris or Black Iris was a darker variation made c. 1901.

*Jewel Porcelain:* A semiporcelain with incised lines for embossed decorations, characterized by rich, heavy color glaze, 1920 to 1960s.

*Lagoon Green:* yellowish green over brown decorations, 1943.

*Limoges Style:* Name used in the early 1890s; it was the application to wet clay pieces of metallic oxides mixed with clay and water, or "slip."

*Lustre:* Undecorated or with incised designs glazed with rainbow luster, 1915.

*Mahogany:* Slip-painted decoration on dark brown ground, 1884; later called Standard Glaze.

*Majolica:* Dark green, red, yellow, blue, and black heavy-gloss glaze. Used primarily on bookends and figurines.

*Mat Glaze Painting:* "A mat glaze with decorations painted in rich, warm reds, yellows, greens, and blues, a process of the greatest difficulty, suggestive of glowing enamels, but with a mat texture," 1904.

*Mat Glazes:* "Distinguished by the absence of gloss. Their texture is in itself delightful, a pleasure to the eye and to the touch, whether the surface be decorated or not. The glaze is no longer designed merely to protect the colors beneath, nor to reveal them as though swimming in a lustrous depth, but is now itself the dominating interest.

"Rookwood Mat possesses hitherto unknown range of color in glazes of astonishing variety of texture. Now it seems solid as quartz, and partaking of its crystalline structure; again one sees a more mellow surface suggesting that of firm, ripe fruit, or again it suggests the quality of old ivory, or of stained parchment; but always showing a slight translucency, a sense of depth, and a pleasure in the feel of it which makes it delightful to the touch.

"On many pieces decoration of flowers is applied or other subjects broadly painted or modeled. Others are treated with simple incised designs, yet always emphasizing those qualities of texture and color which give this type of Rookwood its fine distinction," 1904 (first made 1896).

*Modeled Mat:* Mat glaze with modeled decoration, 1904.

*Ombroso:* "[This] type of glaze was brought out in 1910. The colors are usually in quiet tones of gray and brown, with occasional accents of other colors (green, blue or yellow), and the decorations, if any, of relief modeling or incised designs," c. 1915. *Arts and Decoration,* September 1911: "Three vases delicately modeled and decorated in a simple and exquisite manner, the result lightly touched with color. In the examples of the true Ombroso ware no color is used, except that in the glaze itself, which is modified by the forms and the chemical changes due to the effect of the fire upon the texture and color, but does away with the necessity of painting, either in mineral colors or with the colored slip," 1904.

*Oxblood:* A red crystalline glaze with a gold or silver glitter, 1920; a 1930 Oxblood line was made with no glitter.

*Porcelain:* A semiporcelain covered with glossy glaze, at first plain or low relief designs, by 1923 painted with slip on biscuit piece; pieces are marked with the impressed letter *P* on the base, 1916.

*Sang de Boeuf:* Solid red glaze, 1894.

*Sea Green:* "A variety of Rookwood in which a limpid, opalescent sea-green effect is attained. Beautiful combinations of rich, deep blues, and greens, relieved with glowing touches of golden yellow, red and other warm colors marked this variety," often marked with incised or impressed letter *G,* c. 1907, developed 1894.

*Smear Glaze:* An earlier effort at a dull finish or Smear Glaze mentioned in a 1902 catalog; it was a different method than the matte glaze developed by 1900.

*Soft Porcelain:* Bright glaze, simple forms, 1915–c. 1925.

*Solid Color:* "Pieces comprise many of the richest and deepest reds and browns, some so intense that only actual sunshine will reveal the elusive hue. Others are covered with feathery mottlings, one color often playing

*Vellum celadon green vase, 9 inches tall, 1936. (Wolf's)*

*A jewel jar with cover from about 1930. The 5½-by-6-inch jar is decorated with pink and blue triangles and flowers. (Skinner, Inc.)*

(Left to right) *Rookwood vases dating from 1922, 1923, 1924, 1952, and 1953 (5 inches high). (Smithsonian Institution)*

*This matte-glazed tile with raised pink tulips and green leaves on a cream ground is 6 inches square. It has the impressed marks "RP 416 G627X" and blurred numerals that appear to be 1947. The frame is original. (Private collection)*

almost imperceptibly through another with occasionally a pleasant grayness of surface as though catching light. Some are combinations of gray greens and browns. There have also been a few small pieces of brilliant red, some of the 'Sang de Boeuf' quality, others lighter," 1896.

*Standard Glaze:* "The term given the type which first matured [first produced at the pottery]. It is the familiar low-toned ware, usually yellow, red and brown in color, with flower and figure decoration. It is characterized by a luxuriant painting in warm colors under a brilliant glaze. From a comparatively light and golden scheme the color arrangement varies to deep, rich red, brown, and green combinations in mellow tones," c. 1884.

*Tiger Eye:* "Takes its name from a strange luminosity of the glaze in places where one catches glimpses of mysterious striations, which seem to glow with a golden fire, indefinable in words. These happy accidents of the kiln are necessarily very rare," 1896; "the fire always contributing its uncertain element to enhance or disturb the artists' calculations. Tiger Eye was first made at Rookwood in 1884 and is the earliest of the class of crystalline glazes since so extensively made at Sèvres, Copenhagen, and Berlin, though none have attained this particular effect," c. 1907.

*Vellum:* "This variety of Rookwood Mat Glaze differs from all others, and was first exhibited at the St. Louis Exposition, 1904. It is the fruit of long experiment, and technically considered, is an achievement worthy to be first shown at a World's Exposition, so radical is the departure it makes from any previously known types.

"The name Vellum conveys some idea of its refinement of texture and color. Devoid of lustre, without dryness, it partakes both to the touch and to the eye of the qualities of old parchment. The mat glazes hitherto known have permitted, by reason of their heaviness, of but little decorations other than modeling or very flat and broad painting. The refinements of rendering so generally esteemed in ceramics have been impossible in that me-

(Left) *Blue-stylized daisies are part of the underglaze decoration on this cream-colored vase. The entire piece is covered with a clear bubbled glaze. It is 5½ inches high. The 1943 flame mark appears with the shape number, 6185 F, and an unknown artist's cipher that may be "H.A." (Right) Stylized leaves in relief decorate this 4½-inch-high vase. It is marked with the 1932 flame mark, and the shape number 6217. (Private collection)*

dium. The Vellum on the contrary retains for the artist all those qualities possible hitherto under brilliant glaze alone. It is therefore within bounds to say that Rookwood, in developing this new ware, has taken a step forward as remarkable as any in its history,'' 1904.

*Water Color:* Writer's name for a design type that resembled a watercolor painting with an indistinct outline, c. 1924.

*Wax Mat:* Soft waxy surface, sometimes looks curdled, matte glaze, c. 1930 (developed by Stanley Burt and John Wareham).

*Wine Madder:* Shades of maroon to blue-purple with an orange peel finish, 1943.

# Rose Valley
### *Rose Valley, Pennsylvania*

An arts and crafts colony was founded in Rose Valley, Pennsylvania, in 1901. The members were weavers, potters, printers, writers, musicians, and others who joined together to create a variety of decorative arts, including some unusual furniture.

William P. Jervis (see Jervis Pottery) opened a pottery shop at the colony in 1904. When he left the colony in 1905, the shop closed. Jervis used matte glazes of many colors. Some pieces were made with mottled, wrinkled, or metallic finishes. Pieces were marked with the name Jervis or a cluster of six dots. The colony's publication in 1903 said the pottery was to be marked with the rose and *V* mark.

ROSE VALLEY
*Impressed.*

W Jr Jervis
*Impressed.*

# Roseville Pottery
### *Roseville and Zanesville, Ohio*

The Roseville Pottery was incorporated in 1892. Its founders began business by purchasing the J. B. Owens factory, which had started operating in 1885. When Roseville Pottery incorporated, George F. Young of Lower Salem, Ohio, who had tried teaching, selling Singer sewing machines, and other jobs without success, became the secretary and general manager. C. F. Allison was president; J. F. Weaver, vice president; Thomas Brown, treasurer; and J. L. Pugh became a member of the board of directors.

The firm's first manufacturing line included stoneware jars, flowerpots, and cuspidors. In 1898, the pottery bought a second plant, the Midland Pottery, and made more stoneware. The Linden Avenue plant, built for Clark Stoneware Company in 1892 in Zanesville, Ohio, was also purchased by Roseville Pottery. Painted wares were made at the Linden location until 1900, when the glazed Rozane ware was developed. There is much confusion about the company's production locations among the early reports of the Roseville Pottery plants. The Zanesville Chamber of Commerce Booklet of 1918 says: "The company began operations in Roseville, where they operated two plants. In 1898, they built a pottery in Zanesville, and a little

**ROZANE**
**RPCo**
*Impressed mark, used before 1905–1910; also used on other lines without word "Rozane."*

**AZUREAN**
*Impressed mark, 1902; sometimes appears with RPCo mark.*

*Paper sticker. Stock number and retail price printed in red ink.*

Applied ceramic seal, first used in 1904; name changed for different lines. Mark was also used for Egypto; Mara; Mongol; Royal.

Applied ceramic disk or paper sticker, printed in green ink; used from 1904 on Della Robbia; Rozane I.

Ink stamp, black, blue, or green; used after 1914–1930. May have been used as early as 1910.

Gray on black aluminum foil sticker, used 1914–1934. Possibly appeared as early as 1912.

Impressed mark, from 1914.

Impressed mark, from 1915.

Gray paper sticker, from 1917. Same sticker in gold used on Pine Cone line, 1930s.

Impressed mark, from 1930s. Numbers used with mark represent pattern number and size in inches.

**ROZANE "OLYMPIC" POTTERY**

Black ink stamp, used after 1905–before 1939. Description of scene printed on bottom of each piece.

**ROSEVILLE POTTERY CO. ZANESVILLE, O.**

Red ink stamp mark, after 1905–before 1939.

later another one, still continuing the plants at Roseville."

In 1902 the Muskingum Stoneware Plant in Zanesville became part of the Roseville Pottery. By 1910 all work in the town of Roseville was terminated and the entire Roseville Pottery operation was located in Zanesville. At no time did the Roseville Pottery make artware in Roseville. All of the early production was devoted to utilitarian wares such as stoneware and painted flowerpots.

After the move to Zanesville, George Young decided that the Roseville Pottery (as it continued to be called) should make art pottery. Young hired Ross C. Purdy to create a line. Purdy made a ware that was similar to the underglaze, slip-decorated, brown-colored wares popular at the time. The name "Rozane," combining Roseville and Zanesville, was used as the mark. Later, a light-background Rozane was made, and later still, some other lines with the same mark. Other marks were also used.

John Herold, hired as a designer and art director in 1900, created the Rozane Mongol line. The pottery then began making a competing art line for each new product produced by the Weller Pottery Company. A Japanese artist, Gazo "Fudgi" Fujiyama, was hired to help add oriental designs to the ware. He developed Woodland, or Fujiyama, ware and Rozane Fudji. Frederick Rhead, who had worked for S. A. Weller, was art director from 1904 to 1908. He developed the Della Robbia and Olympic lines. When Rhead left to pursue his career in teaching in St. Louis, Missouri, his brother Harry, from England, replaced him.

In 1917 the Muskingum plant burned and that entire operation was moved to the Linden plant. Frank Ferrell (whose name is sometimes spelled Ferrel) was hired as art director, remaining in that post until 1954. He developed the Pine Cone line, which derived from ideas he had suggested at the Weller plant. It became the most popular line ever made at Roseville. (Earlier, one of Ferrell's rejected Weller designs was produced by Peters and Reed and called "Moss Aztec.")

In 1918 the new trademark "Roseville U.S.A." was adopted.

Raised mark, after 1935–1954.

Raised mark, after 1935–1953.

Raised mark, 1939–1953. Numbers used with mark represent pattern number and size in inches.

*Roseville U.S.A.*

Raised mark, 1939–1953. Numbers used with mark represent pattern number.

*ROSEVILLE ROZANE WARE POTTERY*

Blue ink stamp, 1939–1953.

*raymor by Roseville U.S.A. OVENPROOF PAT. PEND.*

Raised mark, 1950s.

*Lotus L6-9"*

Raised mark, 1950s.

**ROSEVILLE PASADENA PLANTER U.S.A.**

Raised mark, 1950s.

George Young turned the general manager's job over to his son Russell T. Young. In 1931 Russell's mother, Anna Young, became president. The name of the firm was changed to Roseville Pottery, Inc. In 1938 Anna's son-in-law, F. S. Clement, became president. After Clement's death, Robert P. Windisch held the job until he left in 1954. That year, the Roseville Pottery, Inc., including all designs, the plant, and its contents, was sold to the New England Ceramics Company, after which it was sold to Franklin Potteries of Franklin, West Virginia. By 1954, all Roseville Pottery production had stopped.

### PRODUCT

A contemporary description of the work at the Roseville Pottery appeared in "A Visit to Some Zanesville Potteries" in *The Southwestern Book* of December 1905:

> We went first to the Roseville potteries, which occupy a large group of buildings, wherein is manufactured a great variety of ware, including washstand sets, jardinieres, and art ware. Over three hundred persons are employed at this plant, and about five thousand pieces of finished ware are turned out every day.
>
> As our time was limited, and we were both very fond of art pottery, my friend and I visited only the rooms in which the art ware is manufactured.

An ear of corn decorates this Rozane Royal mug. It has dark glaze and is 6 inches high. The mark is "Rozane Royal Scene" and the artist is V(irginia) Adams. (Donald Alexander)

M(ae) Timberlake signed this dark Rozane vase. It is 10 inches high. (Donald Alexander)

J(osephine) Imlay is the artist who signed this Rozane Royal vase with light glaze. It is 8½ inches high. The mark is "5," plus the Rozane Royal emblem. (Donald Alexander)

E. A. (Elizabeth Ayers).
Also worked at Lonhuda; Weller.

G. A. Unknown.

Virginia Adams. c. 1911. Rozane.
Also worked at Owens; Weller.

A. B. Unknown.

C. B. Unknown. Crocus line.

E. B., E. R. B. Unknown.
Della Robbia.

F. B., F. A. B. Unknown.
Della Robbia.

G. B. Unknown.
Della Robbia.

M. B. Unknown.

A. F. Best. Also worked
at Owens; Weller.

Jenny Burgoon.

John Butterworth. Also worked
at Owens; Weller.

E. C. Unknown. Della Robbia.

Charles Chilcote.
Also worked at Owens; Weller; Zane.

Anna Dautherty (?). Also worked
at Weller.

Anthony Dunlavy.

E. Dutro.

Charles Duvall.

Katy (Katie) Duvall. Della Robbia.

Hattie Eberlein. Also worked
at Owens.

M. F. Unknown.

Bill Farnsworth.

Frank Ferrell. 1917–1954. Art
director; developed Ferrella; Pine
Cone. Also worked at Owens;
Peters and Reed; Weller.

Gazo Fujiyama. c. 1900.
Japanese artist. Fudji; Fujiyama;
Rozane; Woodland.

Gussie Gerwick.

Goldie.

C. H. Unknown. 1906. Della
Robbia.

William Hall. Also worked
at Weller (?).

John J. Herold (1871–1923). Hired
1900. Designer, art director; created
Rozane Mongol. Chemist, later
started Herold China Company,
which became Coors China Co. Also
worked at Owens; Weller.

**MH**

*Madge Hurst. Also worked at Weller.*

*Joseph Imlay. (Josephine ?)*

**JI    J Imlay    J.I.**

*Josephine Imlay. Decorated Rozane. Also worked at Weller.*

*George Krause. c. 1915. Technical supervisor.*

*H. L. Unknown.*

**Ht**

*Harry Larzelere. Also worked at Owens.*

**C.L.    Cv    CL    CL    CLL    C L Leffler**

*Claude L. Leffler. Azurean; Rozane. Also worked at Weller.*

**F. M.**

*F. M. Unknown.*

**W**

*L. McGrath. Also worked at Weller (?).*

**B Mallen    BM**

*B. Mallen. Also worked at Owens.*

**M    A**

*Mignon Martineau.*

*Madeline Menet.*

**C Mitchell**

*C. Mitchell. Rozane.*

**)HM**

*Hattie Mitchell (?). Also worked at Owens; Weller.*

**L. Mitchell    LM    LM**

*Lillie (Lilly) Mitchell. Also worked at Weller.*

**M**

*Gorden Mull. Modeler. Married Grace Neff.*

**B. MYERS**

*B. Myers.*

**H . MYERS**

*Helen Myers.*

**M·M**

*M. Myers. Also worked at Weller.*

**W. MYERS**

**W. MYERS**

*Walter Myers (Meyers).*

**C NEFF**

*C. Neff. Rozane.*

**GN**

**G. NEFF**

*Grace Neff. 1911. Artist, decorator. Married Gorden Mull.*

**CN**

*Christian Nielson. Modeler and designer.*

**MN**

*M. N. Unknown. Rozane.*

**KO**

*K. O. Unknown.*

*C. E. Offinger (d. 1962). 1900–1915. Technical supervisor.*

**M. P.**

*Mary Pierce.*

**HP    Pillsbury    HP**

*Hester W. Pillsbury. Also worked at Weller.*

*Ross C. Purdy (1875–1949). Artist; developed Rozane.*

**F Rhead**

*Frederick Hürten Rhead (1880–1942). Brother of Harry Rhead. 1904–1908. Art director; developed Aztec; Della Robbia; Olympic. Also worked for American Encaustic Tiling Company, c. 1910; Avon Faience, 1902–1903; University City, 1909–1911; Weller, 1904. Studio potter, Santa Barbara, California, c. 1914.*

**H Rhead**

*Harry Rhead (1881–1950). Brother of Frederick Hürten Rhead. 1908–1920. Art director; developed Carnelian; Donatello; Mostique; Pauleo. Also worked at Mosaic Tile Co., 1922–1923; Standard Tile Company, 1923.*

**RLS**

**RS**

*R. Lillian Shoemaker (?). Also worked at Owens.*

**AS**

*Allen Simpson.*

*Helen Smith. Also worked at Owens; Weller.*

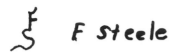

*Fred Steel(e). Also worked at Weller.*

*Tot Steele. Also worked at Owens; Weller.*

*Caroline Frances Steinle (?). Also worked at Rookwood.*

*E. T. Unknown. Woodland.*

*C. Minnie Terry. Also worked at Owens; Weller.*

M . T.

*Madeline Thompson (?). Also worked at Weller.*

Mae Timberlak
M.T. 5

*Mae Timberlake. Also worked at Owens; Weller.*

S.T.  S̄T

*Sarah Timberlake. Also worked at Owens; Weller.*

C U

*C. U. Unknown.*

*Arthur Williams. Also worked at Owens.*

C. Z.
C. 3.

*Clotilda Zanetta. Also worked at Rookwood; Weller.*

*V(irginia) Adams signed this dark Rozane Royal 15-inch tankard. It is marked "5, Rozane Royal" with the Rozane emblem. (Donald Alexander)*

Our guide led us from room to room, showing and explaining to us the various processes through which the clay passes, until it is ready for the admiring purchaser.

We learned that the Ohio clays naturally run to golden browns and yellows, that can be preserved unaltered through the intense heat of the firing to which the ware is subjected.

Most of the potteries use clay from the neighboring hills, but to produce certain kinds of ware, and certain color effects, other ingredients are added; sometimes clays from other sources are used entirely or mixed with the native clays.

The abundant supply of natural gas at Zanesville is a potent factor in the manufacturing of all kinds of pottery. By its use degrees of heat are attained that would be impossible by other methods of firing, and the buildings are kept clean and free from dust.

Led by our guide, we viewed with interest the processes through which the clay is taken, from the time it reaches the factory, fresh from the neighboring hill, until it is transformed into a thing of beauty, fit to grace an artistic home.

The clay is pulverized and thoroughly washed, filtered and mixed with water, to a certain consistency. It is then, either by hand or machine, pressed into a mold, made of plaster of paris. This mold absorbs the water, making a body of clay next to the mold. After three or four minutes, the liquid that remains is poured

No. 956. 8¾ in. high. $9.00 each.  No. 949. 12 in. high. $8.00 each.  No. 882. 9 in. high. $25.00 each.  No. 870. 11 in. high. $15.00 each.  No. 827. 9 in. high. $12.00 each.

*A page from the Roseville 1906 catalog showing the Rozane Royal dark-glazed pieces. (Ohio Historical Society)*

*This 18½-inch-high vase is Rozane Royal with a dark glaze. It is marked "Rozane, RP Co. 865." The vase is signed by the artist Walter Myers. (Donald Alexander)*

*This 10-inch-wide by 9-inch-high Rozane jardiniere has a brown to green to mahogany glaze with orange and floral decoration. The artist's cipher, "WH" (for William Hall), appears at the base. The impressed Rozane mark and "40 4 RPCO" and "2" are on the bottom. (Donald Alexander)*

out. The shell thus left is the future vase. It goes to the finisher who sponges and smooths off all defects.

The underglaze artware is sprayed with a clay liquid in mineral colors, and we marveled at the rapidity with which the blending is done by the young girls in charge of this branch of the work. We were allowed to stand and watch the decorators at work, painting from nature or copy, in mineral colors, giving to each article with skillful fingers its own individual crown of beauty.

After being decorated, the piece is taken to the dry room, where it stays until the water has all evaporated, and then is placed in the kiln.

We were surprised to find how large the kilns are, some of them being twenty feet high inside. The men have to climb on ladders to put on the top of the tall columns of saggers, or boxes of clay, which contain the precious ware. At the right time, after the ordeal by fire, each article is dipped in a liquid glass solution called glaze, and after this, fired for the second time, and is then a finished product.

We were told that we had seen the usual process of manufacturing artware, but variations of this and different processes are used, to produce other effects, and that the artist chemists are allowed to experiment, and often achieve wonderful results.

The greatest care in every detail must be exercised in order to secure perfection.

Most of the decorators were women, and I observed women and girls at work in many other rooms. Such employment must be very pleasant, congenial and suitable, bringing them into constant contact with beauty, in form and color, and it demands the care, patience and attention to detail which women are fitted by nature to give to their work.

About 1900 the Cornelian or Cornelian Twist line was introduced. The unmarked 6-inch vase has a dull green glaze and gold trim. (Donald Alexander)

Myers signed this dark-glazed 16-inch Rozane ewer. It is marked "1 Rozane RP Co 858." A similar piece appears in the 1906 catalog as "Rozane Royal, dark." (Donald Alexander)

A portrait of the actress Maude Adams decorates this Rozane vase with dark glaze. The 13-inch-high piece is marked "Rozane RPCo 812." The artist's initials "AD" (for Anthony Dunlavy) are on the vase. (Donald Alexander)

(Above) A vase pictured in the 1906 Roseville catalog showing the Rozane Royal Light pieces. (Ohio Historical Society)

(Left to right) Rozane Royal 8-inch vase of crackled gray and green glaze. Rozane Ware Egypto candlestick inscribed "More Light to Goethe," 3¾ inches high. And an orange and brown urn with orange flowers. It is marked "R.P. Co." and is in the Rozane Royal line. (Smithsonian Institution)

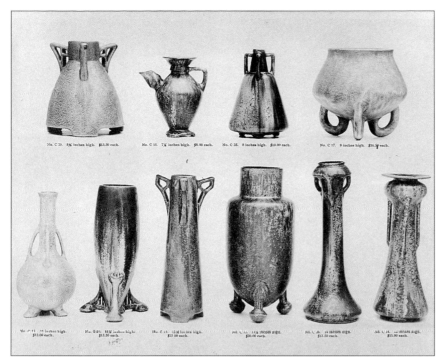

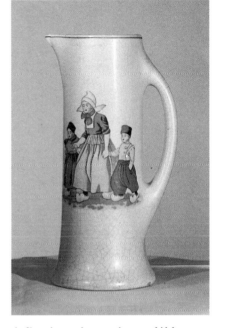

*A page from the 1906 Roseville catalog shows the Crystalis line. (Ohio Historical Society)*

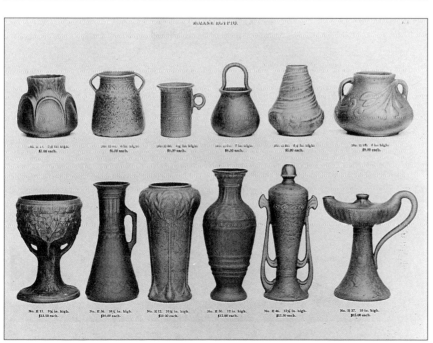

*A Dutch mother and two children are shown in a decal on this pitcher. The line called "Dutch" was introduced about 1900. The figures are multicolored, and a thin blue line appears near the top. The 12-inch-high pitcher is unmarked. (Donald Alexander)*

*A page from the 1906 Roseville catalog shows the Rozane Egypto line. (Ohio Historical Society)*

Other sources say the pieces were made from American clays, mainly from Ohio and Tennessee. The earliest pieces were painted clay. The artwares were made with almost every type of decorative detail, slip decoration, decals, freehand decoration, incised or embossed designs. A few lines, such as Aztec, were decorated by slip squeezed from a bag, just as we decorate today with cake frosting.

The pottery used more modern methods through the years and by 1920 the handmade art pottery was replaced by commercial pottery produced by machine to be sold in quantity. Embossed designs with little freehand decoration were favored.

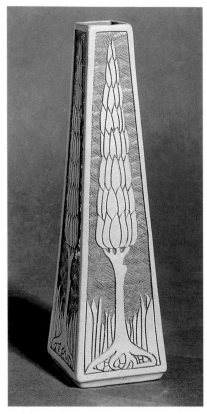

*Frederick H. Rhead designed this vase made by "C.H." about 1906–1908. It is decorated with brown and buff cypress trees. The glossy-glazed piece is 10½ inches high. (Private collection; photograph from The Art Museum, Princeton University, Princeton, New Jersey)*

*This 2¼-inch juvenile cup has an orange band on cream ground. The Sunbonnet Baby is wearing a blue dress and yellow bonnet. The cup is marked "Rv" on the bottom. (J. Walter Yore Company)*

## LINES

*(The date given represents the catalog year when the line was first shown or, if in parentheses, an approximation from other sources.)*

*Antique Green Matte:* overall design of raised vines, solid green matte glaze, brown overglazed patches, 1916.

*Apple Blossom:* colored background of blue, coral, or green, relief apple blossom spray, marked "Roseville" in relief, 1948.

*Artcraft:* geometric relief, may be Red Topea (1930)–1934.

*Artwood:* Art Deco shapes, yellow and brown, green and brown, or gray and wine (late 1940s–1951).

*Autumn:* shaded creamware background, pink, green landscapes, 1916.

*Aztec (Aztec Art):* base color beige, brown, green, cream, or gray, stylized band resembling leaves, flowers, or Indian patterns, 1910 catalog listing, may have been made about 1904.

*Azurean (Azurine):* blue and white background decorated with ships, scenes, portraits, or flowers, high-gloss glaze, marked "R.P. Co." on some pieces, 1902.

*Azurine, Orchid and Turquoise:* solid high-gloss colors of blue, orchid, or turquoise, unmarked (1920), 1952.

*Baneda:* incised band with raised leaf decoration on mottled green and red ground (1933).

*Bittersweet:* shaded background, relief bittersweet vine in natural shades,

A Della Robbia vase, pictured in the 1906 catalog, has incised and painted underglazed decorations of flowers and leaves in blue, green, yellow, and orange. This 11-inch piece has a glossy glaze. It is marked with the Rozane Ware disk in relief and the artist's initials, "W.M.," for Walter Myers. (Private collection, photograph from The Art Museum, Princeton University, Princeton, New Jersey)

This 10½-inch-high Della Robbia vase is decorated with raised fish. The piece is signed "ED" by the artist (E. Dutro?) and has the Rozane Ware seal. (Donald Alexander)

This early Roseville umbrella stand is number 724. The realistically colored peacock is shown against a cobalt blue background. (Skinner, Inc.)

backgrounds of gray, green, or yellow, marked "Roseville" in relief, 1940–1951.

*Blackberry:* mottled green line with autumn-colored blackberry leaves and berries at top, 1933.

*Bleeding Heart:* shaded pink or blue background, relief bleeding hearts in natural colors, marked "Roseville" in relief, 1938, 1940.

*Blue Ware:* high-gloss glaze, blue background, underglaze decorating, 1910.

*Burmese:* solid-color green, white, or black, busts of Burmese men and women decorate bookends, plaques, bowls, candleholders, 1950.

*Bushberry:* dark green, blue, or orange rough background, relief bushberry spray in natural colors, marked "Roseville" in relief, 1940s.

*Cameo:* dark green or beige matte finish background with a border of trees and girls holding hands, 1920.

*Capri:* modernistic shapes, solid, muted colors, celadon, beige, maroon (c. 1950).

*Carnelian I:* drip glaze decoration over matte glaze on specially shaped pieces with elaborate handle; two colorations, one with matte glaze and

Roseville Rozane pieces closely resemble the brown-glazed wares by Rookwood. This Rozane lemonade pitcher is signed by Alfred Best. It is 8½ inches high. (Early Auctions)

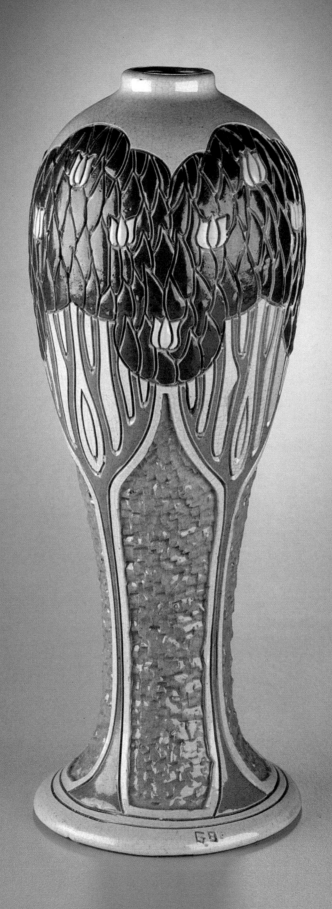

*This Rozane mug has a brown background and is decorated with earth-tone cherries.*

*Dogwood I pattern was made from 1916 to 1918. This green vase is 11 inches high. (Wolf's)*

*Tea sets were made in the Landscape pattern about 1915. This teapot shows views of windmills and ships in blue on a cream background. The pieces are unmarked. (Donald Alexander)*

dark drip top border in two shades of blue, pink with blue, or green with gold, other with textured glaze in mixture of black, purple, yellow, rose, sometimes turquoise; marked with "Rv" cipher (*v* within loop of *R*), 1910–1915 (developed by Harry Rhead).

*Carnelian II:* textured glaze, blended color, handles and shapes less ornate than Carnelian I, 1916.

*Cherry Blossom:* pink, brown, buff, yellow, blue body with vertical bands in relief, natural-color cherry blossom flowers and leaves, 1932.

*Chinese Red:* see Rozane Mongol.

*Chloron:* dark green background, matte finish, embossed classically inspired decoration on cream ground, mark "Chloron" in a semicircle appears on some pieces, 1907.

*This 3-inch-high bowl is in the Persian pattern, made about 1916. It is marked only with the number "14" in red ink. (Donald Alexander)*

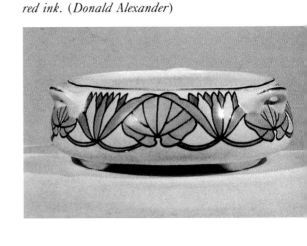

(Left) *A selection of Donatello pieces. The Donatello pattern was introduced in 1915. These unmarked pieces are decorated with orange and green scenes on white ground. (J. Walter Yore Company)*

(Opposite page) *Early, Della Robbia design. The line was introduced in 1906 and featured colorful enameled sgraffito decoration. This vase is 9 inches tall and is marked "Rozane Ware" in relief. (Private collection)*

(Right) *Mottled matte glaze covers these candleholders of the Cornelian line. Each is 3 inches high and 4½ inches in diameter and is marked with a blue underglaze "Rv." (Private collection)*

(Above) *Yellow, blue, and green glazed geometric designs appear on the unglazed gray background of this Mostique vase. The interior is glazed green. The unmarked piece is 12 inches high. (Private collection)*

(Below) *Dahlrose vases are decorated with white flowers on brown ground. The brown and green bowls were made in 1930. They have a barklike appearance and are unmarked.*

*Clemana:* yellow-beige or blue-green background, raised stylized floral decoration and basketweave, sometimes marked "Roseville" in relief, 1934.

*Clematis:* green, brown, or blue background, relief clematis flowers, 48 items, marked "Roseville" in relief, 1944–1945.

*Coat-of-Arms:* banner and shield design, black and red on cream (1916).

*Colonial:* blue spongeware (1900).

*Columbine:* shaded background in red, blue, or brown, relief columbine spray, 44 items, marked "Roseville" in relief, 1941.

*Corinthian:* green and ivory vertical fluting with wreath border, marked with "Rv" cipher, 1923 (developed under George Young).

*Cornelian or Cornelian Twist:* spongeware, yellow and brown or blue, some pieces had raised decorations (1900).

*Cosmos:* green, blue, or earth-tone background, several ridges as part of design around center of vase, raised cosmos flower decoration in natural colors, marked "Roseville" impressed or in relief, 1939.

Yellow sunflowers and green leaves cover this Sunflower vase made about 1930. The unmarked vase is 6¼ inches high. (Donald Alexander)

This Jonquil vase from the 1931 line features white jonquils on green to orange ground. It is unmarked. (J. Walter Yore Company)

This Cherry Blossom vase, 5¼ inches high, was made about 1932 and is unmarked. (Donald Alexander)

*Cremo:* three colors blended together, green at base, yellow center, rose top, swirled stem with single blossom evenly spaced around vase (1910–c. 1915), 1916.

*Cremona:* pink, blue, or cream background, small raised flowers and leaves (1924–1930), 1927.

*Crocus:* stylized geometric and floral designs of various colors, slip decoration, crocus flowers not used as part of decoration, sometimes called Shiny Aztec (c. 1915).

*Crystal Green:* c. 1939. Appears in contemporary pattern lists, but design unknown.

*Crystalis:* crystalline glazed undecorated pieces made on Rozane shapes, marked with Rozane Ware seal, 1906.

(Above) *This 14-inch vase of deep red is undecorated. It is the Rozane Mongol line. (Smithsonian Institution)*

(Left) *One of the most powerful Art Deco designs created by an American pottery is the Moderne pattern made by Roseville about 1936. The vases are 6 and 4 inches high; the bowl is 8 inches across. (Wolf's)*

*This 7¼-inch Baneda line vase from 1933 is unmarked. The piece has a mottled red background with red berries and green leaves. (Donald Alexander)*

*The Laurel line, introduced in 1934, was often marked like this 6¼-inch vase, with a silver-colored paper sticker. (Donald Alexander)*

*Twenty-two different shapes and sizes in jade green, celestial blue, and temple white were made in this Ming Tree line in 1949. This vase is 6½ inches high. It is marked "20, Roseville, U.S.A." (Donald Alexander)*

*Dahlrose:* daisylike flowers with green leaves on mottled beige and cream background (1924–1928).

*Dawn:* pale pink, yellow, or blue matte glaze with simple raised floral decoration, rectangular handles, bases, and feet, impressed Roseville mark, 1937.

*Della Robbia:* background cut away, Greek, Persian, or conventional decorations remained, overglazed, sgraffito decoration later added to some

*(Left) An 8-inch-high Bittersweet basket decorated with orange berries on gray ground and marked with a raised "Roseville U.S.A. 809-8." (Bottom center) The Bittersweet flower bowl is 7 by 2½ inches. It is decorated with orange berries on a gray ground and marked "Roseville U.S.A. 826-6." (Right) The 8-inch-high Iris vase made about 1939 is decorated with white iris on blue ground. "Roseville 9-228" is impressed on the bottom. (J. Walter Yore Company)*

The Roseville Pottery made many experimental pieces that were never accepted for commercial production. This vase, front and back view, is a sample that was rejected in the late 1930s. It is decorated with a cranberry bush in red and yellowish green. (Mary and Terry Turan, Mostly Pottery, Wilmington, Illinois)

Pine Cone was first made in 1935. Vases and candlesticks have pinecone decoration on several different colored backgrounds. The line was marked in many different ways. (J. Walter Yore Company)

pieces, marked with Rozane Ware seal, 1906 (developed by Frederick Rhead).

*Dogwood I:* large dogwood flowers on matte green ground, marked with "Rv" cipher (1916–1918) (developed by Frank Ferrell).

*Dogwood II:* white dogwood flowers on smooth green background, high gloss, 1928.

*Donatella tea sets:* cream background, variety of designs, including forget-me-nots, seascape, landscape, Gibson girl, (1914).

*Donatello:* fluted top and bottom, molded strip featuring cherubs and trees, glazed green and brown shades on white background; early pieces (Donatello first line) had matte glaze, later pieces (Donatello second line), semi-gloss or glossy glaze; sometimes marked with large "Rv" cipher or with impressed "Donatello R.P. Co." mark, 1919 (developed by Harry Rhead, who copied the decoration from a Czechoslovakian jardiniere).

*Dutch:* colored decals of Dutch people, creamware with blue edging (1900).

*Earlam:* two-toned mottled glaze, turquoise and tan or green and tan, slight incised ridge at neck of vase (1930).

*Egypto or Rozane Egypto:* Egyptian-shape vases covered with relief decoration and matte green glaze, marked with Egypto seal, 1905 (made by John Herold).

*Falline:* beige with peapodlike green decorations, 1933.

*Ferrella (Ferella):* shell-like border, mottled body, green and brown or rose with ivory shells and other colors, openings at top between shells, 1931 (named for Frank Ferrell).

*Florane:* shaded matte-glazed ware in tans and browns, simple shapes, marked with "Rv" cipher (1920s and c. 1949).

Roseville Pine Cone vase, 7¼ inches high, incised "Roseville 112-7" under the glaze. (Private collection)

(Left and right) *Two vases in the Moss pattern introduced in 1936. The pieces are decorated with moss on pink to green ground and marked with the impressed Roseville mark.* (Center) *Pink and white flowers decorate the 8-inch-high and 7-inch-wide green Foxglove vase made in 1942. It carries the raised "Roseville U.S.A. 373-8" mark.* (J. Walter Yore Company)

*Spires of flowers decorate this Foxglove jardiniere and pedestal, a pattern introduced in 1942. The piece is 24 inches high and is marked "20 Roseville, U.S.A."* (Donald Alexander)

*Made in 1935, this Morning Glory vase is 5 inches tall and 6 inches in diameter at the rim. The piece is unmarked.* (June Greenwald Antiques)

*Florentine:* rough mottled panels alternating with perpendicular clusters of leaves and berries, brown or ivory, green, and brown, marked with "Rv" ink stamp, 1924–1928.

*Forest:* unidentified line.

*Forget-me-not:* blue or lavender forget-me-nots and green leaves in border, gold trim, cream background (1916).

*Foxglove:* solid-color red, blue or green background, relief foxglove stalk, marked "Roseville" in relief, 1942.

*Freesia:* brown, green, orange, purple, or blue background, relief flowers of yellow, pink, or white, 48 shapes, marked "Roseville" in relief, 1945.

*Fuchsia:* slightly mottled background in dark browns, grays, fuchsia leaves, a few drooping blossoms in natural shades, impressed Roseville mark, 1938.

*Fudji:* see Rozane Fudji.

*Fujiyama or Woodland:* sgraffito decorations (incised designs) surrounding glazed design, small dots made with a needle as background, naturalistic designs, colored flowers, matte finish, gray, yellow, brown, or russet; when dots omitted, ware was called Fujiyama or Rozane Fudji and pieces decorated with stylized designs or insects in the European tradition; sometimes marked "Fujiyama" or with "Rozane Ware," "Woodland," or "Rozane Ware" seal, 1905 (created by Gazo "Fudgi" Fujiyama to compete with Dickens Ware by Weller).

*Futura:* modern shapes and designs in blended glaze, pink, blue, beige, green, matte or high gloss, 1924–1928.

*Gardenia:* shaded pastel background in green, gray, or tan, relief white gardenia flower and green leaves, marked "Roseville" in relief, late 1940s.

*Glossy Pine Cone:* Pine Cone with glossy glaze; sometimes called Pine Cone II, 1945–1953.

*Glossy White Rose:* probably same as White Rose, but with glossy finish.

*Holland:* Dutch boy and girl on ivory-colored stoneware, green, tan, or blue shading at rim and base, 1930 (before 1916).

*Holly:* red to green matte glaze on carved holly leaf decoration, 1915.

Orange berries decorate these vases in the Bushberry design, a 1941 line. The background colors range from green to either orange or blue. The raised "Roseville U.S.A." mark is on each piece. (J. Walter Yore Company)

This 7½-inch-high Gardenia vase of the late 1940s is decorated with a white flower on green ground. It is 13 inches wide. (J. Walter Yore Company)

*Imperial I:* twisted vine forming heart-shaped motif on side of green or blue mottled background, 1916–1919.

*Imperial II:* textured matte glaze, red, blue, green, orange, yellow, violet, white, pink, other colors in various combinations, some pieces have raised designs, 1924–1928.

*Iris:* earth-tone background, raised iris decoration in natural colors, often impressed "Roseville"; sometimes marked "Roseville" in relief, 1939.

*Ivory II:* white matte glaze, mostly used shapes from other 1930s lines, impressed Roseville mark, 1937; an earlier line, c. 1916, called Old Ivory or Ivory.

*Ixia:* pink, yellow, green, matte background shaded to darker color at base, floral spray, unusual pointed solid handles, impressed Roseville mark, 1937.

*Jonquil:* white and yellow jonquils and leaves on mottled light brown body, green interior, 1931.

*Juvenile:* decal decoration on light ground, chicks, bunnies, ducks, sunbonnet girl, pigs, dancing cat, sometimes marked with small "Rv" stamp, c. 1916–1930.

*Landscape:* matte glaze, brown or blue decal landscapes of Holland, 1910; glossy glaze, 1920.

*La Rose:* creamy matte background, delicate floral drape in pastel pink and green, marked with "Rv" ink stamp, 1924–1930.

*Laurel:* medium brown, turquoise, or gold background, stylized laurel branches in wood tones, vertical panels of three incised bands, 1934.

These large and small Zephyr Lily vases have white flowers on blue background. Fifty-two different pieces were included in this 1946 line. The raised "Roseville U.S.A." mark appears on the bottom. (J. Walter Yore Company)

*This Roseville Magnolia vase, 6 inches high, dates from 1943 and is marked "Roseville" in relief. (June Greenwald Antiques)*

*Water Lily, a 1943 design, was decorated with yellow or lilac flowers on orange to brown or pink to green ground. Each piece is marked with the raised "Roseville U.S.A." mark. (J. Walter Yore Company)*

*Lombardy:* scalloped top, paneled, square feet, blue or green, 1924–1928.

*Lotus:* petals of lotus surround opening of the vase like an opening lotus flower, marked "Lotus" in relief, 1951.

*Luffa:* green or brown glaze on background with raised waves, border of pointed leaves and flowers, 1934.

*Luster (Lustre):* metallic luster glaze of orange, purple, or yellow, sometimes marked with impressed "Rv," 1921.

*Magnolia:* rough background, tan, blue, or green, relief magnolia in shaded white glaze, 65 items, marked "Roseville" in relief, 1943–1944.

*Mara, Rozane:* see Rozane Mara.

*Matte Color:* blue, orange, yellow, pink, solid or shaded colors, c. 1927.

*Matte Green:* see Antique Green Matte.

*Mayfair:* solid-color glaze, beige, lime, brown and tan, dark green and tan, marked "Roseville" in relief (c. 1947).

*Medallion:* oval cameo decal decoration with gold floral swags, 1916.

*Ming Tree:* tortured branch shapes in oriental manner decorate irregularly shaped pieces, green, turquoise, or white, 1949.

*Mock Orange:* pale pink, yellow, green background, modern shapes, relief mock orange blossoms in natural colors, marked "Roseville, U.S.A., Mock Orange" in relief, 1949.

*Moderne:* modern shapes, solid-color blue, ivory and pink, brown and green, impressed Roseville mark, c. 1936.

*Monticello (Montacello):* mottled brown, blue, band of darker shade, small modern decoration on band, running over edge of band, 1931.

*Morning Glory:* pastel shade background, overall design of raised white morning glories with green leaves on vine, 1935.

*Moss:* shaded pink to white or green to white background, raised decoration of Spanish moss in natural colors, impressed Roseville mark, 1936.

*Mostique:* Indian-inspired flower or conventional incised designs on pebbly matte background, sometimes marked with large "Rv" stamp, 1915.

*Normandy:* pink grapes and green leaves in top brown band, fluted vertical green and white stripes, matte glaze, 1924–1930.

*Nursery:* nursery rhyme motifs, baby plates, other children's dishes (1916).

*Old Ivory:* ivory color, raised classical designs, sometimes tinted with pink, blue, or green (before 1916).

*Olympic, Rozane:* Greek mythological scenes made by black line transfer, white figures, red background, overglazed, decorations not made by hand, marked "Rozane Pottery," "Rozane Olympic Pottery," "Rv," or "Pauleo Pottery" within impressed circular seal (1905), one of the rarest Roseville lines.

*Orian:* solid contrasting colors inside and out, blue, tan, with drip glaze band at rim or yellow with no band, handles shaped like leaves (1935).

*Panel:* see Rosecraft Panel.

*Pasadena:* planters and flower containers in modern shapes, high-gloss pink or black with border of white drip glaze, marked "Roseville, Pasadena Planter" in relief, 1952.

*Pauleo:* original line used varied glazes, no decorations, 1914; decorated after 1916. Designed by Harry Rhead, named after George Young's daughter-in-law Pauline and daughter Leota, oriental shape with red crackled glaze, metallic brown luster overglaze, later version marbleized.

*Peony:* shaded earth tones of brown, green, or coral, rough background, relief peony in yellow, brown, or green, 65 shapes, marked "Roseville" in relief, 1942.

*Persian:* brightly colored Persian-type motif on light color matte background, 1916.

*Pine Cone:* pine branch and pinecones on green, blue, brown, or pink background, marked "Roseville" impressed or in relief, developed by Frank Ferrell in 1917 but not made until the 1930s.

*Poppy:* pale pink or blue shaded background, raised poppy spray in pastel shades, impressed Roseville mark (1930).

*Primrose:* pastel blue, pink, or tan background, globular-shaped vases, raised primrose decoration, impressed Roseville mark, 1934.

*Raymor:* ovenproof modern stoneware, mix-and-match table settings in brown, green, terra cotta, gray, white, or black, marked "Raymor by Roseville, U.S.A." in relief, 1952 (designed by Ben Seibel).

*Raymor Modern Artware:* vases, ashtrays, other dishes to match Raymor, marked "Raymor modern artware by Roseville," 1952.

*Romafin:* restaurant serving dishes, reddish brown outside, white interior (1918).

*Rosecraft:* lusterware, plain classic shape, undecorated, marked with "Rv" ink stamp, 1916–1917 (developed by Harry Rhead).

A selection of Magnolia vases made about 1943–1944. White flowers appear on pink, blue, green, or orange ground. "Roseville U.S.A." in raised letters appears on each piece. (J. Walter Yore Company)

Pink flowers on green ground decorate Clematis pieces introduced in 1944–45. Each has the raised "Roseville U.S.A." mark. (J. Walter Yore Company)

*The Freesia line was introduced in 1945. The pieces are decorated with pink, yellow, or white flowers on green, orange, purple, brown, or blue background. (J. Walter Yore Company)*

*Rosecraft Black:* classic undecorated shapes, black glaze, 1916.

*Rosecraft Blended:* mottled overall glaze, simple shapes, similar to Rosecraft (c. 1915).

*Rosecraft Hexagon:* dark green, black matte background, hexagonal-shaped body, decoration of slender leaf in a lighter color, marked with "Rv" stamp, 1924–1928.

*Rosecraft Panel:* relief decoration of flowers or female nudes in dark green or brown panels, marked with "Rv" stamp (1920).

*Rosecraft Vintage:* black background with Art Nouveau curved border of browns and yellows, marked with "Rv" stamp (1916), 1924–1928.

*Rouge Flambé:* see Rozane Mongol.

*These pieces of Snowberry-pattern Roseville pottery, a line first made in 1947, are decorated with white berries on a pink to red ground. Each piece bears the raised "Roseville U.S.A." mark. (J. Walter Yore Company)*

*Royal Capri:* metallic gold luster on textured modern vases, marked "Roseville" in relief (c. 1950).

*Rozane I:* first pieces were made with dark backgrounds and underglaze slip painting, finished piece had a high-gloss finish, similar to Rookwood's standard glaze, decorated with portraits, animals, or flowers, marked "R.P. Co." or "Rozane R.P. Co."; later the line used either a light or dark background and name was changed to Rozane Royal; name Rozane Ware written over a rose in a double circle was being used on this ware by 1905.

*Rozane Crystalis:* crystalized flowing glaze (1907).

*Rozane Egypto:* see Egypto.

*Rozane Fudji:* decorated with stylized patterns in European tradition, sometimes marked with Rozane Ware seal, 1906 (created by Gazo "Fudji" Fujiyama); see Fujiyama.

*Rozane Grecian:* blue background and classical white figures, early line.

*Rozane Mara:* iridescent red metallic line similar to Weller's Sicardo, most is unmarked, c. 1904 (developed by John Herold).

*Rozane Matte:* see Matte Color.

*Rozane Mongol:* dark red crystalline glaze, a few pieces were made with a solid red glaze or a silvery overlay, sometimes called Chinese Red or Rouge Flambé, marked with Mongol or Rozane Ware seal (1900–1904) (developed by John Herold).

*Rozane Ware:* raised roselike flowers in pastel colors surrounded by green leaves, stippled cream background, stamped "Roseville Pottery Rozane Ware" (1917).

*Russco:* modern shapes, solid-color glaze, a few with crystalline glaze, 1934.

*Savona:* solid-colored shiny glaze with fluting at bottom, garland of leaves at top, salmon, blue, or lime, 1924–1930.

The Wincraft line was made about 1948. This 18½-inch vase features a raised tulip. It is marked "23 Roseville, U.S.A. 279-18." Advertisements for the line show pieces with other flowers or even geometric designs. It came in apricot, chartreuse, and azure blue. (Donald Alexander)

*A Clematis vase with a green background made in 1944–1945 is 7½ inches high and marked "20, Roseville, U.S.A." (Donald Alexander)*

*Silhouette:* modern-shaped pieces with leaves or nude females in panels, pink, turquoise, beige, or white and turquoise, marked "Roseville" in relief (1952).

*Snowberry:* shaded background, blue, green, or rose, relief snowberry branch, 52 pieces, marked "Roseville" in relief, 1947.

*Sunflower:* mottled background, earth tones, band of natural color sunflowers in raised design (1930).

*Sylvan:* owls or animals and leaves on rough background (1930) (developed by Frank Ferrell about 1916).

*Teasel:* plain shapes, raised curved teasel spray in shaded monotone glaze, beige, blue and gold, pink, light blue, impressed Roseville mark, 1936.

*Thorn Apple:* shaded blue, brown, pink, raised thorn apple branch with white flowers, pods as decoration, impressed Roseville mark, 1937.

*Topeo:* four relief perpendicular designs running from rim, green, blue, pink, red, yellow, 1934; see also Artcraft.

*Tourist:* decals of automobiles on a cream background, matte finish (1906–1916).

*Tourmaline:* shaded blue, peach, yellow, some with ridged banding at neck, 1933.

*Tuscany:* pink, gray, turquoise, sculpted grapes and leaves as handles, 1924–1930.

*Velmoss:* green leaves curved over three horizontal stripes, green, blue, or red background, orange interior matte glaze, 1935.

*Velmoss Scroll:* red roses, green leaves, incised on cream matte background, 1916–1919.

*Roseville Bushberry vase, shape #657. It stands 3 inches high, is marked "Roseville U.S.A." in relief, and dates from 1948. (Private collection)*

*Venetian:* fireproof baking ware, blue or yellow with white interior (early 1900s).

*Victorian:* simple shapes, band of stylized design of leaves, marked with large "Rv" ink stamp, 1924–1930.

*Vista:* large palm trees in relief "growing" from base to top of vase (c. 1925).

*Volpato:* similar to Savona, pieces are ivory-glazed, some marked "Rv" impressed (1918–1921).

*Water Lily:* shaded rough background, blue, brown, or rose, relief water lilies, over 50 items, marked "Roseville" in relief, 1943.

*White Rose:* solid background, coral, blue, or brown, relief white roses, 50 items, marked "Roseville" in relief, 1940.

*Wincraft:* modern assymetrical shapes, background shades to brown at bottom, relief floral or animal decoration, high-gloss apricot, chartreuse, or azure blue glaze, marked "Roseville" in relief, 1948.

*Windsor:* blue or brown background, leaves, pine trees, or geometric designs, 1931.

*Wisteria:* mottled earth-tone brown to blue body with lavender wisteria on green vine at neck, 1933.

*Woodland:* see Fujiyama.

*Zephyr Lily:* shaded background, blue, tan, or green, relief cream-colored zephyr lily with green leaves, 52 items, marked "Roseville" in relief, 1946.

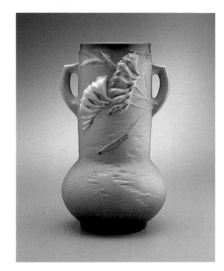

*A 10½-inch jardiniere in Roseville's 1945 Freesia pattern. It is marked "Roseville U.S.A. 126-10" in relief. (June Greenwald Antiques)*

# Shawsheen Pottery
### Billerica, Massachusetts and Mason City, Iowa

Shawsheen pottery was first made in Billerica, Massachusetts, during the spring of 1906. The firm moved to Mason City, Iowa, in 1907.

Edward and Elizabeth Dahlquist, who founded the company, had been trained as potters. Edward Dahlquist studied at the Minneapolis School of Art, the Chicago Art Institute, and the Art Students League in New York. Mrs. Dahlquist also studied at the Minneapolis School of Art and the Chicago Art Institute. She took special instruction from Lucy Perkins, a potter in New York City.

The early pottery done at Shawsheen was hand-coiled, but after moving to Iowa the potters made many pieces on the wheel. The Dahlquists themselves did the designing, throwing, decorating, glazing, and firing, although some of the work may have been done by students in the ceramics classes the couple offered.

Edward joined the University City Pottery in St. Louis for a short time, then returned to Iowa. Shawsheen pottery went out of business in 1911 and the Dahlquists moved to Chicago. Both continued to teach, but stopped making ceramics in 1915. Elizabeth died in 1963, Edward in 1972.

Pieces were marked with the initials "SP."

*Incised.*

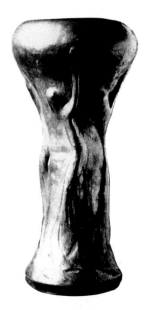

*A Shawsheen vase with molded decoration shown in* Keramic Studio, *May 1911.*

REKSTON

*Impressed.*

*Incised.*

(Above) *A Stockton dark brown pitcher.* (*Thelma Shull*, Victorian Antiques)

(Below) *Stockton sugar bowl, creamer, and teapot with raised ivy leaf pattern around the sides.* (*Thelma Shull*, Victorian Antiques)

# Stockton Terra Cotta
*Stockton, California*

The Stockton Terra Cotta Company was established in Stockton, California, in 1891. Charles Bailey, former manager of the majolica department of the Excelsior Pottery Works in Trenton, New Jersey, convinced several Stockton businessmen that a California pottery could be a successful business. Bailey traveled as a sales representative for various potteries in the East and felt that California was a logical place for a pottery because of the nearby clay beds and cheap transportation.

The firm manufactured drain and sewer pipe and other terra-cotta ware from clays that were found in Calaveras County, California. Art pottery was made from about 1894 to 1895. The ware was called "Rekston," possibly a recombination of the letters in the name Stockton Terra Cotta. It is believed to be the first art pottery made in California.

A successor company, Stockton Art Pottery, began making art pottery in 1896. The production of Rekston artware continued and included vases, pitchers, and tea sets with heavy-colored glazes in mottled and blended colors. Dark green, brown, mustard, pale pink, rose, spattered gold, and yellow were some of the colors used. Most pieces were decorated with naturalistic flowers or ivy leaves, and some of the decorations were raised. Pieces are marked with the round symbol of the firm and the name Rekston. A few were marked "MariPosa Pottery, Stockton, California."

Fire destroyed the company on November 17, 1902, and the pottery was never rebuilt.

## Teco Gates
### Terra Cotta, Illinois
~

William D. Gates was born in Ashland, Ohio, in 1852. The following year his family moved to Illinois, where he attended public schools. He received his degree from Wheaton College in Wheaton, Illinois, in 1875. Gates moved to Chicago to study law, but before he finished, his father died and he returned home to spend two years settling the estate. In 1878 he returned to Chicago, and in 1879 was admitted to the bar. He practiced law for a few years, but when an opportunity arose to make more money, he began a tile business with a plant in Terra Cotta (Crystal Lake), Illinois, and an office in Chicago.

The tile business, founded in 1881 as the Spring Valley Tile Works, was renamed the Terra Cotta Tile Works in 1885. The plant was in an old grist mill. With good clay deposits on the property and the grist mill wheels to grind the clay, Gates went into the manufacture of architectural terra-cotta bricks, drain tile, and pottery. Terra-cotta architectural pieces were in great demand by builders during that time.

A fire in 1887 destroyed part of the factory, but Gates rebuilt and enlarged it, then renamed the company the American Terra Cotta and Ceramic Company. The new factory had a chemical laboratory and kilns, and a nearby farmhouse was turned into a pottery so that Gates could begin experimenting with art pottery. Plain terra-cotta vases had already been made at the factory for several years to be decorated by Chicago's amateur china painters.

In 1902 the Teco (pronounced Tee-koh) line was officially introduced, although similar experimental pieces were produced as early as 1895. The name Teco came from "te" in terra and "co" in cotta. The American Terra Cotta and Ceramic Company, sometimes called Gates Pottery, had money, space, equipment, and many talented artists. None of its art pottery was produced until experiments assured a superior product. Paul and Ellis Gates, sons of William Gates, and Elmer Gorton, all three graduates of the Department of Ceramics at Ohio State University, worked at the pottery.

Many artists and architects were employed as designers. Artists included Fritz W. Albert, N. Forester, Mrs. F. R. Fuller, Ellis D. Gates, Neil H. Gates, William D. Gates, Orlando Giannini, R. A. Hirschfeld, Hardesty Gillmore Maratta, Fernand Moreau, Blanche Ostertag, Kristian E. Schneider, and Holmes Smith. Architects included Jeremiah K. Cady, N. L. Clark, William J. Dodd, Nelson Max Dunning, William K. Fellows, Hugh M. G. Garden, Harold Hals, John L. Hamilton, William LeBaron Jenney, William B. Mundie, George C. Nimmons, Howard Van Doren Shaw, Melville P. White, and the young Frank Lloyd Wright. Kristian Schneider, a modeler for the company, was loaned to Louis Sullivan, the architect, to help with his modeling of architectural details. The archi-

## TECO

*The name Teco was used on experimental pieces as early as 1895. Marks were stamped on the bottom. Paper labels were also used.*

*An advertisement from* Pottery and Glass, *November 1909.*

*Three Teco porcelain vases with crystalline glazes shown in* Keramic Studio, *February 1905.*

(Above) *Teco paper labels.*

tects may have been working on specific buildings and were at Teco only to design special items for their own projects. At least half of the pieces that were produced were designed by William Day Gates.

Though the work with architectural terra-cotta was of prime importance to the company, experiments with the art pottery yielded some beautiful results. Marbled or mottled surfaces were tested on the terra-cotta, with a similar glaze tried on the art pottery. Green matte was a popular standard glaze, but red, buff, and brown finishes were also made. The pottery discovered a metallic luster by chance in 1898, and experiments were repeated until the glaze was finally perfected. Another accident caused a piece of pottery to be covered with a glaze having minute crystals. Once again, more experiments were needed to improve the quality and standardize the finish. Major Gates, William's youngest son, invented a machine to throw three streams of different colors of glaze to produce a mottled effect, and developed both a more efficient pressing machine and a tunnel kiln.

Teco pottery was offered for sale in an advertisement listing "The Gates Pottery, Chicago, Illinois," rather than the firm name. Ads and articles about Teco and its production have been found

*A tile decorated by Hardesty Gillmore Maratta for Teco Gates Pottery as shown in* Sketch Book, *October 1905.*

dating back to 1923. The company closed just four months after the stock market crashed in 1929.

The pottery buildings were purchased in 1930 by George A. Berry, Jr., Gates's attorney. He renamed the company the American Terra Cotta Corporation and made architectural terra-cotta, ceramic wares, and some ornamental pottery. The company later diversified, and in 1972 its branch businesses merged to become TC Industries, Inc. The firm, which currently sits on the site of William Gates's original pottery, is in the commercial heat-treating business and produces ground-engaging tools for construction equipment.

*Teco advertisement. (Erie Art Museum)*

### PRODUCT

The first experimental Teco pottery was in subdued tones of red, then in buffs, and then in browns. Later, the pottery made some pieces with a marbleized finish similar to the finish used on architectural pieces.

An experimental metallic luster glaze, brown with gold flecks, was made in 1898 and later an iridescent crystalline glaze appeared after an accident in an experiment. These glazes were perfected and also used on a porcelainlike body. Since the green matte glaze used by Grueby and other art potteries was popular with customers, Teco developed a green glaze that was "strongly suggestive of Grueby pottery in tone and finish, but again this was a matter of accident and not of deliberate imitation" (according to Walter Gray—see the bibliography). The green Teco glaze was a soft, crystalline moss color on a stonewarelike body. Green-glazed Teco pottery was displayed at the St. Louis Exposition in 1904. The famous vases in the Pompeian Room of Chicago's Auditorium Annex Hotel were examples of this peculiar silvery green glaze. Designed and made by William Gates, they stood 7 feet tall; such large-size pieces were possible because Teco had kilns large enough to fire architectural works.

An unusual type of clay picture occasionally used in a fireplace mantel was made at Teco starting about 1905. The pictures were painted using slip of various colors of liquid clay. The surface was unglazed when it was fired. The tiles used to create a picture were each 3 feet wide and 18 inches high, with the finished view composed of a group of tiles, sometimes as many as seven or eight. Hardesty Gillmore Maratta did most of the tile painting.

By 1911, Teco's pottery line included more than five hundred designs.

*A guide to Teco shapes by number used by workers when filling orders. (Erie Art Museum)*

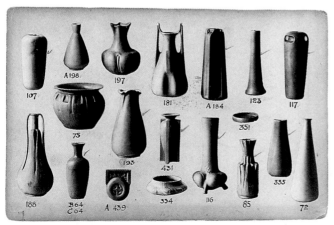

*Teco pottery on display in Chicago in 1912. (Erie Art Museum)*

*The Gates mold shop in about 1903. (Erie Art Museum)*

KOVELS' AMERICAN ART POTTERY

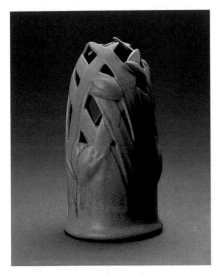

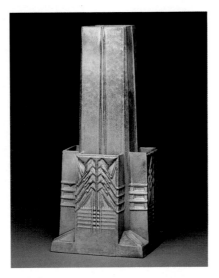

*William J. Dodd designed this 11-inch-high vase, no. 151 in the catalog, to be used for cut flowers. Stems were put into the openings to produce "an exceptionally pleasing and artistic effect." (The Dillenberg-Espinar Collection; photograph from the Erie Art Museum)*

*Frank Lloyd Wright designed this vase, no. 331, for Unity Temple, Oak Park, Illinois. It is 29½ inches high. (Collection of Unity Temple, The Unitarian Universalist Church; photograph from the Erie Art Museum)*

*Hugh M. G. Garden designed vase no. 252. It was used as a vase or lamp base. This piece is 17½ inches high. Another size was also made. (Collection of Stephen Gray; photograph from the Erie Art Museum)*

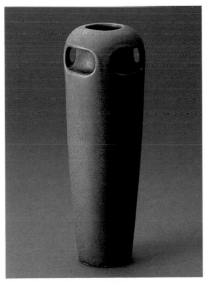

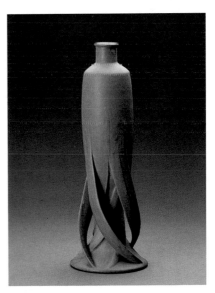

*Vase no. 85 by William J. Dodd. The leaves on this vase were molded separately and added to the 13-inch body after the clay was partially hardened. The leaves are attached only at their base and tip, leaving a space between most of the leaf and the pot. (Collection of Barbara and Jack Hartog; photograph from the Erie Art Museum)*

*Fritz Albert designed vase no. 117. The piece is 10¾ inches high. This design was made in several sizes. (Collection of Joel Silver; photograph from the Erie Art Museum)*

*Vase no. 310, designed by Fritz Albert. It is 18½ inches high. (Private collection; photograph from the Erie Art Museum)*

(Right) *Vases no. 171, left, and no. A418, right, designed by Chicago architect Jeremiah K. Cady. Both are 13 inches high. (Collection of Linda Balahoutis and Jerry Bruckheimer and collection of Patsy and Steven Tisch; photograph from the Erie Art Museum)*

*Leaves are applied to the 10¼-inch body of this vase, no. 191, attributed to Fritz Albert. (Collection of Jean and Martin Mensch; photograph from the Erie Art Museum)*

*Tall green weed holder no. 74 was shape no. 73 customized with a lacy pattern. It is 25⅛ inches high. (Collection of the Chicago Historical Society; photograph from the Erie Art Museum)*

New colors were constantly added, including platinum gray, blue, red, purple, yellow, several peculiar shades of green, and four shades of brown. Sometimes the new glazes were sprayed over the old green glaze and then the pieces were refired. A few "freaks of the kiln" were sold with metallic blue and purple or starred crystallized patterns.

At first, Teco was influenced by the natural woodland and lake setting of the pottery building. Designs suggesting aquatic plants such as lilies, lotuses, flower petals, leaves, branches, stalks, and buds were made. One popular vase resembled an ear of corn.

Almost all of the early pieces of Teco art pottery were flower vases, but garden ornaments of classical design were included in the line. By 1911, soft stone gray pieces for the yard were produced, and garden fountains were made using several types of glaze. A fountain might be of buff-colored clay with a wreath glazed in red, green, or orange.

Tile was also produced during this period. Mantels were made of several colored tiles in green, brown, orange, blue, and gray tones. The popular Teco green glaze was used for many tiles, some of which were in low relief. Landscape decorations were often part of the design. The firm also made tableware and full tea sets in gray, pearly pink, or light pinkish beige.

Teco pottery vases were cast in a mold, but the originals used to make the mold may have been thrown on the wheel or modeled by hand. The clays used were of many colors, including red, yellow, buff, and blue, and were carefully mixed with other minerals for the desired effect. Almost all the clay came from local beds or from Brazil, Indiana. A complete description of the making of a Teco vase can be found in a 1905 *Sketch Book* article by Susan Frackelton—see the bibliography.

## Tiffany Pottery
### Corona, New York

The varied works of Louis Comfort Tiffany are well known. One of America's great artists, Tiffany made glass, pottery, jewelry, enamel on copper, tombstones, paintings, and other salable works of art. It is his pottery, however, that is of interest here.

The Tiffany metal furnaces in Corona, New York, were first fired in 1898 and experiments in making pottery began the same year. But Tiffany pottery was not displayed until the St. Louis Exposition in 1904. The three pieces presented at the exhibit were made from ivory-glazed white semiporcelain clay from Ohio and Massachusetts. In 1905, Tiffany's firm began to make vases as well as pottery lamp bases for its Favrile glass shades.

Tiffany's early pottery lamp bases were an ivory-shaded deep brown. By 1906, most of the bases were tinted green, but a few were white, iridescent, or, by 1911, coated with bronze. Many had matte glazes. All were marked "LCT" on the bottom. The pottery bases were only a limited success. Most of the lamp bases made by Tiffany were of enameled bronze rather than pottery.

Limited quantities of art pottery were made and sold by Tiffany Studios, where the pottery was made, and by Tiffany and Company, the New York retail store. Some were thrown on the wheel, but most were cast in molds. Clara Ruge, writing in *Pottery & Glass* in 1908, found that

> the main body of the pieces are in porcelain (really a semiporcelain), but for the plastic decorations, other clays were also used. Slender forms, which often approach those of the Favrile glassware were most often chosen. The glass shows only the plant motifs in the forms of the objects themselves, but in the ceramics the motifs of plants are also used for the decorations. Water plants, the lotus, the poppy, and many kinds of creepers including the Fuchsia, are employed with good taste.

Tiffany pottery was also decorated with a variety of grains, jack-in-the-pulpits, ferns, mushrooms, Queen Anne's lace, tree branches or leaves, birds, and insects. He also used Near Eastern motifs. A few pieces had abstract designs. The early wares were colored a deep ivory and shaded to brown. Later, green shades in varicolored glaze were applied on the outside of pieces, which were glazed inside with green, brown, or blue. Some pieces have code numbers or letters incised on them. Matte crystalline and iridescent glazes were also tried, as were blue, red, and dull bronze. Bronze pottery was perfected about 1910. One type of pottery was made with a metal sleeve that was shrunk onto the clay, while another was electroplated.

A few pieces are marked with variations of an inscription written into the glaze, such as "L.C. Tiffany," "Favrile Pottery," "Bronze

*Incised after glazing.*

*Incised after glazing.*

*L. C. Tiffany pottery vases made about 1905. (Smithsonian Institution)*

Unusual leaves and flowers and other organic shapes were molded into vases designed by Tiffany. (Left to right) Mint green 10-inch vase with fruit, made about 1905; ochre-glazed 9-inch vase with stylized leaves, c. 1905; green-to-avocado vase with molded branches and flowers, c. 1905, 10 inches. (Sotheby's)

(Left to right) Artichoke-shaped buff-green vase; green and mustard-colored 6½-inch vase with molded leaves; avocado-colored 9½-inch vase with molded fern fronds. All three vases were made about 1905. (Sotheby's)

This vase with molded decoration of tulips is glazed in mottled green semigloss glaze. It is 11 inches high. The piece is marked with the incised "LCT" cipher and the etched mark "P1341 L.C. Tiffany Favrile Pottery." (Private collection; photograph from The Art Museum, Princeton University, Princeton, New Jersey)

This mushroom-decorated vase is glazed with shades of brown to mustard. It was made about 1904–1910 by the Tiffany Pottery and is marked on the bottom. It is 5¾ inches high. (Sotheby's)

Purple and russet green glazes decorate this 4¾-inch vase by Louis Comfort Tiffany, made sometime between 1905 and 1919. (The Museum of Modern Art, New York, Gift of Joseph H. Heil)

Pottery," or "P." The term *Favrile* is one of Tiffany's trademarks, derived from an old English word meaning handmade. As with the bases, the pieces are marked with the letters "LCT" scratched into the bottom clay.

Only glazed pottery was sold at Tiffany and Company. The unglazed pottery was sold at the Tiffany Studios and could be ordered in a special color or bisque finish. The pottery production stopped between 1917 and 1920.

## University City
### *University City, Missouri*

Edward Gardner Lewis, a St. Louis art lover, founded the American Woman's League in 1907. The league, whose goal was to educate women, offered classes in business, languages, photography, art, and pottery. Taxile Doat, the French potter who wrote *Grand Feu Ceramics*, was invited to University City, Missouri, in 1909 to advise the architect designing the league's art pottery facilities.

In 1910 Adelaide Alsop Robineau (see Robineau Pottery) moved there to teach and work. Frederick Hürten Rhead, who had worked for Weller Pottery and Roseville Pottery and would later work at his own studio in Santa Barbara, California, and at the American Encaustic Tiling Company, and Edward Dahlquist, who had worked at Shawsheen Pottery, were instructors.

Doat brought a collection of his pottery from France and many of the shapes were used at University City. Pieces were glazed in crystalline glazes, and Doat's pâte-sur-pâte technique was used.

*Incised.*

*Incised.*

*Incised.*

*Incised.*

*Initials of Edward Garner Lewis.*

*Initials of Edward Garner Lewis with U.C. mark, incised.*

*Initials of Taxile Doat, incised.*

*Incised.*

*Frederick Hürten Rhead in his University City studio, 1911. (Erie Art Museum)*

Both pottery and porcelain were made at the University City Pottery. This 4½-inch pottery bowl with incised and painted decorations is glazed light blue, cream, and pink. The vase was made about 1910–1914. It is marked with the cipher "UC" and "5105." (Private collection; photograph from The Art Museum, Princeton University, Princeton, New Jersey)

A 17½-inch-high University City vase made by Frederick Hürten Rhead. Its incised mark is "UC/FHR/1911/1020." (Bryce Bannatyne Gallery, Santa Monica, California; photograph from the Erie Art Museum, Erie, Pennsylvania)

University City plate made by Taxile Doat in 1914. The plate is porcelain with a colored slip glaze and is 9¼ inches in diameter. (The High Museum, Atlanta, Georgia; Virginia Carroll Crawford Collection)

Most pieces of pottery were marked with the cipher "UC." Many had the artist's initials and the date. Rhead and his wife, Agnes, worked together on two tile arrangements of peacocks, one of Rhead's favorite subjects. The Woman's League experiment ended in 1914, and Doat returned to France the following year.

## University of North Dakota
### *See North Dakota School of Mines*

## C. B. Upjohn Pottery
### Zanesville, Ohio
~

The C. B. Upjohn Pottery Company was established in Zanesville, Ohio, in 1904. Its founder, Charles Babcock Upjohn, had worked for Weller and the Cambridge Art Pottery. Evidently, the firm was not a success because it closed in 1905. Upjohn then went to work for Trent Tile Company of Trenton, New Jersey. He later taught art at Columbia University in New York.

**UPJOHN**
*Impressed.*

## Valentien
### San Diego, California
~

Albert and Anna Marie Bookprinter Valentien worked together as decorators for the Rookwood Pottery in Cincinnati, Ohio. Both had trained at the Cincinnati Academy of Art and later studied in Paris, France. Anna was interested in sculpture and worked for a short time with the French sculptor Auguste Rodin. The couple traveled to San Diego, California, in 1908 because Albert had a commission to paint a series of botanical studies of California wildflowers. He continued this project for ten years.

In 1911 the Valentiens opened a pottery in San Diego. They made cast pieces with matte or vellum glazes. A few pieces had floral or geometric slip decoration. A shape book from the pottery shows they made forty-three plain shapes and forty-eight designs with molded low relief decoration. Each piece was marked with the letters "VP" and a California poppy. The pottery closed by 1914.

The Valentiens continued working as artists in San Diego. Albert died in 1925, Anna in 1947.

*Impressed.*

## Van Briggle Pottery
### Colorado Springs, Colorado
~

Artus Van Briggle was born in Felicity, Ohio, on March 21, 1869. His parents, Eugene and Martha Bryan Van Briggle, had emigrated from Holland. They claimed the two Pieters and Jan Brueghel, the famed Flemish painters, as ancestors.

Even as a child, Artus was a talented artist. He worked in Cincinnati and studied there at the Academy of Art. He worked with Karl Langenbeck of the Avon Pottery in about 1886 and a year later he joined the Rookwood Pottery. In 1893, he studied in Paris, France, at the Julian Art Academy under Jean-Paul Laurens and Benjamin Constant. During that period, he went to the Beaux Arts to study clay modeling and in the summer of 1894 was in Italy studying painting. Back in Paris in 1895, he became engaged to a talented American artist, Anne Louise Gregory.

The time he spent in France influenced Van Briggle in many ways. He became familiar with the Art Nouveau style, which he

*Incised Van Briggle trademark used from 1900. Date sometimes used with this mark 1900–1920.*

*Van Briggle trademark used in later years. Date sometimes used with this incised mark 1900–1920.*

19 AA 15

*Incised mark with date.*

VAN BRIGGLE
COLO SP. '65

Incised mark, used after 1920.
Incised U.S.A. added to mark,
1922–1929.

anna Van
Colo. sp. g.

Incised mark used on high-gloss
pottery, 1955–1968.

This photo of Artus Van Briggle working on his famous Toast Cup was taken
in 1900 in Colorado. The boy is
William C. Holmes. (Van Briggle Pottery Archives)

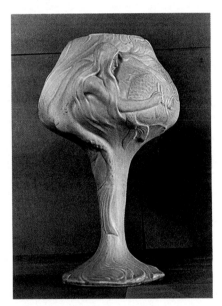

(Above) *The Van Briggle Toast
Cup, also called Chalice, dates from
1900 and stands 11½ inches high.*
(Colorado Springs Pioneers Museum,
Colorado Springs, Colorado)

(Right) *A posed picture of Artus Van
Briggle,* (left), *Harry Bangs* (in
bowler hat), *and an errand boy with
Van Briggle Pottery at the kiln. Among
the vases are the Toast Cup and the
Lady of the Lily.* (Van Briggle Pottery
Archives)

later adapted. He saw Chinese pottery of the Ming dynasty and
determined to reproduce the matte or dead glaze of that earlier
period. And he became familiar with the works of the Berlin and
Sèvres porcelain factories, whose designs influenced his own.

Artus returned to Cincinnati in 1896. He worked at the Rookwood factory as a painter and decorator and also at his own studio.
Because of the tuberculosis he had contracted as a boy, he decided
to move to Colorado Springs, Colorado, in 1899. He worked at
Colorado College and at a home with the local clay and glazes. In
August 1901, the first pieces were fired at the Van Briggle Pottery
located at 615 North Nevada Avenue, Colorado Springs.

By Christmas of that year, he was selling his pottery, and sometime during that same year he exhibited in Paris. The vase he exhibited, "Despondency," was later purchased for the Louvre Museum in Paris for $3,000.

Anne Gregory Van Briggle, Artus's wife, was born in Plattsburgh, New York, on July 11, 1868. As a young girl, she lived with an aunt, then studied painting in New York City from 1889 to 1893. In 1894, Anne and her aunt went to Paris, where Anne had her own studio and painted many pictures, including a portrait of Artus.

Despite their engagement in 1895, Anne did not move to Colorado Springs with Artus until 1900, when she obtained a job as art supervisor in the local high school. They married in 1902. Anne worked with Artus at the pottery until his death on July 4, 1904. At the time, the Van Briggles employed fourteen workmen.

Anne continued the pottery after the death of her husband, and a memorial building, the Van Briggle Art Pottery, was begun in 1907 and completed in 1908. It stood at 300 West Uintah Street, Colorado Springs. Young artists were trained at a school of design at the pottery to continue the work of Artus Van Briggle. In 1908 Anne Van Briggle married Etienne A. Ritter of Denver, Colorado, but she continued to work at the pottery until 1912. She died November 15, 1929.

The pottery was reorganized in 1910 and renamed the Van Briggle Pottery and Tile Company. The new approach did not help lagging sales, and the pottery went into bankruptcy in 1913. The business was taken over by Edwin DeForest ("Ned") Curtis. Then C. B. Lansing took it over from 1915 to 1919, when he sold it to I. F. and J. H. Lewis of Springfield, Missouri. In June 1919, a fire destroyed part of the plant, but it was rebuilt. I. F. later moved to

*This unusual Van Briggle Pottery vase has aqua matte glaze and bronze mountings. The bronze resembles mistletoe with seed pearl berries. The 8½-inch vase is marked "AA" in a rectangle and "Van Briggle, 1904, V 275." (Private collection; photograph from The Art Museum, Princeton University, Princeton, New Jersey)*

*Matte glaze covers this 11½-inch-high vase with raised floral decorations. (Private collection)*

*A Van Briggle stoppered jug with green matte glaze and raised designs. Around the neck are the words "Fire Water." The piece is incised "1902 AA." (See the photograph of the spider vase in the Rookwood entry.) (Smithsonian Institution)*

*This dark green–glazed piece is unmarked, but the design and technique identify it as Van Briggle pottery made about 1902. It is 5 inches high. The spiderlike decoration is on one side, an Indian symbol on the other. The clay used for this vase is very yellow. (Private collection)*

*Two women form the handles of this green matte-glazed vase. It is 7¾ inches high, marked "AA" in a rectangle and "Van Briggle, Colorado Springs, 1906." (Private collection; photograph from The Art Museum, Princeton University, Princeton, New Jersey)*

Phoenix, Arizona, where he died in 1959. In 1969, J. H. Lewis sold controlling interest in the pottery to an employee of eleven years, Kenneth W. Stevenson.

Kenneth Stevenson later became full owner of the pottery. His son Jeff, a ceramic engineer, developed some new glazes and clay bodies. Kenneth's son Craig, a sculptor, created many designs, including a limited-edition series of five near–life-size busts of "Famous American Indians." Kenneth died in November 1990, but his wife, Bertha (Newton) Stevenson, and Craig Stevenson continue to operate the pottery.

The Van Briggle Pottery continued making its typical matte-glazed wares throughout the years. When the factory became too small in 1955, a building of native stone was built at 600 South Twenty-first Street in Colorado Springs. Pottery, including new designs and reproductions of old pieces, is still being made and sold from this address.

*These Van Briggle pieces appeared in a photograph in a German publication about 1901. (Left) Lady of the Lily. (Right) Lorelei. The later version of the Lady of the Lily did not include the flowers on the base. See page 238*

The Van Briggle Pottery Company won many awards, including gold, silver, and bronze medals at the Paris Salon in 1903 and 1904; other medals at the Saint Louis Exposition, 1904, and at the American Pacific Exposition, 1905; and an award at the Arts and Crafts Exhibition, Boston, 1906.

### PRODUCT

The clay used at the Colorado Springs pottery came from a deposit located within five miles of the plant. The deposits of clay ranged from dark red to cream buff. Clays from Georgia and England were also used. The plant had electrical power and machinery for all of the needed clay preparation.

A variety of pieces was made at the pottery, including all types of glazed terra-cotta tiles for window columns, mantels, and chimney tops; roof tiles, tiles for interior decoration and building exteriors, and dry-press tiles for fireplace hearths, wall fountains, garden decorations, and even flowerpots. Some tiles, machine-pressed, were glazed by hand in one color. Another type had designs that were hand-pressed and then decorated in several colors. Still other tiles were three-dimensional, molded, and hand-colored. Van Briggle tile designs can be seen in several buildings in Colorado Springs.

The glazes varied, the best-known being the turquoise Ming (a blue matte glaze still in use). The deep mulberry was lightened in 1946 and

*(Left to right) Van Briggle vases. The relief-decorated vase with daffodils is marked 1903, and is 9½ inches high. The all yellow matte glaze vase is dated 1901, and the 15-inch-high green mottled vase is marked 1904. The other three vases are undated. (Smithsonian Institution)*

*Bronze electroplated Van Briggle bowl made about 1900–1905. It is marked "Van Briggle Colo. Spgs. 702 S. W." (Courtesy of the Western Reserve Historical Society)*

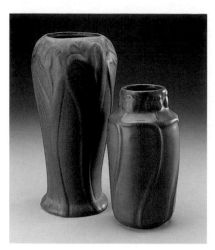

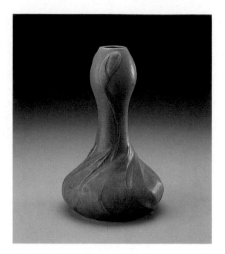

(Left) *This 9½-inch vase is one of a pair. Both are glazed in dark maroon matte glaze. Raised flowers and stems are the decoration. One is marked "Van Briggle, Colo. Spgs.," the other "Van Briggle U.S.A." (Right) Raised stems and flowers decorate this 7¼-inch dark maroon vase. It is marked "Van Briggle 1916." (Private collection)*

*Anna Van vase with turquoise matte glaze. This vase is 16½ inches high. It has been made since about 1925 and is still available at the factory. (Private collection)*

*A light pink matte glaze covers this 8-inch-high vase. It is marked with the Van Briggle square symbol and "Van Briggle, Col. Spgs. 666 16." (Private collection)*

*An undecorated brown-green candlestick, 9 inches high. (Private collection)*

renamed Persian Rose (a two-tone rose to maroon shade discontinued in 1968). Mountain Craig Brown, the brown and green glaze favored at Van Briggle Pottery after 1922, was discontinued in 1935. The Mountain Craig Brown glaze formula and several molds were later lost in a flood at the factory.

A white glaze called "Moonglo" was in use about 1946. High-gloss glazes in black, brown, and dark blue-green were made from 1955 to 1968 on pieces marked "Anna Van." Russet matte glaze was used from 1978 to 1984. Midnight, a black matte glaze, was used from 1979 to 1984. The Van Briggle Pottery also used green, brown, purple, pink, red, blue, lavender, plum, cardinal red, brown, yellow, mustard, black, gray, green, and other colors.

A few pieces were done with as many as three colors. An early article (in *Keramic Studio*, May 1905) mentions a "quaint all over pattern like figures from a cashmere shawl." Van Briggle "adorned his creations with the precious and semiprecious stones of Colorado" (*Pottery and Glass*, August 1908). In 1912, *House Beautiful* noted: "Within the last three years it [Van Briggle Pottery] has been making an iridescent glaze which takes a third firing. The color is put on by hand, making the design more pronounced yet in complete harmony with the colors of the vase." The glaze was not applied by dipping, but was sprayed on with an atomizer. (For a more complete description of the technical aspects of making the pottery, see *Transactions of the American Ceramic Society* X (1908). All these articles are listed in the bibliography.

Lamp bases were produced by 1919. Lampshades using real grasses and butterflies and local flowers were designed to blend with the bases.

The Van Briggle Pottery made several pottery designs that were copper/bronze plated. We have seen a piece of bronze-plated Van Briggle pottery marked "Van Briggle, 702 S. W." According to Robert Wyman Newton, this piece is design number 702 to which lizard handles have been applied, and the "S. W." may be the designer's initials. The firm also did

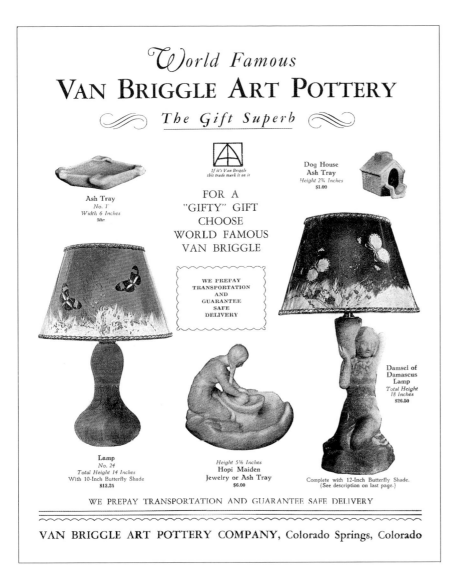

(Left) *A page from a Van Briggle catalog dated 1930.*

(Above) *Despondency vase, 16 inches high, with Persian Rose glaze. (Courtesy of the Western Reserve Historical Society)*

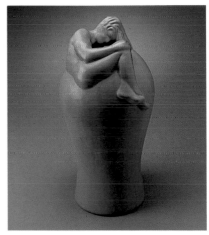

(Above) *Despondency, the vase with a man curled around the top, has been in the line since 1903. This turquoise matte-glazed vase is 16 inches high. (Private collection)*

(Left) *Candlesticks and a flower bowl with frog in high-gloss turquoise. The candlesticks are 4 inches high, the flower frog 3¾ inches high, and the bowl 3 inches wide by 13½ inches long. The bowl bottom has the incised script mark "Anna Van Briggle, Colorado Sprgs." (Private collection)*

*These are small Van Briggle pieces. (Left to right) A green vase, 3 inches high; a darker green-brown bowl, 2 inches high by 3¾ inches in diameter; a round bowl from the 1950s, "Design 847" (the catalog called it "an example of eyelet embroidery in clay. Height 4 inches, Width 5 inches, $3.85" and mentions that it was also available in "Persian Rose" or "Moonglow"); a 5-inch turquoise vase with floral design. (Private collection)*

some silver plating and made "solar apparatus" used in the treatment of tuberculosis from about 1915 to 1919.

Several prominent designs made by the Van Briggle Pottery Company through the years should be mentioned. All have been produced continually since they were first introduced. "Lorelei" was first exhibited in 1903 at the Paris Art Salon. The original is now in the South Kensington Museum in London. The vase shows a figure of a woman draped around it and incorporated into the design. Early examples also show a man at the base of the vase. A picture of the vase appeared in *Brush and Pencil* in October 1901. The details were blurred in later vases and the mold was reproduced several times with slight design changes.

The "Lady of the Lily" vase, which dates from 1901, has a woman reclining against a leaning vase. Early examples have raised flowers on the skirt.

The "Siren of the Sea" is a shell-shaped vase topped by a reclining mermaid. According to a typed company history distributed at the factory during the early 1970s, this piece was an award winner at the St. Louis Exposition of 1904. Other sources claim the piece was designed by Anne Van Briggle, not Artus, in about 1912.

"Despondency," a 14-inch-high vase encircled by a male figure, won first prize at the Paris Salon in 1903. It is now in the Louvre.

The "Toast Cup" is a large cup with a mermaid holding on to a large fish. The piece is also decorated with other nautical and marine life, including seashells. It was first made in 1900 and continued in production until the 1920s.

"Anna Van," a vase held by a standing woman, was made later. Company legend claims it was sculpted by Artus Van Briggle and found in his attic workroom after he died. It does not seem to have been in production until 1925, and many experts believe it was not created by Artus. Several versions of this vase are known, and comparisons suggest that several molds were used.

Many hundreds of other designs for vases, lamps, bookends, ashtrays, cups, and other items have been made through the years. Almost all of them were of a single-color matte glaze with a raised decoration of Art Nouveau inspiration.

### MARKS

The famous "AA" mark was used by Artus and Anne Van Briggle on the very first pieces made in Colorado. It was incised in the clay with the date and the name Van Briggle. The mark appears with some variations because it was always incised by hand.

The "AA" is usually in a rectangle, or is distorted to look like a trapezoid. This mark is found on almost all pieces except the high-gloss pieces marked "Anna Van" that were made from 1955 to 1968.

Many of the pieces were dated from 1900 to 1912. The date was incised by hand on almost every piece from 1900 to 1907. Few dates were used from 1907 to 1912. In early 1912 the date was put to the left of the "AA" mark; by the end of the year it was under the mark. This system of hand-incised dates stayed in use until 1915. Late in 1915, the date and the design number were die-impressed. The date sometimes showed "19" on one side of the "AA" and "15" on the other. From 1916 to 1918, the marks were the same as the earlier system, and after 1919 dates were rarely used. The words "Colorado Springs" were used after 1906. The letters "U.S.A." followed the mark from 1922 to 1929. After 1920, the words "Colorado Springs, Colorado" were added to the mark. This was sometimes done in an abbreviated form. A line of high-gloss glazed ware made from 1955 to 1960 is frequently marked "Anna Van Briggle."

The young women who worked in the pottery sometimes listed other things on the bottom of a piece. The words "Colo Sprgs" were written in script or print, depending on the writer. "Original," used after 1920, means the piece was turned on a wheel and not made in a mold; "hand carved" means that the design was carved into the piece; "hand decorated" means there was slip decoration. Roman numerals have appeared on some early pieces made before 1905. These refer to the type of clay used.

There are other ways to date a piece of Van Briggle. Design numbers were used starting in 1902. The numbers were hand-incised at first, die-stamped from 1904 to 1907, then hand-incised in script from 1907 to 1908. The letters *A* to *E* were sometimes added to the design number from 1902 to 1907, probably to indicate size. Robert Wyman Newton's 1975 "Catalogue of Van Briggle Designs," showing a sketch of each design with its number and date of introduction, is included in *A Collector's Guide to Van Briggle Pottery* by Scott Nelson and in *Van Briggle Pottery: The Early Years* by Barbara Arnest. Detailed information about position of marks, appearance of marks, and other dating information is included.

*The Siren of the Sea has been made since 1904. The frog flower holder in the center of the bowl is a separate piece. A 1935 postcard lists the bowl at $42.50. (Private collection)*

*Lady of the Lily has been made at the Van Briggle Pottery since 1901. This is a vase with turquoise matte glaze made in 1970. An example in Mountain Craig Brown appeared on a color postcard about 1935, priced at $42. (Private collection)*

*The Lorelei vase has been produced since 1901. This turquoise example was made in 1970. It is 10½ inches high and marked "Van Briggle Colo. Spgs." (Private collection)*

## QUICK-DATING TIPS

A quick-tip, year-by-year listing of marks follows. It is quoted, with permission, from Robert Wyman Newton's essay in *Van Briggle Pottery: The Early Years:*

Aside from the trademark, which was always used, variations in markings year by year were as follows:

*1900:* The year only.

*1901:* Roman numeral II, indicating the type of clay.

*1902:* Roman numeral II or III, indicating type of clay; the pattern number, indicating the design.

*1903:* Roman numeral III, and the pattern number.

*1904:* The pattern number and the Roman numeral V, indicating the type of clay.

*1905:* The pattern number; a variety of Roman numerals indicating different clays, e.g. V, X, VV, VX; and Arabic numbers enclosed in circles, indicating individual pottery finishers.

*1906:* The pattern number; some Roman numerals; and finishers began to place their numbers on one side of the trademark with the number of the month the piece was finished *sometimes* on the other side.

*1907:* The pattern number, and the finishers' marks as described above. Roman numerals no longer appeared.

*1908–1911:* All marks remained the same as above except that the year of manufacture did not appear. The conclusion that wares so marked belong to this period (the first years of operation of the new pottery) has been made from the fact that the markings differ from those of prior years only with the absence of the date.

*1912–1916:* Sometimes the pattern number; the date; occasionally marks denoting the finisher and the month of finishing.

*1917–1918:* The year only.

*1919–1920:* The year, e.g. '19, below other markings, but seldom. Glaze partially or completely covers the bottoms of these wares.

*1921–1922:* No indication of dates.

*1922–1929:* Marked U.S.A.

*1930–:* Finishers' numbers; more recently finishers' initials instead of numbers; the number of the month of finishing; no yearly dates. Since 1930 a standard white clay has been used, and the bottoms of all wares are white. Dark clay indicates the piece predates 1930.

## Vance/Avon
### *See Avon Works*

## Volkmar Kilns
### *See Volkmar Pottery and Durant Kilns*

## Volkmar Pottery
### *Tremont and Corona, New York*

∽

Charles Volkmar was born in Baltimore, Maryland, in 1841. His grandfather was an engraver and his father a portrait painter, so it was natural for Charles to be trained as an artist. He went to Paris, France, to study under Antoine-Louis Barye, the bronze sculptor, and Henri Harpignies, the landscape painter. Volkmar returned to the United States after fifteen years, "partly for the purpose of voting for the second term of Lincoln, getting married, and other commendable enterprises" (*International Studio*, January 1909). He later returned to Paris, where he became interested in pottery and underglaze painting. He apprenticed at the Haviland factory and learned about the underglaze decoration done at that time. By 1875 he was exhibiting his oil paintings and pieces of pottery.

Volkmar again returned to the United States in 1879 and set up a kiln in Greenpoint, New York. By 1882 he moved to Tremont in the Bronx, where he continued to make the same type of underglaze decorated pieces, working with limited colors. He made vases and tiles with applied or underglaze decorations, and used blue, brown, or orange as background color. Many pieces were decorated with landscapes and animals. In 1883 he made a series of "barbotine" vases, a slipware-decorated faience.

In 1888 Volkmar moved again and started to make art tile with J. T. Smith at the Menlo Park Ceramic Company in Menlo Park, New Jersey. They made enameled terra-cotta tiles for the Rockefeller mansion in Tarrytown, New York, tiles that matched the marble and onyx used on other walls in the building. Their tiles were installed in a number of buildings, including the Boston Public Li-

*Incised monogram, used 1879–1888.*

**VOLKMAR & CORY**

*Raised mark, used 1895.*

**IV**

*Incised or relief mark, used 1896–1903.*

*Incised or relief mark, used 1896–after 1903.*

**VOLKMAR Corona N.Y. 1896.**

*Incised.*

**VOLKMAR**

*Incised.*

*Charles Volkmar made these 12⅝-inch red earthenware vases about 1881 in Brooklyn, New York. The cow and tree decoration is slip-painting. One of the vases is marked. (The Brooklyn Museum, Brooklyn, New York, gift of Leon Volkmar)*

Although blue and white plates were made at the Volkmar Ceramic Company in Brooklyn about 1895, this 11½-inch-diameter plate was probably a continuation of the series made at Corona, New York, by Volkmar and Cory about 1896. (*Smithsonian Institution*)

Volkmar made this matte green-glazed vase at Metuchen, New Jersey, about 1910. It is 6 inches high and marked with an incised V. (*Collection of the Newark Museum*)

Hand-painted birch trees in brown, green, and blue semimatte glaze decorate this 7¾-inch-square tile. It is marked "Volkmar Kilns, Metuchen, N.J." on the back. A "V" is painted in the lower right-hand corner on the face of the tile. (*Collection of the Newark Museum*)

This Volkmar plate dating from about 1895 is 11½ inches in diameter and is marked with the rectangular incised Volkmar mark. (*Private collection*)

brary and the National Bank Building in New York City.

The partnership ended in 1893. Volkmar organized the Volkmar Ceramic Company and Smith continued at the Menlo Park Ceramic Company.

Volkmar moved again and started a new company, The Volkmar Keramic Company, in Brooklyn, New York. He continued to produce tiles, including a series of plaques with underglaze blue designs, usually of historic buildings or persons. The company also made loving cups, beer mugs, and plates, all of them with the same type of blue decoration.

Volkmar joined Kate Cory in 1896, and under the name Volkmar and Cory in Corona, New York, they worked together for a few months making plaques. They used the familiar blue and white decorations.

After their partnership ended, Volkmar made plain pieces with colored glazes. The ware was thin and light. A few examples from this period had painted decorations, usually landscapes. He also made an underglaze decorated ware called "Crown Point." All of the pieces were made of New Jersey and other United States clay.

In 1903, Volkmar moved his pottery to Metuchen, New Jersey, where the company was known as the Volkmar Kilns, Charles Volkmar & Son. (Volkmar's son Leon became a teacher of pottery at the Industrial School of the Pennsylvania Museum by 1905.) The firm made art pottery, including vases and bowls with a matte finish in dark gray, green, blue, dark red-brown, and pink. Some pieces had linings of a brighter color such as orange. The Volkmars also made decorative underglaze paintings of ducks, foliage, or other natural subjects. Several underglaze decorations were made with a firing between each painting. One of Leon Volkmar's pupils, Jan Hoagland, did some of the designing. The last-known working date of the pottery is 1911. The exact date of closing is unknown, but Charles Volkmar died in 1914.

### MARKS

Volkmar used the "CV" mark from 1879 to 1888. The name Volkmar in an impressed rectangle was used in 1895, Volkmar & Cory in 1895–1896, and Volkmar without a rectangle from 1869 to 1903. The letter *V* was used on some pieces of Crown Point Ware. Leon Volkmar, son of Charles, also used this mark on some of his pieces made as late as the 1920s. Tiles were imprinted "VOLKMAR KILNS, METUCHEN, N.J." or, in raised letters, "MENLO PARK CERAMIC WORKS, VOLKMAR TILE."

## W. J. Walley
### West Sterling, Massachusetts

William J. Walley bought the old Wachusett Pottery in West Sterling, Massachusetts, in 1898 and continued to operate it alone until his death in 1919. Born in East Liverpool, Ohio, on August 3, 1852, Walley went to England as a young boy and worked at the Minton factory until he returned to the United States in 1873. During the 1870s, he made art pottery in Portland, Maine, and was later employed at the Norton Pottery in Worcester, Massachusetts.

At West Sterling, Walley continued his flowerpot business in a small way, and also made artware with fancy glazes. He used local red clay. Many of his pieces were finished in a green matte glaze, but other pieces were various shades of blue, red, brown, and purplish brown, or were an unglazed terra-cotta. He made an assortment of candlesticks, bowls, tiles, vases, mugs, paperweights, and planters. "WJW" was incised on the bottom of most pieces.

## Walrath Pottery
### Rochester, New York

Frederick Walrath, born in 1871, was a studio potter who trained with Charles F. Binns at New York State School of Clay-working and Ceramics in Alfred. While he was a student himself, Walrath taught at the Arts & Crafts School of the Chautauqua Institution in 1903. He worked briefly at Grueby Pottery before he was hired to teach at the Mechanics Institute's Department of Decorative and Fine Arts in Rochester, New York (now the Rochester Institute of Technology), and in 1918 became head ceramist at Newcomb Pottery. His works were displayed and sold from 1904 until his death at age fifty in 1921.

Walrath's early pieces were decorated with crystalline glazes or single-color matte glazes. By 1908, he started using two-color matte glazes. His decorations were usually conventionalized trees, plants, or flowers.

*Incised,*
*W. J. Walley mark.*

*Incised.*

*Frederick Walrath made this vase about 1910. The iris decorations are brown, purple, yellow-green, and green matte glazes. The vase is 9 inches high. It is marked. The original price sticker is attached: "18/6.00." (Collection of the Newark Museum)*

## Walrich Pottery
### Berkeley, California

~

WALRICH

*Incised.*

WALRICH
Berkeley, Cal.

*Incised.*

Walrich Pottery was owned by James A. and Gertrude Rupel Wall. It was first listed in the Berkeley, California, city directory in 1922 and last appears in 1930. Gertrude Wall was an art teacher in the Midwest. She began to work in ceramics in California in 1912. James Wall had worked at the Doulton works in England before he moved to the United States. He could make pottery on the wheel but most of his pieces were cast.

Walrich Pottery was small and made a variety of gift shop items, such as bowls, vases, figurines, candlesticks, bookends, paperweights, covered jars, lamp bases, and tiles. Dinner sets were made to order. The pottery used a variety of matte glazes, but specialized in blue. Many pieces were glazed a single color and had no other decoration. Tiles often pictured California missions or landscapes. Pieces were sold in many department stores and gift shops in California. They were marked with the incised name or a paper label.

James Wall remained in the ceramics industry until he died in 1952. Gertrude Wall taught pottery classes at the University of California Extension Division and did rehabilitation work with inmates at San Quentin Prison. She died in 1971.

## Wannopee Pottery
### New Milford, Connecticut

~

*Printed.*

The New Milford Pottery Company, established in New Milford, Connecticut, in 1887, changed its name to The Wannopee Pottery Company in 1892. The pottery made a mottled glaze ware and porcelain and semiporcelain pitchers with a dull glaze. One type of Wannopee pitcher was decorated with relief medallion heads of Beethoven, Mozart, or President McKinley, another with a bust of Napoleon. The pitchers were white except for two bands of brown and greenish yellow leaves. The pottery also made mottled-glaze Duchess ware, clock cases, and a blue-glazed ware. "Lettuce leaf ware" looked like a majolica leaf molded from a real cabbage leaf.

Wannopee also made an art pottery called "Scarabronze" about

*Lang and Schafer mark.*

*Impressed.*

*Impressed.*

*Lang and Osgood cipher.*

*Printed on lettuce leaf ware.*

*Impressed Scarabronze mark.*

1901. Scarabronze had a metallic-type glaze that resembled old copper. A. H. Noble, the manager of the pottery, developed the ware accidentally while trying to create a new glaze. Scarabronze ranges from dark bronze to sage green and reddish copper in color. The body is made from Connecticut red clay. The pieces also feature slip-painted Egyptian characters and figures. Pieces are marked with an applied or impressed picture of a scarab, and were sometimes marked with a square and the letters "NMPCo." or "L & S" (Lang and Schafer, New York agents who ordered the ware) in a circle. Another agent's mark often used on Scarabronze pieces is made up of the initials of Lang and Osgood.

The pottery closed in 1903.

*"Scarabronze Ware" from Edwin Barber's* The Pottery and Porcelain of the United States, *1909 edition.*

# Weller Pottery
### Zanesville, Ohio

Samuel A. Weller opened a small factory in Fultonham (Muskingum County), Ohio, in 1872 and started by making plain, unpainted flowerpots and other wares. He soon began decorating the pots with house paint and sold them door to door in nearby Zanesville. He also made stoneware on a kick wheel. By 1882, the pottery was so successful that Weller moved into a frame building on Pierce Street on the Muskingum River. In 1888 he leased an extra warehouse on South Second Street and by 1890 he had built a new pottery at Pierce Street and Cemetery Drive. In 1891 he purchased the Sharon Avenue plant that had been used by the American Encaustic Tiling Company. During these years he made painted flowerpots, jardinieres, hanging baskets, umbrella stands, and other pottery pieces.

In 1893 an addition was built on the old plant and the Weller Pottery produced its first artwares. Samuel Weller had seen Lonhuda ware at the Chicago World's Fair and was so impressed that he bought the Lonhuda Pottery and convinced William Long to move to Zanesville to continue the line at Weller. Within a year, Lonhuda was being produced at the Weller Pottery. Although Long left in 1895 after fire destroyed much of the plant, Weller rebuilt the pottery and continued to make a very similar brown artware decorated with underglaze designs that he named "Louwelsa." Louwelsa glaze is characterized by its slight brittleness. It has been known to "explode" if the piece is subjected to too high or too low a temperature.

Just after Long left, Charles Babcock Upjohn was hired as Weller's art director and designer. He introduced Dickens ware in 1900, but left the firm in 1904. In 1902, Weller hired Jacques Sicard and his assistant, Henri Gellée, from France. They made the Sicard line, a pottery with a metallic luster, but left Weller in 1907 and took the secrets of the glaze with them. William Long apparently returned to work at Weller sometime between 1909 and 1912.

During all these years, the Weller Pottery continued making a variety of other art potteries. The Aurelian, Auroral, Turada, and

**LONHUDA**

*Impressed mark, used on Lonhuda pottery made at Weller factory by William Long. "LF" stands for Lonhuda Faience.*

*Aurelian*
**WELLER**

*Incised, 1898–1910.*

**AURELIAN**

*Incised, 1898–1910.*

**SICARDO-WELLER**

*Impressed, 1902–1907.*

TURADA
WELLER

SICARDO
WELLER.

DICKENS WARE
WELLER

*Ink-stamped or impressed half-circle marks, 1896–c.1910.*

LOUWELSA
WELLER

*Ink-stamped marks, 1895–1918.*

**WELLER**

*Incised, 1898–1918.*

*Incised, 1903–1904.*

*Ink stamp, 1920s.*

*Ink stamp, c. 1925.*

*Ink stamp, c. 1925.*

**WELLER**

*Embossed.*

**KKΓ**

*Stamped, used on Hudson pieces specially ordered by Kappa Kappa Gamma fraternity, 1926–1933.*

Weller Pottery
Since 1872

*Incised, c. 1927–1930s. In mold, 1933 on.*

*Written under glaze.*

*Ink stamp, late 1920s.*

---

**WELLER**

*Incised, 1900–1925; small size letters used before 1900.*

Eocean lines were introduced by 1904. Etna, Floretta, Jap Birdimal, Dresden, Etched Matt, Hunter, and L'Art Nouveau were made before 1906.

In 1915 the Weller Pottery was generally considered to be the largest art pottery in the world. Weller had more than forty salesmen and hundreds of workmen.

Weller's prestige lines of pottery were discontinued at the end of World War I and more commercial lines were substituted. The pottery started making wares that would compete with each of the new Roseville Pottery items, with at least one new line appearing each year.

Weller bought the Zanesville Art Pottery on Ceramic Avenue in 1920 and enlarged it in 1924. During the 1920s, John Lessell (Lassell) designed and made the LaSa line, which had a metallic overglaze decoration of trees and landscape. He also designed the Chengtu and Lamar lines.

In 1925 the pottery became a corporation, the S. A. Weller Company, rather than a sole proprietorship. Samuel Weller died on October 4, 1925, and his nephew, Harry Weller, became president of the firm. A fire destroyed one of the three Weller plants in 1927, but it was rebuilt by 1931. Harry Weller died in an automobile accident on September 25, 1932, and the firm was then headed by two of Samuel Weller's sons-in-law, Frederick Grant and Irvin Smith. During the Depression, demand was small and the pottery lines became less elaborate. Two plants were closed in 1936 and all

*Incised, c. 1930.*

**WELLER MATT WARE**

*Incised.*

WELLER
ART
TILES

*Incised.*

---

*Impressed marks, 1900–1930.*

WELLER
ZONA
WARE

No._____
Price_____

*1930s paper label; special label for each line.*

**DicKENS
WELLER**

*Incised.*

WELLER SICARD

*Written on side of piece.*

the pottery was made at the one remaining factory on Ceramic Avenue. Business improved during World War II, but after the war, imports took over the American pottery market. By 1945, some of the space in the pottery was leased to the Essex Wire Company, and in 1948 the Weller Pottery ceased manufacturing.

An article by May Elizabeth Cook in *Sketch Book* described the workings of the famous pottery in 1906:

> Seven miles from Zanesville, in a log cabin, twenty-one feet square, was the first fire kindled in 1872, in one small kiln. Motive power for crushing clays, hauling the finished products to nearest market was supplied by an old white horse. Common red ware alone was made, viz., crocks, tile, etc., from clay found around Zanesville.
>
> Mr. Weller's pottery is now known as one of the large potteries of the world, having floor space of three hundred thousand feet. Twenty-five kilns with natural gas for fuel (which is, by the way, the ideal fuel for firing kilns, as the temperature is the most even to be obtained) are glowing night and day. Hundreds of skilled workmen are employed. The great room in the first story where the clays are first made ready for the artist modeler is of surpassing interest.
>
> The clay body used in the manufacture of the Weller pottery is a combination of several clays, both native and foreign. These have been most carefully tested by chemical analysis and fire tests, until a satisfactory body has been found for the decoration and glaze desired. First there must be found a perfect harmony in body and glaze; and where such a variety of ware in under glaze decoration, matt and luster is made, a great number of tests, in fact hundreds for body, glaze and color must be made. The clay for art pottery, into the composition of which, pipe clay, koalin, quartz and feldspar enter, is prepared with special care. These ingredients are thoroughly mixed in a blunger, a machine not unlike a

(Above) *Raised lavender and tan flowers decorate this Weller vase made about 1896–1905. It is 10 inches high. (Smithsonian Institution)*

(Below) *This matte-glazed vase in L'Art Nouveau pattern was modeled in the form of a plant about 1900. It is 7½ inches high and unmarked. (Smithsonian Institution)*

*This Dickens Ware vase pictures a Native American with the typical sgrafitto decoration. (Early Auctions)*

*A vase with a raised figure decoration pictured in* Pottery and Glass, *August 1908.*

*A jardiniere from either the Weller or the Roseville potteries designed by Frederick Rhead around 1904. The piece, unmarked, measures 11½ inches high and 15 inches in diameter at its widest point. (June Greenwald Antiques)*

Three-dimensional frog and snake climb this Weller vase made about 1905. The 7¾-inch vase has matte green glaze. It is marked with the impressed name "Weller." The same vase was made with the Etna line glaze. (Smithsonian Institution)

This vase made about 1900 is in the form of a bivalve mollusk shell resting on a low pedestal base. It is 6¾ inches high and has a matte glaze. The piece is impressed "Weller." (Smithsonian Institution)

Frederick Rhead was the designer of this Weller Pottery plaque, made about 1904. It has painted underglaze decorations of poppy flowers and seeds in shades of brown, green, white, and blue. The 10½-inch plaque is incised "Weller Faience" on the back. The name "Rhead" appears in sgraffito on the front. (Private collection; photograph from The Art Museum, Princeton University, Princeton, New Jersey)

(Left) Eocean ware (top) and Dickens Ware (bottom) from an advertisement for Weller Pottery, American Pottery Gazette, August 1905.

*Eocean ware from an advertisement in* American Pottery Gazette, *August 1906.*

(Above left) *Weller matte-glazed Dickens Ware vase, 8¾ inches high.* (Above right) *Dick Swiveller is pictured on this glossy glaze Dickens Ware vase. It is 10½ inches high and was made about 1906. (Smithsonian Institution)*

*Weller Sicardo ware vase, 14 inches high, decorated with iridescent peacock feathers. (Wolf's)*

great churn with paddles to cut and blend the clays. Water is added, and as the blunger turns, the clay and water [are] thoroughly mixed into a "slip" and . . . carried from the blunger to a cylindrical sieve, of one hundred meshes to the inch.

The liquid clay or "slip," as it is technically known, is then pumped by hydraulic pressure into presses where the superfluous moisture is pressed out, and we then have great cakes of fine plastic body, blue-gray in color.

From the presses the clay is carried to great pits to be "aged"; it then is ready for the hand of the modeler. Mr. Weller is utilizing every appliance that modern mechanics can supply to facilitate the work of his artist ceramists. The modeling and moulding rooms are on the second floor and are quite picturesque with the many workers in their white blouses and caps. Some are busy at the wheels, while others bearing long boards filled with moulds gracefully balanced on their heads, walk rapidly to the drying rooms where the moulds are placed on shelves to dry.

There is quite a fascination in watching the expert moulder at his wheel, known as a "jigger." The moulds, made of plaster of Paris three inches thick, are in two parts, tightly bound together by a strap, and placed on the rapidly revolving wheel. From a great box of very soft clay, placed at his right, the moulder throws into the mould with his hand the needed amount of clay, then quickly inserts a shaped paddle suspended above the wheel, pressing it against the sides of the revolving mould until an even thickness of clay adheres to the sides. Then the superfluous clay in the bottom is lifted out, [the] inside of the base smoothed, and before one can draw a long breath a workman is carrying away the mould to the drying room and another form almost finished is whirling around on the jigger.

The absorption of the moisture by the plaster mould, soon gives the clay sufficient consistency to take the necessary shape. Subsequent shrinkage allows its removal from the mould. After a partial drying, the vase or jardiniere is dressed or smoothed and has

its decorations applied and the ware then goes again to the drying room. If it is to be decorated in relief, or with handles or feet, they are applied at that stage. If to receive the underglaze decoration, it is taken when bone dry to the studios where the backgrounds are applied. These are sprayed on through an atomizer by compressed air, the vase standing upon a wheel that turns slowly. From this studio it goes to another where the design suited to its form is painted on with liquid clays, in which the colors have been thoroughly blended with the "slip." This process is called by the French "pâte-sur-pâte," and is seen in its greatest beauty in the exquisite work of Solon, the noted artist of the Sèvres and Minton Potteries.

(Above left) *A Weller Sicardo vase, 8½ inches high, signed Sicardo on the side.* (Above right) *This Weller Sicardo vase is 6 inches high and is signed on the side.* (Private collection)

*An assortment of iridescent Weller Sicardo ware made from 1902 to 1907. The iris plate is 10½ inches in diameter.* (Christie's)

*An asterisk before the name indicates an artist listed in Edwin Barber's*
Marks of American Potters.

ABEL  E. A  Ēᴀ

Edward Abel.

ꓦ  V. ADAMS

* Virginia Adams. Also worked
at Owens; Roseville.

W. Allsop (Alsop).

M ᴀnsᴇʟ

M. Ansel.

REA  AX  ꓱ

Ruth Axline. Also worked at
Mosaic Tile.

* Elizabeth Ayers. Also worked
at Lonhuda; Roseville.

J. B. c. 1902. Dickens Ware.

M. B. Unknown.

AꓭBEST  ꓭB  ᴀB Fᴢᴇsᴛ

Anna Fulton Best. Also worked
at Owens; Roseville (?).

L. B.  ꓔB  ꓔB
E. BLAKE  Ꙓ·ꓭ

* Lizabeth Blake. May also be
Elizabeth Blake.

Florence Bowers.

O.B

Oscar Bronkar.

E. Brown

E. Brown.

ᴸᴶB  ᴸᴶB  L.J.B.

* Levi J. Burgess (d. 1943).
1905–1907. Dresden; Louwelsa.
Artist; decorated many vases with
Indian head decoration. Son of
Samuel Weller's sister; lived in
Zanesville and worked at the studio
as an artist from 1905–1907.
Opened art emporium 1909,
decorating business 1912, then a
tearoom; later a commercial
illustrator, Cincinnati.

Jennie Burgoon.

JB

John Butterworth. Also worked at
Owens; Roseville.

C~

C. Unknown.

Sam Celli.

c.c. chilcote

Charles Chilcote (1888–1979).
1904–1905. Apprentice to Charles
Upjohn. Also worked at
Owens; Zane.

Cill

Cill. Unknown.

M·C.
M CIPICH  ᴍ.C.

M. Cipich.

LC

Laura Cline.

NC  nc

Nell Corbin.

Coyleone

K. Coyleone.

A.D.

Anna Dautherty. Dickens; Louwelsa.
Also worked at Roseville (?).

A. DAVIS

A. Davis.

F. D. D.
FOOTIS

Frank Dedonatis.

K. G.  K ᴳ

Katherine (Kathryn) deGolter.

C · J · D
C · J · D

Charles J. Dibowski.

FD

* Anthony Dunlavy. 1901, 1923;
Dickens; Lamar.

C. A. Dusenbery
C A. Dusenbery

C. A. Dusenbery.

NE

N. E. Unknown.

**W₵**

*W. E. Unknown.*

**ENgLANd, ⅁E**

*Dorothy England. See also Dorothy England Laughead.*

*I. F. Unknown. c. 1909. Dickens Second.*

**Ferrell**
**F.F.**

*\* Frank Ferrell. (1878–1961). c. 1900–1905. Also worked at Owens; Peters and Reed; Roseville.*

**F**

*Charles Fouts. Also worked at Owens.*

**Fox, E.**

*E. Fox.*

**H Fuchs**

*Henry Fuchs. Head of the decorating studio, 1925.*

*Gazo (Fudji) Fujiyama.*

*G. Unknown. Louwelsa.*

**H. Gellée**

*Henri Gellee. 1901–1907. Assistant to Jacques Sicard. Returned to France 1907; wounded in World War I at Battle of Verdun; died of pneumonia.*

**MG M.G.**

*\* Mary Gellie. Aurelian; Jap Birdimal.*

**MG**
**M Gibson**

*M. Gibson.*

---

**A G**

*Arthur Goetting.*

**G   C.G.**

*Charles Gray. Also worked at Owens.*

**F. F. H.**

*F. F. H. Unknown.*

**K ∨H**

*K. V. H. Unknown.*

**V. M. H.**

*V. M. H. Unknown.*

**W.H .**
**w.F Hall WH**

*William F. Hall. Also worked at Roseville.*

**D H   H**

*Delores Harvey. Aurelian. Also worked at Owens.*

**A Haubrich   ⅄ H**

*\* Albert Haubrich (1875–1931). 1897–1903. Decorator. Eocean; Louwelsa. Born Biersdorf, Germany; moved to Steubenville, Ohio. Started working for the Weller Pottery Company in 1897. Also worked for Owens; later A. Radford. Activities 1904–1920 unknown; operated interior design business, Columbus, Ohio, 1920.*

**H. H.**

*Hugo Herb. Also worked at Owens.*

**J H   J.H.   J. H.**

*John J. Herold. Also worked at Owens; Roseville.*

**Hood**

*Edith Hood. (Hudson).*

---

**R H   R H**

*Roy Hook. Also worked at Owens.*

**J. HUNTER**

*Jean Hunter.*

**MH**

*\* Madge Hurst. Aurelian. Also worked at Roseville.*

*W. I. Unknown. Aurelian.*

**J.I   JI**

*\* Josephine Imlay. Also worked at Roseville.*

**EJ**

*E. J. (?). Unknown.*

**J. J.**

*J. J. Unknown.*

**g**

*Anna Jewett.*

**K.K.**

*\* Karl Kappes. Louwelsa. Artist.*

**K**
**KeNNedy**

*Kennedy.*

**LK   K**

*L. Knaus. 1902. Applied glaze.*

*Joe Knott.*

**E.L.**

*E. L. Unknown.*

**J. B. L.**

*J. B. L. Unknown. Dresden.*

---

S. L.

*S. L. Unknown. Louwelsa.*

X L

*X. L. Unknown.*

*Rose Langstaff.*

*Dorothy England Laughead
(1895–1982). 1925. Decorator,
modeler, etc. Married a Mr.
Laughead in 1938; used both maiden
and married names in signature. See
also Dorothy England.*

C L Leffler    C. L.

*Claude L. Leffler. Hudson. Also
worked at Roseville.*

Lessell
JL

*John Lessell (Lassell) (1871–1926).
Early 1920s–1925. Head of
decorating department; created
Cheng-tu; Lamar; LaSa; Marengo.
Born Mettlach, Germany. Also
worked for Owens; started pottery in
Newark, Ohio, 1925.*

A V

*A. V. Lewis. Also worked at Owens.*

W. L.

*William A. Long. 1893–1894,
1909–1915. Also worked at Clifton;
Lonhuda; Owens. See Lonhuda
Pottery.*

R Lo

*Rudolph Lorber. 1905–1919. In
charge of modeling new lines. Born
Vienna, Austria; educated in
Bohemia; worked in England.*

M. Lybarger

*M. Lybarger.*

C B M

*C. B. M. Unknown.*

C M M

*C. M. M. Unknown.*

CMC

*Cora McCandless.*

*Margaret McGinnis.*

*L. McGrath. Also worked
at Roseville.*

L McLain

*L. McLain.*

SL
McLaughlin

*\* Sarah Reid McLaughlin. Louwelsa.
Also worked at Lonhuda.*

*Lelia Meloy.*

HM

*\* Hattie Mitchell. Aurelian; Dickens.
Also worked at Roseville.*

L M
LM
L Mitchell

*\* Lillie B. Mitchell. Also worked at
Roseville.*

M.    M.    M
M M.Tchel

*\* Minnie Mitchell.*

Morris

*L. Morris.*

GM   YM

*\* Gordon Mull. 1902. Designer. Also
worked at Mosaic Tile.*

M-M

*M. Myers. Also worked at Roseville.*

MBP

*M. B. P. Unknown.*

hP.

*Lizzie Perone.*

ELP

E.L.P.

*\* Edwin L. Pickens. Dickens,
Dickens Second. Plant supervisor.*

*Mary L. Pierce. Louwelsa line.
Also worked at Owens.*

HP  JP
Pillsbury

*\* Hester W. Pillsbury. Hudson. Also
worked at Roseville.*

C.a.R

*C. A. R. Unknown.*

F N R

*F. N. R. Unknown.*

## A R

*Albert Radford. c. 1900. Modeler. Had worked at Wedgwood in England, then in Trenton, New Jersey; Broadway, Virginia; and Tiffin, Ohio. Also superintendent at Owens; made own pottery in Zanesville, Ohio, 1903; in 1904 moved to Clarksburg, West Virginia. See A. Radford Pottery.*

*Marie Rauchfuss. Before 1899 (?). Also at Owens; Rookwood.*

F. R.   F Rhead

*Frederick Hürten Rhead (1880–1942). Came from Staffordshire, England, in 1902; created the Jap Birdimal, 1904. Also worked at Roseville, 1904–1908; University City, 1908–1911; Arequipa, 1911–1914; Rhead Pottery; American Encaustic, 1920–1927; Homer Laughlin China Company, East Liverpool, Ohio, 1927–1942.*

*\* Eugene Roberts. Hudson. Also worked at American Encaustic.*

HR

*Harry Robinson.*

HMR

*Hattie M. Ross. Also worked at Owens.*

S

*S. Unknown.*

DS

*D. S. Unknown.*

---

*Henry Schmidt.*

*Aloysius J. Schwerber. 1901. Potter and plant foreman.*

N. S.

*Norman Scothorn.*

R
S

*R. Lilliam Shoemaker.*

SICARD

*Jacques Sicard (d. 1923). 1901–1907. Had worked at Clement Massier Pottery in France. Developed metallic luster used on Sicardo. Sicard had heard about William Long's dismissal after Samuel Weller learned Long's secrets of glazing Lonhuda ware. Determined to keep his own secrets from Samuel Weller, Sicard supposedly worked in a secret room and plugged up Weller's peepholes. Returned to France 1907; operated a pottery in Golfe Juan.*

SKOIN

*Skoin.*

*Helen Smith. 1897. Utopian. Also worked at Owens; Roseville.*

Is

*Irvin Smith.*

*Jessie R. Spaulding.*

A.B.S.

*Amelia Browne Sprague.*

*Fred Steel. Also worked at Roseville.*

---

*\* Tot Steele. Also worked at Owens; Roseville.*

*William H. Stemm. Eocean. Also worked at Owens.*

E Sulcer

*E. Sulcer. Louwelsa.*

*C. T. Unknown. Louwelsa.*

*L. B. T. Unknown.*

4.
LT

*L. T. Unknown.*

*\* C. Minnie Terry. Also worked at Owens; Roseville.*

M. T.

*Madeline Thompson (?). Also worked at Roseville (?).*

M. T.

Mae Timberlak

*Mae Timberlake. Hudson; Louwelsa; Pictorial. Also worked at Owens; Roseville.*

S.T.

*Sarah Timberlake. Also worked at Owens; Roseville.*

R. G Turner

*R. G. Turner.*

H. U. Unknown.

Charles Babcock Upjohn (1866–1953). 1895–1904. Dickens. Worked in father's architecture firm; studied art in England, France, and Italy. Although red-green color-blind, he was employed by Samuel Weller as art director and designer. Opened his own pottery in Zanesville, Ohio, 1904; designer for Trent Tile, 1905–1915; art and ceramics professor, Columbia University.

K.W.

K. W. Unknown.

KЅAW

K. A. W. Unknown.

L. W. Unknown.

MFW

M. F. W. Unknown.

Arthur Wagner (1900–1979). c. 1920–1948. Decorator. Also worked for American Encaustic; Mosaic Tile.

N WAlch

Naomi Walch (Truitt). 1927–1936.

CW

Carl Weigelt. 1920s. Lusterwares.

T.g.W.

T. J. Wheatley. Later founded Wheatley Pottery.

Carrie Wilbur.

ƐW

Edna Wilbur.

A Wilson

Albert Wilson.

H.W.

* Helen B. Windle.

LW

Louise Wood.

X

X. (?) Unknown.

Clotilda Marie Zanetta. Also worked at Rookwood; Roseville.

Stylized decorations in gold, blue, and maize on a crackled cream matte glaze decorate this Weller vase. The artist's name, "Ferrell," is in color on the side of the vase. The bottom is marked "WELLER." (Private collection)

After the decoration is applied, the vase is ready for glazing, which in this case will be a bright, clear glaze. This ware with the underglaze decoration is the first art pottery made by Mr. Weller. Its pretty name, Louwelsa, is a combination of the name of his little daughter, Louise, who was born at the time these first experiments were perfected, the first syllable of Mr. Weller's name, and his initials. The usual backgrounds on this ware are orange, shading into the browns with decorations in lighter tones of the same colors and green. The Aurelian, which was the second ware produced, is similar to the Louwelsa in effect, both background and decoration being painted on in rich mahogany tones.

These first experiments were quickly followed by others known as the Jap-Birdimal, Golbrogreen, Eocean, Sicardo, Oriental, Monochrome, Hunter, Floretta, L'Art Nouveau, Dickens and Perfecto, and were the results of many experiments made by artists of various nationalities employed by Mr. Weller. French, Japanese, Austrian, German, and American craftsmen work side by side in the studios, though in reality each is in a little world of his own, working out his dreams in form and color, entirely oblivious of all around him. The Eocean ware mentioned has an underglaze decoration on white clay body. The backgrounds are beautifully blended from pinkish fawn color at the base into soft blue grays. The decorations are in harmonious tones of pinks, grays, and browns. The designs used are flowers, birds, animals, and one

A Weller LaSa vase, 8½ inches high, with a paper label. (Private collection)

Weller Sicardo vase with raised grape vine decoration, 22½ by 9 inches. (David Rago Arts & Crafts Gallery)

This Weller Sicardo ware plaque, 13 by 16 inches, is covered with iridescent glaze. The plaque is of St. Cecelia, the patron saint of music and the blind, and is based on a fifteenth-century bronze relief believed to be the work of Donatello, the Renaissance sculptor. (Smithsonian Institution)

Marked in script, "Eocean Weller 116," this vase stands 9 inches high. (June Greenwald Antiques)

A Jap Birdimal vase, 7½ inches high. It is unmarked. (June Greenwald Antiques)

Weller plaque with painted design of an Apache child. The picture was copied from a photograph by Edward S. Curtis in 1903.

*A lifelike Indian stares from the side of this Louwelsa jardiniere. (Christie's)*

*(Left to right) Weller Pottery Coppertone vase with frog, 9 inches high; Dickens Ware vase showing Dombey and son, 9 inches; Louwelsa vase, 4½ inches; and russet matte vase, 6 inches. (Smithsonian Institution)*

*This glossy Zona umbrella stand decorated with six women in lavender gowns is 20½ inches high. (Wolf's)*

*Roma Line examples in red and green decoration with white ground. The pieces, made in the 1920s, are marked with the impressed word "Weller." Some pieces in this line are unmarked. (J. Walter Yore Company)*

special decoration is known as the Dickens ware, having figures in low relief from Cruikshank's illustrations of Dickens' stories. The floral decorations on this delicate background are particularly good. The Sicardo ware is of special note. It is the crowning product of the metallic luster studio, under the directorship of Monsieur J. Sicard, formerly an associate of Clement Massier, a famous ceramist of Golfe-Juan, France.

M. Sicard, after coming to the Weller Pottery, experimented in the metallic lusters for two years, aided in every way by Mr. Weller, until he achieved the beautiful luster known as Sicardo. The forms which he uses are those thrown on the potter's wheel, and this method, or modeling by hand, gives a character and purity of line to a vase thus made, which can never be obtained by the commercial method of moulding.

The metallic lusters require not only the fine color sense of the artist, but also the skill and knowledge of the chemist; these gifts M. Sicard happily possesses. Accustomed to the use of peat or dead brushwood to fire the kilns in France, M. Sicard could with

difficulty be persuaded to use the natural gas in the kilns in which the luster ware was to be fired. In his first experiments, he insisted on firing the kilns with the wild growths found along the roadsides around Zanesville. Was it not a pretty thought that the wild blossoms, having caught all the glow and richness of the summer, in rainbow tints, should through sacrificial fires transfer their glory to the moulded clay? The large showroom devoted to the Sicardo ware would indicate most satisfactory results from the complicated experiments requiring such care in decoration and firing. Beautiful forms with exquisite tones of flame, rose, blue, green, bronze, purple and crimson, melting into one another like colors in an opal, or in the great arch of the rainbow, are most harmonious and restful. To obtain this beautiful luster, the vases are first treated all over with a metallic preparation, and then decorated in conventional designs, in long flowing lines and curves, with chemically prepared pigments. This glaze is fired at a very high temperature, resulting in a texture and lustrous, changing color much like the Tiffany glass.

Mr. Weller is to be congratulated upon his past successes and the promise of greater ones in the future. At the Weller Pottery both thought and money are being expended most liberally for experiments. A great future and a great opportunity lie before these practical ceramists of our day.

## LINES

*(So many pottery lines were offered by the Weller Company during its years of operation that a complete list is probably impossible. The following is a compilation of the lines offered, approximate dates where possible—early period, pre–World War I; middle period, 1920–1930; late period, 1930–1948—artist and modelers who worked on the line if known, and a description of the line. An asterisk appears before unofficial names used by various authors of articles and books about Weller.)*

\* *Alpha:* cream-colored ware with reticulated rims and geometric designs, some with designs of lions or classical profiles, c. 1911.

*Alvin:* matte glaze, molded raised decoration with fruit, branches, or vines, c. 1928.

*Weller Knifewood pieces shown in an undated catalog, circa 1920. (Ohio Historical Society Library)*

*The kingfisher on this 8-inch-high Weller pitcher is colored brown and green. The line of pottery, made about 1920, is Zona. (Christie's)*

(Above) *Hudson line pieces shown in an undated catalog, circa 1920.* (Right) *Jardinieres and pedestals in several patterns shown in an undated catalog, circa 1920. (Ohio Historical Society Library)*

*Anco:* ivory-colored, dark brown traditional designs, probably middle period.

*Ansonia:* matte glaze in blue or gray, made to appear hand-turned with small ridges in the design (called Fleron if colored green), middle period.

*Arcadia:* matte or glossy glaze, molded leaves and flowers form irregular edges, late period.

*Arcola:* matte glaze, light or dark colors, realistic grapes on vines or roses in relief, middle period.

*Ardsley:* raised cattails, leaves, and water lilies form body of vase, matte glaze, 1928.

*Art Nouveau:* matte or high-gloss glaze, light color molded decoration, typical Art Nouveau decorations featuring women with flowing hair, tendrils, etc., usually marked, 1904.

* *Athens:* tall vases, black, gray, or terra-cotta background, raised classical decorations, glossy or matte glaze, early period.

*Atlantic:* matte glaze, tinted and molded fruit, flowers, leaves, middle period.

*Atlas:* star-shaped top, semigloss, angular sides, many colors, late period.

*Aurelian:* brushed background, high-gloss brown glaze background similar to Louwelsa, brighter colors, red, yellow, brown, sometimes marked "Aurelian" in script, 1898–1910.

*Auroro:* mottled pastel background, gray, pink, overall crazing, fish, flower decorations, slip decorations, high gloss, 1904 (variants called Auroral, Aurora, Auroso).

*Baldin:* matte or glossy glaze, apples on branch, sometimes shaded blue background, other colors, middle period.

*Barcelona:* matte glaze, pink to yellow, pink at base, flower decorations, ridges to imitate hand-thrown pottery, matte glaze, middle period.

*Bedford:* glossy glaze, molded flowers on stems, dark colors, middle period.

*Bedford Green Matte:* green matte glaze, molded flowers on stems, middle period.

*Besline:* luster glaze, monochrome, overglaze woodbine decoration, middle period.

*Blo'red:* blue glaze with red, high-gloss glaze, middle period.

*Blossom:* pink flowers, green leaves, blue or green matte glaze, late period.

*Blue and Decorated Hudson:* matte blue background glaze, slip decoration, flowers or parrots in shaded blue or cream pink, middle period.

*Blue and Ivory:* tinted apple or pinecone decoration, blue background, middle period.

*Blue Drapery:* dark blue matte glaze, red roses, pastel flower, draped vertical folds, c. 1920.

*Blue Ware:* dark blue matte glaze, embossed medieval figures with plants in light colors, middle period.

*Bo-Marblo:* luster glaze, tree design, middle period.

*Bonito:* matte cream glaze, flowers, middle period.

*Bouquet:* molded dogwood blossoms, a lily of the valley, matte glaze, late period.

*Bradley:* fluted garden pots, middle period.

*Breton:* matte glaze, band of stylized flowers and leaves in center, middle period.

*Brighton:* figurines, natural colors, birds, glossy glaze, middle period.

*Bronze Ware:* metallic-looking mottled glaze, middle period.

*Burnt Wood:* realistic-looking tan and brown ware with the appearance of burnt wood, lighter color designs carved out of clay, 1909, middle period.

*Cactus:* figurines ranging in size from about 3 to 12 inches tall, each in a solid color, green, yellow, brown, or beige, 1930s.

*Camelot:* earth tones, ivory geometric designs, glossy glaze, early period.

*Cameo:* large white flowers in relief, pastel green, blue, coral used for background, late period.

*Cameo Jewel:* white "jewels" in relief, cream shaded to dark colors, glassy glaze, early period.

\* *Candis:* ivory and light green, stylized flowers, late period.

*Chase:* relief white dogs and hunter on horseback, dark blue matte background, similar to Wedgwood jasper in appearance, late period.

*Chelsea:* band of flowers near top, dark color to accent fluted sides, matte glaze, middle period.

*Chengtu:* matte glaze, orange-red, 1920–1925, developed by John Lessell.

*Chinese Red:* red glaze developed by Lessell, c. 1920 (perhaps Chengtu).

*Clarmont:* dark background, raised flowers, vines, grapes on band, raised small "beads" near top, bottom, middle period.

*Classic:* evenly placed relief vines forming arches at top of piece with cutout

*A Muskota ware Weller figurine glazed in shades of brown and beige, made about 1920.*

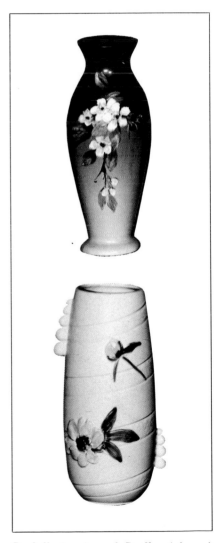

*Rochelle* (top) *and Rudlor* (above) *lines shown in an undated catalog, circa 1920. (Ohio Historical Society Library)*

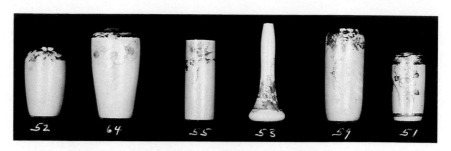

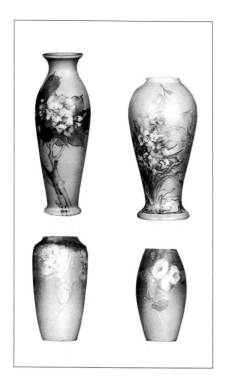

areas beneath the vine, plain light colors, c. 1920.

*Claywood:* similar to Burnt Wood but with dark vertical bars, middle period.

*Clinton Ivory:* raised, molded trees, plants, other decorations, matte glaze, ivory with brown overtones, middle period.

*Cloudburst:* crackled luster glaze, brown, pink, violet, middle period.

*Comet:* matte glaze, stars scattered on surface, pastel or white glaze, late period.

*Coppertone:* blotchy semigloss green over brown glaze, yellow shading, figures of frogs, etc., and vases decorated with lifelike frogs, fish, animals, plants, middle period.

*Copra:* description unknown, possibly a mingling of Louella and Flemish Ware, with large realistic flowers, early period.

*Corleone:* similar to Louwelsa but with green brush strokes, early period.

*Cornish:* relief decoration of leaves and berries, largest leaves near top, mottled background, middle period.

*Creamware:* cream-colored, textured, various styles, early to middle period.

*Cretone:* modern-style deer and leaves, late period.

*Crystalline:* columns of overlapped leaves, matte glaze, late period.

*Darsie:* looped cords with tassels, matte glaze, solid color, late period.

*Delsa:* relief flowers and leaves, matte glaze, leaf handles, late period.

*Delta:* blue slip decorations on blue background, matte glaze, middle period.

*Dickens Tobacco Jars:* Admiral, Turk, Chinaman, Irishman, sculpted heads, incised and colored by hand, matte finish, designed by Charles Upjohn, marked "Dickens Weller," c. 1900.

*Dickens Ware:* first line, solid dark brown, green, or blue background resembling Louwelsa, occasionally a shaded background, slip decorations, flowers, marked "Dickens Ware," 1897–1898, developed by Upjohn.

Second line, shaded background matte or high-gloss glaze, sgraffito decoration of scenes from Dickens, also Indians, monks, fish, birds, golfers, drinking scenes, historical scenes, dark red brown, green, gray, turquoise, and pink, marked "Dickens Ware," sometimes with artist's name, 1897–c. 1905, developed by Upjohn.

Third line, dark background shaded to light, similar to Eocean, high gloss, relief figures from Dickens stories one side, reverse side has a raised black disk with name of scene, sometimes raised white disk with Dickens profile, marked "Weller," 1910, created by Frederick Hürten Rhead.

*Dorland:* scalloped top, ribs, matte glaze, late period.

*Drapery:* see Blue Drapery.

*Dresden Ware* (also called Holland): Dutch scenes, slip-painted, blue, blue figures, matte glaze, 1907–1909.

*Dugan:* relief flowers on low bowls, middle period.

*Dunton:* black background, colorful naturalistic birds and flowers, early period.

*Dupont Ware:* relief roses, colored background, middle period.

\* *Dynasty:* green to blue matte, middle period.

*Eclair:* high-relief roses, white or dark glossy background, middle period.

*Elberta:* buff-colored bands on green matte background, 1931.

*Eldora:* ribbing at bottom, flowers in band at top, matte glaze, colored background, middle period.

*Eocean* (Eosian): underglaze slip decoration, birds, animals, fish, flowers, character study, light eggshell shaded to blue, gray, or brown background, high gloss, marked "Eocean Weller," 1898–1915, similar to Rookwood's Iris glaze.

*Eocean Rose:* same as Eocean except shaded from gray to pink, usually marked "Eocean Rose Weller."

*Etched Matt:* incised decoration, matte gray glaze, similar to second-line Dickens, early period.

*Ethel:* cream-colored background, matte glaze, oval medallion with profile of woman's head (said to be Ethel Weller, Samuel Weller's youngest daughter), roses on stems, bands on cross-hatching top and bottom, c. 1915.

*Etna:* light blue to gray shaded to dark at the top, high gloss, flowers or grapes molded, colored, 1906, mark "ETNA" scratched into base.

*Euclid:* matte glaze, no decoration, middle period.

*Evergreen:* green-blue matte finish, ribbed, late period.

*Fairfield:* band of cherubs at top, fluted base, matte finish, middle period, similar to Roseville Donatello pattern.

*Flemish Ware:* matte glaze, embossed decorations, parrots, cows, grapes, roses, apples, birds, nymphs, c. 1920(?)–1928 (name seems to have been used for other wares too).

*Fleron:* green glaze, made to look hand-turned, middle period, called Ansonia if blue or gray.

*A vase from Weller's Flemish Ware line, about 1915–1928, stands 15½ inches high and is marked "Weller."* (*June Greenwald Antiques*)

The name "Timberlake" is signed on the side (detail below) of this 7-inch vase. It has an aqua to pink crackled matte glaze with pink and white dogwood blossoms. (Private collection)

This 8-inch vase is impressed with the name "Weller." It has a raised iris decoration in pale pink shades on a gray background. (Private collection)

An 8½-inch-high Weller Chengtu vase. It is marked "Weller Pottery" with an ink stamp. (Private collection)

A Weller Softone vase, 9 inches high, made in the 1930s. It is incised "Weller" in script. (Private collection)

*Floral:* ribbed background, blue, green, or white background pastel colors, floral decoration, semigloss, late period, 1931–1948.

*Florala:* cream background, raised molded flowers, pastel tints in rectangular panels, matte glaze, middle period.

*Florenzo:* pastel flowers on ribbed background of cream edged with green, matte glaze, middle period, 1928.

*Floretta:* brown or pastel background, underglaze flowers or fruit in low relief, or incised like second-line Dickens, high-gloss glaze or matte finish, mark "Floretta Weller" in a circle impressed, 1904.

*Forest:* polychrome, tinted color, matte or shiny glaze, hand-decorated forest scenes, c. 1920.

*Forest View:* forest scenes, leaf and berry decoration.

*Frosted Matte:* mottled, almost metallic-looking in many colors, green, yellow, purple, blue, pink, middle period.

*Fruitone:* upright streaks of color, shaded like a piece of fruit, late period.

*Fudzi:* similar to Roseville's Roseanne Fudji, listed in 1906 catalog, artist Gazo Fujiyama.

*Gardenware:* assorted molded figures and garden ornaments, middle to late period.

*Geode:* cream glaze, fluting, scalloped top, 1936.

*Glazed Hudson:* see Hudson.

*Glendale Ware:* scenes of birds with nests, branches, plants, Indians, slightly raised on sky-blue background, matte glaze, 1928.

*Gloria:* matte glaze, beige, black berries in relief.

(Left) *An unmarked vase of the Claywood line with a fish decoration is 2 inches high.* (Right) *A Weller vase from the Coppertone line is 6 inches high, has a mottled green glaze, and is signed "Weller Handmade."* (*Private collection*)

*This Marvo pattern vase marked "Weller Ware" was made about 1930. (Courtesy of the Western Reserve Historical Society)*

*Golbrogreen* (gold-brown-green): gold shaded to green, matte glaze, (1907).

*Golden Glow:* mottled background, leaves, applied handles, 1932.

*Gold-Green:* teapots, dark green with gold transfers, later period.

*Graystone:* outdoor pottery line resembling granite, c. 1931.

*Greenaways:* gray to pink, landscapes, windmills, sea scenes, similar to Dresden Ware, 1909.

*Greenbriar:* pink over green glaze, glossy, made to resemble hand-turning, middle period.

*Greora:* mottled orange-brown, green semigloss, middle period.

*Hobart:* vellum finish, monochrome green, white, human and animal figures, flower holders, 1928 (if shaded glaze, called Lavonia).

*Holland:* see Dresden Ware.

*Hudson:* matte glaze, underglaze slip-painted decorations, realistic flowers, birds, etc., early and middle periods (Glazed Hudson is the same with a glossy finish); Weller produced a variety of Hudson wares, including Blue and Decorated Hudson, White and Decorated Hudson, Hudson Pictorial, and Rochelle.

*Hunter:* brown background, slip decorations of outdoor subjects, birds, butterflies, etc., glossy glaze, signed "Hunter," 1907.

*Ivoris:* ivory background color, relief flowers, semigloss, late period.

*Ivory:* cream color tinged with brown, relief decorations, cupids, swags, etc., matte glaze, 1928.

*Jap Birdimal:* brown, blue, gray, terra-cotta, greenish-yellow background, decorations of birds, trees, animals, Japanese women, designs incised, then

*A vase from the White and Decorated Hudson line made in the 1920s–1930s. The body is cream-colored crackle glazed. The trailing blossom decorations are in the "Japonisme" mode. The 10-inch-high vase is marked "Weller." (Private collection)*

*This 15½-inch-high Hudson vase has a matte blue background with lifelike colored irises. It is signed "Pillsbury" on the side near the base.*

*An unmarked Coppertone Weller frog dating from the 1930s measures 2¼ inches high by 4½ inches long. (Private collection)*

inlaid with slip, covered with high-gloss glaze, 1904, created by Frederick Rhead (sometimes marked "Weller, Rhead").

*Jet Black:* matte black, late period.

*Jewel:* see Cameo Jewel.

*Juneau:* white matte glaze, late period.

*Kenova:* relief decorations of flowers, woman's head, birds, middle period.

*Kitchen Gem:* utility line.

*Klyro Ware:* 7-inch bud vases, two flowers and perpendicular green lines, middle period.

*Knifewood:* looks like carved wood, colored decorations, dogs, swans, other animals, matte glaze, middle period.

*L'Art Nouveau:* see Art Nouveau.

*LaSa:* metallic glaze in gold, reddish gold, silver background, landscape decorations, marked on side near base, 1900–1925, created by John Lessell.

*Lavonia:* matte or glossy glaze, pink shaded to blue, fluted pieces, middle period (see Hobart).

*Lamar:* deep red background with black scenery, trees, middle period, designed by John Lessell.

*Lido:* pastel, relief leaf decoration or just draped, middle period.

*Lonhuda:* brown glazed line, impressed mark, 1894.

*Lorbeek:* cream color, modernistic, middle period.

* *Lorber:* similar to Burntwood, cavorting satyr in relief, early period, named for modeler Rudolph Lorber.

*Loru:* raised leaf design near base, matte finish, late period.

*Louella:* same as Blue Drapery except in pink, gray, or brown, middle period.

*Louwelsa:* shaded fall-colored background of brown, yellow, green, slip decorated with flowers, fruit, Indians, dogs, very similar to Lonhuda, high-gloss glaze, sometimes marked "Louwelsa," 1895–1918, similar to Rookwood's standard glaze, Owen's Utopian, Roseville's Rozane.

*Louwelsa Matte:* slip decorated, pastel matte finish, 1905.

*Lustre:* plain luster glaze, no decoration, middle period.

*Luxor Line:* imitation bark with relief flowers, middle period.

*Malta Ware:* flower holder shaped like birds or figures, pastel, 1928.

*Malvern:* high-relief realistic leaves and flowers on rough background, matte finish, middle period.

*Manhattan:* different color background, traditional stylized flowers and leaves, matte or glossy glaze, middle period (c. 1920).

*Marbelized* (Lessell Ware): luster background decorated with trees, mountains, pink, orange, blue, lavender, gray, or purple luster, sometimes marked "Lessell" on side, middle period.

*Marengo:* burnt orange, stylized trees, middle period.

*Marne:* outdoor pottery sundials and birdbaths, etc., middle period.

*Marvo:* raised ferns and leaves, light green, tan, matte glaze, 1928.

*Matte Floretta:* see Floretta.

*Matte (Mat) Green:* slightly shaded dark green, matte glaze, raised designs of leaves, natural forms, 1905.

*Melrose:* pastel-colored realistic cherries, grapes, or roses in relief, cream background, tinged with color, irregular-shaped vase, middle period.

*Mi-Flo:* flowers, leaves, or diagonal panels in relief, matte glaze, late period.

*Mirror Black:* black glaze, plain, middle period.

*Monochrome:* matte glaze, solid color, early period (1907).

*Morocco:* tree, fruit in carved relief on black or red background, middle period.

*Muskota:* flower holders in bird, animal, human shapes, bowls, jars, light or dark colors, glossy glaze, 1928.

*Neiska:* mottled finish, matte glaze, Ivoris, Velva shapes, late period.

*Nile:* matte glaze, drip decoration, middle period.

*Norona (Narona):* ivory-colored background, classic figures, fruit, or flowers in relief, decorations accented with rubbed brown color, wax, 1909.

*Norwood:* Art Nouveau patterns in relief, stippled background, dark, matte background, 1909.

*Noval:* brown background or white with black edging, applied roses, fruit, middle period.

*Novelty:* animal novelties, wall ornaments, vases, sometimes human forms, various colors, glossy or matte glaze, late period.

*Oak Leaf:* matte glaze, raised oak leaves and acorns, late period.

*Ollas Water Bottle:* gourd-shaped bottle, stem top, plate painted yellow, green, etc., late period, designed by Mrs. Dorothy England Laughead.

*This 7¼-inch-high Selma vase is decorated with a dark blue background and daisies. (Wolf's)*

*Cactus pattern figurines made in the 1930s from an undated catalog. (Ohio Historical Society Library)*

PESCA OLD MAN WITH FISH
HEIGHT 12"
IVORY MATT GLAZE
ON RED BODY

GLOUSTER WOMAN
HEIGHT 11"
IVORIS WHITE GLAZE
TURQUOISE GREEN GLAZE

*Figurines pictured in an undated catalog, circa 1930. (Ohio Historical Society Library)*

*Oriental:* variation of Jap Birdimal, early period.

*Orris:* relief flowers and leaves, basketweave background on some pieces, middle period.

*Panella:* nasturtiums or pansies in relief, matte finish, late period.

*Paragon:* stylized impressed flowers and leaves, matte glaze, late period (c. 1934).

*Parian:* hanging wall baskets, ivory, impressed leaves, geometric designs, matte glaze, late period.

*Pastel:* modern shapes, pastel colors, matte glaze, late period.

*Patra:* scalloped top, mottled, design at bottom, round texture, matte finish, middle period.

*Patricia:* swan handles, glossy pale cream glaze, tinted, late period.

*Pearl:* matte glaze, cream color, decorated with loops of pastel-colored beads, relief decoration, middle period (c. 1920).

*Perfecto:* unglazed, painted decoration, early period (1907).

*Pictorial:* underglaze slip decoration, landscapes, usually pastel, middle period.

*Pierre:* basketweave decoration, dinner sets, late period.

*Pinecone:* pinecone decoration in panel, light color, matte glaze, middle period.

*Pumila:* matte glaze, relief leaves or blossoms form irregular edge at top, 1928.

*Raceme:* half black, half gray globe-shaped vase decorated with muted floral design, late period (called Racene by earlier writers).

*Ragenda:* draped folds make design, dark matte glaze, middle period.

*Raydence:* solid color glaze, flowers at bottom, fluted top, middle period.

*Reno:* plain dark bands decorate middle of light piece, middle period.

*Rhead Faience:* mark used on some Jap Birdimal pieces.

*Roba:* raised flowers and leaves, realistic coloring, looped on crinkled background, matte glaze, late period.

*Rochelle:* slip designs, low relief, high-gloss glaze, similar to Eocean, middle period.

*Roma:* garlands of flowers or other motif on plain background, cream, brown, black, or green, matte glaze, middle period, c. 1919; may be several types, another had raised naturalistic flowers and stems tied with bow on matte vase, some had cattails, kingfishers.

*Roma Cameo:* see Cameo Jewel.

*Rosella:* mugs, pitchers, fluted near base, flower bands, middle period.

*Rosemont:* low relief decoration, flowers, birds on dark high-gloss glaze or rose petals on light background, middle period.

*Rudlor:* relief flowers on horizontal spiral, ribbed piece, matte glaze, late period.

*Sabrinian:* seashell-like piece, sea horse handle, matte glaze, pastel shades, middle period.

*Samantha:* brushed background, no examples known, c. 1897.

*Selma:* high-gloss glaze on Knifewood line, middle period.

*Seneca:* pastel or dark colors, glossy glaze, no decoration, middle period.

*Senic:* matte glaze, blue or green, scenes of nature, 1937.

*Sicardo:* iridescent glaze of metallic shadings in greens, blues, crimson, pur-

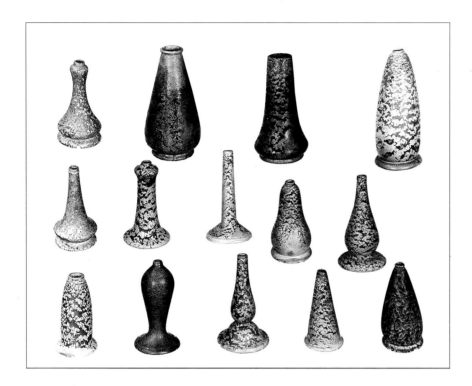

(Left) *Two undated catalog pages illustrate frosted matte ware.* (*Ohio Historical Society Library*)

(Above) *These Weller tiles appeared in an ad in* Tiles and Tile Work, *June 1930. It states that each installation is one-of-a-kind and never duplicated.*

ple, copper tones, with vines, flowers, stars, free-form geometric lines, 1902–1907, usually signed on surface of piece "Weller-Sicard" or "Sicardo," created by Jacques Sicard and Henri Gellée. A Sicardo lion made from a mold of a bronze figure by Antoine Barye has recently been seen.

\* *Silhouette:* solid background, black slip silhouette, rare, late period.

*Silvertone:* matte glaze, pink, blue, green, lavender, realistic cast flowers, fruits, or butterflies, middle period.

*Softone:* drapery design with folds, semimatte glaze, pastel, late period.

*Souevo:* Indian-type decoration, incised, matte glaze, 1909.

*Souvenirs:* various smaller items, mostly made for St. Louis Exposition of 1904.

*Stellar:* black with white stars and comet or white with blue stars and comet, matte glaze, middle period.

*Sydonia:* shell-like shape, leaves at base, middle period.

*Teakwood:* dark woodlike background, flowers, fruits, birds, women's heads, "carved" on surface, matte glaze, middle period.

*Tearose:* kitchen wares, white matte glaze, plain or ribbed, middle period.

*Terra-Cotta:* outdoor birdhouses, baskets, gray, rough surface, middle period.

*Ting:* white or ivory vase, Chinese shape on black pottery base, like teakwood, late period.

*Tivoli:* glossy cream color, black edging on some, borders of flowers, middle period.

*Tupelo:* perpendicular bands of flowers, grapes, pastel colors, ribbed, middle period.

*Turada* (Tourada): background brown, black, dark blue, applied lacy decoration of white, pale orange, light blue, incised then inlaid with slip, high-gloss glaze, usually marked "Turada," 1897–1898.

*Turkis:* vases, mottled yellow-green drip glaze on a glossy red background, c. 1933.

*Tutone:* flowers and leaf-decoration in relief, matte glaze, assorted colors, middle period.

*Underglaze Blue Ware:* mottled dark blue glaze, similar to Coppertone, middle period.

*Velva:* stylized relief flowers and leaves in panels, brown or beige background, late period.

*Velvetone:* blended colors of green, pink, yellow, brown, green, matte glaze, 1928.

*Voile:* matte green-gray background, low relief, fruit trees in tinted colors, 1928.

*Warwick:* matte, fruit trees modeled, middle period.

*Wayne Ware:* ivory with green interior, matte glaze, jardinieres and pedestals, 1928.

*More Weller tiles from the* Tiles and Tile Work *advertisement.*

*Weller Etched Matte:* see Etched Matte.

*Weller Matte Green:* see Matte Green.

*Weller Matte Ware:* similar to Art Nouveau, but deeper color and more distinct pattern, early period.

*White and Decorated Hudson:* matte cream background glaze, slip decoration, flowers or parrots in shaded blue or cream pink, middle period.

*Wild Rose:* light pink shaded, matte background, roses applied or later cast, middle period.

*Woodcraft:* natural-looking tree stumps, logs, wooden surface with realistic animal decorations, polychrome colors, matte glaze, 1928.

*Woodrose:* oaken bucket background, roses for decoration, middle period.

*Zona:* red apples, green leaves, stems, 1920, designed by Rudolph Lorber (same design made by Gladding, McBean & Co. of California as "Franciscan ware"); later line of jars, baskets, pitchers, decorated with kingfisher, cattails, in panels, low relief designs.

*Zona Baby Line:* baby dishes, including plate, cup, bowl and pitcher, glossy cream background, decorated with duck, squirrels, bunny, and bird, or Mary and lamb, c. 1926–1936.

*This advertisement from* Tiles and Tile Work, *April 1930, shows "Venetian Canal Scene," a tile panel made by the Weller potteries for the Carmichael Tile Company of Birmingham, Alabama. (Ohio Historical Society Library)*

*Incised mark.*

WHEATLEY.
No. 2·37·9·43
Price.................
CINCINNATI, O.

*Wheatley label featuring the mark.*

# T. J. Wheatley & Company/ Wheatley Pottery Company

*Cincinnati, Ohio*

Thomas Jerome Wheatley was one of many people influenced by the work of the Pottery Club of Cincinnati and Mary Louise McLaughlin. He also experimented at the pottery of P. L. Coultry about 1879, forming a brief partnership with Mr. Coultry. In 1880, Wheatley established his own firm, T. J. Wheatley & Co., in Cincinnati, Ohio. He built a kiln on Hunt Street, where he did his own preparation of clay and his own molding, glazing, and firing.

Contemporary sources comment that he "has been unselfish in regard to his discoveries of modes and processes, freely communicating them to any who wish to learn and who are welcomed to work at his establishment" (*Harper's New Monthly Magazine*, May 1881). Nevertheless, he once threatened to file suit to prevent other potters from using his patent on glazing. His improvement in underglaze decoration was patented on September 28, 1880. McLaughlin claimed to have developed the method first, but she had never filed for a patent.

Wheatley made some of the largest pieces ever produced in his time. His wares were varied, some covered with a mottled green matte glaze, others with a shiny glaze and floral decorations. He used dark green, blue, and yellow glazes, and many of his pieces had relief decoration. He made art pottery, architectural tiles, and gar-

*A Wheatley Pottery dark and light green vase is 12 inches high, and is marked only with a paper sticker. (Smithsonian Institution)*

*Green matte glaze covers this 14-inch-high vase made by the Wheatley Pottery Company about 1905. (Smithsonian Institution)*

*John Rettig signed this 13⅛-inch-high vase made by T. J. Wheatley. It has wild roses painted under glaze on a blue background. The bottom of the vase has the incised mark "T.J. Wheatley, 1879." (Cincinnati Art Museum, Cincinnati, Ohio; gift of Theodore A. Langstroth)*

den pottery. The pieces were marked with a paper label or with the incised signature "T.J.W.C." Although Wheatley had his own company, he also helped form the Cincinnati Art Pottery Company in 1880. His association with that company ended in 1882, and T. J. Wheatley closed sometime between 1882 and 1884.

In 1897 Wheatley worked for Weller Pottery in Zanesville, Ohio. He returned to Cincinnati about 1900 and started the Wheatley Pottery Company there in 1903. The company made a colored matte glazed artware with relief decorations, a green matte glazed ware, and garden and architectural wares. A fire destroyed much of the pottery in 1910 and the firm made little if any art pottery after that.

Thomas Wheatley died in 1917, but his company continued producing architectural faience and garden pottery. The firm was incorporated in 1921. The Cambridge Tile Manufacturing Company bought the Wheatley Pottery in 1927 and reincorporated it as the Wheatley Tile and Pottery Company. Tiles were marked with the names "Wheatley" and "Cambridge" until 1936.

*Wheatley vase 9½ inches high, 10 inches wide, and 3 inches deep. (Private collection)*

## White Pines
### See Byrdcliffe
~

## Zane Pottery
### Zanesville, Ohio
~

Zane Pottery was officially founded in January 1921, when the Peters and Reed Pottery was purchased by Adam Reed and Harry McClelland. Reed had been a partner of John D. Peters in Peters and Reed, and McClelland had worked for Peters and Reed since 1903. By 1909, McClelland was company secretary of Peters and Reed, and he became president and sole owner of Zane Pottery when Reed died in 1922.

*Impressed.*          *Impressed.*

*This Landsun-glazed vase marked "Zane ware" is 10 inches high. (Private collection)*

*A bowl with Landsun glaze. It is marked "Zane ware" and measures 2½ inches high by 8 inches in diameter. (Private collection)*

(Above) *This 5-inch-diameter bowl is brick red with green. It has a glossy interior. The piece is marked "Zane Ware, Made in USA" in a rectangular style.* (Above right) *This Zane Ware vase with Landsun glaze in shades of blue and yellow is 6¾ inches high. It is marked with the rectangular Zane Ware mark.* (*Private collection*)

McClelland enlarged the plant, continued the Peters and Reed lines, and added more art pottery while continuing to make flowerpots. Using a handpress method, the Zane Pottery made a full line of garden flowerpots, decorative garden pieces, jars, vases, birdbaths, and art pottery. The firm added a line called "Greystone," but since the Weller Pottery had copyrighted that name, Zane changed the name of its line to Stonetex.

Some of the other lines Zane Pottery is known to have produced are Crystaline, a semimatte orange and green glazed ware; Drip, a line covered with one color glaze and a dripped glaze of a second color at the top; Powder Blue, a blue matte finish; and Sheen, a four-color line with a semimatte glaze. The company used a red body at first, changing to a white clay in 1926.

When McClelland died in 1931, his wife became president. In 1941, the family sold the plant to Lawton Gonder, who changed the name to the Gonder Pottery. See Peters and Reed.

## Zanesville Art Pottery
### Zanesville, Ohio
~

**LA MORO**

The Zanesville Art Pottery was founded by David Schmidt (sometimes spelled Schmid) in 1900. Schmidt had moved from Germany

to Pittsburgh, then to Zanesville, Ohio, where he was a roofer and later imported and sold slate for roofs. In 1900, he changed the Zanesville Roofing Tile Company into the Zanesville Art Pottery Company.

The firm made umbrella stands, cobalt blue jardinieres, and pedestals. Cooking bowls in brown and white, and coffeepots and casseroles were also produced. The art pottery was dark brown with Indian heads, flowers, and other underglaze decorations. Its famous art line was called "La Moro." Another line of matte-glazed wares with slip decoration was also marketed. Two known artists' marks used on La Moro are "CS" and "LE." The artists' names are unknown.

The firm was destroyed in a fire in 1901, but was rebuilt. In 1910, another fire and another rebuilding took place. In 1920, the plant was sold to S. A. Weller and became Weller Plant No. 3.

Albert Radford of England worked at the Zanesville Art Pottery as general manager in 1901. He started his own firm in 1903. Otto and Paul Herold, David Schmidt's nephews, worked at the pottery for about six years. Otto worked at the Roseville Pottery from 1914 to 1918, then moved to the American Encaustic Tiling Company and later to Zane Pottery. Paul moved to Chicago and became an artist. In 1936, the two Herold brothers founded their own firm, LePere Pottery. It operated until 1962.

(Above left) *This La Moro vase is decorated with a yellow black-eyed Susan. The 10-inch piece is impressed "LA MORO" on the bottom with the numbers "8 11 5." The artist's initials "C.S." are on the bowl part of the vase.* (Above) *This 7-inch-high La Moro vase is decorated with yellow violets. The artist's cipher "L.E." appears on the rim of the base. The bottom is marked with an impressed "LA MORO 885." (Private collection)*

Tile Companies

(*Overleaf*) Mosaic tiles. See page 298 upper right-hand corner photograph for further detail.

Used on pieces modeled by Herman C. Mueller before 1893.

Paper label.

## A.E.T.Co.

*From 1902, impressed or incised.*

*Incised.*

*In mold.*

## AETCO FAIENCE.

*In mold.*

*In mold.*

Some of the potteries that made vases, figurines, bookends, lamps, and jardinieres also made floor and wall tiles. If a pottery is best known for its tile production, it is listed in this section. If it is best known for other types of pottery, it will be found in the Art Potteries section with a cross-reference in this section. Tile companies listed here did artistic-glazed ceramic and terra-cotta tiles. Firms that made only plain construction tiles are not listed.

## American Encaustic Tiling Company
### Zanesville, Ohio

English-made tiles for flooring and walls were selling so well in the United States that in 1874 a group of Zanesville, Ohio, men decided to try making tiles locally. One of the men, F. H. Hall, had the financial backing of Benedict Fischer and George R. Lansing of New York City, both of whom eventually became officers of American Encaustic Tiling Co. Mr. Hall was evidently successful in making tiles from Ohio clay, because in 1875 the *Zanesville Courier* mentioned that he had patented his system of tile manufacturing. No more is known of Hall and he is not listed in the city directories.

The American Encaustic Tiling Company was founded in 1875, and in 1876 Gilbert Elliott arrived from England to supervise its tile production. In 1877 he planned and directed the manufacture of the company's first commercial installation of tile, the floor of the Muskingum County Courthouse in Zanesville. The firm must have been producing tile in quantity, because in 1877 American Encaustic bought land for more kilns. A new building with six kilns was finished in 1879, the same year the American Encaustic Tiling Company Ltd. was incorporated, with Benedict Fischer, president; George R. Lansing, treasurer; and William G. Flammer, secretary.

George A. Stanberry probably joined the company in 1876. He was a mechanical engineer, born in Zanesville, but he had evidently worked in Europe. He developed the machinery that made it possible for the firm to produce floor tiles in quantity. By 1879, he was general superintendent of the plant.

The problem facing the company was to convince American architects that the locally made tiles were of the same quality as those from Europe. To prove its point, the company not only manufactured the tile, but also laid it and guaranteed it. It was not long before the American tile was accepted, and by 1880 the floor of the New York State Capitol Building in Albany, New York, consisted of American Encaustic Tiling Company tiles.

The first glazed tile was made at the plant in 1880, and by 1881 embossed tiles were being made. The firm continued to grow, and by 1889 the owners decided to move the plant to New Jersey. But the citizens of Zanesville raised $40,000 to keep the plant in Zanesville, where a new factory site was purchased in 1890. The citizens gave the company the land for the site, developed the natural gas,

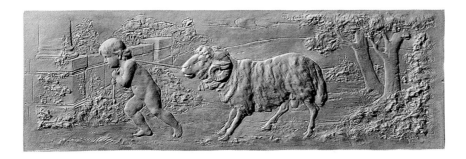

and furnished free water and adequate railroad lines. The new plant, the largest tile works in the world, was opened in 1892. At the dedication, 15,000 souvenir tiles were distributed.

The factory made tiles of all types. In 1893, Edwin Barber described the processes in his book *The Pottery and Porcelain of the United States:*

> Encaustic or inlaid floor tiles are made by both the plastic and the damp-dust processes, and the geometrical designs for these are prepared by competent designers who are employed by the company for this purpose. Relief tiles are also made here to a large extent, designed by Mr. Herman Mueller. . . . Special designs have been produced in single panels, twelve by eighteen inches in dimensions, of which we have seen some female water carriers of Grecian type. Plastic sketches of large size have also been executed for special orders. Among other styles produced at this factory are imitation mosaic tiles, damask, and embossed damask-finished tiles. By a peculiar treatment, pictures and portraits are also reproduced on a plain surface. [Some tiles appeared to be photographs on the tile. These were made by a special process. The portrait was modeled, then covered with black translucent glaze. The variations in glaze thickness produced color tones of gray and black] . . . Some of the most artistic productions of this factory are the eight, ten and fifteen tile facings, with raised designs of classic female and child figures. . . . This company has recently produced a new style of unglazed floor tiling, in elegant designs and attractive coloring which is designated by the name and trademark of "Alhambra.". . . The tinted arabesque designs are inlaid to the depth of about one eighth inch, simulating mosaic work.

*A white and yellow border edges this 4-inch-square polychrome tile marked "AET Faience." (Smithsonian Institution)*

*This framed American Encaustic tile is glazed a pale gray. It is 6 inches wide and 18 inches long and is marked "A.E.T." (Barrett Durkes)*

*Tiles were often made to surround a fireplace opening. This tile was used at the top of the fireplace. It is 6 by 18 inches. (Private collection)*

*This fireplace top tile with a peacock and a lounging woman measures 6 by 18 inches. (Private collection)*

*A pair of figures, 7 inches high, 5½ inches long, and 3½ inches wide. Each is marked with the impressed mark "AET Co." in a rectangle. (Private collection)*

The firm was making 6-by-6-inch tiles in 1906, but later changed to 4¼ by 4¼ inches. In 1909, George Stanberry died and Harry D. Lillibridge became plant superintendent. The firm continued to prosper. In 1919, American Encaustic had a shop in New York City where workmen cut tiles for mosaic work. That year, American Encaustic also purchased a plant in California. Half the tiles used in the Holland Tunnel in New York City were made by the American Encaustic Tiling Company.

Frederick Rhead was hired as a designer in 1917. He soon headed the research department. Plaques, plates, tiles, figurines, vases, fountains, and other wares were made at this time. The firm started to make faience tiles by the 1920s. Rhead used many animal designs. He headed the research for bathroom fixtures and soda fountain tiles from 1920 to 1927. His second wife, Lois Rhead, worked at the factory as a designer and modeler. She produced some pieces of pâte-sur-pâte.

In 1932, the firm began having financial problems and the California branch of the company was sold. The Zanesville plant was closed in 1935 and reopened in 1937 as the Shawnee Pottery. Some of American Encaustic's employees found work at the Mosaic Tile Company of Zanesville, and Mosaic apparently purchased much of American Encaustic's stock and molds.

### SPECIAL SOUVENIR TILES

Tiles were made in limited numbers for special events:

*A. E. Tiling Co., Ltd.* Paperweight tile, 1896 calendar on back.

*American Encaustic Tile Company.* Dedication tile, April 19, 1892, blue glaze, 4 by 4 inches, 15,000 said to have been made.

*Association of Interstate Mantel and Tile Dealers.* New York, February 1911, white tile, hand-colored flowers, gold border, 5 by 7 inches.

*William Jennings Bryan.* Democratic presidential candidate, 1896, 3-inch square, blue glazed, biography pasted on back.

*D. W. Caldwell.* Portrait, president of Nickel Plate Railroad, 6-inch square, biography on reverse.

*The Courier Company.* Zanesville, Ohio, paperweight, 1896 calendar on back.

*Walter Crane Tiles.* Crane was an English illustrator of books; about 1891, tiles were made from the original plates used to illustrate *The Baby's Opera* and *The Baby's Own Aesop.* At least eleven designs known; each tile marked with the Crane monogram and the letters "AET CO" on the back, a crane standing on a *W* inside a *C* pictured on the front. Similar tiles were made by the Mosaic Tile Company, but the Crane monogram was omitted.

*Cyrene Commander.* November 10, 1902, meeting, Louisville, Kentucky, a 2½-inch circle.

*Admiral George Dewey.* Six-inch plaque in color.

*Eastern Ohio Teachers Association.* Zanesville, November 10–11, 1916, worn on ribbon.

*Benedict Fischer.* Portrait, founder of A.E.T.C., tile 7 by 9 inches, brown glaze.

*The Foraker Club.* Zanesville, Ohio. Foraker was governor of Ohio from 1886 to 1890 and aspired to the presidential candidacy in 1903; circular 3-inch tile set in a badge, date unknown.

*Garret A. Hobart.* Republican vice-presidential candidate in 1896 (vice president from 1897 until his death in 1899), 3-inch square, blue glazed.

*William McKinley.* Republican candidate for president in 1896, 3-inch square, blue glazed.

*William McKinley.* In color on a blue background.

*Republican State Convention.* Zanesville, 1896. Blue glazed tile 1½ by 3 inches, given to delegates.

*Arthur Sewall.* Democratic vice-presidential candidate 1896, 3-inch square, blue glaze, biography pasted on back.

*Weller's Outing.* Buckeye Lake, August 6, 1904, 2-inch circular tile.

*A rack of tile border samples, probably dating before 1920. The tile strips can be removed from the tin rack. Each has an identification number on the back. (Private collection)*

*An American Encaustic 6-inch-square tile. (Private collection)*

*A 6-inch dark green tile marked "A.E. Tile Co." (Private collection)*

(Opposite page) *This large tile, 9½ by 14 inches, is marked on the back with the incised AET Co. symbol in a circle and the painted symbols "8165 Dec. 82." It is a red clay tile with carved decorations. (Private collection)*

## ARTISTS, DESIGNERS, SUPERVISORS

*Felix Alcan.* (c. 1919). Supervised the artists in New York City who cut the mosaics.

*Karl Virgil Bergman.* (1889–1955) From Brussels, Belgium. Worked for the Mosaic Tile Company, for American Encaustic Tiling Company until 1919; left to work in Flint, Michigan, for five years, then founded his own company, Continental Faience and Tile, in Milwaukee, Wisconsin.

*Ira Chandler.* Designer.

*Lillian Cross.* (c. 1903). Employee whose name was found scratched on the back of tile.

*Alma Hale.*

*Ernest R. Hartshorne.* From England; worked about 1910 as head of the design department; also worked at Mosaic Tile Co.

*Karl Langenbeck.* (1861–1938) Born in Cincinnati, Ohio. Graduated from the College of Pharmacy in Cincinnati, Polytechnic School of Zurich, Switzerland, and Technische Hochschule of Berlin. Chemist and superintendent of the Rookwood Pottery 1885–1886, also founded the Avon Pottery in Cincinnati in 1886; it closed in either 1887 or 1888. From 1890 to 1893, was the chemist for American Encaustic; in 1894, helped found the Mosaic Tile Company of Zanesville.

*Harry D. Lillibridge.* Superintendent in 1909.

*Herman C. Mueller.* (1854–1941; some records say he was born in 1858, but his obituary says he died in 1941 at age 87). Had studied in Nuremberg and Munich, arrived in the United States in 1878. Modeled for American Encaustic beginning in 1887, left in 1894 to found Mosaic Tile Company, also in Zanesville. Left Zanesville in 1903 to work at the Robertson Art Tile Company in Morrisville, Pennsylvania; in 1908, founded the Mueller Mosaic Co. in Trenton, New Jersey.

*Campaign tiles and other special tiles were often made by the factory. Garret A. Hobart, vice presidential candidate in 1896, is pictured on this blue-glazed intaglio tile from the election of 1896. The picture was reproduced by a special process. The biography of the candidate was pasted on the back of the 3-inch-square tile. (Charles Klamkin)*

*Alfred Nicklin.* Nephew of Richard Nicklin, headed the design department after his uncle.

*Richard Nicklin.* Headed the design department.

*Christian Nielson.* Modeler and designer from 1894 to 1902; became superintendent of the Roseville Pottery.

*Harry M. Northrup.* Worked at the Zanesville Art Pottery and then Mosaic Tile Company until 1917; after serving in World War I, returned to American Encaustic Tiling Company as head of glazing, casting, and decorating. Left to work for the Roseville Pottery Company in 1935, then worked for the U.S. Air Force.

*Peter Patterson.* Designer.

*Frank Philo.* A ceramicist who later worked in mining and tile manufacturing in California.

*Frederick Hürten Rhead.* (1880–1942) Came from Staffordshire, England, in 1902. Head of research department for American Encaustic Tiling Company from 1917 to 1927. Worked for Weller (1902–1904); Roseville Pottery (1904–1908); Jervis Pottery (1908–1909); University City, St. Louis, Missouri (1909–1911); Arequipa Pottery, San Francisco, California (1911–1913); Steiger Pottery (1913); Rhead Pottery, Santa Barbara, California (1914–1917); Homer Laughlin China Company, East Liverpool, Ohio (1927–1942).

*Loiz (Lois) Whitcomb Rhead.* (b. 1892) Worked at Rhead and American Encaustic Tiling Company. Frederick Hürten Rhead's second wife.

*Eugene Roberts.* Decorator, worked with Frederick Rhead and Harry Northrup. Also worked at Weller.

*Mayme Rock.* Employee whose name was found scratched on a tile.

*George Ruston.* English designer.

*Henry Scharstine.*

*Nannie Shunk.* (c. 1903). Employee whose name was found scratched on the back of a tile.

*Leon Victor Solon.* (1872–1957) From England, son of Louis Marc Solon. Worked as a designer for American Encaustic Tiling Company in New York City from 1912 to 1925. Had worked at Minton's beginning in 1896, became art director there in 1900, emigrated to America 1909.

*Paul Solon.* Another son of Louis Marc Solon, worked as designer about the same time as his brother Leon.

*George A. Stanberry (Stanbery).* Employee superintendent from about 1876 to 1909.

*Walter P. Suter.* Designer.

*J. Hope Sutor.* Artist.

*Boris Trifinoff.* A Russian designer.

*Gertrude Trittipo.*

*Von Housenett.* An Austrian designer.

*Arthur Wagner.* Artist who also worked with Frank Lessell.

*William Jennings Bryan is pictured on this 3-inch-square intaglio blue-glazed tile produced for the presidential election of 1896. (Charles Klamkin)*

## Batchelder Tile Company
### Pasadena and Los Angeles, California
~

Ernest Allan Batchelder was born in Francestown, New Hampshire, in 1875. He studied to be an art teacher at the Massachusetts Normal Art School and the Harvard Summer School of Design. In 1901 he took a job at Throop Polytechnic Institute in Pasadena, California. From 1904 to 1909 he taught both in California and at the Handicraft Guild in Minneapolis, and also traveled to Europe. His work was inspired by the Arts and Crafts designers and he wrote a series of articles for *The Craftsman* magazine.

In 1909 Batchelder founded a workshop in Pasadena to make leather, pottery, copper, silver, jewelry, and enameling. The first tiles made by the workshop were probably made for his new house. The Moravian tiles by Henry Chapman Mercer inspired his work. He ordered tiles from the Pennsylvania pottery and used some of them with his own tiles in his living room. He made his tiles in a backyard kiln and soon needed more space.

Frederick L. Brown became his partner in 1912 and the company moved to a small factory and was named Batchelder and Brown. In 1920 Lucien H. Wilson became a partner and the company, renamed Batchelder-Wilson, moved to Los Angeles. The tiles were so popular that the firm grew to 175 employees and processed six tons of material each day. By 1925 the tiles were warehoused and sold in New York City and were installed in buildings in many major cities. The company closed during the Depression in 1932. The inventory was sold to Pomona Tile Manufacturing Company and the Bauer Pottery Company. Ernest Batchelder returned to making pottery in 1936. He made slip-cast bowls and vases he called Kinneloa. He died in 1957.

Batchelder made wall and floor tiles, fountains, door frames, fireplace mantels, and many special order architectural pieces. Early tiles were often incised and modeled with vines, flowers, birds, animals, and sometimes Mayan Indian designs. Many tiles were fired, glazed, then refired. Colored engobe (slip) was rubbed on the surface and the tile was given a single firing. No glaze was used. Later tiles had flat designs and incised lines.

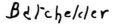

*Batchelder*
*Incised.*

**BATCHELDER**
**LOS ANGELES**
*In mold, after 1916.*

*A Viking ship is carved on this tile marked "Batchelder, Los Angeles." It is 4 inches square with brown and blue glaze. (Smithsonian Institution)*

*A Batchelder 3¾-inch-square tile with carved design. The color is produced by rubbing colored slip (very liquid clay) on the tile, and then baking the tile. It is marked with the impressed "Batchelder, Los Angeles," two-line mark. (Private collection)*

## Beaver Falls Art Tile Company
### Beaver Falls, Pennsylvania

Francis William Walker organized the Beaver Falls Art Tile Company Limited in Beaver Falls, Pennsylvania, in 1886. At first the company made only plain tiles, but after a few months, embossed intaglio tiles and stove decorations became the company's most important products. Mr. Walker, who was a chemist, developed a soft-colored glaze that was free from crazing, which made the tiles especially desirable for stove decorations. The glazes were pale blue, green, purple, or other pastel shades.

Professor Isaac Broome, who joined the factory in 1890, was one of the most famous artists who worked at American pottery and tile factories. Broome was born in Valcartier, Quebec, in 1835. He moved to Philadelphia when he was fifteen and studied art with Hugh Cannon, with private tutors, and at the Pennsylvania Academy of Fine Arts. After a year of study in Europe, he returned to the United States and tried twice, unsuccessfully, to establish a business to make terra-cotta vases and architectural pieces. During the same period, Broome did portrait painting and sculpting and became better established as an artist.

In 1875, Broome went to work for Ott and Brewer of Trenton, New Jersey. He developed an improved kiln and designed many of the sculpted pieces made by the firm for the 1876 Centennial. Broome also experimented with ceramics and porcelain. The pieces

*In mold.*

BEAVER FALLS. ART TILE CO. LTD.
BEAVER. FALLS. .PA.

*In mold.*

*Three Beaver Falls aquamarine tiles, each 3¹/₈ inches in diameter. There is a "B" under the glaze on the left side of the front of the tile at the top, and the back is marked "P53, B.F.A.T. Co." The middle tile is marked "B" under the glaze at the back of the neck of the figure and the back is marked "B.F.A.T. Co." The tile at bottom is marked "B" under the glaze on the right near the hat band and the back is marked "B.F.A.T. Co." (Barbara White Morse,* Spinning Wheel Magazine*)*

*A woman in a feathered hat decorates this 3-inch stove tile. It is glazed green and marked "Beaver Falls Pa 23 P." (Private collection) To see how a stove tile was used, see the stove pictured on page 290.*

*This stove tile is 2 inches in diameter and has a dark brown glaze. The back is marked "Beaver Falls" in a semicircle. (Private collection)*

(Far left) *"Sappho" is the name of this Beaver Falls Art Tile modeled by Isaac Broome.* (Popular Science Monthly, *January 1892*) (Left) *This light blue tile is decorated with a vine pattern. When lined up with other tiles, a continuous design is formed. The 6-inch tiles are marked "Beaver Falls Art Tile Co. Ltd. A 156."* (*Private collection*)

he designed for the Centennial were so popular that he was sent to the French Exposition of 1878 as "Special Commissioner on Ceramics for the United States Government and the State of New Jersey." The job lasted two years.

In 1883, he joined the Harris Manufacturing Company, which soon became the Trent Tile Company of Trenton, New Jersey (see Trent Tile Company). He made designs for tiles, marking some with the letter *B* on the face of the tile. Broome left Trent Tile in 1885 and founded the Providential Tile Works in Trenton before finally joining the Beaver Falls Art Tile Company in 1890.

In 1927, the Beaver Falls Art Tile Company was absorbed by the Robert Rossman Corporation. It went bankrupt in 1930.

Several types of tiles were made by the Beaver Falls Art Tile Company. Many of them had raised designs of people's heads or full figures. Large panels representing the Muses were made. The latter were approximately 6 inches high and 18 inches long, while tiles showing only heads were 12 inches square. The star-studded tile picturing George Washington is one of the most famous.

## Cambridge Art Tile Works
### Covington, Kentucky
〜

The Cambridge Art Tile Works opened in Covington, Kentucky, in March 1887. Three Cincinnati men, A. W. Koch, F. W. Braunstein, and Heinrich Binz, founded the tile works. They planned to make enameled and embossed tiles. Heinrich Binz was a German tile

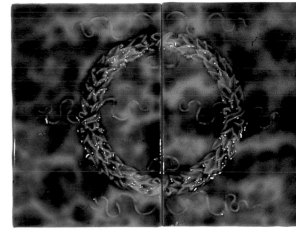

*Two matching Cambridge tiles are each 6 by 9 inches. The wreath was part of a fireplace tile trim.* (*Private collection*)

*"Poetry" is a modeled Cambridge tile 6 by 18 inches with a green glaze.* (*Smithsonian Institution*)

## Cambridge
*Incised, or in mold.*

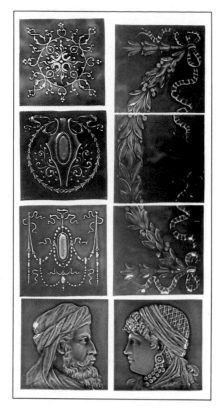

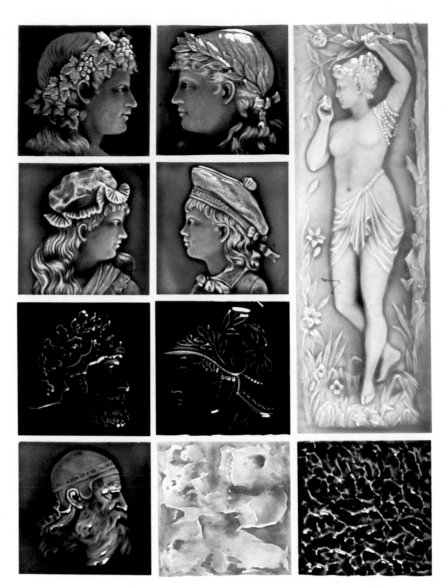

(Above and right) *These Cambridge tiles were made in Covington, Kentucky, about 1887–1899. (Smithsonian Institution)*

*"Night" and "Morning" are a pair of decorative Cambridge Art tiles. Each is 6 by 18 inches and glazed light brown. The tiles were modeled by Ferdinand Mersman. (Smithsonian Institution)*

maker who had been making glazed bricks in Covington with two brothers by the name of Busse.

In 1889, the Cambridge Art Tile Works merged with the Mount Casino Tile Works to form the Cambridge Tile Manufacturing Company. The company used clay from Kentucky and South Carolina. Several talented designers were hired, including Ferdinand Mersman, who had worked at the Rookwood Pottery. Mr. Mersman became the principal designer, with Clem Barnhorn as a modeler. Ivory and gold-toned tiles were popular pottery products. The company also made stove tiles, teapot stands, and brightly colored architectural tiles.

In 1927, the Cambridge Tile Manufacturing Company bought the Wheatley Pottery of Cincinnati, Ohio. The new company was renamed Wheatley Tile & Pottery Company and moved from Covington to Cincinnati in 1929. The manufacturing of art tiles was discontinued the same year.

# Enfield Pottery and Tile Works
### Enfield, Pennsylvania
~

Enfield Pottery and Tile Works was established about 1906. The company made pottery with a heavy enamel glaze until about 1910, then produced tiles similar to those made by the Moravian Pottery and Tile Works. It remained in operation until about 1928.

*Paper label.*

*The Enfield Pottery and Tile Works made this 4-inch-square dark brown and green tile about 1907. (Smithsonian Institution)*

*The Enfield Pottery and Tile Works also made pottery. This cup is 10 inches high. It shows a bicycle rider in a raised design. The exterior glaze is blue-green over red clay and the interior is glazed white. The piece is a puzzle jug; water could pour out the holes in the sides or the handle. (Smithsonian Institution)*

(Below) *An Enfield Pottery tile fireplace shown in* The American Magazine, *February 1916.*

(Left) *An Enfield Pottery puzzle pitcher, 5½ inches high. The name "Enfield" is incised on the bottom. (Private collection)*

Molded.

```
J.G.&J.F.LOW.
ART TILE WORKS.
   CHELSEA,
MASS.,U.S.A.
  COPYRIGHT
BY J.G.&J.F.LOW
     1885
```

Molded.

```
  J.&J.G.LOW,
    PATENT
ART TILE WORKS,
   CHELSEA,
MASS.,U.S.A.
COPYRIGHT 1884,
by J.G.&J.F.LOW.
```

```
  J.&J.G.LOW.
    PATENT
ART TILE WORKS
    CHELSEA,
       MASS. U.S.A.
COPYRIGHT 1883 by J.G.&J.F. LOW.
```

*Molded.*

*Other marks included the registered
trademark with a small circle
enclosing the crossed keys, "J. & G.
Low" with the city and state in a
rectangle, and "Pat'd/Fed 18/1879"
in a circle. Sometimes the tile is
marked with the name of the firm
that sold it (such as J. S.
Conover & Co.).*

*A yellow-green glazed tile pictures
monks walking. The framed piece is 20
by 15 inches and was made about
1881. (Skinner, Inc.)*

# Low Art Tile
## Chelsea, Massachusetts

John Gardner Low was a skilled artist long before he began producing tiles in Chelsea, Massachusetts. He was born on January 10, 1835, in Chelsea, the son of John Low, a civil engineer. His artistic ability was apparent while he was still a boy. At the age of twenty-three, John went to France for three years and studied in Paris with Thomas Couture and Constantine Troyon. Many of his oil paintings of landscapes and peasants were auctioned in Boston in April 1861.

Low hoped to make his living as an artist, and for several years he did paintings and murals, including a drop curtain for the Chelsea Academy of Music. He did not make enough money as a painter, so in 1870 he began working in ceramics. (The Low Tile catalog at the Boston Public Library has a chronology listing 1873 as the date Low started his ceramic work.) Low first joined the Chelsea Keramic Art Works, operated by James Robertson. He worked there a year or more, learning the techniques and experimenting with his own projects. A visit to the Centennial Exhibition in 1876 led him to use new colors and oriental designs.

In 1877, with financing by Low's father, construction began on the J. and J. G. Low Art Tile Works. The building was located at 948 Broadway, on the corner of Stockton Street. It was a well-equipped factory, not just a small craft shop. In 1878, John G. Low hired George W. Robertson, of the family that founded the Chelsea Keramic Art Works, to work at the tile works. George Robertson was paid $75 per week, which was a high salary at that time. The first firing of tile took place on May 1, 1879. The quality was excellent, and five months after the first tiles were made, Low Art Tile was awarded a silver medal at the Cincinnati Industrial Exposition.

In 1880 Low was awarded a gold medal in Crewe, England, for the best English or American tiles shown at the exhibit of the Royal Manchester and Liverpool Agricultural Society Exhibition. The award caused much comment in the industry, as reported by *Popular Science Monthly* in January 1892: "This record, probably unsurpassed in ceramic history, serves to illustrate the remarkably rapid development of an industry new in America, but old in the East; it shows the resources at command of the American Potter." However, researchers have found no record of the award in England, as noted by Barbara Morse in *Spinning Wheel*, July-August 1971.

Low tiles and "plastic sketches" were exhibited again at the Fine Arts Society of London, England, in 1882. The work was praised for its artistic and ceramic features.

In 1883 John Low, John G. Low's father, retired from the business, and his grandson, John Farnsworth Low, joined the company. The firm name was changed to J. G. and J. F. Low Art Tile Works. In addition to tiles, other forms of pottery, including vases and jugs, were introduced, as was a new major product, art tile soda fountains.

(Left) *A selection of tiles from* Plastic Sketches of J. G. and J. F. Low, *1887. Notice that the tiles are shown unglazed in the pictures although the finished product was glazed. The cipher "AO" for Arthur Osborne appears on almost every piece. (Photograph from the Boston Public Library)*

(Above) *Floral decorations on Low tiles were not uncommon. This green tile, with 7½-inch edges, was made about 1885. (Smithsonian Institution)*

(Below) *This Low Art Tile modeled by Arthur Osborne is 7¾ by 24 inches and is glazed a yellow-green. The design for the tile appears in the book* Plastic Sketches of J. G. and J. F. Low, *1887. The words "Copyright 1881, JG and JF Low" and the title "Eureka" are printed on the face of the photograph in the book. (Smithsonian Institution)*

(Above) *Arthur Osborne made this "Sterine" wax plaque after he left Low and returned to England. The 8-by-6-inch plaque has a raised design colored in a lifelike manner. The front of the plaque is marked with the "AO" cypher found on Low tiles. The back is stamped "Osborne (copyright) Made in England." (Private collection)*

*This relief-scene tile with a glossy brown glaze is 17½ inches tall by 9½ inches wide and is signed "A.O." for Arthur Osborne. The tile dates from the late nineteenth century. (Skinner, Inc.)*

*An ornate cast-iron frame, apparently original, was used for this Low tile made about 1885. The tile is 6 inches square and is glazed yellow-brown. (Smithsonian Institution)*

*The "Semper Fidelis" tile was modeled by Arthur Osborne about 1885. It is 7 by 11 inches and is glazed a yellow green. (Smithsonian Institution)*

The firm operated until about 1902, when it may have been forced out of business by new tariff laws that permitted the importation of foreign kaolin (clay) at a low price. Liquidation of the company took place in 1907, the same year John G. Low died. The tile works survived a disastrous fire that burned much of Chelsea in 1908.

### PRODUCT

J. G. Low tiles were made by several methods. When John Low first began operations in 1877, he had probably never seen tile made mechanically in a factory. He experimented with various methods, glazes, and clays, and finally developed a relief tile via a method that had been used for years in England. The "dust" process, as this method was called, was a popular way to make ceramic buttons, and the technique was patented in England about 1840. Dry powdered clay was slightly moistened and subjected to great pressure in a machine press with a die. The design of the die was impressed on the tile, then the tile was fired and glazed. Low also made "wet" or "plastic" tiles. This method was similar to that used in making any sort of pottery. The damp or "plastic" clay was pressed into molds where it was allowed to dry and shrink. The tile was then easily removed from the mold, and had a raised design on one side. The tiles were placed on cloth-covered plaster blocks, where they were allowed to dry for a day. Artists often touched up the relief design by undercutting it with hand tools. The tiles were placed in drying rooms for several weeks and then were fired and glazed. These tiles were unmarked and indented in the back to follow the curves of the tile design.

John Low also developed an original method of tile manufacture which he called the "natural" process. First, a flat tile was shaped. Then a leaf, grass, lace, or a similar delicate object was placed on the tile and forced into the clay surface with pressure from a screw press. A piece of tissue paper was then placed over the impressed tile. Clay dust was put on the tissue paper and pressed against the paper by the same screw press. The result was a sort of sandwich of two tiles, with the paper in between. The bottom tile had an impressed design, the top tile a raised design. The two tiles

*Stove tiles were used as decorations. The round tile has a small notch so it could be held in place on the stove. This "Sterling Stove" was made at the Rice Stove Works in Rochester, New York, about 1886. Notice the three Low tiles. The center tile is turquoise, the side tiles yellow. (From the collections of Henry Ford Museum & Greenfield Village)*

Arthur Osborne made this plastic sketch for Low. (*Robert Koch*)

This 7½-inch-square tile was made about 1885. (*Smithsonian Institution*)

The Quick Meal Company's trademark chicken emerging from an egg is shown on this unmarked oval blue-green tile. The back of the 3¼-by-3-inch tile shows it was made by impressing the clay into a mold in the manner of Low tiles. Other clues from the Quick Meal Company, which manufactured stoves, suggest that this is a Low tile. (*Private collection*)

were separated and both the relief and intaglio versions were completed with glaze. Low later improved the method by making an impressed tile of paraffin wax, which he coated to make a mold to be used for hundreds of relief tiles.

The J. G. and J. F. Low Art Tile Works also made hand-modeled tiles. The tiles were made by workmen who pressed them by hand into a mold and then undercut the design by hand, making a very high-relief product. These tiles often have rough backs and show the fingerprints of the workmen. They are also marked on the back with the name of the factory impressed on ridges (Barbara Morse, "Tiles to Treasure, Low Art Tiles," p. 18).

All of the tiles were made from Connecticut feldspar, Carolina kaolin, and clays from Missouri and New Jersey. Tiles were made in many sizes, but the most common were 6 by 6 inches or 4 by 4 inches. Narrow border tiles were used on stoves or as trim. Round tiles, also used on stoves, were made in quantity and are often unmarked.

A special product of the tile company was what Low called "plastic sketches." These were low-relief pictures made by an artist using clay instead of oil paints. Nearly all the sketches were made by Arthur Osborne, an English artist who had worked for the Chelsea Keramic Art Works. He was hired by Low by 1879 and continued working with him until 1893 or later, when for some reason he decided to return to England. Osborne was an imaginative artist who designed tiles and did sketches inspired by the oriental, Moorish, African, and Egyptian cultures and from nature, mythology, and other sources. His plastic sketches were up to 18 inches in length and were of farm scenes, animals, birds, monks, cupids, and beautiful women. Each was signed "AO" on the face of the sketch. (Two books titled *Plastic Sketches*, by J. and J. G. Low, 1882, and J. G. and J. F. Low, 1887, can still be found in the Boston Public Library that show many of these designs.) The identical signature "AO" was used by Osborne for the copyrighted "Sterine" wax plaques he made in England beginning at the turn of the century. The plaques are still being made by W. H. Bossons, Ltd., of England. Osborne died in 1952.

John G. Low began working on his tile soda fountain in 1883. He applied for a patent for his designs in 1888. Earlier soda fountains had been made of marble, but Low felt that glazed tiles would be an improvement

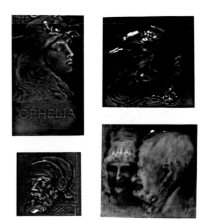

Tiles by J. and J. G. Low Art Tile Works, Chelsea, Massachusetts, from 1881 to 1885. Several are marked on the face with the Arthur Osborne "AO." (*Smithsonian Institution*)

(Right) *J. and J. G. Low marked this 6-inch square brown tile.* (Far right) *This framed tile is signed on the front with an "A" in a circle. The 6-inch-square green tile has the same design as one of the plastic sketches pictured in the Low book.* (*Private collection*)

(Above) *"The J. and J.G. Low Art Tile Works, Chelsea, Copyright 1885"* is marked on the back of these pictured tiles. Each tile is 4½ by 6¼ inches. The Abraham Lincoln and Ulysses S. Grant tiles are both medium blue. (*Smithsonian Institution*)

and would reduce the cost. His patent was not accepted at first, but with a few changes and the services of several lawyers, it was finally granted in 1889. The Low tile soda fountains were sold in all parts of the country. The most elaborate one ever made was shown at the Columbian Exposition in Chicago in 1893. It was 16 feet high, 20 feet long, and was covered with panels picturing cupids, human figures, and dolphins.

The factory also made pottery and tile-decorated objects for several years starting about 1882. These included clock cases, ewers, flower holders, fireplace tiles, planters, and inkwells. Candlesticks, boxes, paperweights, lamps, and trivets were made of brass with tile decoration. Stoves were of cast iron with tile inserts. Vases, jugs, and cups were styled in the Japanese manner, with designs of flowers, animals, leaves, or scrolls (*Scribner's Magazine*, November 1902). The pieces were small to medium in size, ranging up to about 10 inches in height. The body of the piece was made of clay similar to the white tile. The body surface was decorated with glazes in many colors, ranging from dark cream to chocolate, and with shades of red, green, blue, gray, and yellow. Several colors were often used on one piece. Low ware was frequently mistaken for oriental pottery. The tiles were made in many colors, including yellow, gray, brown, orange, blue, rose, and white, but most of them were earth-tone greens and browns.

Low Art Tile products were held in high regard, as described by Edwin Barber in his book *The Pottery and Porcelain of the United States*, p. 353:

> The Lows never imitated other work, either domestic or foreign. They have never made hand-painted, mosaic, printed, encaustic, or floor tile, and they have never employed men who were trained in other tile works. Consequently, their products are characterized by a marked originality, both in style and design, which has caused them to be extensively imitated, both at home and abroad.

# Moravian Pottery and Tile Works
## *Doylestown, Pennsylvania*
~

The family of Henry Chapman Mercer arrived in Bucks County, Pennsylvania, in 1684. Henry was born in Doylestown in 1856. His family was one of wealth and position; they were members of Congress, judges, and businessmen. Henry attended a local boys' boarding school, then went to Mohegan Lake School near Peekskill, New

## MORAVIAN

*Stamped or impressed.*

*Mark of the Moravian Pottery and Tile Works, about 1900. (Collection of Moravian Pottery and Tile Works)*

York. He graduated from Harvard in 1879. He started law school at the University of Pennsylvania, but he soon left to read law at two private firms. After passing the university's annual exam in 1881, he was certified to practice law.

In the 1880s, Henry Mercer became interested in antiquities and helped found the Bucks County Historical Society. He published a book in 1885 about the discovery of the Lenape stone, which contained a pictographic history of the Delaware Indians. For the next ten years, he worked in the fields of archaeology and anthropology and became curator of American prehistoric archaeology at the Museum of the University of Pennsylvania. In 1893, he was associate editor of the *American Naturalist* and a member of the U.S. Archaeological Commission for the Columbian Exposition. He was given a grant in 1895 to make an expedition to the Yucatan, where he worked for several months but could find no evidence of prehistoric man. In 1897, he began to write about colonial America and published an article about tools.

That same year, in Doylestown, he started experimenting with the manufacture of tiles, another of his many interests. Anyone who visits the Mercer Museum in Doylestown can appreciate the scope of this collector.

*A sconce called "Deer Riding Wolf" is 11 by 4½ inches and was made between 1900 and 1930. (Collection of Moravian Pottery and Tile Works)*

*The Spray of Tulips, tile no. 223, is buff clay with blue slip. It was made sometime during the 1920s. (Private collection, by courtesy of Moravian Pottery and Tile Works)*

*The Swan and Tower tile, no. 32, was made circa 1910–1920. It measures 7 by 5½ inches. (Collection of Moravian Pottery and Tile Works)*

*"Musicians: Harp" is the name of this 6-by-4-inch tile that was made sometime between 1915 and the 1940s. (Collection of Moravian Pottery and Tile Works)*

*Dragon of Castle Acre, tile no. 59, is 4 by 4 inches and was made in 1912. (Collection of Moravian Pottery and Tile Works)*

*A 4-by-4-inch tile called "Aves" dates from the 1920s. (Private collection, by courtesy of Moravian Pottery and Tile Works)*

*This Trinity tile is 7 by 5½ inches and dates from about 1900. (Collection of Moravian Pottery and Tile Works)*

*The City of God tile, no. 282, is 5½ inches square. The tile dates from around 1900. (Collection of Moravian Pottery and Tile Works)*

Mercer studied tools as a hobby and he bought quantities of all types with the hope of comparing American tools with those made in other countries. He visited many factories, including pottery companies. While studying potters' tools, he became interested in the manufacture of pottery, though no one told him about the difficulties involved or of the problems in building a working kiln. Mercer experimented and tried several potters and potteries before he decided to go to Germany, where he could learn the "proper" way to make pottery from the experts.

He built a kiln soon after returning home and made goblets, pots, and tiles. He soon realized that tiles were the items that would sell best. He named his pottery the Moravian Pottery and Tile Works because his earliest tiles were Moravian-inspired. The firm made tiles for floor pavements (the Capitol building in Harrisburg, Pennsylvania), fireplaces, walls, and ceilings, as well as large decorative tile panels.

Mercer also built a new residence, a huge concrete "castle" he named Fonthill, which was completed in May 1912. Before Fonthill was finished, he began work on a new fireproof concrete building for his pottery that was finished in November 1912. The structure, located near Fonthill, incorporated tile decorations and included a high, vaulted ceiling that some contemporary architects warned would collapse. He built a third concrete structure, a museum, in 1916. All of Mercer's strange concrete pottery buildings still stand as museums that house his tool collection. The buildings illustrate to the public the advanced architectural construction of Mercer's design.

Throughout its operation, the Moravian Pottery and Tile Works remained a small plant with about sixteen artists and workmen. When Mercer died in 1930, he willed the company to Frank King Swain. Swain died in 1954 and his nephew Frank H. Swain became manager. Swain sold the pottery in 1956 to Raymond F. Buck, who

This "Bible Fireplace" was featured in an article about tiles in International Studio in 1922. Notice the Adam and Eve tile in the upper right corner. (International Studio, *March 1922*)

This 2-by-2½-foot Moravian tile is perforated. The design is copied from the Balcony of Desdemona in Venice. The colors are black, buff, red, and green. (Keramic Studio, *May 1909*)

Large tiles were made by the Moravian Pottery and Tile Works for special purposes. This flower box is 2 feet by 2 feet by 3 inches thick. The red and green mosaics are from the carved balustrade at the Church of Saint Apploinaris, Ravenna, Italy. (Keramic Studio, *May 1909*)

An armored knight on a charging horse is the relief pattern on this Moravian Pottery tile. It is glazed with glossy ocher and blue. The tile is 4¹⁄₁₆ inches high by 7⁵⁄₁₆ inches wide. The pattern, made about 1910, was called "Knight of Margam." (Collection of the Newark Museum)

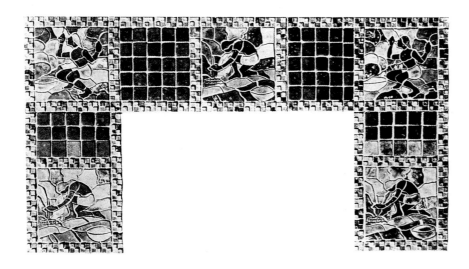

These fireplace tiles illustrate Native Americans making fire and smoking. (Keramic Studio, *May 1909*)

*This Moravian Pottery and Tile Works
mural panel was made about 1922.*
(International Studio, *March 1922*)

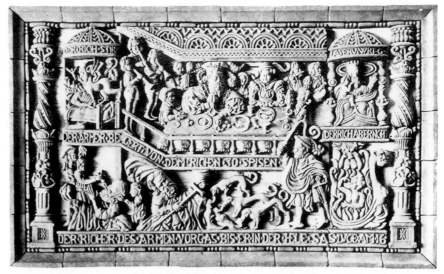

*This Moravian Pottery and Tile Works
tile in green, brown, red, yellow, and
black is 15 by 22 inches. This is the
same type of tile design showing Adam
and Eve as the one in the Bible fireplace
picture. The tiles were assembled into
sets to tell a story. The selection was the
decision of the buyer.* (Smithsonian Institution)

*This Moravian tile mosaic depicts
Christopher Columbus leaving Spain.
The image comes from a German design
of the sixteenth century. The colors are
black, red, blue, yellow, green, and
buff.* (Keramic Studio, *May 1909*)

made ordinary tiles. The county bought it in 1968 and the traditional Moravian tiles are again being produced there.

*The Moravian Pottery and Tile Works made this tile called "Dragon Pattern" about 1910. It is glazed blue and yellow tan and is 3½ inches square. (Collection of the Newark Museum )*

### PRODUCT

The first wares made at the Moravian Pottery and Tile Works came from common red clay found nearby. Too soft for pots, the clay proved very satisfactory for tiles. The tiles were covered with a heavy glaze. Other tiles were made from white New Jersey clay. White tiles were usually colored blue or green; red tiles were glazed with other colors. The body color sometimes showed through the glaze and changed the apparent shade, so Mercer tried to use a body color that would not interfere with the glaze color.

The designs for the tiles were created by Mercer. His first designs were inspired by the Moravian stove plates that he had collected from the Philadelphia region. Later he made medieval, Indian, and other tile designs, including plants and animals. Other sources of inspiration came from English floor tiles and German and Spanish tile designs of the earlier centuries, as well as from tapestries and archaeological finds.

About 1908 he began making "brocade" tiles, high-relief designs of irregular shapes. The colored clay was cut into small units, creating designs in silhouette. These designs were often set in concrete. The overall effect was that of a mosaic decoration, though the pieces were large slabs, not the tiny mosaic pieces. Some of the tiles were glazed and some were made from colored clay without glaze, so that some tiles had a shiny finish while others had a matte appearance. Some floor tiles were half glazed, the raised unglazed portion protecting the glazed surface from wear. Mercer used all techniques, including smear glaze, modeling, sgraffito, and slip decoration. He made no attempt to create uniformity or realism. Colors were placed arbitrarily, sometimes resulting in an orange sky or yellow tree. The pieces of tile were often cut to the shape of the figure in the design rather than square. Square tiles were dried on racks or metal trays and were often irregular in shape. The installation of these irregular tiles required wide joints and many critics objected to this look.

*A relief pattern of a lion in blue-green and tan glazes decorates this tile called "Etin." It is 5⁵⁄₁₆ inches square. (Collection of the Newark Museum)*

Plain geometrically shaped tiles glazed brown, black, green, blue, buff, or red were also available, as were special designs featuring the customer's business or family. The tiles usually included the company mark or the word "Moravian" stamped into the clay.

In 1901 Henry Mercer began making art pottery and selling it through his tile catalogs. He made boxes, inkwells, cups, mugs, and bowls. In 1904 he added sconces, flowerpots and, later, candleholders. Designs were similar to some of his tile designs, and the boxes and inkwells were actually made from tiles. Many of the pieces were inspired by ancient pottery.

## Mosaic Tile Co.
### Zanesville, Ohio

The Mosaic Tile Company of Zanesville, Ohio, was started by Karl Langenbeck and Herman Mueller in 1894. The two men had been working for the American Encaustic Tiling Company—Langenbeck as a chemist and Mueller as a modeler—but they wanted a larger

*Impressed.*

THE MOSAIC TILE
COMPANY
ZANESVILLE OHIO
NEW YORK
N.Y.

*Mark embossed on back of Lincoln
hexagonal tile.*

ZANESVILLE
POST NO-29
AMERICAN
LEGION
HOME
BUILDING FUND
MFG BY
THE MOSAIC
TILE CO.
ZANESVILLE
OHIO

*Mark embossed on back of General
Pershing oval tile.*

*Mosaic Tile Company tiles of Abraham
Lincoln (3 inches), General John J.
Pershing (3½ by 5¼ inches), and
Woodrow Wilson (3 inches). (Private
collection)*

*Sample rack of Mosaic Tile Company
tiles. These were probably used in bathrooms. (Private collection)*

*Two sample racks of trim tiles, proba-
bly dating before 1920. The tile strips
can be removed. Each has a style number on the back. (Private collection)*

share of the profits. Mueller had modeled for Matt Morgan Art
Pottery in Cincinnati, Ohio, and the Kensington Art Tile Company
of Newport, Kentucky. A group of investors joined the two men in
forming Mosaic Tile. A building and kiln were constructed, and a
staff was hired.

The firm grew and buildings were added. At first Mosaic produced only floor tiles from local buff clay. But when the firm began
using a new method of manufacture that employed perforated patterns to apply clay, production became less expensive. Soon other
types of tiles were added to the line, including "Florentine mosaic,
a dull finish floor tile inlaid with colored clays under pressure." The
floor tiling was popular with the building trades and the firm opened
an office in New York City in 1901. Langenbeck and Mueller left
the company by 1903.

William M. Shinnick, who worked at the plant, continued to
become more active in the management until he was named general
manager in 1907. The firm continued to grow and prosper, and by
1918 it had branch offices not only in New York but also in San
Francisco, Boston, Baltimore, and Philadelphia. Although Shinnick
was interested in new methods and new products, it was not until
1918 that faience tiles were made for walls in a variety of pastel
colors. Other plain and ornamental vitreous and semivitreous (low
porosity) tiles were produced, including ceramic mosaic, art mosaic,
white wall tiles, and fireplace tiles. About 1920, Harry Rhead of the
Roseville Pottery Company was hired to supervise the manufacture
of faience tiles. He left in 1923 to found the Standard Tile Company
of South Zanesville.

The Mosaic Tile Company flourished and many important struc-

*This beige, brown, black, and green tile was made about 1905–1915. It has both matte and semimatte glaze. The 5-inch-square tile has a molded design of an elephant standing on a ball with the company monogram. (Collection of Carol Ferranti Antiques; photograph from The Art Museum, Princeton University, Princeton, New Jersey)*

*The tile-covered Mosaic Tile Company building was erected at 445 West 41st Street, New York City, in 1928. It was torn down in 1954. (Ohio Historical Society Library)*

tures featured their tiles: the Stevens, Drake, Morrison, and Sherman hotels in Chicago; the Roosevelt mansion in Hyde Park, New York; the Will Rogers Memorial in Fort Worth, Texas; and the New York subways, among others.

When the Depression slowed the construction business, the firm began to make hot plates, badges, boxes, bookends, souvenirs, and wall panels. In 1959 the company stopped making faience tile, and in 1967 Mosaic Tile closed.

### ARTISTS

Ruth Axline (also worked at Weller); Harry Ayres; Ira Chandler; Sydney Cope, from England, 1929–1934 (Nelson McCoy Pottery 1934–1961); David Fink; George D. Ford; Kenneth Gale (?); Kenneth Garrison; Roy Greene; Robert Hartshorne (also worked at American Encaustic Tiling Company); Cecil Jones; Karl Langenbeck, chemist (see American Encaustic); Horace M. Langley; Charles Lenhart; Herman Mueller, modeler (see American Encaustic); Gordon Mull (also worked at Weller); Alfred Nicklin (also worked at American Encaustic); Harry M. Northrup (see American Encaustic); Peter Patterson; Charles Penson; Harry Rhead, supervisor (see Roseville Pottery under Art Potteries section); James Riley; David Schaum; William Shinnick, general manager; Byron Shrider; Mary Vore; Bernard West.

### SPECIAL TILES

Aesop's Fables tiles; Simon Bolivar, 3¼-inch hexagonal, blue basalt with white bust; Abraham Lincoln, 3¼-inch hexagonal, blue basalt with white bust; Charles A. Lindbergh, rectangular, printed picture; Douglas MacArthur, 4-inch printed tile, brown; William McKinley, 3¼-inch hexagonal, blue basalt with white bust; John Joseph Pershing, 3¼-by-5-inch oval, blue basalt with white bust; Franklin D. Roosevelt, 12-inch plaque, brown; William Shinnick, round printed tile; Woodrow Wilson, 3¼-inch hexagonal, blue basalt with white bust; Zanesville Sesquicentennial, 1947.

## Mueller Mosaic Tile Company
### Trenton, New Jersey

The Mueller Mosaic Tile Company of Trenton, New Jersey, was organized by Herman Mueller in 1909. Fifteen years earlier, he had cofounded the Mosaic Tile Company in Zanesville, Ohio. In 1903,

*Impressed.*

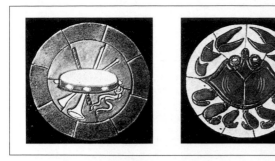

(Above and right) *A collection of Mueller pieces from a catalog, date unknown. (Courtesy of the New Jersey State Museum)*

*This gaping turtle is a fountain spout. It was made about 1910, is glazed brownish green, and measures 6 by 6 by 3½ inches. (Smithsonian Institution)*

**PARDEE**

*Incised mark.*

he had joined the Robertson Art Tile Company, Morrisville, Pennsylvania, a branch of the National Tile Company of Anderson, Indiana.

Mueller Mosaic Tile made mosaic tiles for bathrooms, swimming pools, mantels, walls, and floors, as well as art faience panels and decorative signs. The company catalog described the tiles in 1909 as "Florentine Mosaic," "Roman Faience Mosaic," "Oriental," and "Modern." The mosaics were incised and irregularly shaped; the Oriental and Modern lines had simple geometric shapes. The firm closed shortly after Mueller died in 1941. See also Mosaic Tile Co.

## C. Pardee Works
### *Perth Amboy, New Jersey*

The C. Pardee Works of Perth Amboy, New Jersey, was founded before 1893. The firm made paving bricks, sewer pipe, and floor and glazed tiles. By 1892, they were producing art tiles to be used as wall decorations. These tiles included intaglio-modeled heads of Emperor Wilhelm II, Benjamin Harrison, Grover Cleveland, and James

(Right) *This tile was made by the C. Pardee Works, probably as a campaign item, in 1884. The 6-inch glazed-purple tile pictures Grover Cleveland, the Democratic presidential candidate. (Smithsonian Institution)*

(Below) *A group of* Alice in Wonderland *tiles made about 1920. Each is marked "C. Pardee Works" and is 4¼ inches square. (Skinner, Inc.)*

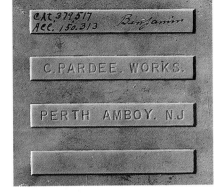

*Mark on tile back.*

*Impressed.*

PROVIDENTIAL

TRENTON

N.J.

*Impressed.*

THE PROVIDENTIAL
TILE WORKS
TRENTON, N.J.

*Impressed.*

*Mark on tile back.*

G. Blaine. Printed tiles were made as souvenirs of Niagara Falls, Plymouth Rock, Salem, and many other historic places. The firm made hand-painted underglaze tiles, printed underglaze and overglaze tiles, and inlaid and relief pattern tiles.

The Pardee Works bought the Grueby Pottery in 1921 and moved it to New Jersey. Tiles are marked in raised letters "C. PARDEE WORKS/PERTH AMBOY N.J."

## Providential Tile Works
### *Trenton, New Jersey*

The Providential Tile Works of Trenton, New Jersey, was started in 1885, but did not sell its first product until 1886. Isaac Broome, of the Trent Tile Company, was the company's first designer and modeler. (See Beaver Falls Art Tile Company; Trent Tile Company.)

Scott Callowhill, another designer and modeler there, came from the Royal Worcester Works in England in 1885. He had also worked at Doulton in Lambeth, England, and at the Phoenixville (Pennsylvania) Pottery. Several tiles designed by Mr. Callowhill were listed in Edwin Barber's *The Pottery and Porcelain of the United States.*

*This tile panel called "Indolence" was made by Providential Tile Works and pictured in* Popular Science Monthly *in 1892.*

*A 3-inch stove tile is marked "P.T.W.T.N.J." for Providential Tile Works, Trenton, New Jersey; the pale gray-green tile was held in place by a screw through the center hole. (Private collection)*

*A 6-inch tile by the Providential Tile Works. (Private collection)*

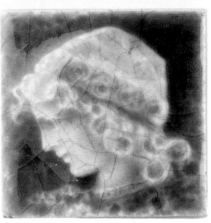

*This 2-inch stove tile of a woman's head is marked "Providential." It is glazed brown. (Private collection)*

*A brown-glazed tile marked "Providential Tile Works, Trenton, New Jersey, Design 244" is 6 inches square. (Private collection)*

**TRENT**

*Impressed mark.*

These included a 6-by-12-inch tile, "Mignon," after Jules Lefebvre, and a 6-by-18-inch tile after Benjamin W. Leader's *February Fill-Dyke.*

Fred Wilde, who had also been employed by the Maywood Tile Company in New Jersey and the Robertson Art Tile Company of Morrisville, Pennsylvania, worked for Providential. So did Joseph Kirkham (of the Kirkham Art Tile & Pottery Company, Barberton, Ohio, c. 1895, and Kirkham Tile and Pottery Company, Tropico, California, 1898).

Providential made glazed tiles that were either plain or in relief. The firm experimented with colored glazes on the same piece, with the raised portion a different color than the base. Underglaze decoration, gilded, and cloisonné-like decorated tiles were made from about 1890 to 1910. The firm closed in 1913.

## Trent Tile Company
### Trenton, New Jersey
~

The Harris Manufacturing Company of Trenton, New Jersey, was organized in 1882 and soon changed its name to the Trent Tile Company. Isaac Broome was the designer and modeler from 1883 to

*A profile of General Ulysses S. Grant made by the Trent Tile Company about 1885. (The Brooklyn Museum, Brooklyn, New York; gift of Arthur W. Clement)*

*This amber-colored Trent tile is 6 inches square. (Smithsonian Institution)*

*A 6-inch-square Trent tile made with mottled green and brown glaze. (Private collection)*

*This golden amber tile, 4 1/4 inches in diameter, is marked "4R20 Trent." It is attributed to the artist Isaac Broome. (Barbara White Morse and* Spinning Wheel Magazine*)*

1886, when he was replaced by William Wood Gallimore. Gallimore stayed for about seven years.

Gallimore came from Great Britain, where he had worked as a potter and designer at the Belleek Pottery of Ireland and the Goss Pottery of Stoke-on-Trent, England. Before joining Trent, he had also worked at the Ceramic Art Company of Trenton, New Jersey, and other American firms. Edwin Barber, in his *Pottery and Porcelain of the United States*, says:

> For six years, he [Mr. Gallimore] was at the Belleek Potteries in Ireland, where he lost his right arm by the bursting of a gun. Since the loss of his arm, Mr. Gallimore has done his modeling with his left hand, and he has accomplished better work with one arm than he did when in possession of both.

The Gallimore designs often portrayed boys and cupids.

The firm made dull lustered tiles in a patented form called "alto-relievo" (high relief), glazed and enameled tiles in all sizes, and 6-by-18-inch mantel facings. Trent Tile Company also made matte-finished tiles by sandblasting the tiles after they were glazed.

The company went into receivership in 1938. It was purchased by the Wenczel Tile Company and is still in business in Trenton.

*A Trent stove tile, 3 by 4 1/4 inches, was used by the Murdock Company of Boston. It says, "May Gode Betide Our Ain Fireside, Murdock Parlor Crate Co.—Boston." (Private collection)*

## United States Encaustic Tile Company
### *Indianapolis, Indiana*

The United States Encaustic Tile Company of Indianapolis, Indiana, started working in 1877. The building was destroyed by fire, but by 1879 a new and larger building was completed. Robert Minton Taylor of England was employed at the tile works from 1881 to

*In mold, raised circles.*

**U-S-E-T-W**

**IND.**
**INDIANAPOLIS**

*Incised.*

A page from the catalog of the United States Encaustic Tile Co. showing floor tile patterns in 1879. Scale: ¾ inch to a foot. (Photo from the William Henry Smith Memorial Library, Indianapolis, Indiana)

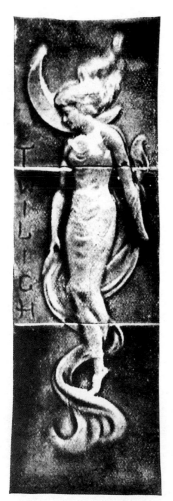

*"Twilight" is the name of this mantel tile made by the United States Encaustic Tile Works and designed by Ruth M. Winterbotham. It was part of a series that also included "Dawn" and "Midday." (Popular Science Monthly, January 1892)*

*Hamlet and Ophelia are depicted on a pair of 6-inch-square brown-glazed tiles. The backs of the tiles are marked "U-S-E-T-W-Indianapolis-Ind." (Private collection)*

1883. In 1886, the ownership changed and the firm was renamed The United States Encaustic Tile Works. The company became U.S. Tile Corporation in 1932, but closed in 1939.

The company made floor, wall, and fireplace tile. Early tiles were unglazed or had a brightly colored glaze. In 1893, a matte-finish glazed tile was developed but was not sold until thirteen years later. The firm made relief tiles in three- and six-section panels. Many of them were made for use on mantels. Ruth M. Winterbotham modeled some of the tiles. The company used clay from Indiana, South Carolina, and Kentucky.

The St. Louis Post Office and the Iowa State House at Des Moines, Iowa, commissioned special tile in the early 1880s. An old tile floor, designed for a saloon during the 1890s, was made to be set with $10 and $20 gold pieces. According to company legend, the floor was popular with customers who liked to walk on money. It was a great idea until the day some workmen stole the floor.

*A stylized flower is centered on this green-brown glossy-glazed 4-inch-square tile. It is marked "United States Encaustic Tile Co. Indianapolis, Ind." (Private collection)*

*A page from the catalog of the United States Encaustic Tile Co., Indianapolis, Indiana.*

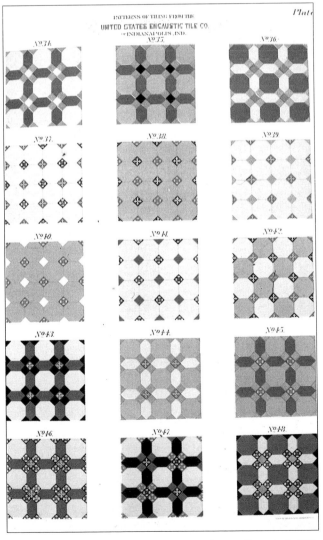

*A page from the catalog of the United States Encaustic Tile Co., Indianapolis, Indiana.*

# Additional Tile Companies

**ALHAMBRA TILE COMPANY**
*Newport, Kentucky 1892*

**AMERICAN TERRA-COTTA & CERAMIC COMPANY**
*See Teco Gates in Art Potteries section.*

**ARCHITECTURAL TILE COMPANY**
*Keyport, New Jersey 1909–1910*

**ATLANTIC TILE AND FAIENCE COMPANY**
*Mauer, New Jersey 1910–1912*

Successor to Architectural Tile Company. Bought by American Encaustic Tiling Company.

**ATLANTIC TILE MANUFACTURING COMPANY**
*Matawan, New Jersey 1910–1920*

Merged with Mosaic Tile Company.

**BOSTON TERRA-COTTA COMPANY**
*Boston, Massachusetts 1880–1893*

Successor to Boston Fire Brick Company. Founded by George M. Fiske, R. G. F. Candage, and James Taylor. Bought by the Perth Amboy and New York companies.

**BROOKLYN VITRIFIED TILE WORKS**
*Brooklyn, New York 1898–c.1918*

Successor to New York Vitrified Tile Works. Owned by A. H. Bonnell.

**CAMBRIDGE TILE MANUFACTURING COMPANY**
*See Cambridge Art Tile Works.*

**CANTON ROOFING TILE COMPANY**
*East Sparta, Ohio c.1913*

Merged with United States Roofing Tile Company.

**CERAMIC TILE WORKS**
*Toledo, Ohio 1890–1892*

May have become the Toledo Art Tile Company, 1893–1896.

**CHELSEA KERAMIC ART WORKS**
*See Dedham Pottery in Art Potteries section.*

**CHICAGO TERRA-COTTA COMPANY (WORKS)**
*Chicago, Illinois 1868–1879*

Founded by Albert H. Hovey and J. F. Nichols. James Taylor, an English potter, hired in 1870. Also made some artware vases.

**CLAYCRAFT POTTERIES**
*Los Angeles, California 1921–1932*

Employed Fred H. Robertson and his son, George B. Robertson.

**COLUMBIA ENCAUSTIC TILE COMPANY**
*Anderson, Indiana 1889–1897*

Founded by B. O. Haugh and George Lilly. Became National Tile Company.

**CONKLING-ARMSTRONG COMPANY**
*Philadelphia, Pennsylvania 1894*

Founded by T. F. Armstrong and E. N. Conkling. Successor to Stephens, Armstrong & Conkling. See Stephens & Leach.

**EMPIRE FLOOR AND WALL TILE COMPANY**
*Zanesville, Ohio 1909–1929*

Founded by John B. Owens as the J. B. Owens Floor and Wall Tile Company (after J. B. Owens Pottery closed).

**FAIENCE MANUFACTURING COMPANY**
*See Art Potteries section.*

**GENERAL TILE**
*Zanesville, Ohio dates unknown*

**GLADDING, MCBEAN AND COMPANY**
*Lincoln, California 1875–1986*

Acquired Pacific Art Tile Company, 1922. Acquired West Coast plant of American Encaustic Tiling Company, 1933. See also Santa Catalina Island Company. Became part of Wedgwood group, 1979. Closed, 1986.

**GRUEBY FAIENCE COMPANY**
*See Art Potteries section.*

**HAMILTON TILE WORKS**
*Hamilton, Ohio 1896–1901*

Founded by A. Mezner. Reorganized in 1897 as Hamilton Tile and Pottery Company. Became Ohio Tile Company.

**HARTFORD FAIENCE COMPANY**
*Hartford, Connecticut 1894–c.1929*

Founded by Eugene Atwood.

**HYZER AND LEWELLEN**
*Philadelphia, Pennsylvania c.1870–1893*

**INDIANAPOLIS TERRA-COTTA COMPANY**
*Indianapolis and Brightwood, Indiana 1893–1918*

Successor to Stilz, Joiner and Company. Became subsidiary of American Terra-Cotta & Ceramic Company (see Teco Gates in Art Potteries section).

**INTERNATIONAL TILE AND TRIM COMPANY**
*Brooklyn, New York 1882–1888*

Founded by English father and son, both named John Ivory. Frederick H. Wilde, also English, joined firm in 1885. Bought by New York Vitrified Tile Works.

## KENSINGTON ART TILE COMPANY
*Newport, Kentucky 1885–1886*

Mary Louise McLaughlin and Herman Mueller were designers.

## KIRKHAM ART TILE & POTTERY COMPANY
*Barberton, Ohio 1891–1895*

Founded by Joseph Kirkham, O. C. Barber, George W. Course, Joseph B. Evans, and Charles Baird. See Providential Tile Works and Kirkham Tile and Pottery Company.

## KIRKHAM TILE AND POTTERY COMPANY
*Tropico, California 1898–1900*

Founded by Joseph Kirkham; funded by a Mr. Richardson and a Mr. Chanler. Sold to a group of investors from Ohio and Trenton, N.J. Frederick H. Wilde was later hired to run the plant after Kirkham sold it, but he did not stay long.

## LONG ISLAND CITY WORKS
*Long Island, New York 1879–1880*

## LYCETT
*See Faience Manufacturing Company in Art Potteries section.*

## MALIBU POTTERIES
*Malibu, California 1926 1932*

Founded by May K. Rindge and Frederick Hastings. Rufus B. Keeler built and managed pottery.

## MARBLEHEAD POTTERY
*See Art Potteries section.*

## MATAWAN TILE COMPANY
*Matawan, New Jersey 1898–c.1940*

## MAYWOOD ART TILE COMPANY
*Maywood, New Jersey 1892–1905*

Foundry and machine shop until 1892. Frederick H. Wilde was superintendent, c. 1898–1900.

## MCKEESPORT TILE COMPANY
*McKeesport, Pennsylvania c.1895*

## MENLO PARK CERAMIC COMPANY
*Menlo Park, New Jersey 1888–1893*

Charles Volkmar (see Volkmar Pottery in Art Potteries section) was a partner.

## NATIONAL TILE COMPANY
*Anderson, Indiana 1897–c.1914*

Successor to Columbia Encaustic Tile Company.

## NEW JERSEY MOSAIC TILE COMPANY
*Matawan and Trenton, New Jersey c.1920*

## NEW YORK ARCHITECTURAL TERRA-COTTA COMPANY
*Long Island City, New York 1886–c.1920*

Founded by Orlando Bronson Potter and Asahel Clarke Geer.

## NEW YORK VITRIFIED TILE WORKS
*Brooklyn, New York c.1888*

## NEWCOMB POTTERY
*See Art Potteries section.*

## NORTHWESTERN TERRA-COTTA COMPANY
*Chicago, Illinois 1877–1956*

Founded as Northwestern Terra-Cotta Works; incorporated in 1888. Made Norweta art pottery, 1907–c.1920, then acquired Chicago Crucible Company and made that company's art pottery wares for a few years.

## OHIO ENCAUSTIC TILE COMPANY
*Zanesville, Ohio 1883–1887*

## OHIO TILE COMPANY
*See Hamilton Tile Works.*

## OLD BRIDGE ENAMELED BRICK AND TILE COMPANY
*Old Bridge, New Jersey c.1893*

Founded by W. E. Rivers.

## OVERBECK POTTERY
*See Art Potteries section.*

## OWEN TILE MANUFACTURING COMPANY
*Tarrytown, New York late 1880s–early 1890s*

## J. B. OWENS TILE COMPANY
*See Owens Pottery in Art Potteries section.*

## PACIFIC ART TILE COMPANY
*Glendale, California c.1900–1904*

First U.S. tile manufacturer west of Mississippi River. Became Western Art Tile Company.

## PARK PORCELAIN WORKS
*West Philadelphia, Pennsylvania c.1884*

## PENNSYLVANIA TILE WORKS COMPANY
*Aspers, Pennsylvania c.1894*

## PERTH AMBOY TERRA-COTTA COMPANY
*Perth Amboy, New Jersey 1879–1907*

Founded by E. J. Hall and W. C. Hall. Merged with Atlantic Company.

## PERTH AMBOY TILE WORKS
*Perth Amboy, New Jersey c.1908*

## PITTSBURGH ENCAUSTIC TILE COMPANY
*Pittsburgh, Pennsylvania 1876–1882*

Managed by Samuel Keys. Became Star Encaustic Tile Company.

## JAMES RENWICK
*New York, New York c.1853*

Architect who experimented with terra-cotta.

## ROBERTSON ART TILE COMPANY
*Morrisville, Pennsylvania 1890–c.1980*

Founded by George Robertson as Chelsea Keramic Art Tile Works. Some early tiles modeled by Hugh C. Robertson (see Dedham Pottery in Art Potteries section). Robertson left for California in 1895 and Arthur D. Frost became manager. Employed Herman Mueller, 1903–1909. Became Robertson Manufacturing Company.

## ROOKWOOD POTTERY
*See Art Potteries section.*

## J. L. RUE POTTERY CO.
*South Amboy and Matawan, New Jersey 1860–1906*

Successor to Swan Hill Pottery. Moved to Matawan in 1880.

## SANTA CATALINA ISLAND COMPANY
*Santa Catalina Island, California 1923–1937*

Ceramics plant built by William Wrigley, Jr., and David Renton. Molds and right to "Catalina" name sold to Gladding, McBean and Company, 1937–1947.

## SATURDAY EVENING GIRLS CLUB
*See Paul Revere Pottery in Art Potteries section.*

## SOLON & SCHEMMEL
*San Jose, California 1920–1954*

Founded by Albert Solon and Frank Schemmel. Became Solon & Larkin, 1937. Became Larkin Tile Company, 1947.

## SOUTH AMBOY TILE COMPANY
*South Amboy, New Jersey c.1900*

## SOUTHERN TERRA-COTTA WORKS
*Atlanta, Georgia c.1871–1890s*

Founded by P. Pellegrini; incorporated in 1875 when Jack Castleberry bought an interest.

## SPARTA CERAMICS COMPANY
*East Sparta, Ohio 1919–1950s*

Acquired by United States Ceramic Tile Company, 1950s.

## STANDARD TILE COMPANY
*South Zanesville, Ohio c.1923–1940s*

## STAR ENCAUSTIC TILE COMPANY
*Pittsburgh, Pennsylvania 1882–c.1920*

Successor to Pittsburgh Encaustic Tile Company. Both companies were managed by Samuel Keys, an Englishman whose successful experiments with tiles in 1867–1871 have made him the first to make encaustic tiles successfully in the United States.

## STEPHENS & LEACH
*West Philadelphia, Pennsylvania 1886–1893*

Became Stephens, Leach & Conkling, 1887. Became Stephens, Armstrong & Conkling, 1888. Acquired by New York Company, 1893.

## TARRYTOWN TILE COMPANY
*Tarrytown, New York c.1880–1900*

May have succeeded Tarrytown Pottery Company.

## TIFFANY POTTERY
*See Art Potteries section.*

## UNITED STATES CERAMIC TILE COMPANY
*Canton, Ohio 1913–present*

Founded as United States Roofing Tile Company. Successor to United States Quarry Tile Company. Acquired by Spartek, Inc., in 1974.

## UNITED STATES POTTERY COMPANY
*Bennington, Vermont c.1850–1858*

Founded by Christopher Fenton, managed by Oliver Gager. Made inlaid floor tiles used at 1853 World's Fair at Crystal Palace in New York City.

## UNITED STATES QUARRY TILE COMPANY
*See United States Ceramic Tile Company.*

## UNITED STATES ROOFING TILE COMPANY
*See United States Ceramic Tile Company.*

## UNIVERSITY OF NORTH DAKOTA POTTERY
*See North Dakota School of Mines in Art Potteries section.*

## VOLKMAR CERAMIC COMPANY
*See Art Potteries section.*

## WELLER POTTERY
*See Art Potteries section.*

## WENCZEL TILE COMPANY
*Trenton, New Jersey 1915–present*

Bought Trent Tile Company, c.1938.

## WESTERN ART TILE COMPANY
*Glendale, California 1904–c.1916*

Successor to Pacific Art Tile Company. Employed Frederick H. Wilde before he worked for the successor to Kirkham Tile and Pottery Company.

## WHEATLEY POTTERY COMPANY
*See Art Potteries section.*

## WHEELING TILE COMPANY
*Wheeling, West Virginia c.1913*

## WINKLE TERRA-COTTA COMPANY
*St. Louis, Missouri 1889–1942*

Founded by Joseph Winkle. Successor to Winkle Terra-Cotta Works, 1883–1889.

## ZANESVILLE MAJOLICA COMPANY
*Zanesville, Ohio dates unknown*

# Bibliography

An extensive bibliography was included in our first book about art pottery, *The Kovels' Collector's Guide to American Art Pottery* (Crown, 1974). These sources were also the basis for this book, but we have not included any of those written before 1915 in the following bibliography. Other information has come to us through private correspondence with relatives of the potters and experts in the field. If you wish to know more about the sources of information in this book, please contact us through Crown Publishers.

## GENERAL POTTERY BOOKS

Anderson, Timothy J., Eudorah M. Moore, and Robert W. Winter, eds. *California Design: 1910*. Pasadena Center exhibition. Pasadena: Anderson, Ritchie & Simon, 1974.

Barber, Edwin A. *Marks of American Potters*. Philadelphia: Patterson and White, 1904.

————. *The Pottery and Porcelain of the United States*. 3d ed., rev. New York: G. P. Putnam's Sons, 1909.

Bowman, Leslie Greene. *American Arts & Crafts: Virtue in Design*. Exhibition catalog. Los Angeles County Museum of Art. Boston: Bulfinch Press, 1990.

Bray, Hazel V. *The Potter's Art in California 1855 to 1955*. Seattle: University of Washington Press, 1980.

Bruhn, Thomas P. *American Decorative Tiles 1870–1930*. Catalog. William Benton Museum of Art. Storrs, Conn.: University of Connecticut, 1979.

Clark, Edna Maria. *Ohio Art and Artists*. Richmond, Va.: Garrett and Massie, 1932.

Clark, Garth, and Margie Hughto. *A Century of Ceramics in the United States: 1878–1978*. New York: E. P. Dutton, 1979.

Clark, Robert Judson, ed. *The Arts and Crafts Movement in America: 1876–1916*. Princeton, N.J.: Princeton University Press, 1972.

Cooper-Hewitt Museum. *American Art Pottery*. Seattle: University of Washington Press, 1987.

Dale, Sharon. *Frederick Hurten Rhead: An English Potter in America*. Erie, Pa.: Erie Art Museum, 1986.

Darling, Sharon S. *Chicago Ceramics & Glass: An Illustrated History from 1871 to 1933*. Chicago: Chicago Historical Society, 1979.

Evans, Paul. *Art Pottery of the United States*. 2d ed., rev. New York: Feingold & Lewis, 1987.

Henzke, Lucile. *American Art Pottery*. Camden, N.J.: Thomas Nelson, 1970.

Herr, Jeffrey. *California Art Pottery: 1895–1920*. Exhibition catalog. Northridge, Calif.: California State University, 1988.

Jervis W. P. *A Pottery Primer*. New York: O'Gorman Publishing Company, 1911.

Kaplan, Wendy. *"The Art That Is Life": The Arts & Crafts Movement in America: 1876–1920*. Boston: Little, Brown and Company, 1987.

*The Ladies God Bless 'Em: The Women's Art Movement in Cincinnati in the Nineteenth Century*. Cincinnati Art Museum exhibition. Cincinnati: Cincinnati Art Museum, 1976.

Levin, Elaine. *The History of American Ceramics*. New York: Harry N. Abrams, 1988.

Lehner, Lois. *Lehner's Encyclopedia of U.S. Marks on Pottery, Porcelain & Clay*. Paducah, Ky.: Collector Books, 1988.

Metropolitan Museum of Art. *In Pursuit of Beauty: Americans and the Aesthetic Movement*. New York: Rizzoli, 1986.

Neslon, Marion John. *Art Pottery of the Midwest*. Exhibition catalog. Minneapolis: University of Minnesota, 1988.

Peck, Herbert. *The Book of Rookwood Pottery*. New York: Crown Publishers, 1968.

Stiles, Helen. *Pottery in the United States*. New York: E. P. Dutton, 1941.

Volpe, Ted M., and Beth Cathers. *Treasures of the American Arts and Crafts Movement: 1890–1920*. New York: Harry N. Abrams, 1988.

Watkins, Lura Woodside. *Early New England Potters and Their Wares*. Cambridge, Mass.: Harvard University Press, 1950.

## ARC-EN-CIEL

Purviance, Evan. "American Art Pottery." *Mid-America Reporter* (November 1972).

Radford, Fred W. *A. Radford Pottery: His Life and Works*. Privately printed, 1973 (Fred W. Radford).

Schneider, Norris F. "Many Small Art Potteries Once Operated in Zanesville." *Zanesville Times Recorder* (February 4, 1962).

————. "Veteran Mosaic Tile Employee Compiles Outstanding Display." *Zanesville Times Recorder* (October 30, 1960).

## AREQUIPA

Blasberg, Robert. "Arequipa Pottery." *The Western Collector* VI (October 1968), 7–10.

Lamoureux, Dorothy. "In Search of Arequipa." *Journal of the American Art Pottery Association* IV (January 1989), 4–7.

## EDWIN BENNETT

"Baltimore, Maryland's Bennett Pottery." *Spinning Wheel* (November 1958), 22.

## BROUWER AND MIDDLE LANE

Evans, Paul. "Brouwer's Middle Lane Pottery." *Spinning Wheel* (December 1973), 48–49, 54.

## BRUSH POTTERY

Brush Pottery Company. Catalogs: 1927, 1930, 1962.

Evans, Paul. "The Confusing McCoy Potteries." *Spinning Wheel* XXIX (January–February 1973), 8–9.

Sanford, Martha and Steve. *The Guide to Brush-McCoy Pottery*. Privately printed, 1992 (230 Harrison Ave., Campbell, CA 95008).

Schneider, Norris F. "Brush Pottery." *Zanesville Times Recorder* (September 9 and 16, 1962).

## BUFFALO POTTERY/DELDARE

Altman, Seymour and Violet. *The Book of Buffalo Pottery*. Atglen, Pa.: Schiffer, 1987.

Garrett, Brice. "Buffalo Pottery and the Larkin Company." *Spinning Wheel* XIX (January–February 1963), 18–19.

Gernert, Dee Albert. "Buffalo Pottery's Deldare Ware." *Spinning Wheel* XIX (March 1963), 14–15.

## BYRDCLIFFE

Delaware Art Museum. *Life by Design*. Exhibition catalog, 1984.

## CAMARK POTTERY

Brewer, Don. "Camark." *Depression Glass Daze* (June 1982), 25.

Derwich, Jenny B., and Mary Latos. *Dictionary Guide to United States Pottery and Porcelain (19th and 20th Century)*. Franklin, Mich.: Jenstan, 1984, 52–53.

Gifford, David Edwin. "Arkansas Art Pottery: A Historical Perspective." *Journal of the American Art Pottery Association* VI (January-February 1991), 3–9.

———. *Arkansas Art Pottery Bibliography*. Conway, Ark.: University of Central Arkansas Archives, 1989.

Huxford, Sharon and Bob. *The Collectors Encyclopedia of Weller Pottery*. Paducah, Ky.: Collector Books, 1979.

### CAMBRIDGE ART POTTERY

*Trade Marks of the Jewelry and Kindred Trades*. New York and Philadelphia: Jewelers' Circular–Keystone Publishing Co., 1904.

Wolfe, John C., Jr. Correspondence with authors, February 7, 1972.

### CLEWELL

*The Bronze Productions of C. W. Clewell of Canton, O.* Advertising leaflet.

### COWAN POTTERY

*American Studio Ceramics: 1920–1950*. Exhibition catalog. Minneapolis: University of Minnesota, 1988.

Boros, Ethel. "Playing the Antique Market." *The Plain Dealer* (November 12, 1967).

Borsick, Helen. "Pottery Lights Up a Brilliant Ohio Epoch." *The Plain Dealer* (August 24, 1969).

Brodbeck, John. "Cowan Pottery." *Spinning Wheel* XXIX (March 1973), 24–27.

"Cowan." *Pottery Collectors' Newsletter* II (September 1973), 143–47.

Cowan Potters, Inc. Catalogs: 1928, 1930, 1931, and undated.

*Cowan Pottery 1925 Catalog*. Privately reprinted (Donald H. Calkins, 1068 Sylvan Ave., Lakewood, OH 44107).

*Cowan Pottery Museum*. Privately printed, 1978 (Rocky River Public Library, 1600 Hampton Rd., Rocky River, OH 44116).

Milliken, William M. "Ohio Ceramics." *Design* (November 1937).

Robbins, Carle. "Cowan of Cleveland, Follower of an Ancient Craft." *The Bystander of Cleveland* (September 7, 1929).

Western Reserve Historical Society. Files: Artists list from Edward Winter, Jan. 4, 1965; "The Cowan Pottery Collection at the W.R.H.S."; "Cowan Potters, Inc."; letters from Rhoda M. Hanna, March 20 and June 22, 1965, and August 13, 1969; letter from Richard O. Hummel, January 27, 1966; information from Dr. William Milliken, Dec. 17, 1964.

### PAUL E. COX POTTERY

Ormond, Suzanne, and Mary E. Irvine. *Louisiana's Art Nouveau: The Crafts of the Newcomb Style*. Gretna, La.: Pelican, 1984.

Poesch, Jessie. *Newcomb Pottery: An Enterprise for Southern Women, 1895–1940*. Smithsonian Exhibition Catalog. Atglen, Pa..: Schiffer, 1984.

### CRAVEN ART POTTERY

Vodrey, William H., Jr. "The Record of the Pottery Industry of the East Liverpool District." *Bulletin of the American Ceramic Society* 24:8 (1945), 286.

### DEDHAM POTTERY

Dedham Pottery Co. "A Short History of the Dedham Pottery." Threefold pamphlet, c. 1930 (author unknown).

*Dedham Pottery 1938 Catalog*. Privately printed, 1987 (P.O. Box 826, Halifax, VA 24558).

Dunbar, Leila. "Dedham Pottery." *The Inside Collector* (September 1990), 83–87.

Evans, Paul F. "The Art Pottery Era in the United States 1870 to 1920, Part One." *Spinning Wheel* (October 1970).

———. "The Robertson Saga, I. The Creative Years: 1891–1943." *The Western Collector* (May 1967).

Hawes, Lloyd E. *The Dedham Pottery and the Earlier Robertson's Chelsea Potteries*. Dedham, Mass.: Dedham Historical Society, 1968.

———. "Hugh Cornwall Robertson and the Chelsea Period." *Antiques Magazine* (March 1966), 409.

Ray, Marcia. "ABC's of Ceramics." *Spinning Wheel* (June 1967), 18.

### FAIENCE MANUFACTURING COMPANY

Lycett, Lydia. "China Painting by the Lycetts." *Atlanta Historical Bulletin* VI (July 1941).

St. John, Wylly Folk. "Hand Painted China." *Atlanta Journal and Constitution Magazine* (February 12, 1967).

### FLORENTINE POTTERY CO.

*Geological Survey of Ohio*. Bulletin 26. Columbus, Ohio, 1923.

Murphy, James L. "Shards Give Identity to Florentine Art Pottery." *AntiqueWeek*, Vol. 24 (October 14, 1991), 2.

### FRACKELTON

Carroon, Robert G. "The Pottery Industry in 19th Century Milwaukee." *Historical Messenger of the Milwaukee County Historical Society* 27 (March 1970).

Crowley, Lilian H. "It's Now the Potter's Turn." *International Studio* 75 (September 1922), 539.

Stover, Frances. "Susan Goodrich Frackelton and the China Painters." *Historical Messenger of the Milwaukee County Historical Society* 10 (March 1954).

Weedon, George A. *Susan S. Frackelton & The American Arts and Crafts Movement*. Privately printed, 1975 (BOOX Press, 1245 N. Water St., Milwaukee, WI 53202).

### FULPER POTTERY

Blasberg, Robert W. *Fulper Art Pottery: An Aesthetic Appreciation: 1909–1929*. Exhibition catalog. New York: Jordan-Volpe Gallery, 1979.

———. "Twenty Years of Fulper." *Spinning Wheel* (October 1973), 14–18.

Folk, Thomas C. "John Kunsman: Fulper's Master Potter." *Arts & Crafts Magazine* (Summer 1991), 32–37.

*Fulper Catalog*. Privately reprinted, 1991 (Ann Kerr, P.O. Box 437, Sidney, OH 45365).

Fulper Pottery Company. *Vasekraft—Fulper Catalogue*, after 1915.

Rehl, Norma. *The Collectors Handbook of Stangl Pottery*. Privately printed, 1979 (Norma Rehl, P.O. Box 556, Milford, NJ 08848).

———. *Stangl Pottery*, Part II. Privately printed, 1982 (Norma Rehl, P.O. Box 556, Milford, NJ 08848).

Stangl Pottery. *Stangl: A Portrait of Progress in Pottery*. Privately printed, 1965 (P.O. Box 2080, Trenton, NJ).

*Vasekraft: 1805 Fulper Pottery Company Catalog*. Privately printed (Hunterdon County Historical Society, Flemington, NJ 08822).

Volpe, Tod M., and Robert W. Blasberg. "Fulper Art Pottery: Amazing Glazes." *American Art & Antiques* (July-August 1979), 76–84.

### GAY HEAD POTTERY

Evans, Paul F. "The Niloak Pottery." *Spinning Wheel* (October 1970).

### GRUEBY FAIENCE CO.

Blasberg, Robert. "Grueby Art Pottery." *Antiques* (August 1971), 246.

*Grueby 1981 Exhibition Catalog*. The Everson Museum of Art of Syracuse and Onondaga County. New York, 1981.

Luther, Louise R. "Tribute to a Remarkable Woman, Another Dimension of Grueby Pottery." *Spinning Wheel* (March 1972), 40–41.

McDowell, C. "Grueby: American Art Pottery." *A Collectors Annual* No. 5, 102–3.

## HAMPSHIRE POTTERY

Evans, Paul F. "Hampshire Pottery." *Spinning Wheel* (September 1970).

"First Hampshire Pottery Was Made 100 Years Ago." *The Antique Trader* (December 21, 1971).

Kendall, A. Harold. *The Story of Hampshire Pottery.* Privately printed, 1966 (A. Harold Kendall, East Surry Rd., Keene, NH 03431).

Pappas, Joan, and A. Harold Kendall. *Hampshire Pottery Manufactured by J.S. Taft & Company, Keene, New Hampshire.* Privately printed, 1971 (Forward's Color Productions, Inc., West Rd., Box 567, Manchester, VT 05254).

## HEROLD CHINA AND POTTERY CO.

Derwich, Jenny B., and Dr. Mary Latos. *Dictionary Guide to United States Pottery & Porcelain.* Franklin, Mich.: Jenstan, 1984, 67.

## HULL POTTERY

Coates, Pamela. *Hull.* Privately printed, 1974 (5121 South Harlan, Indianapolis, IN 46227).

Crooks, Guy E. "Brief History of the Pottery Industry of Crooksville, 1868–1932." *Crooksville-Roseville Pottery Festival Souvenir Program* (1967), 37–38.

Felker, Sharon L. *Lovely Hull Pottery.* Radnor, Pa.: Wallace-Homestead Book Co., 1974.

———. *Lovely Hull Pottery, Book 2.* Radnor, Pa.: Wallace-Homestead Book Co., 1977.

Foraker, David. "Hull Pottery, Crooksville, Ohio." *The Western Collector* IX (January-February 1971), 4–8.

Roberts, Brenda. *The Collectors Encyclopedia of Hull Pottery.* Paducah, Ky.: Collectors Books, 1980.

Weiss, Grace M. "Hull Art Pottery." *The Antique Trader* (September 25, 1973), 46.

## IOWA STATE POTTERY

Dommel, Darlene. "Iowa State College Art Pottery." *Journal of the American Art Pottery Association* V (March-April 1990), 1, 4–7.

"The Prairie-Style Art Pottery of Iowa State College." *Art Trader* (December 1, 1982), 70–71.

Russo, Susan. "A Collaboration in Clay, Iowa State's Prairie Pottery." *The Palimpsest, Iowa's Popular History Magazine* 68 (Fall 1987), 113–29.

## JALAN POTTERY

Evans, Paul. "Jalan: Transitional Pottery of San Francisco." *Spinning Wheel* (April 1973), 24.

## JUGTOWN POTTERY

Breese, Jessie Martin. "Jugtown, N.C." *Country Life* XLII (October 1922), 64–65.

Crawford, Jean. "Jugtown Pottery." *The Western Collector* VI (July 1968).

———. *Jugtown Pottery: History and Design.* Winston-Salem, N.C.: John F. Blair, 1964.

Goldsmith, Margaret O. "Jugtown Pottery." *House Beautiful* 52 (October 1922), 311, 358, 360.

Hoagland, Jane. "Jugtown Pottery." *Art Center New York Bulletin* I (April 1923), 167–68.

"Interested in Jugtown Ware?" *Pottery Collectors' Newsletter* I (October 1971).

Mock, Esther. "An American Craft with a Pedigree." *Early American Life* (June 1973), 42–43, 86.

———. "The High Craft of Jugtown." *Hobbies* (November 1972).

Salem College Collection. Winston-Salem, North Carolina.

## KENTON HILLS

Cox, Warren E. *The Book of Pottery and Porcelain.* Vol. I. New York: Crown Publishers, 1944.

## KNOWLES, TAYLOR AND KNOWLES

Crutcher, Jean. "Lotus Ware." *Antique News* 2 (October 1964).

Garrett, Brice. "Ohio's Lotus Ware." *Spinning Wheel* (January-February 1966), 16–17.

"Lotus Ware." *Spinning Wheel* (November 1967).

*Pottery Festival Catalogue.* East Liverpool, Ohio, 1968–1972.

Ramsay, John. "East Liverpool Ohio Pottery in the Museum of the East Liverpool Historical Society." *American Collector* (April 1948).

———. "Lotus Ware." *Glass and China* 47 (October 1942), 55–57.

## LONHUDA POTTERY

Hall, Foster E. and Gladys C. "The Lonhuda Pricing Formula." *Newsletter* (1972).

"Lonhuda." *Spinning Wheel* (November 1967), 17.

"Lonhuda Pottery." *Mid-America Reporter* (December 1971).

Purviance, Louise and Evan, and Norris F. Schneider. *Weller Art Pottery in Color.* Radnor, Pa.: Wallace-Homestead Book Co., 1968.

Schneider, Norris F. "Lonhuda: Originated by William A. Long." Reprint from *Sunday Times Recorder,* Zanesville, Ohio, 1971. *Pottery Collectors' Newsletter* I (January 1972).

———. "Weller Pottery." *Zanesville Times Signal* (March 16, 1958).

## MARBLEHEAD POTTERY

Baggs, Arthur E. "The Story of a Potter." *The Handicrafter* I & II (April 1929), 8–10.

Binns, Charles F. "Pottery in America." *The American Magazine of Art* VII (February 1916), 131.

Crowley, Lilian H. "It's Now the Potter's Turn." *International Studio* 75 (September 1922), 539.

Little, Flora Townsend. "A Short Sketch of American Pottery." *Art & Archaeology* 15 (May 1923), 219.

MacSwiggan, Amelia E. "The Marblehead Pottery." *Spinning Wheel* (March 1972).

Marblehead Historical Society. *Marblehead Pottery—An American Industrial Art of Distinction.* Reprint from Marblehead Pottery Catalogue, 1919.

The Marblehead Potteries. *Marblehead Pottery Supplementary Catalogue.* Marblehead, Mass., 1924.

Russell, Elizabeth H. "The Pottery of Marblehead." *House Beautiful* 59 (March 1926).

## MARKHAM POTTERY

*The Markham Pottery Book.* Privately reprinted catalog, 1991 (Ann Kerr, P.O. Box 437, Sidney, OH 45365).

Scott, Douglas. "Markham Pottery." *American Clay Exchange* (November 1983), 13.

## MATT MORGAN POTTERY

Coleman, Duke. "Matt Morgan . . . More Than a Potter." *American Art Pottery* (November 1977).

## J. W. MCCOY POTTERY CO.

Coates, Pamela. *The Real McCoy.* Cherry Hill, N.J.: Reynolds Publishers, 1971.

Evans, Paul. "The Confusing McCoy Potteries." *Spinning Wheel* XXIX (January-February 1973), 8–9.

Huxford, Sharon and Bob. *The Collectors Catalog of Brush-McCoy Pottery.* Paducah, Ky.: Collector Books, 1978.

———. *The Collectors Encyclopedia of Brush-McCoy Pottery.* Paducah, Ky.: Collector Books, 1978.

———. *The Collectors Encyclopedia of McCoy Pottery*. Paducah, Ky.: Collector Books, 1978.

Lynn, Evelyn. "What About McCoy?" *The Antique Trader* (January 23, 1973), 50–51.

Nelson, Marianne. "The Nelson McCoy Sanitary Stoneware Company." *Joel Sater's Antiques News* (February 11, 1972).

Sanford, Martha and Steve. *The Guide to Brush-McCoy Pottery*. Privately printed, 1992 (230 Harrison Ave., Campbell, CA 95008).

Schneider, Norris F. "Brush Pottery." *Zanesville Times Recorder* (September 9 and 16, 1962).

Zanesville Chamber of Commerce. Booklet, 1918.

### NELSON MCCOY POTTERY

Coates, Pamela. *The Real McCoy*. Vols. I and II. Cherry Hill, N.J.: Reynolds Publishers, 1971 and 1974.

Nichols, Harold. *McCoy Cookie Jars: From the First to the Latest*. Lake Mills, Iowa: Nichols Publishing, 1987.

For additional bibliography, see J. W. McCoy Pottery Co.

### MERRIMAC POTTERY

Lunt, Miss Wilhelmina V. (curator, Historical Society of Old Newbury, Newburyport, Mass.). Correspondence with authors, May 1972.

### NEWCOMB POTTERY/NEW ORLEANS ART POTTERY

Blasberg, Robert W. "Newcomb Pottery." *Antiques* (July 1968), 73–77.

———. "The Sadie Irvine Letters: A Further Note on the Production of Newcomb Pottery." *Antiques* (August 1971), 250–51.

Collier, Alberta. "She Unveiled Vistas for Others." *Dixie* (March 14, 1971), 8–10.

Cox, Paul E. Baton Rouge, La. Correspondence with authors, April 1968.

———. "Potteries of the Gulf Coast." *Ceramic Age* 25 (date unknown).

———. "Technical Practice at the Newcomb Pottery." *Journal of the American Ceramic Society* I (July 1918).

Crowley, Lilian H. "It's Now the Potter's Turn." *International Studio* 75 (September 1922), 539.

Grady, Susan W. (Isaac Delgado Museum of Art, New Orleans, La.). Correspondence with authors, March 1972.

Henzke, Lucile. "Newcomb Art Pottery." *Spinning Wheel* (September 1968), 12.

———. "Newcomb College Pottery." *Pottery Collectors' Newsletter* 1 (January 1972), 51.

Irvine, Mary Ellen. New Orleans, La. Correspondence with authors, March and April 1972.

Irvine, Sadie. New Orleans, La. Correspondence with authors, April 1968.

Kendall, John Smith. *History of New Orleans*. Vol. 2. Chicago and New York: Lewis Publishing Company, 1922.

Little, Flora Townsend. "A Short Sketch of American Pottery." *Art & Archaeology* 15 (May 1923), 219.

Ormond, Suzanne, and Mary E. Irvine. *Louisiana's Art Nouveau*. Gretna, La.: Pelican, 1976.

Poesch, Jessie. *Newcomb Pottery: An Enterprise for Southern Women, 1895–1940*. Smithsonian Exhibition catalog. Atglen, Pa.: Schiffer, 1984.

Smith, Kenneth E (manager, Ceramic Division, American Art Clay Co., Indianapolis, Ind.). Correspondence with authors, March 1972.

———. "The Origin, Development and Present Status of Newcomb Pottery." *American Ceramic Society Bulletin* 17 (June 1938), 257.

Swanson, Betsy. New Orleans, La. Correspondence with authors, March 1972.

*Two Decades of Newcomb Pottery*. Exhibition catalog. New Orleans: Art Department, Newcomb College, Tulane University, 1963.

### NILOAK POTTERY

Crowley, Lilian H. "It's Now the Potter's Turn." *International Studio* 75 (September 1922), 539.

Dixson, Jeannette H. "Niloak Pottery." *Hobbies* (March 1973), 109.

Doherty, Bob. "Niloak Swirl Pottery Production." *American Clay Exchange* IV (March 1984), 2.

Dunnahoo, Pat. "Cheap Glass Killed Once-Thriving Pottery Industry." *Arkansas Gazette* (June 28, 1970), E–4.

Evans, Paul. "The Niloak Pottery." *Spinning Wheel* (October 1970), 18.

Gifford, David Edwin. "Arkansas Art Pottery: A Historical Perspective." *Journal of the American Art Pottery Association* VI (January-February 1991), 3–9.

Goolsby, Erwin. "Niloak Pottery." *Old Bottle Magazine* (April 1970), 35.

Heissenbuttel, Orva. "Niloak Pottery, Little Known Ware of Art Nouveau Period." *Tri-State Trader* (March 13, 1971), 1.

Johnson, Gini. "'Mission' Control, Don't Call It 'Mission'!" *Pottery Collectors' Newsletter* 2 (November 1972), 21.

Kistler, Ralph H. Salt Lake City, Utah. Correspondence with authors, January 24, 1970.

Malone, Cecil T. Little Rock, Ark. Correspondence with authors, July 1970, November 1970, and January 1972.

Mauney, Kenneth. "Arkansas Man Collects Ozark Pottery." *Collectors News* (date unknown).

———. Dumas, Ark. Correspondence with authors, February 1970, September 1970, December 1971, and January 1972.

———. *Niloak of the Ozarks*. Privately printed, 1972 (Kenneth Mauney, P.O. Box 517, Dumas, AR 71639).

———. *Niloak Pottery Catalog*. Privately printed, 1971 (Kenneth Mauney, P.O. Box 517, Dumas, AR 71639).

*Niloak Pottery*. Privately printed (Pottery Shack, 108 N. Cooper Ave., Cincinnati, OH 45215).

Rainey, Arlene. Letter to the editor. *Spinning Wheel* (June 1971).

Shipman, Mrs. C. B. Mount Lake Terrace, Wash. Correspondence with authors, January 1972.

Smith, Judy. "Niloak Pottery, Benton, Arkansas." *Pottery Collectors' Newsletter* V (November 1976), 97.

Weiss, Grace. "Niloak Pottery." *The Antique Trader* (April 17, 1973), 63.

### NORTH DAKOTA SCHOOL OF MINES

Barr, Margaret Libby, Donald Miller, and Robert Barr. *University of North Dakota Pottery: The Cable Years*. Fargo, N.Dak.: Knight Printing Company, 1977.

Cable, Margaret. "Post-Ware Ceramic Opportunities in North Dakota." (publication and date unknown).

"Ceramic's Mrs. Pachl Retires to the Ozarks." *Grand Forks* (N.D.) *Herald* (June 7, 1970).

"Ceramics Veteran to Retire July 1." *Grand Forks Herald* (May 29, 1949), 21.

Dommel, Darlene. "University of North Dakota Pottery." *Spinning Wheel* (June 1973) 30–31.

"Former Ceramics Head at U Honored." *Grand Forks Herald* (April 25, 1951).

Grantier, Charles. Letter to the editor. *Spinning Wheel* (October 1972).

University of North Dakota. Clippings from files on Margaret Kelly Cable, Julia E. Mattson, and Margaret Davis Pachl.

### ODELL & BOOTH BROTHERS

Keno, Leigh. "Odell & Booth Brothers." *Arts & Antiques* III (March-April 1980), 96–101.

### GEORGE E. OHR

*The Biloxi Art Pottery of George Ohr.* Privately printed, 1978 (Mississippi State Historical Museum, Mississippi Department of Archives and History).

Blasberg, Robert W. *George E. Ohr and His Biloxi Art Pottery.* Privately printed, 1973 (J. W. Carpenter, R.D. 1, Box 274, Port Jervis, NY 12771).

———. *The Unknown Ohr.* Milford, Pa.: Peaceable Press, 1986.

Carpenter, J. W. "Geo. Ohr's 'Pot-Ohr-E'." *The Antique Trader Weekly* (September 19, 1972), 32.

Clark, Garth, Robert A. Ellison, Jr., and Eugene Hecht. *The Mad Potter of Biloxi: The Art & Life of George E. Ohr.* New York: Abbeville Press, 1989.

Ellison, Robert A., Jr. "George Ohr: Small Wonders of a Giant's Vision." *Arts & Crafts Quarterly* III (Summer 1990), 18–23.

*The George E. Ohr Exhibition Catalogue.* The University of Mississippi, 1983.

Hecht, Eugene. "George Ohr: Modern Potter." *Antiques and the Arts Weekly* (October 27, 1989), 1–2, 103–8.

———. "The Long Lost 1903 Handbill of G.E. Ohr." *Arts & Crafts Quarterly* III (Spring 1990), 14–18.

———. "An Ohr Primer: Part II, A Chronology with Beasties." *American Art Pottery* (June 1982).

Kovel, Ralph and Terry. "The Mad Potter of Biloxi." *The Western Collector* X (May 1972), 18–20.

Ohr, George E. "Some Facts in the History of a Unique Personality: Autobiography of Geo. E. Ohr, the Biloxi Potter." *Crockery & Glass Journal* 54 (December 12, 1901).

### OUACHITA POTTERY

Gifford, David Edwin. "Arkansas Art Pottery: A Historical Perspective." *Journal of the American Art Pottery Association* VI (January-February 1991), 3–9.

Hudgins, Mary D. Correspondence with authors, 1974.

### OVERBECK POTTERY

Crowley, Lilian H. "It's Now the Potter's Turn." *International Studio* 75 (September 1922), 539.

*International Studio* 75 (September 1922), 546.

Little, Flora Townsend. "Overbeck Motifs Drawn from Nature: Were Made at Cambridge City, Ind." *Tri-State Trader* (July 24, 1971), 1.

———. "Overbeck Pottery." *Spinning Wheel* (May 1972), 10–12.

———. "Overbeck Pottery Collection Sold: New Value Scale Set." *Tri-State Trader* (date unknown).

———. "A Short Sketch of American Pottery." *Art & Archaeology* 15 (May 1923), 219.

"Overbeck Home Purchased by Hagerstown, Ind., Couple Recently." (publication and date unknown).

Postle, Kathleen R. *The Chronicle of the Overbeck Pottery.* Indianapolis: Indiana Historical Society, 1978.

### OWENS POTTERY COMPANY

Hahn, Frank L. Correspondence with authors, 1991.

Hall, Foster E. and Gladys C. *The Owens Pricing Formula.* Punta Gorda, Fla. (date unknown).

"J. B. Owens Pottery Co." *Spinning Wheel* (January-February 1968).

*Owens Collectors Newsletter* I (July 15, 1991).

Purviance, Evan. "American Art Pottery." *Mid-America Reporter* (October 1972), 18.

Purviance, Louise and Evan, and Norris F. Schneider. "The J. B. Owens Pottery Company." *Zanesville Art Pottery in Color.* Radnor, Pa.: Wallace-Homestead Book Co., 1968, plates 12 and 13.

Schneider, Norris F. "Dutchman Creates Owens Utopian." *Pottery Collectors' Newsletter* VII (May 1978), 34–35.

———. "Veteran Mosaic Tile Employee Compiles Outstanding Display." *Zanesville Times Recorder* (October 30, 1960).

Zanesville Chamber of Commerce. "J. B. Owens Floor and Wall Tile Company." Booklet, 1918.

### PAULINE POTTERY

Allan, Alice. "Pauline Pottery." (date unknown).

Platt, Dorothy Pickard. *The Story of Pickard China.* Hanover, Pa.: Everybodys Press, 1970.

Shull, Thelma. "The Pauline Pottery." *Hobbies* 48 (October 1943), 56–58.

Whyte, Bertha Kitchell. "Pauline Pottery of Edgerton, Wisconsin." *Spinning Wheel* (April 1958), 24–26, 38.

### PAUL REVERE POTTERY

Binns, Charles F. "Pottery in America." *The American Magazine of Art* 7 (February 1916), 131.

Blasberg, Robert W. "Paul Revere Pottery." *The Western Collector* VII (January 1969), 13–16.

Crowley, Lilian H. "It's Now the Potter's Turn." *International Studio* 75 (September 1922), 539.

Guagliumi, Arthur. "The Saturday Evening Girls: Opening a Door to America." *Pottery Collectors' Newsletter* IV (October-November 1975), 151.

Little, Flora Townsend. "A Short Sketch of American Pottery." *Art & Archaeology* 15 (May 1923), 219.

Paul Revere advertising brochure. (date unknown).

"The Paul Revere Pottery, An American Craft Industry." *House Beautiful* 51 (January 1922), 50.

Pochmann, Ruth Fouts. "The Paul Revere Pottery, 1912–1942." *Spinning Wheel* (November 1963), 24.

"The Story of Paul Revere Pottery." Pamphlet (date unknown).

Wallach, Mrs. Philip. Correspondence to Mr. Jacoby, director of North Bennett Street Industrial School, March 1972.

### PETERS AND REED

Gonder catalogs: 1943, 1950, others undated.

Hershone, Jeffrey, Sherrie, and Barry. *The Peters and Reed and Zane Pottery Experience.* Privately printed, 1990 (P.O. Box 950670, Lake Mary, FL 32746).

*The Peters & Reed Pottery Company,* undated catalog.

Schneider, Norris F. "Lawton Gonder." *Zanesville Times Signal* (September 22, 1957).

———. "LePere Plant." *Zanesville Times Signal* (November 11, 1956).

———. "Peters & Reed Pottery." *Zanesville Times Signal* (September 15, 1957).

Zanesville Chamber of Commerce. Booklet, 1918.

## PEWABIC POTTERY

*Arts and Crafts in Detroit 1906–1976*. Exhibition sponsored by Founders Society, Detroit Institute of Arts and the Center for Creative Studies—College of Art and Design. Detroit: The Detroit Institute of Arts, 1976.

Brunk, Thomas W. *Pewabic Pottery: Marks and Labels*. Detroit: Historic Indian Village Press, 1978.

"Ceramics." *Antiques* (March 1965), 324.

Flu, E. B. "The Pewabic Pottery at Detroit—A Unique Institution." *The Ceramic Age* (January 1927), 13–16.

Hegarty, Marjorie. "Pewabic Pottery." *Detroit Institute of Arts Bulletin* XXVI (1947), 69–70.

Holden, Marion L. "The Pewabic Pottery." *The American Magazine of Art* 17 (January 1926), 22.

Lacey, Betty. "Pewabic Pottery in Detroit." *National Antiques Review* (March 1971), 22.

Letter to the editor. *National Antiques Review* (June 1971), 6.

"Michigan State University Revives Pewabic Pottery." *Impresario, Magazine of the Arts* (February-March 1968), 16.

Pear, Lillian Myers. *The Pewabic Pottery: A History of Its Products and Its People*. Radnor, Pa.: Wallace-Homestead Book Co., 1976.

"Pewabic." *Art Digest* 3 (June 1929), 20.

"Pewabic Pottery, An Introduction to the MSU/Pewabic Pottery." *Pottery Collectors' Newsletter* 1 (July 1972), 135.

*Pewabic Pottery Commemorative Exhibit Catalog*. Privately printed, 1977 (Ars Ceramica Ltd., P.O. Box 418, Ann Arbor, MI 48017).

"Pewabic Pottery Detroit." *Antiques* (March 1965), 324.

Roehm, Mary. "An Update Pewabic." *Flashpoint* 3 (April-June 1990), 2.

Stratton, Mary Chase. "Pewabic." *American Ceramic Society Bulletin* 25 (October 15, 1946).

## PISGAH FOREST POTTERY

Camp, Helen B. "A Craftsman of the Old School." *International Studio* 78 (October 1923), 54.

Johnston, Pat H. "O.L. Bachelder: Omar Khayyam Pottery." *Pottery Collectors' Newsletter* 1 (August 1972), 145–48.

*The Pottery of Walter Stephen*. Journal of Studies of the Ceramic Circle of Charlotte in Conjunction with The Mint Museum of History, vol 3. Charlotte, N.C.: Ceramic Circle of Charlotte, 1978.

Ray, Marcia. "Pisgah Forest Pottery." *Spinning Wheel* (January-February 1971), 16.

Roberts, Ralph. "Pisgah Forest Pottery: A Half Century of North Carolina Mountain Art." *AntiqueWeek* 19 (March 23, 1987), 1.

## POTTERY CLUB OF CINCINNATI

Crowley, Lilian H. "It's Now the Potter's Turn." *International Studio* LXXV (September 1922), 539.

Evans, Paul F. "Cincinnati Faience: An Overall Perspective." *Spinning Wheel* XXVIII (September 1972), 16–18.

Little, Flora Townsend. "A Short Sketch of American Pottery." *Art & Archaeology* XV (May 1923), 219.

Nelson, Marion John. "Indigenous Characteristics in American Art Pottery." *Antiques* LXXXIX (June 1966), 846.

"Overtures of Cincinnati Ceramics." *Cincinnati Historical Society Bulletin* XXV (January 1967), 72–84.

## A. RADFORD POTTERY

*Pottery Collectors' Newsletter* (April and September 1972).

Purviance, Evan. "American Art Pottery." *Mid-America Reporter* (November 1972), 7.

Radford, Fred W. *A Radford Pottery, His Life and Works*. Privately printed, 1973 (Fred W. Radford).

Schneider, Norris F. "Many Small Art Potteries Once Operated in Zanesville." *Zanesville Times Recorder* (February 4, 1962).

## RED WING

DePasquale, Dan and Gail, and Larry Peterson. *Red Wing Collectibles*. Paducah, Ky.: Collector Books, 1985.

———. *Red Wing Stoneware*. Paducah, Ky.: Collector Books, 1983.

Dommel, Darlene. "Red Wing and Rum Rill Pottery." *Spinning Wheel* (December 1972), 22–24.

———. "Red Wing Pottery." *The Antique Trader* (October 23, 1973), 59.

Simon, Dolores. *Red Wing Pottery with Rumrill*. Paducah, Ky.: Collector Books, 1980.

## RHEAD POTTERY

*Rhead Artists & Potters: 1870–1950*. Exhibition catalog. Geffrye Museum. London: Inner London Education Authority, 1986.

## ROBLIN POTTERY

Evans, Paul F. "The Art Pottery Era in the United States: 1870 to 1920, Part Two." *Spinning Wheel* (November 1970), 52.

Hawes, Lloyd E., M.D. *The Dedham Pottery and the Earlier Robertson's Chelsea Potteries*. Dedham, Mass.: Dedham Historical Society, 1968.

## ROOKWOOD POTTERY

Alexander, Mary L. "New Crystal Glaze Described as Rookwood's Masterpiece." *The Cincinnati Enquirer* (December 2, 1943).

"Auto Dealer Is New Owner of Pottery, Attorney Reveals." *The Cincinnati Enquirer* (October 1, 1941).

Bopp, H. F. "Art and Science in the Development of Rookwood Pottery." *Bulletin of the American Ceramic Society—Communications* 15 (December 1936), 443–45.

Burt, Stanley. *Record Book of Ware at Art Museum*. Cincinnati: Cincinnati Historical Society, 1978.

*Catalog of Rookwood Art Pottery Shapes, Part 1*. Privately reprinted, 1971 (P-B Enterprises, 93 Lucas Ave., Kingston, NY 12401).

*Catalog of Rookwood Art Pottery Shapes, Part 2, 1907–1967, Shapes 1303–7301*. Privately reprinted, 1973 (P-B Enterprises, 93 Lucas Ave., Kingston, NY 12401).

Crowley, Lilian H. "It's Now the Potter's Turn." *International Studio* 75 (September 1922), 539.

Cummins, Virginia R. "Albert Robert Valentien." *Pottery Collectors' Newsletter* 6 (March 1977), 19.

———. "Clara Chipman Newton." *Pottery Collectors' Newsletter* 7 (July-August 1978), 50–55.

———. "Clotilda Marie Zanetta." *Pottery Collectors' Newsletter* 7 (November 1978).

———. "Elizabeth Barrett, Jens Jensen, Wilhelmine Rehm." *Pottery Collectors' Newsletter* 6 (October 1977), 81–82, 89.

———. "Fannie Louise Auckland—Rookwood Decorator." *Pottery Collectors' Newsletter* 6 (May 1977), 35–40.

———. "Rookwood." *Pottery Collectors' Newsletter* 5 (June 1976), 1.

———. "Rookwood Pottery (New Monograms)." *Pottery Collectors' Newsletter* 1 (June 1972), 119.

———. *Rookwood Pottery Potpourri*. Silver Spring, Md.: Cliff R. Leonard and Duke Coleman, 1980.

Davis, Chester. "The Later Years of Rookwood Pottery, 1920–1967." *Spinning Wheel* (October 1969), 10–12.

Dietz, Ulysses G. *Newark Museum Collection of American Art Pottery*. Salt Lake City: Gibbs M. Smith, 1984.

Freeman, Helen. "The Rookwood Pottery in Cincinnati, Ohio." *House Beautiful* 47 (June 1920), 499–501.

Hall, Foster E. and Gladys C. *The Rookwood Pricing Formula*, undated leaflet.

Johnston, Pat H. "Rookwood Pottery at the Paris Exhibition of 1900." *Pottery Collectors' Newsletter* 9 (1980).

"June Auction Notes." *Pottery Collectors' Newsletter* 1 (July 1972), 142.

Kircher, Edwin J. *Rookwood Pottery, An Explanation of Its Marks and Symbols*. Privately printed, 1962.

———, and Barbara and Joseph Agranoff. *Rookwood: Its Golden Era of Art Pottery, 1880–1929*. Privately printed, 1969.

Koch, Robert. "Rookwood Pottery." *Antiques* (March 1960), 288.

Kolakowski, Gail. "Louise Abel." *Pottery Collectors' Newsletter* 3 (July 1974), 138–40.

Laing, Trudy. "Rookwood Art Pottery." *The Gallery* (January-February 1972), 11.

———. "Rookwood Art Pottery Exhibited at Frame House Gallery, Oct. 3–Nov. 7." *Tri-State Trader* (November 20, 1971), 19.

———. "Rookwood's Japanese Artist." (April 1972), (publication unknown).

Landsdell, Sarah. "Rookwood Pottery Having a Revival." *Pottery Collectors' Newsletter* 1 (November 1971), 13.

Letter to the editor. *Spinning Wheel* (March 1970), 45.

Little, Flora Townsend. "A Short Sketch of American Pottery." *Art & Archaeology* 15 (May 1923), 219.

Macht, Carol M. "Rookwood Pottery." *Ceramics Monthly* (January 1966), 29.

Nelson, Marion John. "Indigenous Characteristics in American Art Pottery." *Antiques* LXXXIX (June 1966), 846.

Newton, Clara Chipman. "Rookwood Pottery." *Pottery Collectors' Newsletter* 5 (September 1976), 69–73 (reprint of c. 1901 article).

"Nineteenth-Century View of Rookwood." *Antiques* (January 1962), 118

Peck, Herbert. "The History and Development of Rookwood Bookends." *The Antique Trader* (February 20, 1973), 48.

———. "New Evidence Points to Alfred L. Brennan as Creator of Famous Rookwood." *Pottery Collectors' Newsletter* 1 (May 1972), 110.

———. "Rookwood Pottery and Foreign Museum Collections." *Connoisseur* (September 1969), 43.

———. "Rookwood Pottery Paperweights." *Pottery Collectors' Newsletter* 2 (November 1972), 17.

———. "Rookwood Pottery, Plaques and Tiles." *Pottery Collectors' Newsletter* 2 (February 1973), 56.

———. *The Second Book of Rookwood Pottery*. Privately printed, 1985 (174 Swan Lake, 4550 N. Flowing Wells Rd., Tucson, AZ 85705).

———. "Some Early Collections of Rookwood Pottery." *Auction* (September 1969), 20–23.

Peck, Margaret. *Catalog of Rookwood Art Pottery Shapes*. 2 parts. P-B Enterprises, 1971–1973.

"Pottery Party Line." *Pottery Collectors' Newsletter* 1 (April 1972), 100.

Ray, Marcia. "ABC's of Ceramics." *Spinning Wheel* (April 1968), 21.

Rookwood Factory Catalogs. Assorted, dates unknown.

"Rookwood—One of America's Finest Potteries." *The Antique Trader* (August 29, 1972), 2.

"Rookwood Paperweights." *Pottery Collectors' Newsletter* 2 (December 1972).

"Rookwood Pottery Soon to Be Reopened." *Cincinnati Times-Star* (September 30, 1941).

"Rookwood Works Bankrupt, Voluntary Petition States; List of 95 Creditors Filed." *The Cincinnati Enquirer* (April 17, 1941).

Rosenkrantz, Linda. "A Rookwood Tile." *American Heritage* (November 1990), 35–36.

Ruge, Clara. "American Ceramics—A Brief Review of Progress." *International Studio* 28 (March 1906), 21–28.

Sheridan, Millicent M. "Rookwood—A Good Field to Explore." *Hobbies* 57 (July 1952), 84, 99.

Shull, Thelma. "Rookwood Pottery." *Hobbies* 47 (October 1942), 66–67.

Stout, Wilber, et al. "Art Pottery." *Geological Survey of Ohio*. 4th ser., Bulletin 26. Columbus, Ohio: J.A. Bownocker, State Geologist, 1923.

Taylor, William Watts. "The Rookwood Pottery." *The Forensic Quarterly* (University of the South, Sewanee, Tenn.) 1 (September 1910), 203–18.

Trapp, Kenneth R. "The Bronze Work of Maria Longworth Storer." *Spinning Wheel* (September 1972), 14–15.

———. "Japanese Influence in Early Rookwood Pottery." *Antiques* (January 1973), 193–97.

———. *Ode to Nature: Flowers and Landscapes of the Rookwood Pottery, 1880–1940*. Privately printed, 1980 (The Jordan-Volpé Gallery, 457 Broadway, New York, NY 10012).

———. "Rookwood's Printed-Ware." *Spinning Wheel* (January-February 1973), 26–28.

———. *Toward the Modern Style: Rookwood Pottery, The Later Years, 1915–1950*. New York: Jordan-Volpe Gallery, 1983.

———, ed. *Celebrate Cincinnati Art*. Cincinnati: Cincinnati Art Museum, 1982.

*2,292 Pieces of Early Rookwood Pottery in the Cincinnati Art Museum in 1916*. Cincinnati: The Cincinnati Historical Society, 1978.

Vlissingen, Arthur Van, Jr. "Art Pays a Profit." *Factory and Industrial Management* 79 (February 1930), 301–3.

Volpe, Tod M. "Rookwood Landscape Vases and Plaques." *Antiques* (April 1980).

Yaeger, Dorothea. "Rookwood, Pioneer American Art Pottery." *American Collector* (July 1943), 8–9, 19.

### ROSEMEADE WAHPETON POTTERY

Barr, Margaret Libby, Donald Miller, and Robert Barr. *University of North Dakota Pottery: The Cable Years*. Fargo, N.Dak.: Knight Printing Company, 1977.

Schneider, Mike. "Distinctive Clay Makes Rosemeade Recognizable." *AntiqueWeek* 25 (August 24, 1992), 1.

Weiss, Grace M. "A Native of North Dakota: Rosemeade Pottery." *The Antique Trader* (February 27, 1973), 68.

### ROSEVILLE POTTERY

Alexander, Donald E. *Roseville Pottery for Collectors*. Privately printed, 1970 (Richmond, IN).

"Answers." *Pottery Collectors' Newsletter* 1 (January 1972), 52.

Buxton, Virginia Hillway. *Roseville Pottery for Love or Money*. Nashville, Tenn.: Tymbre Hill Publishing Company, 1977.

Clifford, Richard A. *Roseville Art Pottery*. Winfield, Kans.: Andenken Publishing Company, 1968.

Henzke, Lucile. "Roseville Pottery, Part One." *Spinning Wheel* (November 1969), 16–17, 56.

———. "Roseville Pottery, Part Two." *Spinning Wheel* (December 1969), 22–24.

Huxford, Sharon and Bob. *The Collectors Encyclopedia of Roseville Pottery*. Paducah, Ky.: Collector Books, 1976 and 1980.

*Patterns Manufactured by Roseville Pottery Incorporated.* Ohio Historical Society Library Files.

Purviance, Evan. "American Art Pottery." *Mid-America Reporter* (April 1972), 17; (May 1972), 15; (June 1972), 14; (August 1972), 28; and (September 1972), 4–5.

Purviance, Louise and Evan, and Norris F. Schneider. *Roseville Art Pottery in Color.* Radnor, Pa.: Wallace-Homestead Book Co., 1970.

———. "Roseville Pottery." *The Western Collector* (July 1969), 302–7.

"Roseville Pottery." *Spinning Wheel* (April 1968), 21.

*Rozane Ware Catalog, 1905.* Ohio Historical Society Library files.

*Rozane Ware Catalog, 1906.* Roseville Pottery Company. Privately reprinted, 1970 (Norris F. Schneider, Zanesville, OH 43702).

Schneider, Norris F. "Veteran Mosaic Tile Employee Compiles Outstanding Display." *Zanesville Times Recorder* (October 30, 1960).

Snook, Josh and Anna. *Roseville Donatello Pottery.* Radnor, Pa.: Wallace-Homestead Book Co., 1975.

Stout, Wilber, et al. *Art Pottery: Geological Survey of Ohio.* 4th ser., Bulletin 26. Columbus, Ohio: J.A. Bownocker, State Geologist, 1923.

Zanesville Chamber of Commerce. *The Roseville Pottery Company.* Booklet, 1918.

### STOCKTON TERRA COTTA

Shull, Thelma. "The Stockton Art Pottery." *Hobbies* 54 (August 1949), 94–95.

———. *Victorian Antiques.* Rutland, Vt.: Charles E. Tuttle Company, 1963.

### TECO GATES

Chicago Historical Society. Various file clippings.

Crowley, Lilian H. "It's Now the Potter's Turn." *International Studio* 75 (September 1922), 539.

Darling, Sharon S. *Teco Art Pottery of the Prairie School.* Erie, Pa.: Erie Art Museum, 1989.

Frackelton, Susan Stuart. "Our American Potteries, Teco Ware." *Sketch Book* 5 (September 1905), 3–19.

Gray, Walter Ellsworth. "Latter-Day Developments in American Pottery-II." *Brush and Pencil* 9 (1902), 239–96.

Little, Flora Townsend. "A Short Sketch of American Pottery." *Art & Archaeology* 15 (May 1923), 219.

"Teco Potteries, Terra Cotta, Illinois." *Pottery Collectors' Newsletter* 1 (August 1972), 151–52.

"Teco Potteries, Terra Cotta, Illinois: More on Teco Pottery by a Teco Collector." *Pottery Collectors' Newsletter* 1 (August 1972), 151–52.

Williams, Margaret Gates. Correspondence with Mr. Jedlic.

### TIFFANY POTTERY

Eidelberg, Martin P. "Tiffany Favrile Pottery, A New Study of a Few Known Facts." *Connoisseur* (September 1968), 57–61.

Koch, Robert. *Louis C. Tiffany's Glass-Bronzes-Lamps.* New York: Crown Publishers, 1971.

———. *Rebel in Glass.* New York: Crown Publishers, 1967.

### C. B. UPJOHN POTTERY

Schneider, N. F. *Zanesville Times Recorder* (September 16, 1962), A-6.

———. *Zanesville Times Signal* (March 23, 1958), D-44.

### VAN BRIGGLE POTTERY

Arnest, Barbara M., ed. *Van Briggle Pottery: The Early Years.* Colorado Springs: Colorado Springs Fine Arts Center, 1975.

Bayer, Ralph E. "Van Briggle Pottery." *The Western Collector* (March 1969), 110–15.

Bogue, Dorothy McGraw. *The Van Briggle Story.* Privately printed, 1968 (Dentan-Berkeland Printing Company, Inc., Colorado Springs, CO).

Crowley, Lilian H. "It's Now the Potter's Turn." *International Studio* 75 (September 1922), 539.

Knauf, Sandra. "The Van Briggle Connection: Carving a Niche in the American Arts and Crafts Revival." *Flashpoint* 5 (April-June 1992).

Koch, Robert. "The Pottery of Artus Van Briggle." *Art in America* 52 (June 1964), 120–21.

Laing, Trudy. "Young Van Briggle, Artist Probed Glaze Secrets." *Collectors' Weekly* (June 13, 1972), 1–3.

Myers, William C. "Dating Van Briggle Pottery." *American Clay Exchange* (February 28, 1986), 9.

Nelson, Scott H., et al. *A Collector's Guide to Van Briggle Pottery.* Indiana, Pa.: A.G. Halldin Publishing Co., 1986.

Newton, Robert Wyman. "Catalogue of Van Briggle Designs." In Nelson, et al. *Collector's Guide to Van Briggle Pottery,* and Arnest, *Van Briggle Pottery: Early Years.*

"Pottery at the Arts and Crafts Exhibit, Craftsman Building, Syracuse." *Keramic Studio* (May 1903–April 1904), 36.

Rawson, Jonathan A., Jr. "Recent American Pottery." *House Beautiful* 31 (April 1912), 148.

Riddle, Frank H. "The New Pottery and Art Terra Cotta Plant of the Van Briggle Pottery Company at Colorado Springs, Colo." *Transactions of the American Ceramic Society* X (1908), 65–75.

Ruge, Clara. "Development of American Ceramics." *Pottery & Glass* 1 (August 1908), 3.

Russack, Fran. Correspondence with authors.

Sasicki, Richard, and Josie Fania. *Van Briggle Art Pottery: An Identification & Value Guide.* Paducah, Ky.: Collector Books, 1993.

Van Briggle Art Pottery. Various leaflets, booklets, etc.

### WALRATH POTTERY

Eidelberg, Martin. "Art Pottery." In *The Arts and Crafts Movement in America: 1876–1916,* ed. Robert J. Clark. Princeton, N.J.: Princeton University Press, 1972, 119–86.

### WALRICH POTTERY

*Pottery Collectors' Newsletter* II (February 1973), 62.

### WELLER POTTERY

Fanale, James. "Weller Louwelsa: Something for Everyone." *Pottery Collectors' Newsletter* VI (June 1977), 51–52.

Fruge, Eloise. "Third Line Weller Is Rarest." *Collectors' News* (date unknown).

Garrett, Brice. "Weller Ware." *Spinning Wheel* (May 1965), 8–10.

Hall, Foster and Gladys. Correspondence to "Pottery Party Line." *Pottery Collectors' Newsletter* 2 (November 1972), 24.

———. "The Weller Pricing Formula." (publication and date unknown).

Henzke, Lucile. "A Visit with Naomi Walch, a Weller Artist." *Pottery Collectors' Newsletter* II (June 1973), 103–7.

———. "Weller's Dickens Ware." *Spinning Wheel* (October 1968), 16–18.

———. "Weller's Sicardo." *Spinning Wheel* (September 1969), 26–28, 67.

Huxford, Sharon and Bob. *The Collectors Encyclopedia of Weller Pottery.* Paducah, Ky.: Collector Books, 1979.

Markham, Kenneth H. "Weller Sicardo Art Pottery." *The Antiques Journal* (September 1964), 18.

McDonald, Ann Gilbert. *All About Weller*. Marietta, Ohio: Antique Publications, 1989.

———. "Franciscan Monks on Weller Dickensware." *Pottery Collectors' Newsletter*, c. 1980.

———. "Unnamed Weller Lines." *American Art Pottery* (November 1979), 1, 3.

———. "Weller Looks Elegant in White, Ivory, Cream." *AntiqueWeek* 23 (March 4, 1991), 1, 40.

Purviance, Evan. "American Art Pottery." *Mid-America Reporter* (December 1971), 8; (January 1972), 30; (February 1972), 13; and (March 1972), 10.

Purviance, Louise. "American Art Pottery." *The Antique Reporter* (April 1973), 4.

Purviance, Louise and Evan, and Norris F. Schneider. *Weller Pottery in Color*. Radnor, Pa.: Wallace-Homestead Book Co., 1971.

———. *Zanesville Art Pottery in Color*. Radnor, Pa.: Wallace-Homestead Book Co., 1968.

Ray, Marcia. "ABC's of Ceramics, Part Thirteen." *Spinning Wheel* (July-August 1968), 32 and "ABC's of Ceramics, Conclusion." *Spinning Wheel* (September 1968), 38.

*S. A. Weller: Manufacturer, Fine Art Pottery*. Reprint. Zanesville, Ohio: Zanesville Ceramic Press.

Schneider, Norris F. "Albert Haubrich, Weller Pottery Decorator." *Pottery Collectors' Newsletter* 1 (May 1972), 107–8.

———. "Plant Ceased Work in 1948." *Zanesville Times Signal* (April 13, 1958).

———. "Sicardo Ware, Pottery Guards Secret Process." *Zanesville Times Signal* (March 30, 1958).

———. "Weller Pottery." *Zanesville Times Signal* (March 16 and April 6, 1958).

———. "Weller Pottery: Charles Chilcote Recalls His Experiences at the Weller Pottery Art Studio." *Zanesville Times Recorder* (December 1968).

Stout, Wilber, et al. "Art Pottery." *Geological Survey of Ohio*. 4th ser., Bulletin 26. Columbus, Ohio: J.A. Bownocker, State Geologist, 1923.

*Weller Pottery*. Reprint of advertising leaflet. Zanesville, Ohio: Zanesville Ceramic Press, undated.

"Weller Pottery." *The Antique Trader* (May 16, 1972), 53.

Zanesville Chamber of Commerce. "S.A. Weller Potteries," 1918.

### T. J. WHEATLEY & COMPANY/WHEATLEY POTTERY COMPANY

"Wheatley Pottery Co." *Antiques* (June 1966), 850.

### ZANE POTTERY

*Zane Ware Catalog*. No. 22. Privately reprinted (A. Wunsch, 4207 Ludwig Lane, Bethpage, NY 11714).

For additional bibliography see Peters and Reed.

### ZANESVILLE ART POTTERY

Purviance, Evan and Louise. *Zanesville Art Tile in Color*. Radnor, Pa.: Wallace-Homestead Book Co., 1973.

Purviance, Louise and Evan, and Norris F. Schneider. *Zanesville Art Pottery in Color*. Radnor, Pa.: Wallace-Homestead Book Co., 1968.

Schneider, Norris F. "Many Small Art Potteries Once Operated in Zanesville." *Zanesville Times Recorder* (February 4, 1962).

———. "Miss Minnie Terry, Zanesville Pottery Decorator." *Pottery Collectors' Newsletter* VIII (November-December 1979), 53–54.

———. *Zanesville Art Pottery*. Privately printed, 1963 (Norris F. Schneider, Zanesville, OH).

"Zanesville Art Pottery." *Zanesville Times Signal* (November 11, 1956).

Zanesville Chamber of Commerce. *The Zanesville Art Pottery Company*. Booklet, 1918.

### GENERAL TILE BOOKS

Barnard, Julian. *Victorian Ceramic Tiles*. Greenwich, Conn.: New York Graphic Society, 1972.

McClinton, K. M. *Collecting American Victorian Antiques*. New York: Charles Scribner's Sons, 1966.

### AMERICAN ENCAUSTIC TILING COMPANY

Davis, Chester. "The AETCO Tiles of Walter Crane." *Spinning Wheel* (June 1973), 18–20.

Evans, Paul F. "Victorian Art Tiles." *The Western Collector* V (November 1967).

Newark Museum Association. *New Jersey Clay Products*. (date unknown).

Purviance, Louise and Evan. "American Art Pottery." *The Antique Reporter* (June 1973).

———. "American Art Pottery." *Mid-American Reporter* (December 1972–January 1973).

———. *Zanesville Art Tile in Color*. Radnor, Pa.: Wallace-Homestead Book Co., 1973.

———, and Norris F. Schneider. *Zanesville Art Pottery in Color*. Radnor, Pa.: Wallace-Homestead Book Co., 1968.

Schneider, Norris F. "A.E. Tile Company." *Zanesville Times Recorder* (May 21 and 28, 1961); (June 4, 1961); and (October 27, 1963).

———. "Souvenir Tile." *Zanesville Times Recorder* (October 30, 1966).

"Sleuths: AETC and Mosaic Tiles." *American Clay Exchange* 5 (June 30, 1985), 10.

Taft, Lisa Factor. *Herman Carl Mueller: Architectural Ceramics and the Arts and Crafts Movement*. Exhibition catalog. Trenton, N.J.: New Jersey State Museum, 1979.

Zanesville Chamber of Commerce. *American Encaustic Tiling Company, Ltd*. Booklet, 1918.

### BATCHELDER TILE COMPANY

Taylor, Joseph A. "Ernest Allan Batchelder." *Flash Point* (The Quarterly Bulletin of the Tile Heritage Foundation) 5 (October–December 1992).

### BEAVER FALLS ART TILE COMPANY

Evans, Paul F. "Victorian Art Tiles." *The Western Collector* V (November 1967).

Morse, Barbara White. "Tiles Made by Isaac Broome, Sculptor and Genius." *Spinning Wheel* XXIX (January-February 1973), 18–22.

### CAMBRIDGE ART TILE WORKS

Evans, Paul F. "Victorian Art Tiles." *The Western Collector* V (November 1967).

### LOW ART TILE

"Charles Dickens: 1812–1870." *Antique Dealer & Collectors Guide* (December 1972).

Davis, Robert E. *The Imagical World of Bossons*. Roswell, Ga.: W.H. Wolfe Associates, 1982.

Evans, Paul F. "Victorian Art Tiles." *The Western Collector* 11 (November 1967).

J. G. and J. F. Low Art Tile Works. *An Illustrated Catalogue of Art Tiles*. Chelsea, Mass., 1884. Reprinted 1990 by Tile Heritage Foundation, P.O. Box 1850, Healdsburg, CA 95448.

King, Emma D. "Low Tiles." *Spinning Wheel* (January 1957), 14–15.

"Low Art Tile." *Spinning Wheel* (December 1970).

"Low Art Tile." *The Western Collector* (November 1967).

"Low Tiles." *Spinning Wheel* (November 1967).

Morse, Barbara White. "Buying a Low Art Tile Stove." Part 1. *Spinning Wheel* (November 1970), 28.

———. "Chelsea Ceramic Charm and Comfort." *The Antiques Journal* (October 1972), 13–15, 40.

———. "I Collect Low Art Tiles." *Yankee* (November 1970), 132–35, 142–47.

———"John Gardner Low and His Original Art Tile Soda Foundation." Part 1. *Spinning Wheel* (July–August 1971), 26–28.

———. "John Gardner Low and His Original Art Tile Soda Fountain." Part 2. *Spinning Wheel* (September 1971), 16–19.

———. "Low 'Art Tiles' Today: A Primer for the Novice Collector." *National Antiques Review* (September 1973), 26.

———. "Tiles to Treasure, Low Art Tiles." *Spinning Wheel* (March 1969), 18–22.

Newark Museum Association. *New Jersey Clay Products*. Booklet. Newark, N.J. (date unknown).

Watkins, Lura Woodside. "Low's Art Tiles." *Antiques Magazine* XIV (May 1944), 250–52.

### MORAVIAN POTTERY AND TILE WORKS

Barnes, Benjamin H. *The Moravian Pottery, Memories of Forty-Six Years*. Doylestown, Pa.: The Bucks County Historical Society, 1970.

Blasberg, Robert W. "Moravian Tiles: Fairy Tales in Colored Clay." *Spinning Wheel* (June 1971), 16.

The Bucks County Historical Society. *The Mercer Mile*. Doylestown, Pa.: The Bucks County Historical Society, 1972.

Crowley, Lilian H. "It's Now the Potter's Turn." *International Studio* 75 (September 1922), 539.

Fox, Claire Gilbride. "Henry Chapman Mercer: Tilemaker, Collector, and Builder Extraordinary." *Antiques* (October 1973), 678.

Moravian Pottery and Tile Works. Catalog, 1982.

Reed, Cleota. *Henry Chapman Mercer and the Moravian Pottery and Tile Works*. Philadelphia: University of Pennsylvania Press, 1987.

Tachau, Hanna. "America Re-Discovers Tiles." *International Studio* 75 (March 1922), 74.

### MOSAIC TILE CO.

Dawson, B.A. "Zanesville Is a Tile Town: Mosaic Tile Co. Is a Large Industry." *The Zanesville (Ohio) News* (November 5, 1939), 9.

Mosaic Tile Company. Catalog, 1959.

Newark Museum Association. *New Jersey Clay Products*. Booklet. Newark, N.J. (date unknown).

Ohio Historical Society Library. *The Mosaic Tile Company Historical File*, August 1967.

Purviance, Louise and Evan, and Norris F. Schneider. *Zanesville Art Pottery in Color*. Radnor, Pa.: Wallace-Homestead Book Co., 1968.

Savino, Guy. "Colorful Skyline Marker Falls in 3d Tube Clearing." *Newark (N.J.) News* (April 27, 1954).

Schneider, Norris F. "Mosaic, Largest U.S. Tile Plant." *Zanesville Times Signal* (September 10, 1944).

———. "Mueller Co-Founder of Mosaic Tile Company." *Zanesville Times Recorder* (March 7, 1971).

———. "Souvenir Tile." *Zanesville Times Recorder* (October 30, 1966).

———. "Veteran Mosaic Tile Employee Compiles Outstanding Display." *Zanesville Times Recorder* (October 30, 1960).

Taft, Lisa Factor. *Herman Carl Mueller: Architectural Ceramics and the Arts and Crafts Movement*. Exhibition catalog. Trenton, N.J.: New Jersey State Museum, 1979.

Wires, E. Stanley. "Aesop's Great Fables: How Tiles Have Interpreted." *Antiques Journal* (May 1970), 10.

Zanesville Chamber of Commerce. Booklet, 1918.

"Zanesville History Recorded in Tile." *The Zanesville (Ohio) Signal* (March 19, 1940).

### MUELLER MOSAIC TILE COMPANY

"Adding Color to Our Architecture." *Trenton* (March 1926), 1–3.

*Mueller Tile Catalog*. Mueller Mosaic Company, Manufacturers. Trenton, N.J. (date unknown).

Taft, Lisa Factor. *Herman Carl Mueller: Architectural Ceramics and the Arts and Crafts Movement*. Exhibition catalog. Trenton, N.J.: New Jersey State Museum, 1979.

### C. PARDEE WORKS

Newark Museum Association. *New Jersey Clay Products*. Booklet. Newark, N.J. (date unknown).

### PROVIDENTIAL TILE WORKS

Newark Museum Association. *New Jersey Clay Products*. Booklet. Newark, N.J. (date unknown).

### TRENT TILE COMPANY

"An Ancient Art Applied to Modern Sanitation: Trent Tile Company's Products Help Keep Nation Clean." *Trenton* (February 1928), 4, 21, 24.

Evans, Paul F. "Victorian Art Tiles." *The Western Collector* V (November 1967).

Hastedt, Karl G. "Wenczel Tile Co." *Trenton* (July 1957), 6–8, 26–29.

Shull, Thelma. "Glass and China Decorative Tiles." *Hobbies* 49 (July 1944), 64.

### UNITED STATES ENCAUSTIC TILE COMPANY

Shull, Thelma. "Glass and China Decorative Tiles." *Hobbies* 49 (July 1944), 64.

United States Encaustic Tile Works. "Fiftieth Anniversary of the United States Encaustic Tile Works, Indianapolis, Indiana; in Continuous Operation for Fifty Years on the Present Site, 1877–1927." In *Fifty Years Ago on Tinker Street in Indianapolis*. Privately printed, 1927 (Indianapolis, IN).

# Index